A Manual of Ancient Sculpture

Also from Westphalia Press
westphaliapress.org

A Manual of Ancient Sculpture

Egyptian, Assyrian, Greek, Roman

with One Hundred and Sixty Illustrations, a Map
of Ancient Greece, and a Chronological List of
Ancient Sculptors and Their Works

by George Redford, F.R.C.S.

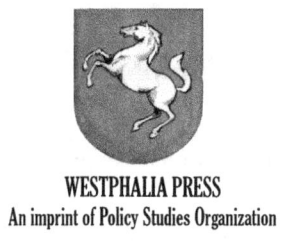

WESTPHALIA PRESS
An imprint of Policy Studies Organization

Westphalia Press
An imprint of Policy Studies Organization
1527 New Hampshire Ave., NW
Washington, D.C. 20036
info@ipsonet.org

ISBN-13:978-1-63391-712-5
ISBN-10: 1-63391-712-6

Cover design by Jeffrey Barnes:
jbarnesbook.design

Daniel Gutierrez-Sandoval, Executive Director
PSO and Westphalia Press

Updated material and comments on this edition
can be found at the Westphalia Press website:
www.westphaliapress.org

A

MANUAL OF ANCIENT SCULPTURE

EGYPTIAN—ASSYRIAN—GREEK—ROMAN

BY GEORGE REDFORD, F.R.C.S.

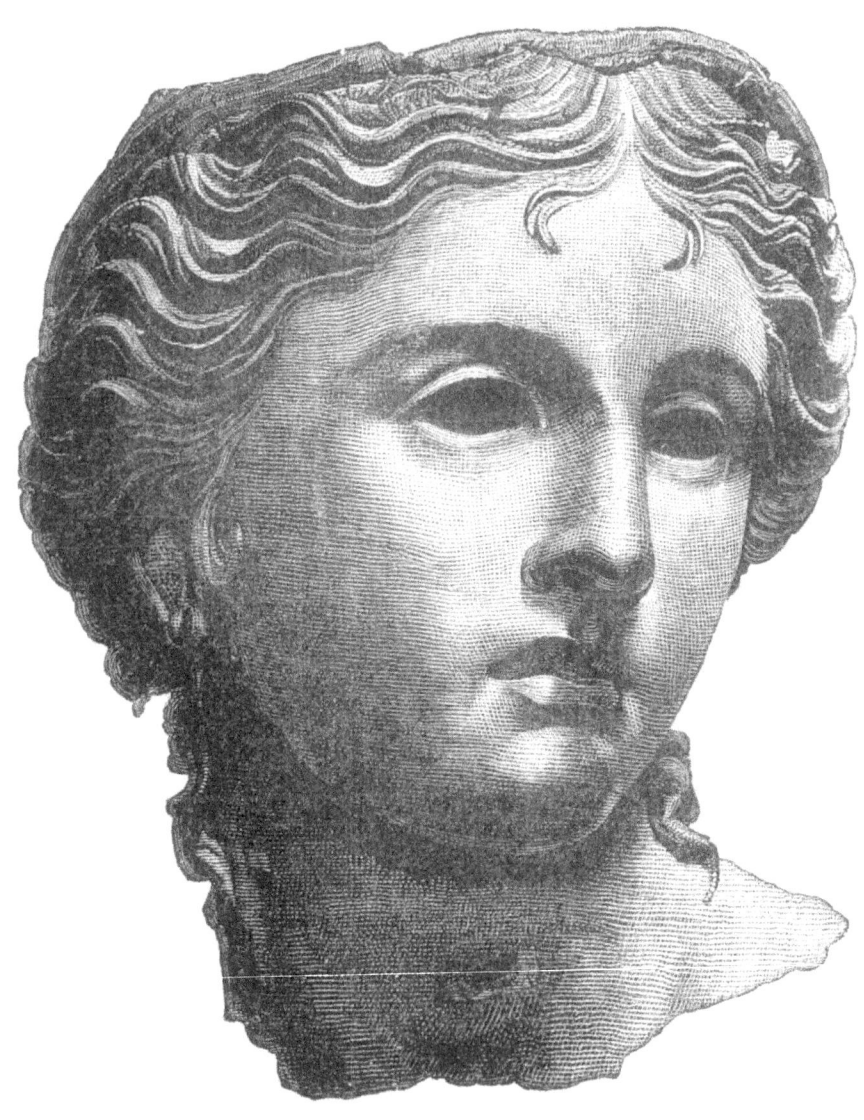

BRONZE HEAD OF ARTEMIS. HEROIC SIZE. (*See page* vi.)

In the British Museum Bronze Room.

A

MANUAL OF ANCIENT SCULPTURE

EGYPTIAN—ASSYRIAN—GREEK—ROMAN

WITH NUMEROUS ILLUSTRATIONS, A MAP OF ANCIENT GREECE
AND A CHRONOLOGICAL LIST OF ANCIENT SCULPTORS
AND THEIR WORKS

Second Edition, Enlarged

WITH ADDITIONAL ILLUSTRATIONS AND EXAMPLES DESCRIBED

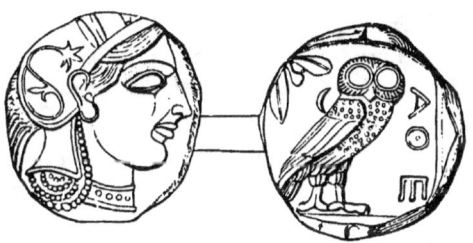

BY

GEORGE REDFORD, F.R.C.S.

Registrar of the Crystal Palace Collection of Sculpture, 1853-4
Curator of the Art Treasures Exhibition, Manchester, 1857
Commissioner for the National Exhibition of Works of Art, Leeds, 1868

LONDON

SAMPSON LOW, MARSTON, SEARLE, & RIVINGTON

CROWN BUILDINGS, FLEET STREET

1886

BRONZE HEAD OF ARTEMIS.

"*This head, which is of the finest period of Greek art, has been called Aphroditè, but is more probably Artemis. It has been broken off from a statue, the hand of which is exhibited in Case 44.*"—*British Museum Guide Book, by* Mr. Newton, *Keeper of Greek and Roman Antiquities at the British Museum.*

The back and crown of the head are wanting. The eye sockets are hollowed, as having originally had eyes of glass or enamel.

It is said to have been found in Armenia, where it was bought by the Turkish Pasha, who sold it to Signor Castellani, of whom it was purchased, with the hand, by the British Museum Trustees for a very large sum—it is said, £10,000—a price which some think not too high for its value as an example of rare beauty.

PREFACE TO FIRST EDITION.

THE Study of Antique Sculpture has two principal directions, the Historic or Archæological, and that on the side of Art. Each view has its own special interest, and both contribute mutually to the elucidation of the general subject; but while the one has comparatively little direct relation to the cultivation of the fine arts, the other is constantly concerned with artistic practice as well as the principles. The great truths which ancient art evolved, and which remain as firmly established as those which science has determined, belong to art, not to archæology. Feeling this to be so, I have endeavoured to lay before the reader the view of an art student, as that which is more directly the intention of this volume. This course seemed not only the one which chiefly concerns the interests of art, and calculated to conduct to the full appreciation of the beautiful in sculpture, but, at the same time, the more practical and the more suitable for a short treatise with illustrations. To have attempted more in the historical section, even had it been possible within the limits, and had I been qualified to deal fully with so large a subject in all its varied relations, would have been to distract attention from the main point. Enough, however, it is hoped, has been said of the history of sculpture to lead those who are disposed to follow out the archæological view, to seek the fuller information to be found in the many elaborate works upon the subject. It may·be some solace for the lack of much that would certainly be indispensable to a bulkier work, to bear in mind that the views of archæologists are liable to modification and some-times to serious revolution, while much is constantly left as matter of opinion and controversy. The archæological side of art is always fruitful in speculation, with a considerable border-land of disputed ground, while the art view is more safely occupied in the perception of the beautiful, the comprehension of the principles which regulate all works of art and which are specially disclosed in sculpture, and the understanding of the characteristics of the various styles. There is no difficulty in arriving at certain broad distinctions in the examples that have fortunately been preserved to us, and this will, it is hoped, be facilitated by the numerous engravings.

The arrangement of the subject under the sections of Technic, Æsthetic, Historic, and Examples, is so far new that it is offered with some diffidence. I adopted it only after having sought in vain for any model to follow which seemed systematic, and at the same time free from the complexity of more elaborate and exhaustive works.

Being a handbook only, this volume does not pretend to do more than open out the principal paths which lead to the great mountain region that has to be climbed before any wide and comprehensive view can be obtained of ancient sculptural art.

G. R.

CRICKLEWOOD, LONDON, N.W.,
    March, 1882.

PREFACE TO SECOND EDITION.

AN impression of 2500 copies having been sold within about three years, a second edition of this 'Manual' is consequently required. The author may be permitted to congratulate the public as well as himself on the fact. It testifies to the existence of a large body of students not to be daunted by the difficulties . of a subject so subtle and intricate as ancient sculpture, provided the writer avoids abstruse questions and unnecessary technicalities.

If my readers were not dissatisfied with the first edition, I venture to promise them that they will find the second both carefully revised and enriched with fresh matter of interest. ·

As 'The Athenæum' in an appreciative review cordially recommended the 'Manual' when it originally appeared, and commended my plan of treating the subject under the sections of *Technic, Æsthetic, Historic,* and *Examples* as "not only well suited for the instruction of the tyros whom the book more particularly addresses, but might well be adopted for a work on a more exhaustive and serious scale," I may say, with some regret, that circumstances forbid me to undertake the elaborate treatise thus suggested. But I shall hope that some one fully capable and with more leisure may be prompted to adopt such a plan to the construction of a full and scientific exposition of the noblest and most consummate of all the branches of ancient art.

G. R.

CRICKLEWOOD, *March,* 1886.

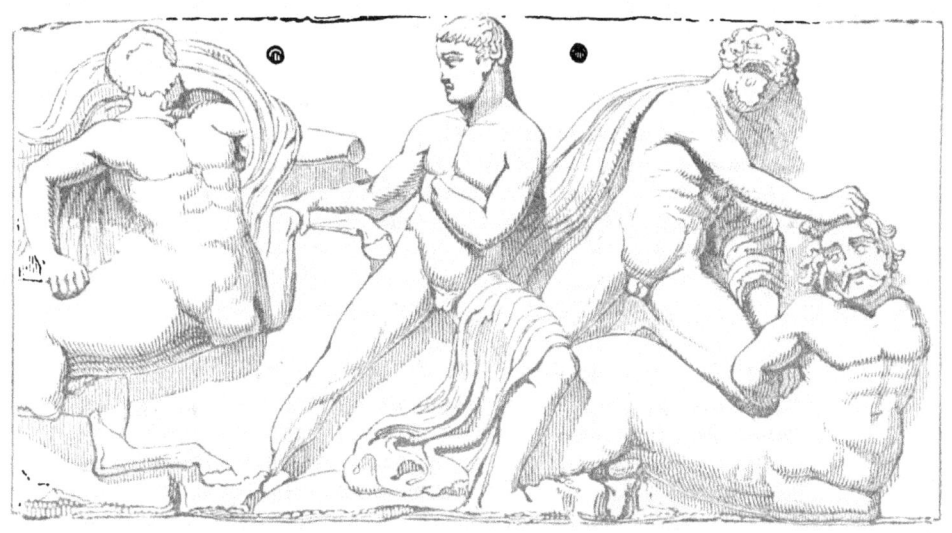

BAS-RELIEF IN MARBLE FROM THE TEMPLE OF APOLLO AT PHIGALIA.
CONTEST OF CENTAURS AND LAPITHAE.
In the British Museum.

CONTENTS.

SECTION I. TECHNIC.

SECTION IV. EXAMPLES.

AN ALPHABETICAL LIST OF ENGRAVINGS *is given in the Index.*

The Author has to acknowledge his obligation to the Directors of the Crystal Palace Company, who were kind enough to allow electrotypes to be taken from some of the wood engravings in their "Guide Book to the Greek and Roman Courts."

A

MANUAL OF ANCIENT SCULPTURE

EGYPTIAN—ASSYRIAN—GREEK—ROMAN

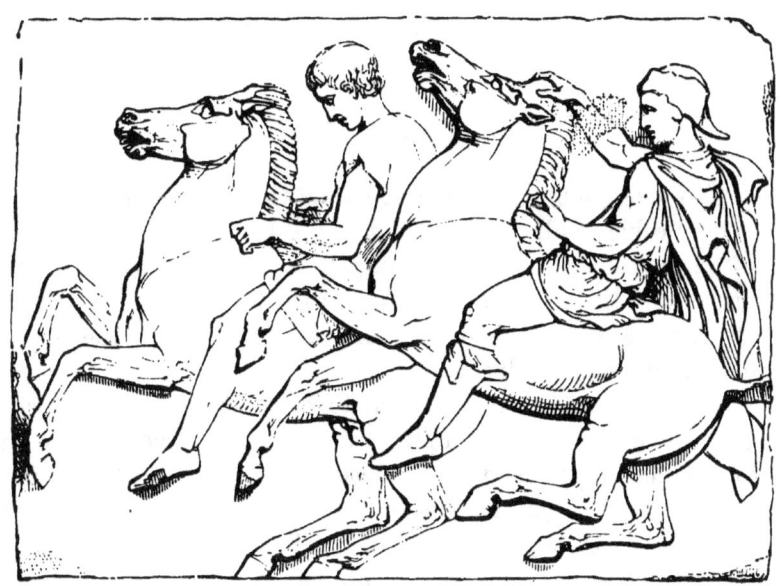

FIG. 1.—BAS-RELIEF FROM THE PARTHENON FRIEZE.

ANCIENT SCULPTURE.

EGYPTIAN, ASSYRIAN, GREEK, ROMAN.

BEFORE entering upon the different styles of ancient sculpture it is necessary to understand what sculpture is, and the various forms it has taken. First, as to what it is in regard to technic and material; next as to what it is in æsthetics. The history and examples of the various styles will then be more readily followed.

The subject, therefore, may be conveniently treated in four sections—

I. TECHNIC. II. ÆSTHETIC. III. HISTORIC. IV. EXAMPLES.

Some of the chief statues in the great museums of Europe are described in this last section.

A.S.

SECTION I.—TECHNIC.

THE word SCULPTURE, derived from the Latin *sculpo*, to carve, is applicable to all work cut out in a solid material in imitation of natural objects. Thus carvings in wood, ivory, stone, marble, metal, and those works formed in a softer material, not requiring carving, such as wax and clay, all come under the general denomination of sculpture.

But sculpture, as we are about to consider it, is to be distinguished by the term STATUARY, from all carved work belonging to ornamental art, and from those beautiful incised gems and cameos which form the class of GLYPTICS, a word derived from the Greek γλύφω, to carve, as well as from the works of the medallist. It must be borne in mind, however, that the sculptor does not generally carve his work directly out of the marble; he first makes his statue or bas-relief in clay, or sometimes in wax. It is scarcely necessary to say that the most primitive sculptor naturally took clay for his work, as the potter did for his "wheel." This method enabled him to "sketch in the clay," and to perfect his work in this obedient material. Michelangelo and such great masters could dispense with this, and when they chose could carve at once the statue from the block. The ancient Egyptian sculptors, and after them the Assyrians, carved their gigantic figures from the living rock. The rock-cut temples of India show similar work. (Figs. 3, 57).

Carving is, however, of secondary consideration—with the exception of the special work of great masters just referred to—and it is the modelling in the clay which is the primary work. Sculpture is therefore properly styled "plastic art," from πλάσσω, to fashion or mould. The "model," as it is termed technically, is afterwards to be "moulded" by the exact application of liquid plaster of Paris (sulphate of lime; gypsum, deprived of its water or unslaked), in a proper manner. By means of the mould thus formed, a cast of the original clay statue or bas-relief is taken by a similar use of the liquid plaster. This liquid plaster has the property of solidifying, or "setting," as it is technically called, by a kind of crystallization, and it thus takes any form to which it is applied. The clay model, therefore, is like the original drawing of a painter, a master work. It is something more ; it is the result of a previous step, for the sculptor has probably made a drawing before taking the clay in hand. In all bas-reliefs the sculptor first draws his design on a slab and fills it in afterwards with the clay, proceeding

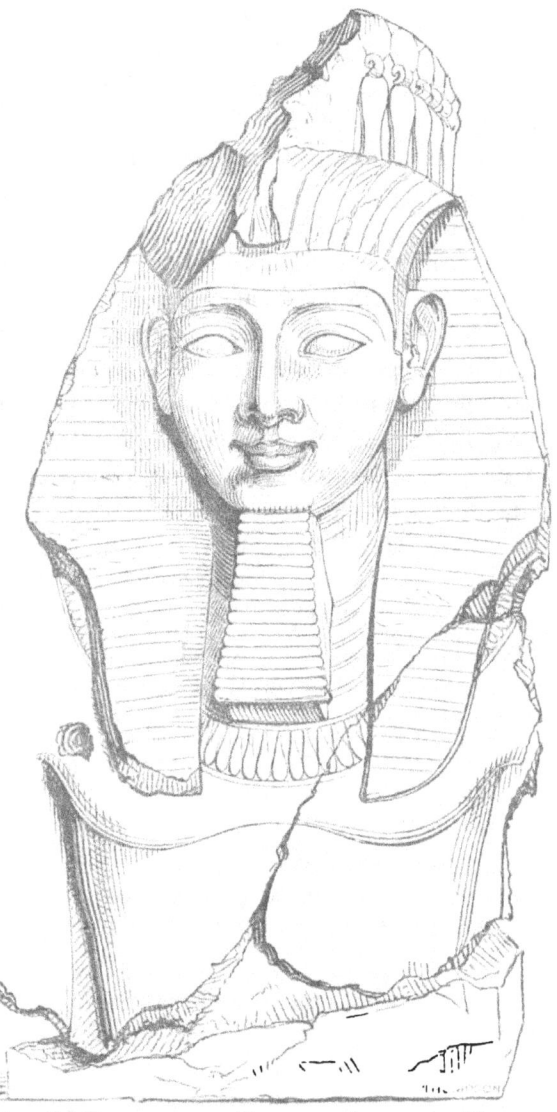

FIG. 2.—PART OF THE EGYPTIAN STATUE OF MEMNON IN RED GRANITE. *In the British Museum.*
The face measures 3¼ feet from top of forehead to chin.

then to model the forms. The sculptor, therefore, is less a carver than a designer, a draughtsman, and a modeller. This being so, he invented a method of mechanical measurement by which most of the carving could be done by skilled labour; the sculptor taking it up to give the finish which a master hand alone can bestow. That this was an ancient practice is shown by an example in the Museum of St. John Lateran at Rome of an unfinished statue of a captive, which has been left with the "points" on the surface; so placed by the master as a guide for the workman.

In the process of "pointing," the model and the block of marble are each fixed on a base called a scale-stone, to which a standard vertical rod can be attached at corresponding centres, having at its upper end a sliding needle so adapted by a moveable joint as to be set at any angle, and fastened by a screw when so set. The master sculptor having marked the governing points with a pencil on the model, the instrument is applied to these and the measure taken. The standard being then transferred to the block-base, the "pointer," guided by this measure, cuts away the marble, taking care to leave it rather larger than the model, so that the general proportions are kept, and the more important work is then left for the master hand.

The process of pointing, which was probably employed in some shape by the ancient sculptors, though not so accurately as in modern times, is of course not applicable to metal statues.

The nature of the material in which a sculptor carves necessarily influences the character of his work; the harder the stone the more difficult to give it the pliant forms of life. The most ancient and the grandest in size of all works of sculpture are in those kinds of hard stone, such as basalt, granite, and porphyry, which cannot be worked sufficiently by the chisel, as they would either break the edge of the tool if the steel were too hard, or turn it if too soft. It is very remarkable that the most ancient and perfect Egyptian statues (Fig. 2) should have been formed out of these very hard stones; and as the ancient Egyptians were not acquainted with steel, they must have been dependent on bronze of various degrees of hardness for their cutting tools.

That it was part of the grand scheme of the Egyptians to raise monuments that would defy injury and the decaying effects

of time, and that they succeeded, is shown by numerous statues
cut out of large blocks of the hardest stone, perfect after the
lapse of at least four thousand years, and likely to remain so till
they encounter the fire that made the igneous rocks out of which
they are hewn. These statues too, it should be clearly understood,
are remarkable for excellence in the work, both as to the form and
proportions, and in the finish given to the details of the features,
the dress, and the ornaments ; and they show a degree of fine
work in the polishing, which compels at once the admiration and

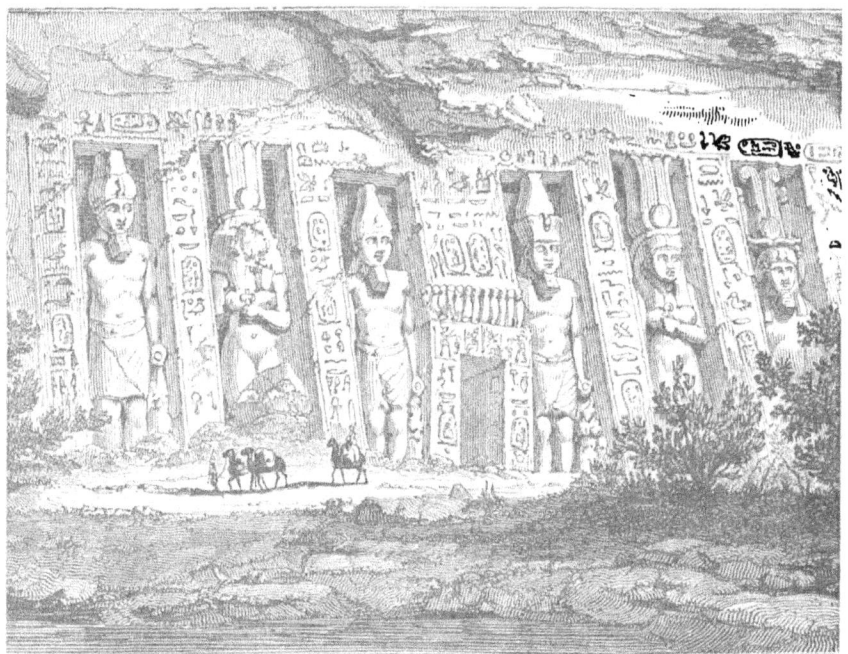

FIG. 3.—COLOSSAL STATUES CARVED IN THE ROCK ; IN THE TIME OF RHAMSES II.
(B.C. 1200).   *On the banks of the Nile.*

astonishment of the world.   It is conjectured that it was done
by immense labour with the chisel, the drill, and the wheel of
the lapidary, aided with sand and emery for polishing.   No
ancient iron tool has ever been found; but this may be on
account of the rusting and decay of this metal.   Sir G. Wilkinson found a chisel made of an alloy of tin and copper, not hard
or brittle, the edge of which was easily turned by striking it

against the very stone it had been used to cut.   He thought the
Egyptians possessed some method of hardening bronze.*

Assyrian sculpture was confined to bas-relief and high-relief

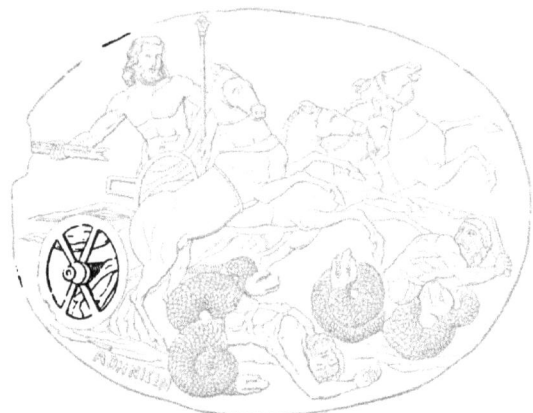

FIG. 4.—CAMEO. GIGANTIMACHIA.
Naples Museum.

approaching the round, in the softer stones, limestone and
alabaster; small objects only, such as the incised cylinders used
as seals, being worked in the hard stones.

Hard Stones.   Greek and Roman sculptors made many statues
and bas-reliefs in hard stones.   There are fine examples in the
Vatican collection, but, as might be expected from the nature of
the material, none that equal in beauty of form and expression

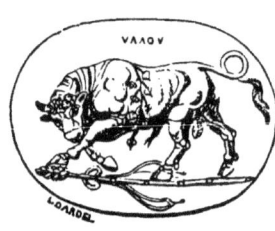

FIG. 5.—THE BACCHIC BULL,
SIGNED ΥΛΛΟΥ (OF HYLLOS).

the works in marble and bronze.   The
Vatican also contains the most remarkable collection of sculpture of this kind
in existence, in the groups of animals,
all in the most spirited actions of sport
or combat, placed in what is called
"the Hall of the Animals."   The extremely difficult nature of such work
may be understood when it is seen

* In a tomb at Kertch of the 4th century B.C. were found bronze arrow-
heads the file could not cut.   An alloy of phosphorus with bronze is very
hard; possibly the ancients made this by using bones and animal matter
in the melting of the metal.

that the ordinary method of the chisel and mallet in the most skilful hands would be quite unavailing in this hard material and upon so small a scale. The treadle-wheel, the drill, and the file are brought to aid the chisel, and even these require the use of emery upon the wheel of the lapidary, in the method by which the hardest gems are cut. In fact these works come rather under the class of glyptics than sculpture. Here it

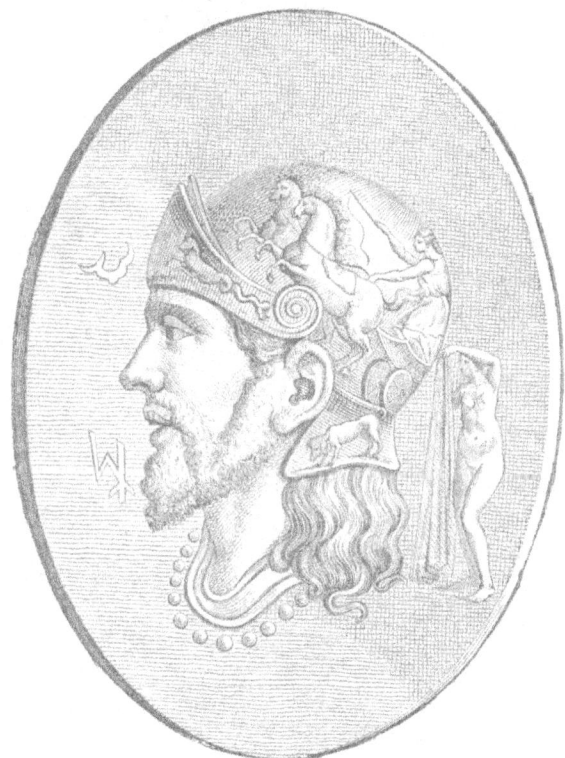

FIG. 6.—AN ENGRAVED GEM IN AMETHYST, CALLED BY AGOSTINI, KING MASSINISSA. *In the Florence Museum.*

may be explained that the wheel referred to is a tool capable of extremely nice application. It is not like the wheel of a grindstone, but more like that of the glass-cutter, being a disc of copper of varying diameter, fitted on the free end of a spindle, which is made to revolve like the common lathe worked by the foot, and the stone is brought into contact with it, guided by the

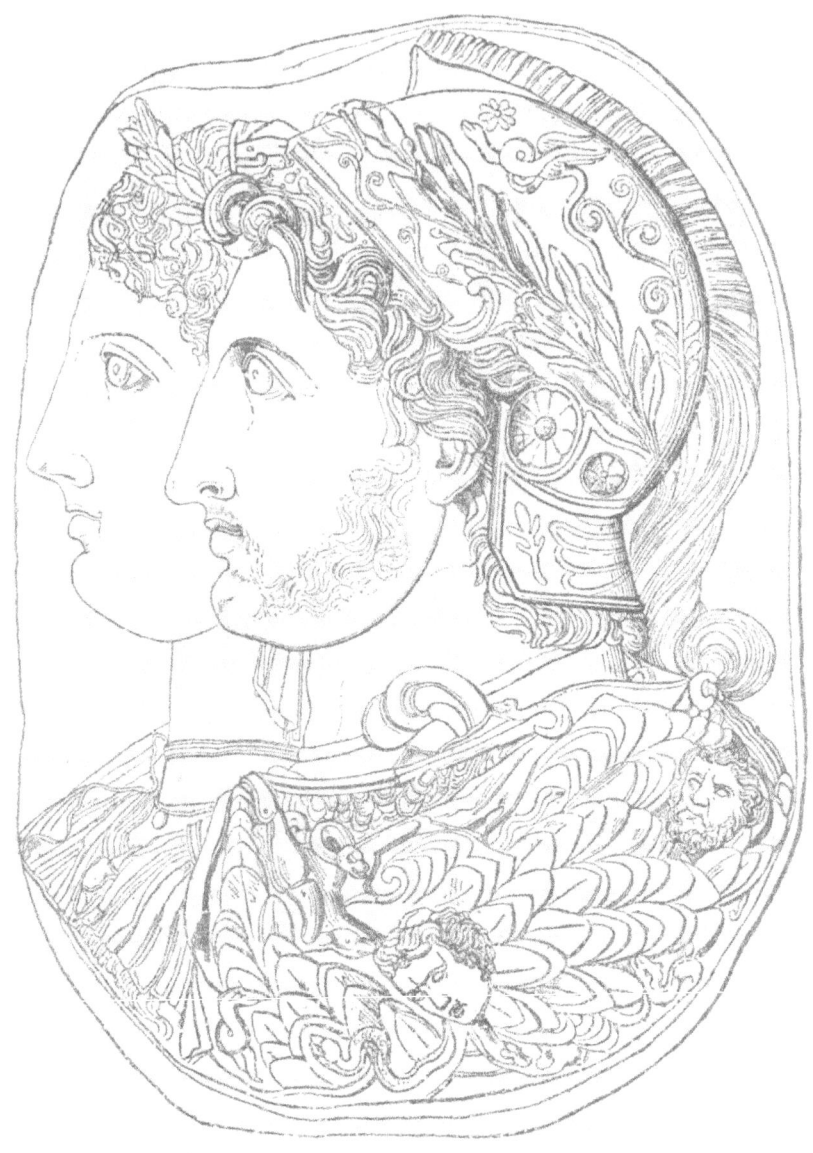

Fig. 7.—The Gonzaga Cameo in Onyx. Ptolemy I. and Eurydice.
Roman Work. *In the St. Petersburg Museum.*

delicate hand and eye of the artist. The cutting edge of this disc is armed with the fine particles of emery, and sometimes diamond dust kept moist with oil, which become embedded in the yielding metal, and thus convert it into the finest and most searching file, so sharp that even the diamond itself, the hardest substance in nature, is cut in the most accurate manner. The last touches are given with the diamond point fixed in a tool, and sharper than a needle. Many of the most beautiful examples of ancient classic art (Figs. 4 to 6), and many of the Italian Renaissance, exist in the form of intaglii and camei. The great masters who have left their names engraved upon the face of these gems

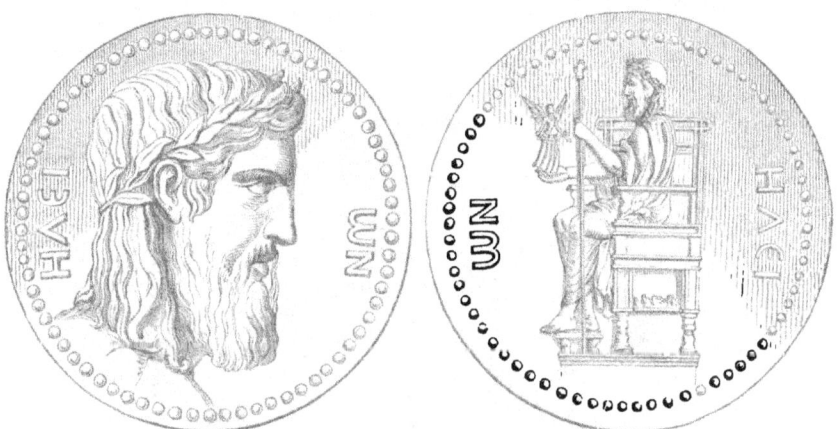

FIG. 8.—COIN OF ELIS—ZEUS OF PHEIDIAS.

FIG. 9.—COIN OF ELIS—ZEUS OF PHEIDIAS.

hold a place parallel with the greatest sculptors of the age of Perikles. When it is remembered that the glyptic sculptor works entirely from his mind—impromptu as it were—some idea may be formed of the profound knowledge he must have of the beauty of the human and animal form, and the amazing mastery he must possess over the most unyielding material.

The medallist both of ancient and modern times is an artist scarcely less able and accomplished than the gem-cutter. The die he carves out of the metal is a fine work of the chisel, the punch, and the drill; with the grinding method of the lathe to give polish and delicacy. This is done by what is technically called "lapping out," which is a term taken from the use of the "lapstone" or "whet-stone," applied somewhat in the manner of the disc in the gem-engraver's work.

The coins of Greece offer many fine examples of beautiful work, besides affording invaluable records of renowned statues, such as the Jupiter Olympius (Figs. 8, 9), the Venus of Knidos, the Palatine Apollo, and the Colossus of Rhodes—long since lost—which were copied on them during the life-time of Pheidias, Myron, Praxiteles, and other great sculptors.

The medallions by the great men of the Renaissance in Italy,

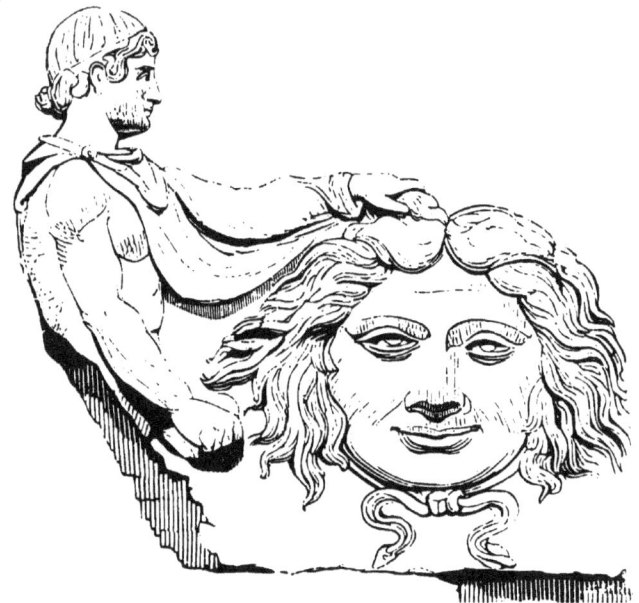

F.G. 10.—Perseus with the Gorgon Head.
Terra Cotta.

France, and Germany, both the early works which were cast in a mould and the later ones produced by stamping with the die, are unsurpassed by any antique works of their kind for portrait character and beauty of work.

Terra cotta. Clay modelled and dried in the sun, or hardened by the fire, was naturally one of the early forms in which sculpture was developed. At once ready to hand and easily modelled, it was adopted for the same reasons that made clay convenient for the ordinary vessels of every-day use. So we find countless numbers of ancient figures of deities, animals, grotesque monsters, in baked or simply sun-dried clay, all more or less barbaric and archaic in style, whether found in Mexico or Cyprus, in Egypt or Assyria, in Etruria or the Troad. These have escaped destruction chiefly on account of their not being of any value as bronze and marble were, and partly from their

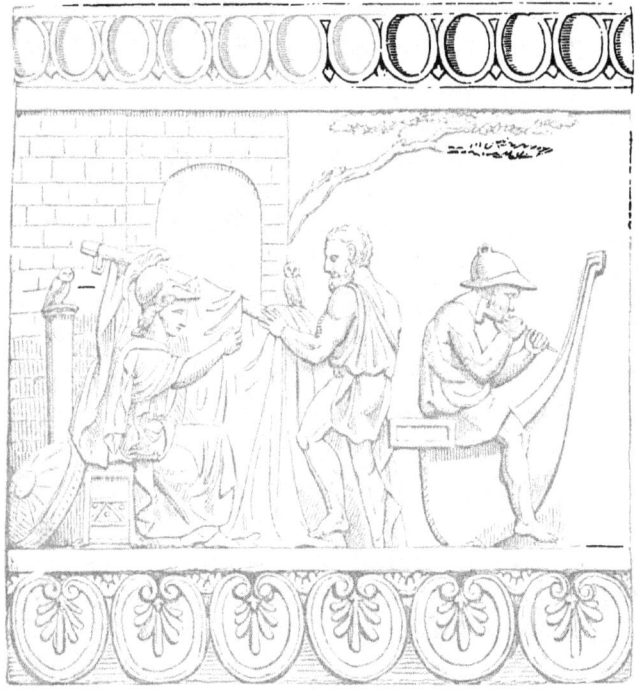

FIG. 11.—BAS-RELIEF. ATHENA PRESIDING OVER THE BUILDING OF A SHIP. *Terra Cotta.*

great durability in resisting decay. The ancient Egyptians and Assyrians applied a vitreous glaze to terra cotta objects, thus making them more decorative and more durable; but they never carried out this process as it was perfected in after-times by the Chinese, and especially by those two distinguished sculptors of the Renaissance, Luca and Andrea della Robbia.

Terra cotta was obviously chosen by the sculptors of Greece and Rome, as it is by modern artists, with the view of preserving

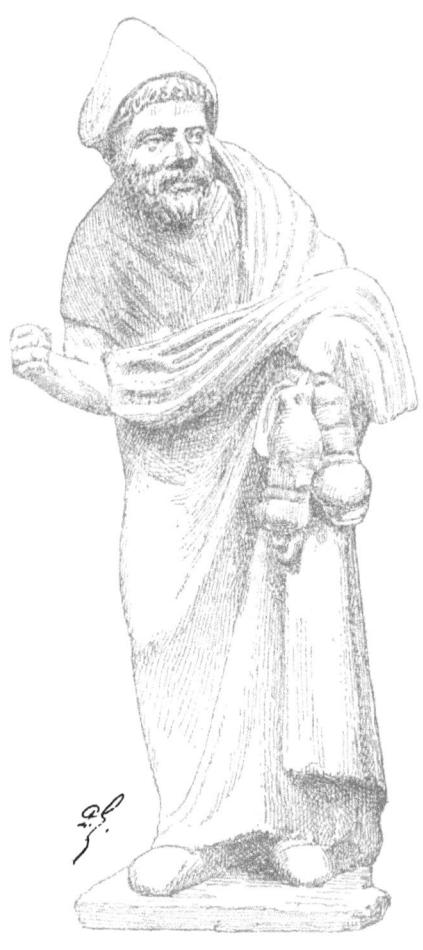

FIG. 12.—A SLAVE. *Terra Cotta.*
Found at Tanagra.

the exact spirit and freedom of the original, whether as a sketch or as a finished work. Although some shrinking under the action of the fire has to be allowed for, and occasionally an accidental deformity may occur from this cause, yet what is perfect in the firing is certain to possess the excellence of the work in the fresh clay; as it escapes the chances of over-finish and the loss of truth and animation, which too often befall bronze and marble. As it left the hand of the master the fire fixes it, converting the soft clay into a material as hard as marble, and more capable of resisting damp and heat. Winckelmann remarks, ' Ancient works in terra cotta are as a rule never bad " (lib. i. ch. ii.).

Some interesting examples of work in terra cotta are little figures which have lately been found in almost countless numbers at Tanagra in Boeotia : some of these are in the British Museum and in the Louvre. A great number of these were shown in the *Exposition rétrospective* of Paris, in 1878. (Fig. 12.)

Ivory. Another ancient form of sculpture to be noticed, though no example of it remains, is very important as it is known to have been that employed by the greatest master of the art— Pheidias, for his grand colossal statues of Zeus (Fig. 16) and

Athenę in the temples of those gods. This is called *Chryselephan-tine*, on account of the combined use of gold (χρυσὸς) and ivory (ἐλέφας); the nude parts of the figure being of ivory, probably with colour applied to the flesh and features, and the drapery of gold. The statue was substantially but roughly made in marble, with wood perhaps upon it; the ivory being laid on in thick pieces (Figs. 13, 14, 15). Much interesting research has been given to this form of sculpture, by De Quincy especially, but it is not necessary to enter into details which are so largely

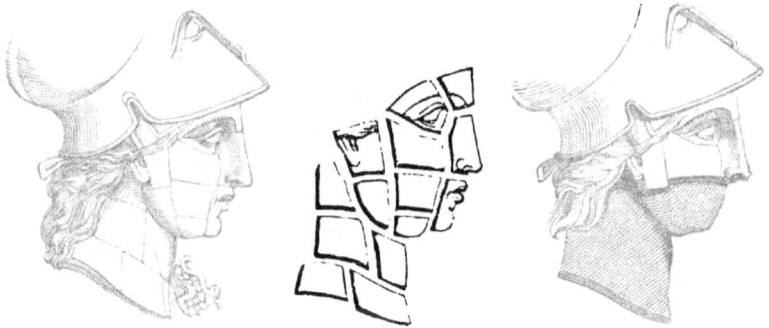

FIGS. 13, 14, 15.—SHOWING THE SUPPOSED METHOD OF WORKING IVORY IN PIECES LAID ON.

conjectural. The use of ivory denoted a very decided intention to imitate nature as closely as possible, though in colossal proportions. Ivory and gold statuary was revived during the time of Hadrian, who had a colossal statue of Jupiter made and placed in the temple at Athens.

That statues made of such valuable materials, to do honour to the god, should have fallen under the hand of the spoiler was inevitable; so that no examples of this work exist. A small reproduction of the chryselephantine statue of the Zeus was made under the direction of the Duc de Luynes in Paris some years ago in order to see the effect of such work. Many fine statuettes in ivory have been carved by modern sculptors of the sixteenth and seventeenth centuries, and by those of more recent times, especially by the late Baron de Triqueti.

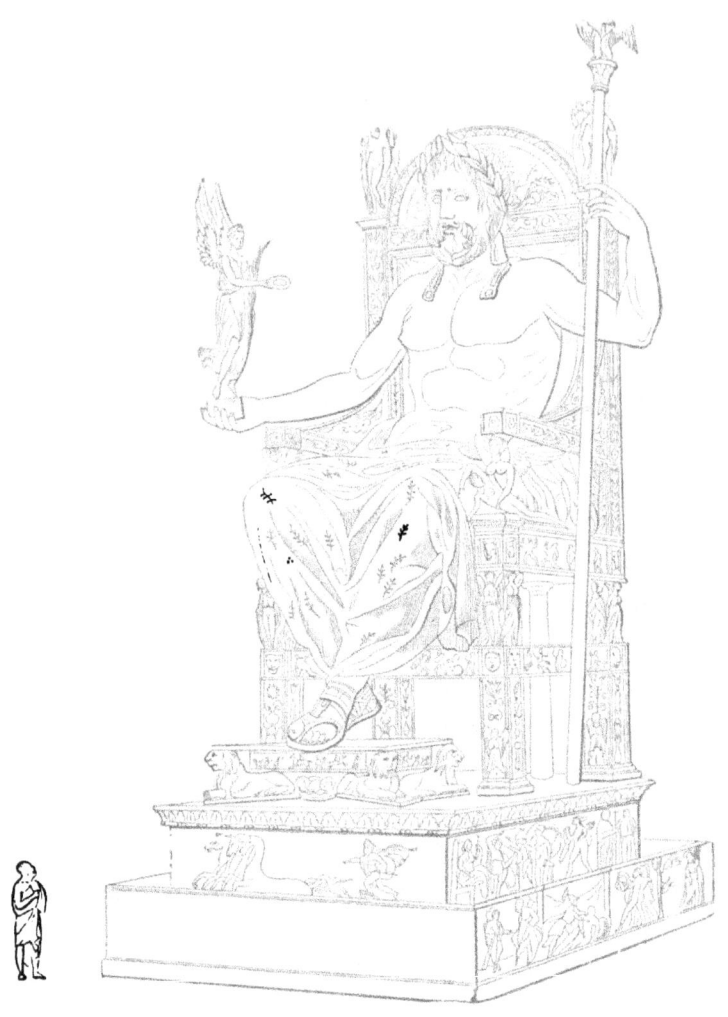

FIG. 16.—THE CHRYSELEPHANTINE STATUE OF ZEUS BY PHEIDIAS.

As restored by Quatremère de Quincy.   Height 45 feet.

*The height of the temple in which this statue was placed was 68 feet to the spring
of the roof.*

Wood. Statues of wood of various kinds were made by the most ancient sculptors of Egypt, Assyria, and Greece. Many small figures in wood, the work of the Egyptian carvers, are to be seen in the museums; and the mummy cases show the practice of carving the head while the trunk is left only partly shaped out of the block. A wooden statue of Sethos I. is in the British Museum. A life-size statue in wood of Ra em ke, with the arms separate from the trunk, and the legs also carved " in the round," from the museum of Boulak at Cairo, was exhibited in the Paris Exposition of 1867.

The Greeks called their wood statues ξόανα, from ξέω, to polish or carve. The statue of a god was called ἄγαλμα κίων—a column is taken to mean also a statue (Plutarch). Castor and Pollux were represented by the Lacedemonians simply as two pieces of wood joined by a ring, hence the sign II for the twins in the Zodiac. The small figures of men and animals, called by the Greeks *Dædalides* as supposed to be made by Dædalus (a name derived from δαιδάλλω, to work skilfully) and his school of artificers, were carved in wood. As we saw when speaking of the origin of the plastic art in the rude clay, and wood figures serving as images of the gods, these were the work of the mechanical producers of the toy-like figures with movable arms, which were dressed up with draperies and wreaths, and painted for festive celebrations. Figures of this nature were universal, and were carried about probably wherever settlers wandered, as forming part of their religious customs. So far as any date has been given to these, it may be said to be from about the 14th to the 7th century before our era. Pausanias (ix. 3) refers to the festival of the Dædala, in which a dressed up wooden statue of Plataea in a chariot was carried in procession, according to the ancient myth. Plutarch also refers to the same festival, calling the wooden statue *Dædala*. Pausanias (who wrote in the second century of our era) also describes similar figures of Bacchus, Ceres, and Proserpine, which he saw in a Nymphaeum between Sikyon and Philontum; in these statues the head only was seen, the rest being covered with drapery.*

* See 'Lectures of Raoul Rochette' for much curious matter concerning the *Dædala.*

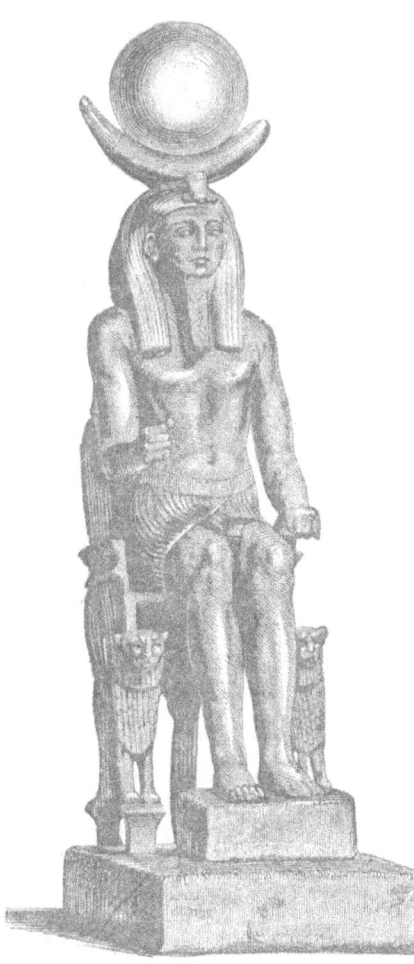

FIG. 17.—OSIRIS. EGYPTIAN STATUE IN BRONZE.

In the Louvre.

The ancient Greeks began by representing their deities by simple blocks of stone (λίθοι ἀργοί), which were gradually hewn into square forms. At length a human head was added, of Hermes or any other god, and they were called ' *Hermes*,' and when used as boundary marks, ' *Termes*,' hence the word *terminal* in sculpture for busts squared at the shoulder.

Bronze. This was one of the most important forms of ancient statuary. Unfortunately we have to rely almost entirely upon ancient writers for any descriptions of the great works of the Egyptian and Greek sculptors in bronze, and upon those copies of them in marble, which tradition tells us are such. The original bronze works have long since perished, some by fire, and others by the hand of the spoiler. Most of them will be noticed when speaking of the history and examples of sculpture. For the present we have to attend to that which concerns the material and the methods of working in it. The word *bronze* is of comparatively modern origin, being similar to the Italian *bronzo*, which is, in all probability, derived from *bruno*, signifying the brown colour of the metal. The ancient Greek word for it was χαλκός,* and

* Mr. Gladstone says *Chalkos* was copper, and that bronze was the metal called Kuanos.—*Juventus Mundi*, p. 532.

the Romans called it *aes*. The words *rame* and *ottone* in Italian, and *airain* in French, mean the metal called in English *brass*, and are sometimes incorrectly used by translators for the Latin *aes*. Brass is an entirely different alloy from bronze; it is composed of copper and zinc, while bronze is an alloy of copper and tin. It is found by analysis of ancient bronze, called *aes*, that it does not contain any zinc; neither is any zinc found in metal used by the ancients. Small proportions of gold, silver, lead, and iron were mixed by the ancient

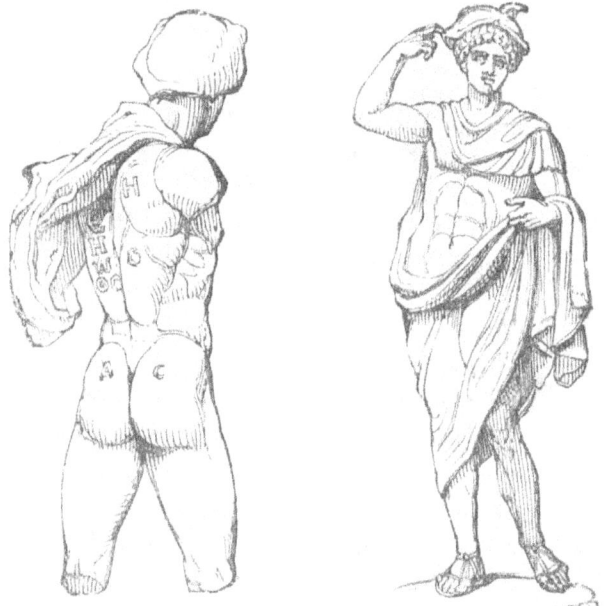

FIGS. 18, 19.—BRONZE FIGURES. *In the British Museum.*

metal-workers with their bronze to give various colour to the work; and this was a point to which much study was directed. Different kinds of *aes* are spoken of, such as the *aes Corinthiacum*, *aes Deliacum*, *aes Aegineticum*, *aes hepatizon*—on account of its liver colour—and others; but the precise composition of these is not known. The analysis of bronze—taken from some nails from the treasury of Atreus at Mycenae, a Greek helmet and a piece of armour (bronzes of Siris, Figs. 21, 22) in the British Museum, and a bronze sword found in

A.S.

France—gives in 100 parts, 87·43 copper, 12·53 tin, varying to 88 copper and 12 tin. The *aes Corinthiacum* was most highly esteemed, and is said to have been discovered accidentally by the running together of gold and bronze articles at the burning of Corinth by Lucius Mummius, B.C. 146. Pliny ('Hist. Nat.' xxxiv. 3) speaks of three kinds of Corinthian bronze. 1. *Candidum*, being made whiter with the addition of silver. 2. Golden-coloured, from the addition of gold. 3. A mixed alloy of gold, silver, and bronze. The *hepatizon* was inferior to the Corinthian, but was said to be better than the metal of Delos and Aegina. Mr. Gladstone, in that remarkable book of his, the 'Juventus Mundi,' which abounds with interesting matters of suggestion and instruction, says, referring to the making of the famous shield of Achilles by Hephaistos, — "The metals used were gold, silver, tin, and chalcos, which has been

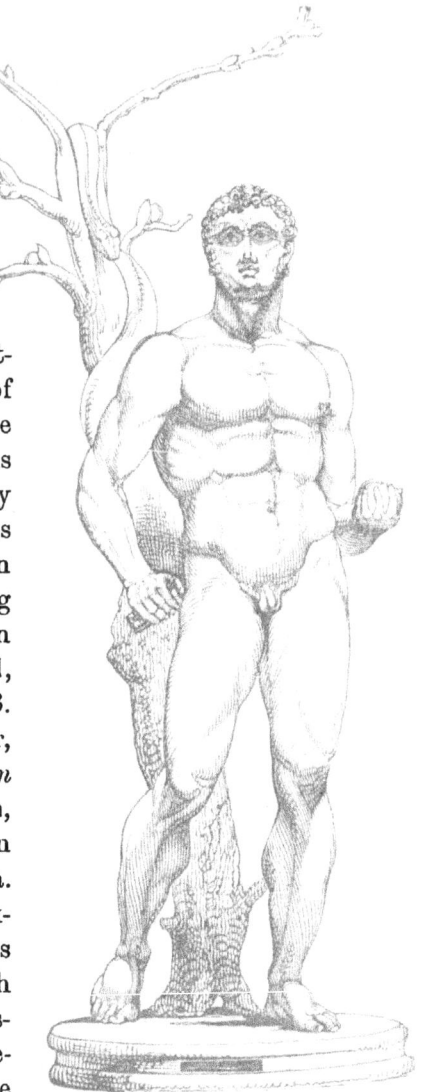

FIG. 20.—HERCULES HOLDING THE APPLE OF THE HESPERIDES.

Bronze, 30 inches high, found in 1775 at Jebely, Sira.

In the British Museum.

by mere license of translators interpreted as brass,—for there was no brass till long ages after Homer had rolled away,—which has been more plausibly taken to mean bronze, but which, after a good deal of inquiry, I am satisfied can only mean copper. . . If chalcos be not copper, then copper is never mentioned in Homer. . . One of Homer's epithets for chalcos is eruthros, *red ;* and this it is impossible under any conditions to apply to bronze. . . Surgical instruments made of copper alone have been discovered recently in a tomb at Athens. . . Chalcos in Homer was a very cheap and common metal ; tin a very scarce and rare metal, used in small quantities, and even approaching in some degree what we term a precious metal." Mr. Gladstone thinks it very improbable, therefore, that defensive armour and utensils could have contained an eighth part of tin, so as to be of the composition of our bronze. He thinks that the six deities in the planetary worship of the East were connected with the six pure metals, and a seventh, Kuanos, which he thinks may be bronze. In order of value he places them—gold, silver, tin, kuanos, iron, chalcos, lead. " Tin was used in small quantities for ornaments, and plated on copper. The only articles entirely made of it were the greaves of Achilles ; and these proceeded from a divine, not a human, workman (' Iliad,' xxi. 582-590, 594)." The alloy of gold and silver, called electrum, was so named after the word for amber (ἤλεκτρον), from its resemblance to the colour of that substance. Helen is said to have dedicated a cup made of elektron, of the exact size and form of her own breast, in the temple of Athene at Lindos (' Plin.,' xxxiii. 23).

The ancient bronze-workers sought to obtain effects of colour ; as Pliny states that Aristonidas made a statue of *Athamas* that showed the blush of shame in the face, by the rusting of the iron mixed with the bronze. Plutarch mentions a *Jocasta dying*, the face of which was pale, the sculptor Silanion having mixed silver with the bronze. A representation of the *Battle of Alexander and Porus* was like a picture, from the different colours of the metal employed. Possibly these effects were obtained by inlaying with metals of different colours.

The primitive bronze-workers began by hammering solid metal into shapes, before they arrived at the knowledge of casting. The " toreutic " art, although not definitely known at present,

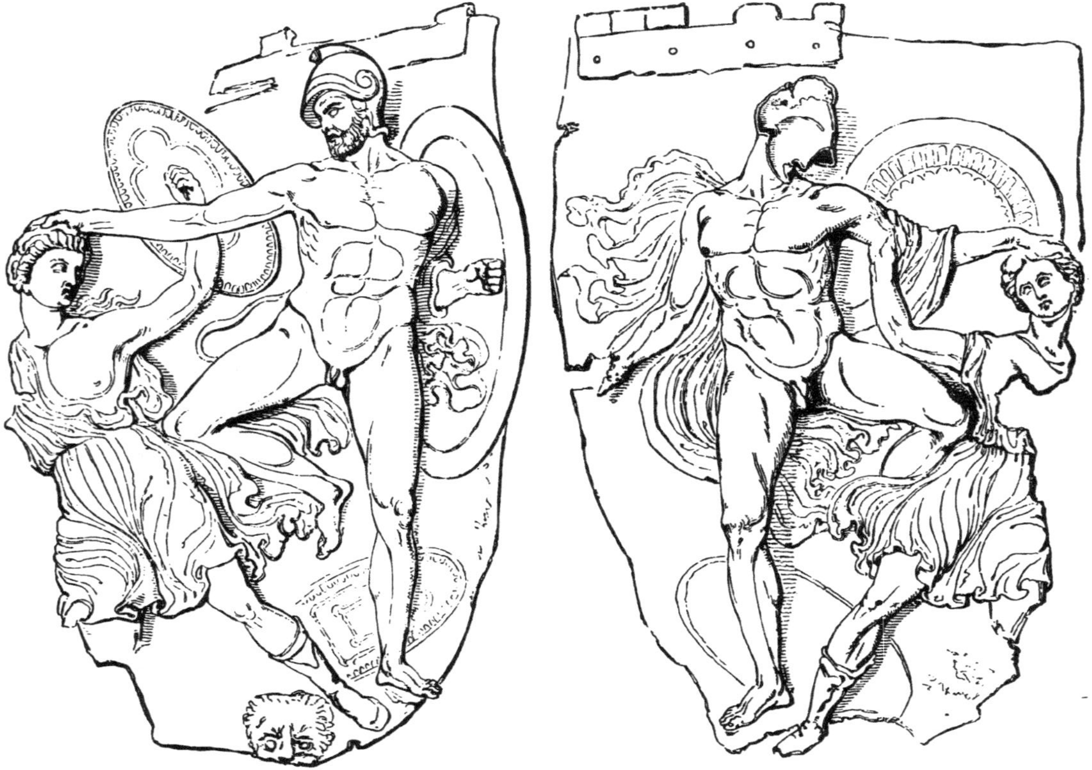

FIGS. 21, 22.—THE BRONZES OF SIRIS—THESEUS AND AN AMAZON. SHOULDER PIECES OF ARMOUR. NOT CAST, BUT REPOUSSÉ.

was probably that of hammering, punching, and chiselling plates of metal, either separately or with a view to fixing them upon stone or wood. Much ancient work was of this kind, as the famous shield of Achilles, described by Homer; the chest of Kypselos,* made about 700 B.C. ; and the ornamental work of the temple of Jerusalem. The Greek word for hammer, σφῦρα, gave the name of σφυρήλατον to work of this kind. Pliny refers to solid hammered work and hollow plate work, "holosphyraton" and "sphyraton." Diodorus Siculus speaks of statues of this kind in the gardens of the palace of Ninus and Semiramis; and Pausanias mentions a solid bronze statue of Dionysus at Thebes, the work of Onasimedes. Many examples are to be seen in museums. The hollow statues were built up in pieces, fastened together with nails, rivets, and dovetails, and it is not improbable that some method of soldering was practised, and perhaps "welding."

The casting of metal in moulds of a very simple kind for small ornaments like rings, the pendants of necklaces, buttons, and bosses, must have followed upon the discovery that metals could be melted in the fire. There are many allusions to this in the Bible (Job xxviii. 1, 2), and to the refiner and purifier of "gold seven times purified."

As the sculptor improved in his art of modelling he would be able to make better moulds. He would soon observe that his solid statue was not only a costly work but a very heavy one. He would find that solid arms broke off at the trunk from mere weight, or that his whole figure had collapsed from the same simple cause. Thus he would be led to seek some means of overcoming these defects in his cast statues, which, though an improvement upon his hammered ones in their correctness of form, were not so durable. This was accomplished by the discovery of a contrivance for casting metal in a hollow form. It was done pretty much as it is at the present day, by fixing a solid but removable mass within the mould, technically called a " core," so that it did not touch the sides except at certain small

* Pausanias, who describes the subjects on it, says the artist of this is not known, but he suspects he was the Corinthian Eumelos, from comparison with other works of his.—Lib. v. c. 19.

points necessary for support. The space between this and the surface of the mould was that to be taken by the molten metal. There is in the British Museum a bronze in which the casting has failed, and the "core" is seen left within. As to the date of this important improvement nothing satisfactory can be stated. Theodorus of Samos is named by Pausanias, and Rhæcus of Samos by Herodotus, as the inventors in bronze work

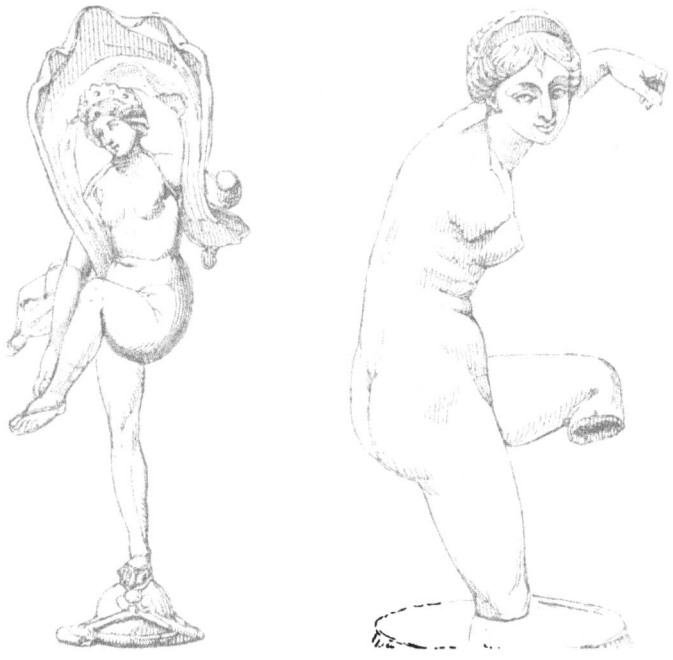

FIGS. 23, 24.—BRONZE STATUETTES.

In the British Museum.

who distinguished themselves so much that their names are handed down as the first to arrive at perfection in the method. Gitiades of Sparta, Glaukias of Aegina, and Glaukos of Chios were other sculptors in bronze of the sixth to the seventh century B.C.

There is still another method of casting, which though common in later times, there is some reason to consider was employed by the ancients for some of their smaller works, such as the statuettes and other objects abounding in the museums (Figs. 23, 24). This is when a wax model, after having been completed by the sculptor, is encased in clay or plaster of Paris, and the molten metal, for small objects, is then poured into it to melt the wax, or the wax is melted out through vent-holes, and so takes the form of every minute and delicate part of the work precisely as it left the hand of the sculptor. The original model is thus destroyed, and the bronze as a solid casting takes its place in the permanent work ; hence it has been termed by the French a ' *cire perdue.*' This method, which was practised by Cellini and before him by the great Italian medallists of the Renaissance, has great advantages in securing the spirit of the master-work. Some large and beautiful works have been cast in this way in recent years, one of the most remarkable being the group of *Two Gladiators*, by M. Gérome, the distinguished painter.

It must be explained with reference to bronze casting with a *core*, that this necessary contrivance has to be formed with very considerable care and practical skill. The mould, which is obliged to be formed of pieces which fit together, in order that the model may be taken out, is first well soaked in oil ; then melted wax is applied to the inner side of the moulded parts in such thickness as may be required in the metal of the completed statue. But as no hollow metal statue would be strong enough to support its own weight, or to be fixed on its pedestal as it is to stand permanently in the attitude designed, a sort of skeleton of iron bars is made to take the general form of the figure, and this strong framework is firmly fixed within the mould. We have then the mould with its wax lining, so to speak, enclosing the iron skeleton, or " *armature* " as it is called, with an opening left in the proper place to allow of pouring in the liquid plaster of Paris mixed with pounded brick, which is to fill up the space around the armature, and set into a solid mass close up to the wax lining. Therefore, if at this stage the mould were taken to pieces again, the sculptor would behold his statue as one of apparently solid wax. Practically this is done in order that he

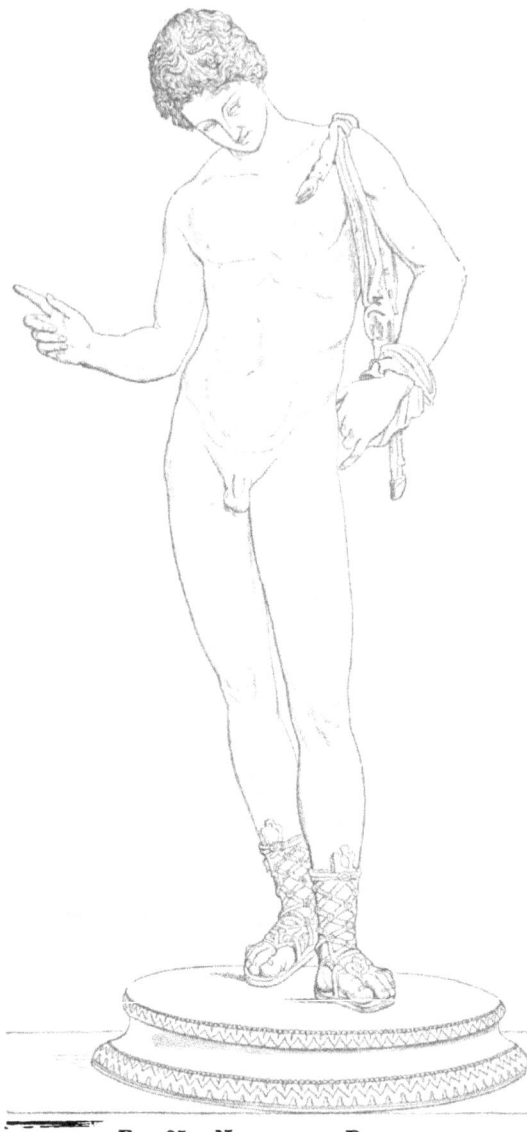

FIG. 25.—NARCISSUS. BRONZE.
Height 20 inches. Found 1830.
Naples Museum.

may satisfy himself of the success of the work so far, and correct it where necessary, especially where the joints of the mould have left any projecting pieces or lines on the wax, which would prove troublesome to remove in the final bronze casting. Then the model is again placed in the mould, and finally closed up, preparatory to melting out.

The wax, having served its purpose, is then got rid of by applying heat to melt it out of the mould —a process requiring care and time. Thus the mould is once more left empty, except the core, and ready for the operation of casting, which it is not necessary to enter into, since sculptors are no longer, as Benvenuto Cellini was, their own foundrymen. It remains to say that the core is removed by providing openings in certain convenient parts of the statue, either at some line of junction in the mould; or in larger work, where the limbs and trunk are cast separately. The iron armature is usually left in the legs when required, as it usually is in equestrian statues, and others needing support.

Galvano-plastique, or the use of electricity to deposit a thin layer of metal in a pure state upon a model, is an important invention or application of science to art, which has been recently carried out with perfect success. The fountain statues by Monti in the Crystal Palace are good examples.

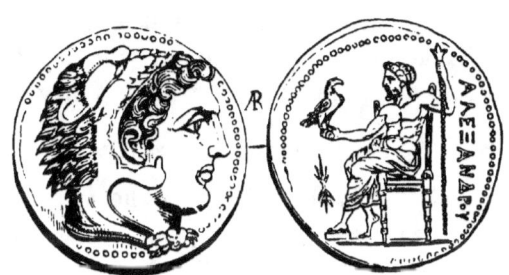

FIG. 26.—GREEK COIN OF ALEXANDER.

THE VARIOUS FORMS ADOPTED IN
ANCIENT SCULPTURE.

HAVING described the various materials and methods employed in sculptural art, we are in a condition to classify the different forms adopted, and arrange them under the proper terms.

All sculpture is measurable; and it has three dimensions—height, width, and depth. Sculpture in "the round," *i. e.* statuary proper, has also circumference or girth that may be measured.

SCULPTURE IN RELIEF.

1. *Bas-relief,* or "*basso relievo*" is the term used when the work projects from the general plain surface or ground, the forms being rounded as in nature.*

2. *Flat-relief,* or "*stiacciato*"—if the work is very little raised, the forms being not so projecting as in nature.

3. *Half-relief,* or "*mezzo-relievo*"—if more raised, but not free from the ground in any part, as in the Parthenon and other friezes (Fig. 1).

4. *Full-relief,* or "*alto-relievo*"—in which parts of the figures are entirely free from the ground of the slab; as in the metopes of the Parthenon (Fig. 27).

5. *Sunk-relief,* or "*cavo-relievo*"—in which the work is recessed within an outline but still raised in flat relief not projecting above the surface of the slab, as seen in the ancient Egyptian carvings.

* The Assyrian bas-relief work is peculiar, and was, no doubt, as suggested by Mr. Fergusson, painted, as were later works of the kind by the Greek sculptors. The Assyrian reliefs may be regarded, indeed, as sculptured pictures. Mediæval reliefs of all kinds were also painted, very commonly.

6. *Intaglio*—invented by the famous ancient sculptors in hard stones and gems. In this the figure is cut into the stone or metal, so that a cast taken from it, as in a seal, gives a *mezzo-relievo* or even an *alto-relievo*. When the gem is transparent the figure appears as if in relief, with very beautiful effect (Fig. 6).

Much of the Renaissance and modern sculpture combines the four first-named kinds of work on different planes in degrees of

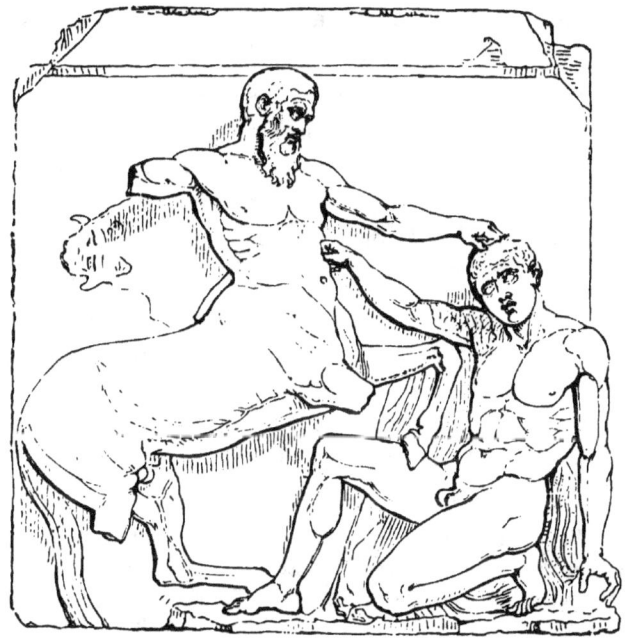

FIG. 27.—ALTO-RELIEVO. ONE OF THE METOPES OF THE PARTHENON.

distance, with some under cutting; thus departing from true relief in sculpture and approaching the pictorial form.

The beauty and character of bas-relief depend much upon the representation of outline. The projection is small in proportion to the distinctness and continuity of line enforced by this method, so conspicuously seen, in its most masterly style, in the frieze of the Parthenon (see Fig. 1). Besides the requisite of a fine conception of beauty and expressive forms, the greatest executive skill and tact are necessary to keep within the limits of sculptural art, so as to maintain the composition free from crowding, or the pressing out of form of one figure by another, and to give to each figure the full necessary space to stand and move in the action represented.

STATUARY.

STATUARY proper, which is so called from the Latin *stare*, to stand, is SCULPTURE IN THE ROUND, or as the French express it, " *en ronde bosse.*" *   A statue is therefore seen on every side. Statues are—1. Standing. 2. Seated. 3. Recumbent. 4. Equestrian. Statues are classed into five forms as to size :—

1. *Colossal*—above the heroic standard.
2. *Heroic*—above six feet, but under the Colossal.
3. *Life Size.*
4. *Small Life Size.*
5. *Statuettes*—half the size of life, and smaller.

The *Bust* (a name derived from the Latin, *Bustum*, a tomb, or rather a place for cremation) naturally came to be used for those portraits of deceased relatives which were placed in the entrance of dwelling-houses, by the Romans, who were the first to show the great love for portraiture not only of public characters but of their friends and relatives.

* The Egyptian statues, though never carved entirely "in the round," although in a standing or seated attitude, and never having the limbs entirely free, either from the trunk of the figure or the block out of which they are cut, are something more than alto-relievi. They have an æsthetic quality of expression and meaning which well dignifies them with the appellation of statues.   In the British Museum are ten archaic Greek statues of seated figures like the Egyptian colossi, which were found at Miletus.   Assyrian colossal figures are nearly all either alto or bas-reliefs ; only two or three statues have been discovered, and these are like the Egyptian statues, or standing with long drapery, showing only the front part of the feet, and being part of the block, so that the figure does not stand any more than the Egyptian statues, and the arms are not sculptured in the round, but fixed.   All sculptors, however, have to study how to conceal the means of support for their marble statues.   Sometimes this is afforded by the trunk of a tree, as in the famous Fighting Gladiator, or the lion's skin and club planted on the rock on which the ponderous Hercules of Glycon leans.

The ancient sculptors represented with great beauty the various mythological creatures described in their fables ; some of which are of the human form varied—as the Amazon, the Faun, the Syren, the Nereid, the Cyclops, the Janus or *bifrons* (double-faced), and the Hermaphrodite, uniting the characteristics of Hermes and Aphrodite. In other instances they invented the combinations of the human with the brute form of fabulous creatures described in ancient mythology : these are —(*a*) *Sphinx.* Lion with head of man or woman. (*b*) Man with eagle or hawk head. (*c*) *Minotaur*—Man with head or body of the bull. (*d*) *Centaur*—Man or woman with part of the trunk and limbs of the horse. (*e*) *Satyr*—Man with hind quarters of a goat. (*f*) *Triton*—Man with fish-tail. (*g*) *The Giants*—Men with serpents for legs. (*h*) *Harpy*—Woman and bird. Other strange creatures were of brutes only, as the *Hippocamp*—Horse and fish, with fins instead of hoofs ; the *Chimaera, Griffin, Dragon, Dog Cerberus* with many heads, &c.

COLOSSAL STATUES.

The most ancient statues were generally colossal, and carved in the hardest granite. The four Egyptian colossal seated figures hewn out of the living rock at the entrance of the temple at Ipsamboul, or Aboo Simbel, are 61 feet high.*

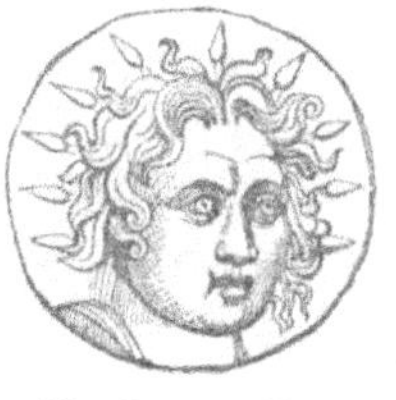

FIG. 28.—COIN OF RHODES.
Head of the Colossus.

But larger than these was the bronze Colossus of Rhodes, one of the seven wonders of the world (Fig. 28). This stupendous figure was 70 cubits high, and was long *said* to have stood with one foot on each side of the entrance to the harbour so that ships could sail under the legs. This is now proved to have been a fabulous story, by the discovery of the foundation stones for the statue. The ancient Egyptian cubit (not the Royal cubit) was, according to Mr. Sharpe, 17·7212 inches, so that

* Two of these were made of the full size of the ancient statues, the head of one having been moulded by, Mr. Bonomi in Nubia, which is in the British Museum, and which was used as a model for these reproductions under his direction in the Crystal Palace. They were, however, destroyed by fire about 10 years ago.

it would be about 115 feet high. The Athene *Promachos*, a bronze figure by Pheidias, placed on the Acropolis, to be seen at sea beyond the Piraeeus, was between 50 and 60 feet high. His statue of Athene within the Parthenon, a chryselephantine statue, was 47 feet high. His statue of Zeus, in the same materials, in the temple at Olympia, was a seated figure, 45 feet high in that position. Some of these colossal statues were built up in sections, and nailed, clamped, or dove-tailed together. Several other colossi are mentioned in history ; one in later Roman times, when Zenodorus made a bronze statue of Nero as Sol, 110 feet high. It was not completely executed, as the art was then partly out of use, but in A.D. 75, it was con-secrated as a Sol, and was afterwards changed into a Com-modus by adapting his head (see Pliny, H. N. xxxiv. 18).

It is interesting to remember that the Colossus of St. Charles Borromeo, placed on a hill near Arona, his birthplace, in 1697, is 66 feet high, standing on a pedestal 40 feet high ; it is formed of sheets of copper beaten out, and supported on a column of masonry ; the head, hands, and feet are cast in bronze.

The statue of Arminius, designed by Bandel, and erected in 1875, is also of hammered copper. It is 45 feet high, and stands on a pedestal 90 feet high, on the top of the Grotenberg, near Detmold.

The largest colossal statue of modern times is the " Bavaria," designed by Schwanthaler of Munich, and cast in bronze by Stiegelmayer, both of whom died unfortunately before their great work was completed in 1848. This draped figure of a German maiden is 54 feet high, the lion at her side is 27 feet high ; the group standing on a pedestal 30 feet high, in front of the Rumeshalle, on an eminence outside the west-gate of Munich.

Some rather large bronze statues have of late years been made by English sculptors. The most remarkable of these are the equestrian statue of George III. on an artificial rock at the end of the long walk at Windsor ; the equestrian statue of the Duke of Wellington which stood on the arch at Hyde Park Corner—now at Aldershot ; the figure in the Park, called the Achilles, which is a copy of one of the celebrated antique marble statues of Castor and Pollux on Monte Cavallo, at Rome ; the seated statue of Prince Albert in the Hyde Park Memorial, 12 feet high, of bronze gilt; the four Lions by Landseer at the base of the Nelson Column.

THE SCULPTOR'S 'CANON' OF PROPORTION.

To know the proper proportions of the figure is a matter of the utmost value in all sculpture, even more so than in painting, as the statue is measurable in every direction and viewed on every side. The work of making colossal statues is therefore not only one of artistic labour and expenditure of money, it requires also a careful study of the proportions of the human figure. It would have been impossible for the ancient Egyptian sculptors to carve out of the living rock those four tremendous figures at the entrance of the temple at Aboo Simbel, or indeed any of the numerous other statues on this scale, unless they had arrived at a rule of proportion for the figure. Without this their colossi would have been only rude monsters. Such a rule they had discovered and laid down in a "canon," as it is called, similar to that which was followed by the Greek sculptors after them, and especially made known by Polykleitos, whose name it received. Polykleitos, who flourished B.C. 452—412, was the greatest master of the school of Argos and Sikyon. He was instructed by Ageladas, and was fellow-student with Myron and Pheidias, who was his senior. Though there is some uncertainty as to the precise terms of the canon of Polykleitos, there can be no doubt that it had for its unit of measurement some part of the human figure. Ever since the time of Vitruvius Pollio, who wrote his well-known treatise on architecture and other branches of art in the first century of our era, it has been an accepted tradition that his version of the canon of Polykleitos was the correct one. He says (lib. iii. cap. 1):—"Nature has so composed the human body that the face from the chin to the top of the forehead and the roots of the hair should be a tenth part; also the palm of the hand from the wrist joint to the tip of the middle finger; the head from the chin to the highest point, an eighth; from the top of the chest to the roots of the hair, a sixth."

The rule of eight heads or ten faces derived from this has

remained to the present time. But Leonardo da Vinci differs from Vitruvius as to the proportions from the top of the chest to the roots of the hair, and states it to be a seventh instead of a sixth. Another similar difference is to be observed between Vitruvius and Leonardo; the foot being stated to be a sixth part of the height by the former, and a seventh by the latter. Mr. Bonomi, who was educated as a sculptor by Nollekens, and who gave much attention to this subject, remarks upon this point :—" The foot in the best antique statues is usually more than a seventh, and less than a sixth." * Prof. Schadorw states that the foot is as 10 to 66 as the height, not as 10 to 60, according to Vitruvius. Leonardo made a diagram in which a circle is applied so as to embrace the figure with extended arms; the circle is described from the navel as the centre (Fig. 29) : this he also took from Vitruvius :—" Item corporis centrum medium naturaliter est umbilicus." But it cannot be overlooked that a circle described from the navel does not show that it is the centre of the body; on the contrary, a circle drawn from this point would cut the line of the top of the head and a spot a little below the tuberosity of the tibia, or leg-bone. Leonardo added a square, of which each side is equal to the height of the body, and marked it into four horizontal divisions, which are certainly correct, viz. in the erect figure equal distances are found to extend from—1. the sole to the lower border of the patella; 2. from that to the pubes; 3. to the nipples; 4. to the crown of the head. The arms being extended horizontally, the tips of the middle fingers touch the sides of the square of Leonardo; the length of the outstretched arms is therefore the approximate measure of the height of the body in men and women, but, as might be expected, there are few persons—only six in eighty-four, according to Mr. Bonomi's measurements—in whom these proportions are exact. The other measurements of proportion given by Leonardo may be accepted, such as across the widest part of the shoulders in a man one-fourth of the height: from the elbow to the tip of the middle finger one-fourth of the height: from the elbow to the top of the shoulder is the eighth of the height of a man : the length of the ear is one-

* The 'Proportions of the Human Figure,' by Joseph Bonomi, 1872.

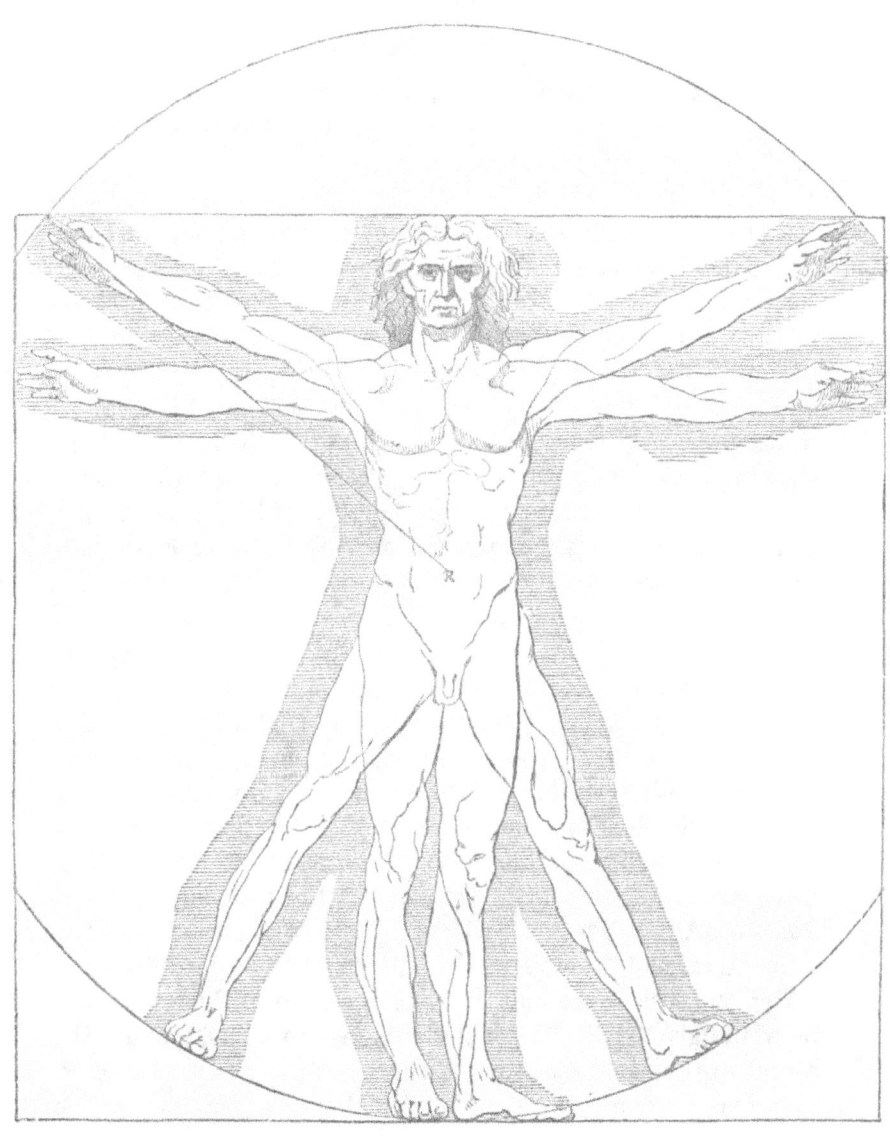

FIG. 29.—LEONARDO DA VINCI'S DIAGRAM.

*Showing that a circle of which the navel is the centre, embraces the extremities;
and that the extended arms to the ends of the fingers equal the height of the
figure.   But showing that the navel is not the centre of the body, as he stated.*

A.S.

third of the face : the greatest width of the hips is one-fifth of
the height. His observations upon the variations to be followed
in representing men, women, and children of certain characteristic types may also be relied on.

This subject, which is of great practical importance to
sculptors, has lately received much elucidation from M. Charles
Blanc, in his 'Grammaire des Arts du Dessin,' who supports
his views by the discoveries of Lepsius of Egyptian measures
of proportion and sculptors' canons, and by the observations of
Schadow (the late eminent professor at Dusseldorf) on the canon
of Polykleitos. To all this may be added the valuable measurements previously given by Clarac ('Musée de Sculpture,' 1841),
showing that eight heads are not the correct rule for the antique
statues. He also notices the variations in width, which though
of less moment are still a matter of great importance in reference
to characteristic forms or typical statues. The figure of woman
is narrower at the shoulders and broader at the hips than in
man (see Plate III. in Bonomi's 'Proportions'). The width of
the thigh and the calf of the leg is generally greater also. The
rule of an equilateral triangle, having its angles at the nipples
and the pit of the neck, holds equally in man and woman,
as does also that of three widths of the face, from the zygomas,
between the shoulders across the chest. M. Blanc, remarking
that the proportion of 10 faces has been so widely adopted,
mentions that a Spanish sculptor of the sixteenth century,
Juan de Arphe, wrote a book, very rarely seen, entitled ' Varia
Comensuracion,' * modifying the proportions of Vitruvius, and
taking the nose as the unit, it being one-third of the face. Thus
he would give 31 lengths of the nose instead of 30, making the
height of the figure seven heads and three-quarters. This, however, does not appear to be correct, for M. Blanc lays down as the
common proportion that there should be more than eight heads,
not less; the small head belonging only to athletes. Winckelmann
says a good deal rather vaguely about the number three being the
ratio, as it was that of perfection, according to Plato (' Timæus,'
p. 477), as that two things cannot exist without a third—a

* The original I have seen once, in Dr. Laing's library. The reprint is
to be met with more frequently.

beginning, middle, and end. In the growth of man three years gives the half of the full size. The face has three nose lengths, but the head has not four, but three and three-quarters. He considers that the foot was the unit employed by the ancients, and the height was determined by this, not by the head or the face. Still, after measuring many Egyptian figures, he is compelled to admit that the foot in them is not the unit of proportion; but in most of the Greek statues he found that it is. His instances, however, do not prove the correctness of his view as to the foot. M. Charles Blanc, in quoting Diodorus Siculus, a contemporary with Vitruvius, who states that the Egyptian sculptors divided the figure into $21\frac{1}{4}$ parts of equal length, says that he himself tested this with the statues at Karnac, and found that they were divisible according to the horizontal lines upon those in the temple of Ombos into about $22\frac{1}{4}$.

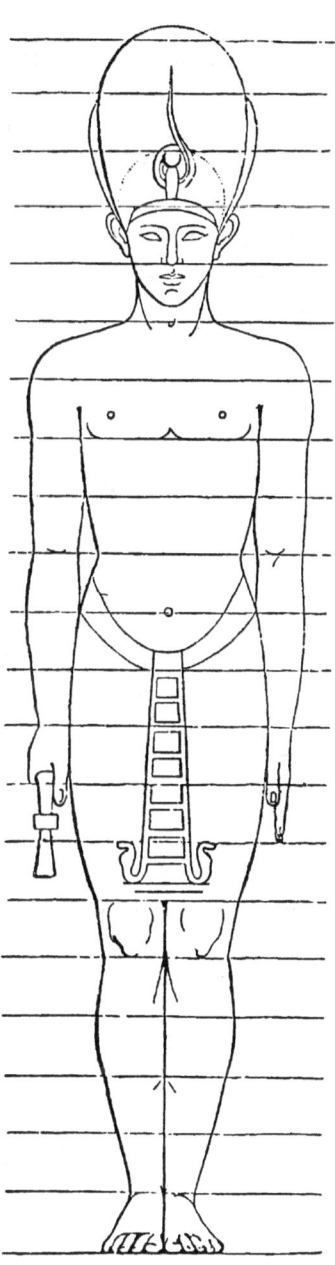

FIG. 30.—EGYPTIAN FIGURE HOLDING A KEY.

Divided by lines into 19 equal parts from the sole of the foot to the top of the head, and $21\frac{1}{4}$ to the top of the cap. Taken from a statue found by Lepsius and figured in his 'Choix de Monuments funéraires.' Each division corresponds to the length of the middle finger as shown.

M. Blanc concludes that the ancient canon was forgotten. He
points out that the length of the head and face from chin to
crown varies with age, that the nose being formed of bone and
cartilage cannot be invariable, and its point of juncture with
the forehead is not marked. It is necessary, then, to seek
some other member as the unit of proportion. He then goes on
to say that Chrysostome Martinez, in the text to his anatomical
plates, points out that the bones of the hand in their growth
preserve a constant proportion to the length of the body. He
thinks that the ancient Egyptians observed this, especially as

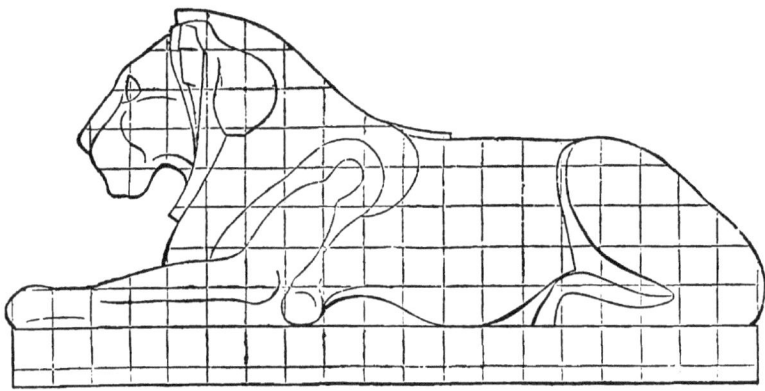

FIG. 31.—PROPORTIONS OF EGYPTIAN LION.

the hand was always regarded as the interpreter of the soul, and
had great importance in the mysterious science of Hermes : that
the *medius* (middle finger), as the finger of destiny, was chosen
as the unit of proportion. Referring to the great work of
Lepsius * he found a figure, divided into 19 parts (Fig. 30),
holding a key in the right hand, and letting the left hand fall
by the side of the thigh with the fingers extended, the eighth
line of division falling precisely at the knuckle of the closed
right hand holding the key, and the articulation of the *medius*,
while the tip of this finger touched the seventh line. This
figure, he considers, is the solution of the problem. The same
number of divisions is to be seen on a tablet with a lion

* Leipzig, 1852.

recumbent, in which the *carpus* and *meta-carpus* together (the paw) fill one space (Fig. 31).

The statement of Diodorus, above-noticed, that the Egyptian figures had a rule of 21½ divisions, is curiously confirmed, in this figure of the Lepsius collection having 21½, if the head-dress is counted in the height. So far M. Blanc; but it was well known long before that the Egyptian sculptors and painters worked by " squaring on " the figures to slabs and walls; and several, not to say many, examples seen in the museums show these lines either still on the work left unfinished, or under the colour on the surface. In the British Museum is " an ancient tablet on which is an outline exhibiting the canon of the proportions of the human frame, in use among the painters and sculptors in the age of Amunopth III., about 1250 years before our era " (*see* Bonomi on the Canon of Vitruvius, 1857, and Sharpe's 'Chronology and Geography of Egypt,' 1849). This tablet has two figures, each squared over, the one seated, and of larger proportions than the other. The seated figure has the feet and top of the head, without the usual high cap, exactly included in 15 squares; the standing figure of a female is also precisely included, but in 19 squares. Bonomi remarks in a note upon John Gibson's canon, the remarkable coincidence that this eminent sculptor divided the figure into 19 equal parts, of which two were to be taken as a radius for a circle, &c., and that this was the same as the Egyptian canon above referred to.*

M. C. Blanc having obtained measures of the Ægina statues in the Munich Museum, and of the *Achilles* and the *Athlete* in the Louvre, finds that the height is regulated by the *medius*, as are most of the other proportions—that from the navel to the pectoral muscles being rather less than in the Egyptian figure. The

---

* I once took occasion to ask Mr. Bonomi, who was a great friend of mine, and from whom I learnt much of Egyptian art, whether he had seen the work of M. Charles Blanc, and he told me he had not, and therefore he was not aware that the canon of Vitruvius was discovered to be an incorrect tradition as to the famous canon of Polykleitos. I think it will be found on examination that the key held by the Lepsius figure represents two medius lengths, and these are equal to one hand; also that 21 medius lengths, and a fraction over, are the rule for Egyptian figures, as Diodorus Siculus had stated.

Achilles is considered by Visconti to be taken from the bronze of Alkamenes; therefore it is a contemporary work with any of Polykleitos. Now, from the most careful measurements taken by M. Longperier, then keeper of the Louvre, it was found that this statue measured 2 metres, 33 millimetres, including the reliefs of the helmet. Allowing for these as equal to the loss by the slightly bent attitude of the head, the height was taken to be 2·035 millimetres. The length of the *medius*, compared with the distance from the bottom of the nose to the roots of the hair, was found to be ·107 mm., which multiplied by 19 gives 2·033 mm. Still further evidence is found in the two fingers in basalt marked with unequal divisions, which are in the Louvre collection, some single, some with two, joined—the index and *medius*.* These confirm the view as to the canon, and in hieroglyphics they are known to be employed to signify the sign numeral of unity. Two joined mean *justice, right, rule*, and naturally, *measure*. The subdivisions on these measures, however, have not yet been explained.

Unfortunately both the written canon of Polykleitos, and the statue canon in marble he made of a guard of the Persian king, armed with a lance—a '*Doryphore*'—are lost. But it is known that Pythagoras of Rhegium was acquainted with the *canon* which his contemporary Polykleitos treated of. They both lived in Olympiad LXXXVII, 5th century B.C., and Laertius says (lib. viii. in 'Pythagora'): Καὶ ἄλλων ἀδριαντεποιὸν Ῥηγῖνον γεγονεναι φασὶ Πυθαγόραν πρῶτον δοκѣντα ῥυθμѣ καί συμμετρίας εστοχασθαι—which points distinctly to measurement first taught by him who learnt from the Egyptians, as Diodorus says, Telekles and Theodoros, sons of Rhœkos, who lived in the eighth century B.C., and who made the Pythian

---

* M. Blanc observes that Paolo Pino—in his 'Dialogo di Pittura,' Ven. —states that from the top of the index finger to the middle phalanx is the same as from the chin to the opening in the lips, and this is also the measure of the mouth and the ears. The ungual phalanx of the same finger is the measure of the eye, and the space between the two eyes. The space from the nose to the opening of the ear is the length of the *medius*. He also mentions that Dr. Henszlmann finds that the *medius* is the unit of proportion in Egyptian architecture. ('Méthode des Proportions dans Architecture Egyptienne Dorique et de Moyen Age,' Paris, 1859.)

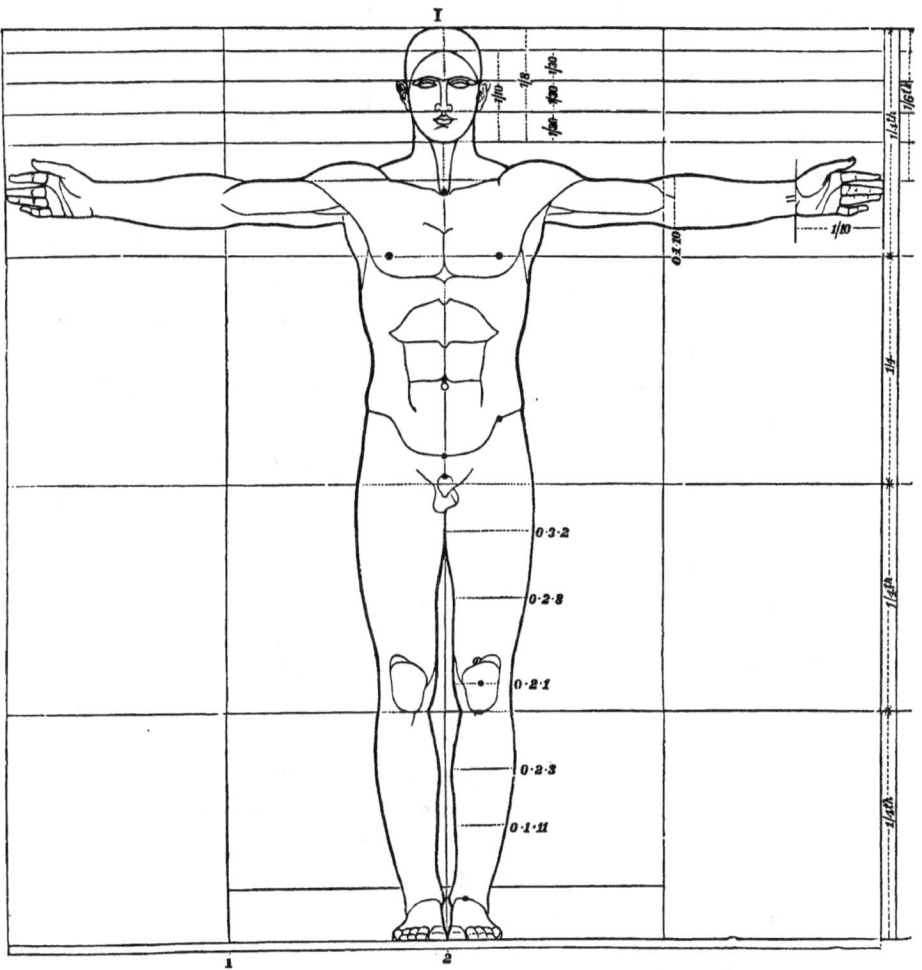

Fig. 32.—The Proportions of the Human Figure.

As handed down to us by Vitruvius—and described by Joseph Bonomi
in his 'Proportions of the Human Figure.'

Apollo for the Samians. So regularly was the work done, although the one sculptor made one-half (vertical half) at Samos and the other was made by Theodoros at Ephesus, when adjusted appeared as the perfect work of one sculptor.

But we arrive somewhat nearer to what was the precise nature of the canon of Polykleitos by what Galen has said of beauty. Freely translated, this would be: "The beautiful is not in the elements, but in the harmony of the parts of the body, of finger with finger, and all these with the *metacarpus* and the *carpus* (the bones of the hand), and of all these with the *cubitus* (fore-arm), and of the *cubitus* with the arms, and of all with all, according as it is written in the Canon of Polykleitos."

Τὸ δὲ κάλλος οὐκ ἐν τῇ τῶν στοιχείων, ἀλλ' ἐν ῇτ τῶν μορίων συμμετρίᾳ συνίστασθαι νομίζει, δακτύλου πρὸς δάκτυλον δηλόνοτι, καὶ συμπάντων αὐτῶν πρός τε μετακαρπίον καὶ καρπὸν, καὶ τούτων πρὸς πῆχυν, καὶ πήχεως πρὸς βραχίονα, καὶ πάντων πρὸς πάντα, καθάπερ ἐν τῷ Πολυκλείτου κανόνι γέγραπται—(Galen, ' de Hippocratis et Platonis Decretis,' l. v. p. 225, Ed. Ven. 1565).

From the well-known terms of the Greek 'measures it is obvious that the parts of the hand were taken as the standard from great antiquity, whether from the Egyptians, or simply from the practice as arising amongst all primitive nations. It is remarkable that while the Egyptians seem to have taken *length* as the measure, the Greeks took the *breadth* of the hand and fingers. To this day also by us the *breadth* of a hand is the measure used in describing horses. The following will suffice to show the Greek measures derived from the hand :—

Δακτυλος—a finger-breadth—Roman, *digitus*.

Κόνδυλος—(a knuckle), two fingers'-breadth.

Παλαισή or παλαστῆς, δῶρον, δοχμή or δακτυλο δοχμη—a hand's breadth.

'Ορθοδωρον—the length of the open hand.

Λιχάς—the span from thumb to fore-finger.

Σπιθαμή—the span from thumb to little finger.

Πυγμή—from the elbow to knuckle joints.

Πυγων—from the elbow to first joint of little finger.

Πῆχυς—(*Cubitus*) from elbow to tips of fingers.

Galen, as an anatomist, founded his statement on the bones ; and no doubt every sculptor who has relied upon safer and sounder knowledge of the figure than his own eye and feeling for proportion afforded, has been guided by the study of the bones of the human figure.

The proportions of the Human Figure as handed down to us by Vitruvius, and enclosed in a divided square, are described by Mr. Bonomi (Fig. 32).

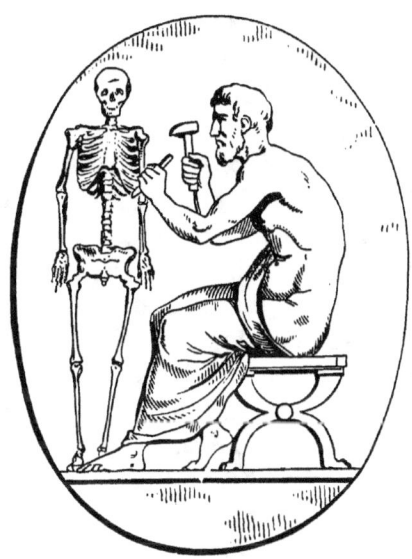

FIG. 32*a*.—PROMETHEUS CARVING A SKELETON.
From an antique gem.

Mr. John Marshall, F.R.S., the Professor of Anatomy at the Royal Academy, has invented a rule of proportion of which the unit is one inch, the length of the top bone of the middle finger, and according to which the general height of the male figure is 67 units or 5 ft. 7 in. This agrees very closely with the average of 500,000 American recruits for the army, which is 67·3.

"The head, neck, and trunk proper contain 36 units or 4 parts of 9 units each. The limbs are attached to the trunk at two points distant 2 heads or 18 units (*i. e.* between the *axes* of the shoulder and hip-joints), one of these points being 1 head

4 units (13 units), the other 3 heads 4 units (31 units), from the top of the head. The three successive segments of the upper limb (arm) measure 19, 9, and $7\frac{1}{2}$ units respectively; while those of the lower limb are 18, 14, and 9 units." The inch corresponds with the length of the top bone of the middle finger. (For further information see 'Athenæum,' no. 2783: Review of Mr. Marshall's book.)

That strict rules of symmetrical proportion should be followed, is necessary in all statuary, but more especially in that which is architectonic, or designed to serve as embellishment to architecture. The knowledge of the figure acquired by such sculptors as Pheidias, Alkamenes, and Praxiteles, and in after times by Donatello, Giovanni di Bologna, and Michelangelo, inspired them with the admiration of the beautiful, and enabled them to express an ideal of grand beauty, not so guided by religious dogma or priestly authority with its rule of measurement, but rather as creations of their art guided by a taste and feeling which rarely failed to direct them aright. We shall see in speaking of the æsthetic in sculpture how the ancient rules of symmetry were modified in giving liberty and spontaneity to the sculptor. It was the greatest sculptor of modern times— Michelangelo—who said, in reference to these rules of proportion, that the sculptor should have " his compasses in his eye." M. Charles Blanc, with his accustomed *esprit*, observes of this *mot*, that "sculptors and painters especially dread the rule of geometry. They regard rule as a fetter upon the liberty of their invention, but without dreaming that this great man (Michelangelo), before he expressed himself thus, had for so long a time had the compasses in his hand." This points to a profound truth in all practical art, that no man can be a great artist unless he have the power of drawing in the true proportions of the beautiful. If he have this gift, and has enlarged and strengthened the faculty by accurate observation and close study of the lines of nature, whether he designs on the scale of nature, on a colossal scale, or one so minute as that adopted by the great Greek gem-cutters, his figures will be in accord with the proportions developed in the most beautiful examples of antique art, and in Nature.

It must be evident that the most gifted sculptor would always be glad to assure himself by reference to any laws of form and proportion that can be formulated into a canon, such as we have been considering.

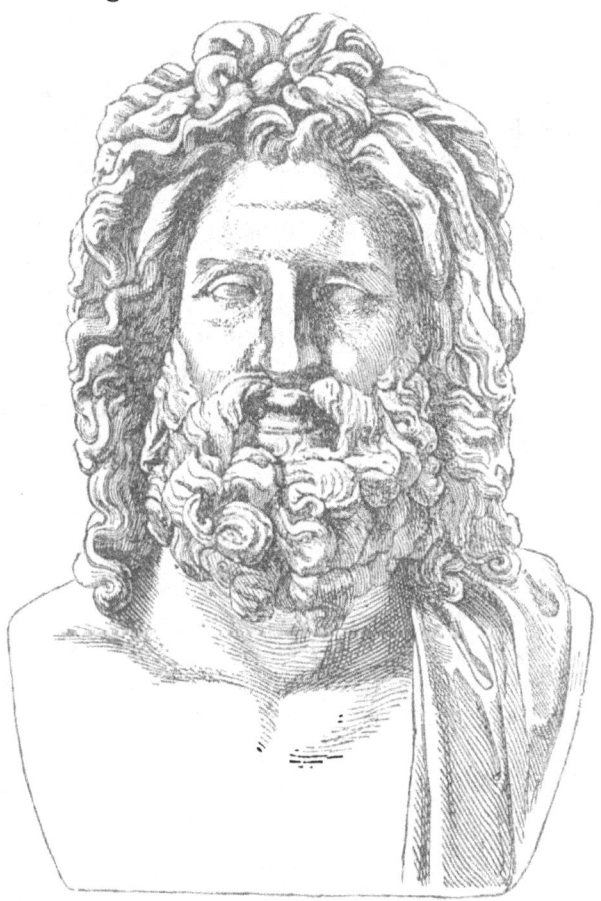

FIG. 33.—COLOSSAL BUST OF JUPITER. *In the Vatican.*
Found at Otriculum during the time of Pius VI.

CHARACTERISTIC TREATMENT OF PARTS OF THE FIGURE.

The method and character of work differ so much in sculpture of different periods, as well as in the works of different sculptors of the same period, that it is necessary to state some particulars upon this point, which however refer chiefly to technical execution.

THE HEAD in fine statues has a certain proportion to the height of the body. In archaic work it is nearly always too large, with dumpy bodies and thick limbs, the muscles of which are exaggerated and forced into lumps, and the joints made too prominent, with a view to show enormous strength. The forehead is massive and full at the brow in Jupiter, Neptune, Mars, Hercules, but not projecting from the line of the nose. The hair is carved in numerous round curls, having in some statues no connection or flow of continuous line. This was a quick and ready mode, but from being cut mostly with the drill, it shows great formality and dryness; in others it is in long straight rolls. In the bas-reliefs of the Harpy Tomb, the hair is wiry and collected on the forehead in bunchy curls. It is similar to this in the archaic statue of Artemis (Fig. 63), and in the two little acroter statues of Athene found in the Ægina ruins are long tails of hair falling on the neck, and the curls are arranged in two or three rows.

It is necessary to note some modes of treating the hair which were adopted as significant of the deities represented.*

Jupiter (Zeus).—Has the hair rising from a point at the top of the forehead, and falling all round the head in massive lion-like curls as in the bust (Fig. 33). Pheidias when asked by Panaenus where he found his idea of the head of Jove for his great statue at Elis (Fig. 16), replied it was in Homer's description of the god.† The beard of the Jupiter is equally marked in its full curling masses. The head of Laocoon is obviously borrowed from the Pheidian Jove, but it was an error in æsthetic knowledge to adopt the physiognomy of a deity.

---

* The fashion of wearing the hair and wigs as seen in many Roman busts need not be entered into. The stiff forms of the hair and beard in Egyptian, Assyrian, and Archaic Greek statues represent probably the effect of intertwining it with gold or silver threads.

† 'Η καὶ κυανέῃσιν ἐπ' ὀφρύσι νεῦσε Κρονίων
Αμβρόσιαι δ' ἀραχαῖται ἐπιρρώσαντο ἄνακτος
Κρατὸς ἀπ' ἀθανάτοιο μέγαν δ' ἐλέλιξεν Ὀλυμπον

('Iliad,' i. v. 528.)

He said, and nodded with his shadowy brows;
Waved on the immortal head the ambrosial locks,
And all Olympus trembled at the nod.—(Lord Derby's translation).

The same is noticeable in the fine head of Æsculapius in the British Museum, purchased in 1866 with the Blacas collection.

Apollo.—Has the hair falling in rich curls upon the neck and flowing at the temples, often gathered in a sort of knot on the front of the crown—κρωβύλος—as in the Apollo Belvedere. The Adonis of the Vatican has the hair on the neck in the manner of the Apollo, and is now called by that name. The Apollo Sauroctonos (see *Examples*) has the hair like a woman, and with a fillet. This form is of the soft feminine style, called " androgunaikal."

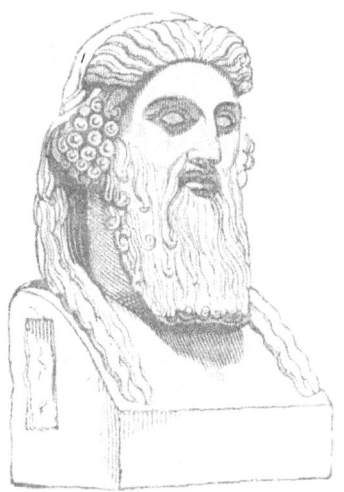
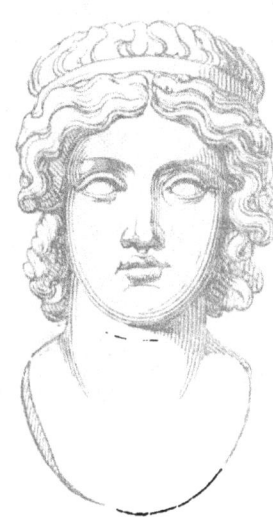

FIG. 34.—INDIAN BACCHUS. FIG. 35.—APOLLO.

Bacchus (Dionysus).—Has the hair falling in curls on the neck. The god is bearded in the early heads distinguished as the 'Indian Bacchus' (Fig. 34), but not in later work. Praxiteles first made Dionysus youthful.

Cupid (Eros).—Curls on neck (Fig. 124, Cupid and Psyche). A tuft-like curl on the fore part of the hair is given to genii.

Diana (Artemis).—Knot on the top (Figs. 36, 37), like Apollo.

Hercules (Heracles).—The hair curled thick upon the forehead, like the hair between the horns in a young bull: as indicating great strength. It stands in close, strong curls all over the head set on a " bull neck " (Fig. 20). The Hercules of

Ionia has the skin of the lion's head worn over the hair; seen also in the coins and gems.

Hercules (Herakles).—A young Hercules with laurel-wreath may be mistaken for an Alexander the• Great or other king (Winckelmann). The heads of Alexander have more resemblance to Zeus, whose son he wished to be considered, in the hair rising off the forehead like the Olympian Jove of Pheidias (Fig. 38, coin). Hyllus, the son of Hercules, is represented with a ram's horn on the left side of the head, as seen also in the coins of Alexander.

Mercury (Hermes).—Curly hair, but not on the neck (Fig. 134). In the older hieratic type the hair is smooth and wiry

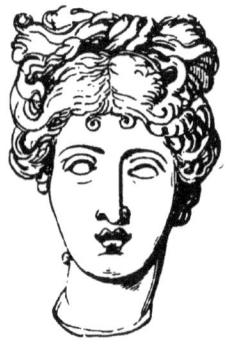 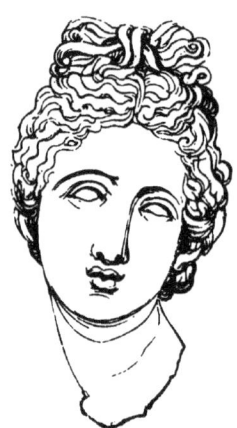

Fig. 36.—Artemis. *Brit. Mus.*   Fig. 37.—Artemis. *Brit. Mus.*

on the crown, with stiff regular ringlets below a fillet, and long plaited tail; the beard stiff and pointed.

Neptune (Poseidon).—Long curls as if wet, parted at the forehead.

Pluto (Plouton, Hades).—Long, straight hair hanging on the shoulders, and low on the forehead, somewhat like Zeus, as the ruler of the lower world.

Venus (Aphrodite).—The hair parted on the top, and gathered into full wavy tresses towards a knot, higher than in the maiden style. Sometimes bound with a fillet or a band of metal, as in the Venus of Cnidos, seen on the coins (Fig. 145).

Amazons have the hair parted and in full waves from the

front, gathered back and fastened in a thick knot at the lower part of the occiput. This is also the form generally adopted for virgins by the Greek and Roman sculptors, and followed by the moderns for maidens and martyrs.

Greek women frequently gathered the hair into a knot on the top of the head, called Κόρυμβος.

Gladiators and Athletes.—Hair in short stubbly curls, from having been cut, as in the Discobolus (Fig. 127). The hair of the so-called 'Dying Gladiator' shows that it was not intended for a gladiator; his shaggy sticking-up hair is that of the half-savage Gauls.

Satyrs and Fauns.—The hair in stiff short curls, standing up at the points, to give the character of the hair of wild animals. In the famous Faun of the Capitol (Fig. 130), the hair falls in more full curls on the neck. Pan was called Φριξοκόμις—in English " frizzed haired."

THE EYES.—These are very differently represented according to the date of the work. In archaic statues and bas-reliefs, the eye is very nearly level with the brow, and the lids, instead of being curved as in nature, are straighter, and the borders of the lids elongated towards the cheek and inclined upwards; the face being in profile the eye is often shown in full. The eye is made out in some examples without much modelling, but with chiselled lines, the pupil being also marked with a line and a dot, giving a stare. The narrow eye with the outer corners elevated belongs to Fauns and Satyrs. But as any marking of the eye is little seen in statues to be viewed from a distance, it became necessary to make the brow more prominent and marked, so as to cast shadow, and the ball of the eye was left plain. In coins before the time of Pheidias the pupil was marked, and strongly afterwards in those of Alexander (Fig. 38). In all the finest statues,

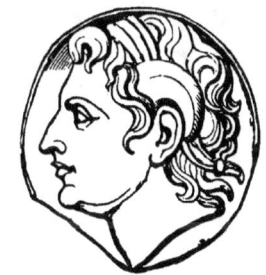

FIG. 38.—COIN OF ALEXANDER.

however, the ball of the eye is quite plain. In many it is hollowed out deeply, to represent the dark of the pupil, and also the form and colour of the iris: but this is not in strict keeping with sculptural art. It is constantly adopted in modern works up to the present time, many sculptors actually representing the reflected high light on the globular form of the eye by leaving a speck of marble or bronze. The eyes in the colossal figures of Castor and Pollux, known as the Monte Cavallo groups, are strongly cut into in this way, and the coloured part (the *iris*) is raised from the ball of the eye quite an eighth of an inch. The magnificent onyx cameo (Fig. 7), the Gonzaga cameo, now in the museum of St. Petersburg, of Ptolemy I. and his queen Eurydice, shows the eyes strongly marked.

In bronze statues the eyes were deeply drilled often, to show the pupil with light and shade upon it, and engraved or chiselled for the iris. But in many fine works the whole of the ball of the eye seen was cut away, as in the bronze head of Artemis (*see* Frontispiece), and the space filled with enamel, coloured to represent the natural eye. Gems were also used for this purpose, and coloured glass, so as to give the appearance of actual life. Probably this arose from the common custom of painting statues with wax and colours—the *circumlitio* which Pliny describes—which, with the gilding of the hair and the ornaments of diadems, ear-rings, and bracelets, was resorted to on any great festival. (*See* description of Venus de Medici, Sec. IV. *Examples.*)

In the Jupiter, Juno, Apollo, and Athene, the eyes are large,* the ball being full and round, and rather short in the horizontal axis. The eye of Athene has the upper lid rather low upon the ball, so as to give the serious and chaste look of the virgin deity. Venus has rather small eyes, with the lids somewhat closed, giving that charm of languor which the Greeks admired, and named ὑγρόν—literally, "moisture."

The eyebrows crown the beauty of the eye, and their beauty consists partly in the constant change of form they undergo with every passing expression, in which they play an important part, and which has so much effect without being noticed as forming the countenance. They are formed by very delicate gradation of

---

* The appellation of " ox-eyed " to Juno is not, however, the proper one for the Greek of Homer—Βοῶπις—the syllable Βο being merely an expletive, signifying large, and having nothing to do with Βοῦς, an ox, whose eyes in the Italian and Spanish beast are so large and prominent.

line, and by the diminution in the fineness of the hairs from the centre to the angle of the brow, indicating the form of the bone.

The form of the brow is always carefully modelled in antique work, but the hairs of the eyebrow are not marked distinctly, such detail not being in accord with the antique style. The Venus of Melos, the Ludovisi Juno, the Apollo Belvedere, and especially the bronze head of Artemis (*Frontispiece*), are examples of this. Praxiteles is said to have excelled in modelling and carving the eyebrow. Theokritos praised eyebrows that joined at the root of the nose; and Porphyrogenitus describes Ulysses as Συνοφρυς, but though there are some portrait busts, as that of Julia, the daughter of Titus, with joined or meeting eyebrows, yet this was not considered a beauty by the ancients. Augustus had meeting eyebrows, according to Suetonius, but this peculiarity is not seen in his busts as it is in those of Lucius Verus strongly marked.

THE MOUTH, next to the eyes, is the great feature of expression; it follows in its beautiful undulating lines, more freely and more fully, the thoughts as well as the words which come from it, like water from the mountain spring. To represent this mobile feature in bronze, in hard stone, and marble, is the most taxing effort of a sculptor, as it is that which most tries the mettle of the painter. We see what importance the Greeks attached to it by their inventing the masks worn by actors in their large theatres. The tragic, with its square, wide-open lips and eyes; the comic, with its round mouth and eyes half-closed and slanting.

The lips in the archaic statues are closed, but the angles of the mouth are curved up to give a smile, and in the dying warriors of the Ægina pediment (Fig. 74) this peculiar smile is very marked.

The lower lip in the *Minerva* is fuller and rather more projecting, supported by a larger chin than in the other female deities, giving gravity and sternness. *Venus* has the lips more delicately modelled, and a little parted. *Apollo* has the lips parted. " Marmoreus tacita carmen hiare lyra " (Propertius).

Diana has a full under lip and arched upper, the chin being strongly formed, and the nose straight.

A.S.

Jupiter has a full under lip ; the moustache and beard indicating the strong forms beneath.

The Deities are never represented laughing, and never show any sign of emotion.

Satyrs and *Fauns* show the teeth if laughing. The teeth are seen in the Monte Cavallo colossi. They are also carved in the Laocoon.

In portrait statues of Roman emperors the mouth has the lips invariably closed firmly.

THE CHIN.—This, in antique statues of deities, is always full, prominent, round, and without any dimple.

THE NOSE, in all fine Greek statues, is nearly on a line with the profile of the forehead. Except in portrait busts there is no example of a high bridge or scarcely any rise—nothing like an aquiline nose—in antique Greek or Roman sculpture, though it is so in Egyptian and Assyrian heads. In archaic Greek statues the nose is rather turned up, as in those found in Cyprus by Cesnola and others, many of which are in the archaic room of the British Museum (Fig. 64). This important organ has so generally been destroyed in the antique statues that the types are not so clear as in other features. Jupiter has the nose straight, the full length of its proportion—a quarter of the head—thick at the root and broad at the bridge, and towards the end, the nostrils wide and full; a massive nose. Hercules has a shorter nose, broad bridge and root, but thinner than in the Jupiter at the tip and the nostrils. The Apollo nose has more upward curve at the end than in the Jupiter, and his sister Diana shows a similar tendency, as does Venus also. Minerva has the long, straight, sharply-cut nose, with thin close nostrils occupying a space equal to an eye in length. In Fauns and Satyrs the nose is flattened at the bridge, and spread out at the nostrils, the openings of which are exposed. The extreme Satyric nose approaches that of the goat, and the openings in the nostrils slant upwards.

THE EAR.—No part was more scrupulously studied in its complex forms by the ancient sculptors than the ear; for this reason it is one of the tests of genuine work. Even in the minute work of the glyptic artist the ear was a point of excellence on which he prided himself, and on which he never neglected to bestow his best skill. Any defect or want of finish here is a sure sign that the work is not of a high order. In portraiture the ancient sculptor was careful to observe the individual character of the ear, and there is no part more distinctive, perhaps. Marcus Aurelius had a very open meatus or passage to his ear, and this would be enough to conclude whether a separate ear belonged or not to his bust (Winckelmann). This character is the reverse of that seen in the ears of Gladiators, Athletes, and especially of Hercules, who have the opening small and the cartilages strongly developed, though flattened. The ears of Fauns are elongated at the top like those of an animal ; the ears of Satyrs more so, and both often have goat's horns. The Centaur (Fig. 44) has pointed ears.

THE CHEST.—A full and finely-proportioned chest, according to the general character of the figure, whether of a Jupiter or an Apollo, a Hercules or a Neptune, is always given. The proportions in width and symmetry have been given in speaking of the figure generally. The salience of the pectoral muscles, and the serrati seen upon the ribs, and the forms of the cartilages with the muscles at the central line of the body (*linea alba*), are strongly marked in Hercules and Neptune. In Apollo these parts are softened, especially in the young god.

In statues of Minerva the chest is invariably covered with the ægis, which was originally the skin of the goat Amalthea that suckled Jupiter as an infant, and which he wore with the Gorgon's head when he conquered the Titans ; hence he is called by Homer Αἰγίοχος, the ægis-bearer. This was afterwards covered with scales of armour. Beneath both, however, the form of the woman's bosom is always shown, though not so prominently as in Venus, Ceres, and Proserpine. The Fates (Fig. 94) show the breast very fully. Amazons have the left breast large and full ; they are said to have cut off, or branded, the right breast of their female infants, because it interfered with the use of the bow in war. But it must be borne in mind that the breast was never at all prominent in fine antique statues, and the nipples were always small, and in Venus coming to a round pointed form which was considered the most beautiful. This, however, is a virginal form. The Diana has also this form, except as the goddess of the Ephesians, when it becomes exaggerated all over the body, and multiplied (πολυμαστος). The nipple is placed in many statues exactly in the centre of the breast, which is not as it is in nature, except in very exceptional instances. It should be a little towards the outer side, and from the dependance, a little below the centre of a circle. In the Parthenon frieze figures, the natural model is followed with most remarkable truth.

THE ABDOMEN.—This yielding part of the trunk, which varies much under different circumstances, is never represented bulging or flaccid in antique statues. The beautiful undulating forms of the muscles and broad tendinous bands that unite in keeping the viscera in place in a vigorous man or woman have always attracted the admiration, and occupied the highest skill of ancient and modern sculptors. We have only to look at the Theseus and Ilyssus of the Parthenon, and the nude figures of Michelangelo on the Medici Tomb, to see this. The instances in which any violent action is shown are few, such as the Laocoon, in which the strong marking of the edge of the rib cartilages by the spasm of the abdomen muscles is finely studied. In the Apollo Belvedere a certain compression of the abdomen appears, which always accompanies the holding of the breath during an effort, and would confirm the suggestion that the god had just let fly the arrow, and was watching its effect. The Clapping Faun (Fig. 39) is another example of this compression. This statue should be compared with the Meleager and the Mercury as well as the Adonis of the Vatican, in which these muscles are in repose. These muscles in the Farnese Hercules are much exaggerated, and turgid with fat, especially at the crest of the ilium (hip-bone). In the Torso Belvedere they are very finely treated in union with those of the chest, and suggest some strong action, and in the Hermes (Fig. 134). A sure mark of debased work is a swollen form in the muscles of the trunk, and especially where the bones of the pelvis show where the "walls" of the abdomen start from this line, marked in nature only by a gentle swell of the soft parts. The veins on the abdomen are exaggerated in statues of Hercules of a debased style, under the mistaken notion that they represent strength. These veins are only slightly shown in fine statues.

THE HIPS.—The greater natural width of the body at this part in the woman than in the man has been already noticed. It does not, however, amount to much, and in the antique it is always kept within rather than beyond this limit of proportion, as in the Venus of Melos. Even in the well-known Venuses of the Naples Museum, of which the Venus Callipyge is one, this rule is kept. Not even in Roman work was there any of the exaggeration that is to be noticed in some modern statues of the Venus type. The Venus of the Capitol, and the Medici Venus, are examples of careful natural study (Figs. 143—147).

THE BACK.—No part of the figure was more carefully and intelligently studied than the muscles of the back—those of the shoulders which aid in the strong exertion of the arms, and of the neck in the attitude of the head, and those which hold the body erect and direct its movements, acting on each side of the bony column of the spine, having firm roots of attachment, so to speak, on the solid base of the pelvis and the sacrum (hip-bones). The finest examples are the Theseus (Fig. 91), the Ilyssus, the Torso Belvedere, the Wrestlers, the Venus of Melos, and the Medici Venus. The true love and admiration of the natural beauty of the human figure which inspired the great Greek sculptors is finely shown in the care bestowed upon this most difficult part of the figure in statues which could not be seen at all from behind, as in the pediment of the Parthenon. The back is therefore one of the great test points in a statue.

THE THIGHS AND LEGS, as well as the UPPER and FORE-ARM, in antique statues, are always studied with careful attention to the differences between the man and woman, and in men the varied forms indicating the character of the person are represented. The arm of Apollo is somewhat soft and feminine in the muscles ; so also is that of Mercury, though slim and wiry. The legs correspond. The limbs of Achilles and Hercules are of course strongly developed. The Antinous and Adonis have the forms undulating and smooth. In Jupiter the limbs are massive and powerful, the muscles being full, but not with the hard and sharper contour of the Neptune, Hercules, and Vulcan. The knees of the

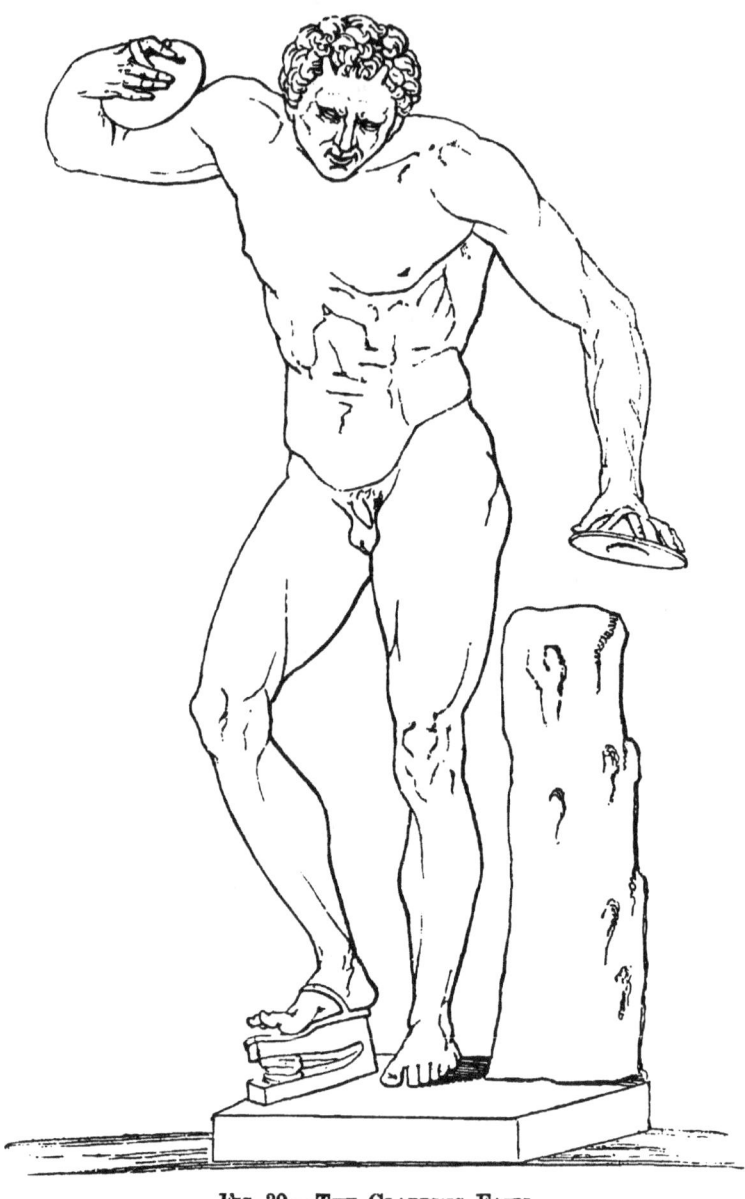

FIG. 39.—THE CLAPPING FAUN.

The head and arms are restorations by Michelangelo. The *scabellum* on the
foot is found on other bacchanal figures.   Marble.   Ht. 4ft. 8½in.

In the Museum, Florence.

Apollo Belvedere and Apollo Sauroctonos are considered the most perfect.

In the late and debased Roman work the forms of the muscles about the knees are dropsical and baggy, showing ignorance of the natural state of the muscles and their true form.

In the statues of the finest time the veins are rarely shown, neither are the tendons at the wrists, and on the backs of the hands and feet. But in the Laocoon the superficial veins on the shoulder and arm, as well as on the thigh and leg, are prominently carved. The Fighting Gladiator shows similar taste in the display of tendons and muscles. This became rather to be admired, displaying knowledge of form and great energy of life ; but as seen in statues of the decadence, where it is common, it is nearly always at fault as regards the correct situation and form of the veins. This kind of work tends to the gross and exaggerated and indicates poor art.

THE HANDS.—So far as the hands and feet can be studied in those rare examples of antique work that remain, it is observable that the forms of the bones were little made out, though they are indicated with perfect truth. Neither the tendons nor the veins on the back of the hands are ever seen strongly marked. The fingers are tapered, but never turned back, as in the modern hands supplied to the Medici Venus. The nails are never long or filbert-shaped, but rather short, broad and rounded. The best examples of antique hands are in one of the sons of Niobe (*Florence Mus.*), the hand stretched on the ground ; a group of Mercury embracing Herse (*Farnese Palace*) has the two hands of Herse and one of Mercury antique ; and one hand of the Hermaphrodite is perfect (*Villa Borghese*). The left hand of the *Apoxyomenos* (Fig. 121) is also a good example of true antique work.

THE FEET.—The sandal of the ancients was favourable to the natural growth of the foot. As a rule, therefore, this part is thoroughly understood by the antique sculptor, who admired the feet. Aspasia and Polyxena are said to have had beautiful feet. The Meleager and the Apollo Belvedere have good feet, and in these the details are rather subdued, though the pliant forms of the ankle and toes are finely rendered. The

nails are rather flatter than in modern statues, arising from the
absence of cramping by shoes.   If the hands and feet are badly
carved the statue is probably a feeble work.

By consulting the Index, the reader will find engravings of
most of the statues mentioned.

DRAPERY.

The great importance of the drapery given to the antique
statues, such as we see in the highest style in the Parthenon
figures, especially of the Fates (Fig. 94), is so universally admitted
that it is not necessary to enforce it here.   It may be remarked,
however, that such is the beauty of fine drapery, that, next to
the portrayal of the nude, it is the highest test of the style and
merit of sculpture.   It is so because to model and carve the folds
so that the beauty of the figure should be displayed, and yet so
far concealed, demands the subtlest art.   To show the action of
the figure also in the forms of the drapery is equally part of the
design.   Goethe, whose critical observations in art were so
instructive and so profound, called drapery " The thousand-fold
echo of the form."   The finest examples that can be pointed
out are those of the Parthenon marbles.   In some, as in the
Fates, we see what dignity and grace, combined with infinite
variety and beauty of line, is given to this superb group, although
the heads, and all that could give expression of an intellectual
kind, are gone.   This is a good example of drapery in grand
repose.   Movement is rendered with consummate art in many
instances, such as those in the Parthenon frieze : in the ' Victory '
of the Nikè Apteros Temple (Fig. 101) and the Sandal-tying
figure (Fig. 102) as well as in other bas-reliefs such as ' The
Dancers ' (Fig. 110), of which the ' Mænad ' (Fig. 108) is a very
striking example.   Some statues of much later time and of far
inferior style, being by Roman sculptors, have the drapery
treated with much nobleness and fine perception of the beauty
that can be given to it (Fig. 40, Thalia).   The representation of
drapery by zigzag folds and stiff impossible forms clinging to the
figure is peculiar to archaic work, and is to be taken generally as

distinctive of early sculpture, always remembering that it was imitated afterwards in the pseudo-archaic statues.

The style of the drapery, whether in statues, bas-reliefs, or pictures, is spoken of as distinguished by " motive " and " cast," the two words being taken from the artist's intention, in displaying the movement or momentary attitude, to indicate these by the forms of the folds and the general composition of the drapery. Technically, he aids his imagination by " casting " an experimental drapery of the material he decides to represent, over the living model before him, and selects after much study those forms which satisfy him, rejecting certain folds which are not essential to the design, which may be trivial and too full of detail that would " cut up " the composition of the work. The clothing of the ancient Greeks was of such light material, sometimes so thin that the forms were fully seen under it, that it evidently lent much to the sculptor, and encouraged him to observe and admire it. In this way the dress of the ancients taught the sculptor as much of drapery as the athletic games did of the nude. The materials used were woven cloths of flax and cotton (from Cos). Silken and woollen cloths dyed or woven in colours, and sometimes with gold, were, it would seem, adopted in times subsequent to the great period in sculpture (Winckelmann). This, however, may be doubtful as to the time. Thukydides speaks of the thin dresses of the women during the plague at Athens (lib. ii. p. 64). The fine and numerous folds, and the ease with which they follow the form of the figure in the statues by Pheidias, are considered to be due to linen cloth. And it was at Elis that flax was cultivated and so delicately woven (Pausanias, lib. v. ; Pliny, lib. xix. c. 4). Cotton cloth was worn almost solely by women, it being effeminate for a man to wear it, either amongst Greeks or Romans (Pliny, lib. ii. c. 27). It was often striped and ornamented with flowers. These fabrics were sometimes made so thin and transparent as to be compared to clouds, and Euripides describes the mantle with which Iphigenia covered her face as so clear it could be seen through. Silk of changing colours, as we should say, "shot," appear to be shown in the draperies of the figures in the famous painting of Roman work of the third

century known as the Nozze Aldobrandini,—the marriage of
Peleus and Thetis—in the Vatican. Woollen fabrics were used
in the same way for coloured garments.

Different forms of Drapery.—Women wore three—the tunic,
the robe, and the mantle. The first of these corresponds to the
modern chemise ; it is seen in the Flora Farnese, the Amazon of
the Vatican (Fig. 118), and in the Thalia of the British Museum
(Fig. 40). It was called a *chiton,* and had no sleeves, being
fastened on the shoulders with a button. Cybele and Isis alone
have sleeves, but they are foreign to the Greeks. The long
falling robe was a simple garment of two broad pieces, open at
the sides, as seen in dancing figures, and fastened at the shoulders
with several buttons (Fig. 63, Artemis). The complexity of
the hanging folds led to the archaic sculptor getting out of the
difficulty by his conventional forms of the zigzag edges. This
robe was held up to the figure by a girdle of some kind, both by
young girls and older women, tied close up under the breasts,
and not at the waist above the hips, which Homer describes as
Βαθυζωνος—low-*girdled.* But the Amazons wore the girdle
like men, round the waist, as the mode adopted for fighting.
In the beautiful little bronze, however, in Naples Museum, of
the Amazon falling wounded from her horse the girdle is not
at the hips ; and it is noticeable also that the right breast is
shown, the left being deficient.

Venus when draped has two girdles—one high up, the other
quite below the hips, fastened in front (Fig. 147).

The Peplos—mantle—originally that which belonged to
Pallas. It was cut round, and probably also square, the corners
having loops with which to fasten it up. It was worn sometimes fastened at the throat with a brooch, and often carried
carelessly on the arm, allowing part to fall round the hips, as
in the fine statue of Thalia (Fig. 40). To follow out the subject
of dress would involve more space than can be given to it here,
and it is not necessary, as it can be so fully studied in the
dictionaries of Greek and Roman antiquities.

The *chlamys* is the cloak so finely shown in the Apollo
Belvedere ; it was fastened at the shoulders by a button or
brooch.

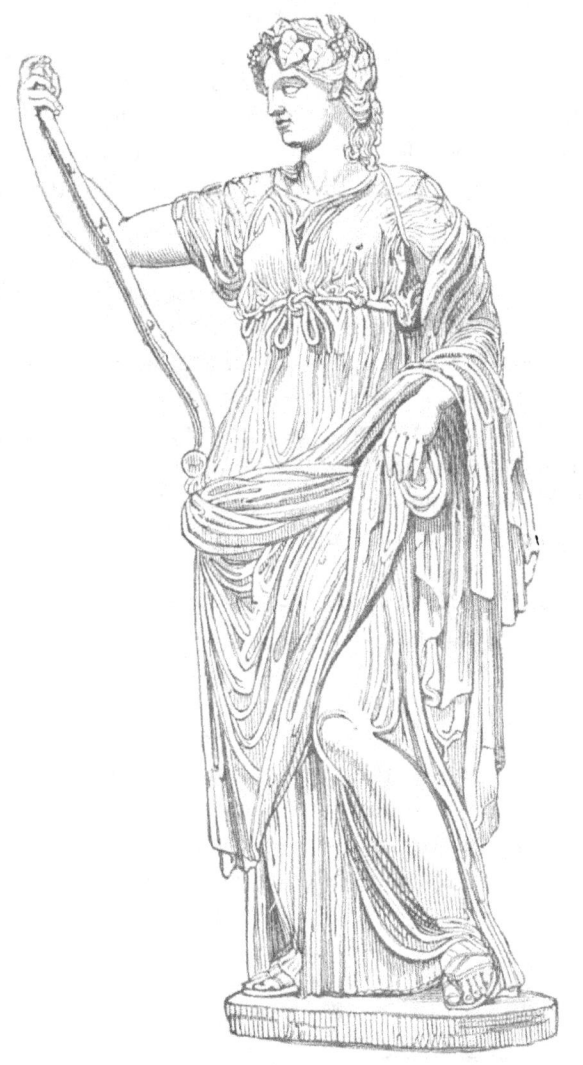

FIG. 40.—THALIA, THE MUSE OF COMEDY.

Wearing the chiton and peplos; and holding the pedum.

In the British Museum.

Drapery should be observed as having the following character-istic disposition in bas-reliefs and statues :—

1. Hanging in perpendicular folds or pleats, dependent on the weight of the fabric.

2. Fitting the form loosely, and showing it through, as in the beautiful bas-reliefs from the Temple of Nikè Apteros (Figs. 101, 102).

3. Stretched or suspended in diagonal folds, as between the knees of seated figures (Fig. 84), particularly remarkable in the Phigalian sculptures, and in one of the Fates of the Parthenon.

4. Flying—with figures in strong action, as in many of the Parthenon bas-reliefs and metopes. Exaggerated into twisting forms in the sculptures of the Theseus temple and the Phigalian friezes (Figs. 98, 99).

5. Clustered—the ends or borders gathered, as by the hand or a loop. Remarkable in the Amazon (Fig. 118).

The principle which governs movement in drapery has been pointed out by Flaxman. Drapery in repose takes the forms as classified above ; but when the figure moves, the perpendicular folds change according to the degree of movement : if slow, towards gentle curves from the fixed point of support to the free end ; if more rapid, the curve becomes more complex and undulating, and to some extent floating on the air. A draped figure moving against a wind doubles the floating power, and increases the curves at the free ends, straightening them in the line of support.

COLOURED MARBLES AND COLOURED SCULPTURE.

A distinction is of course necessary between colouring statues and bas-reliefs, and forming them out of various coloured mate-rials. That both processes were constantly practised from early to the best times of Greek art, under Pheidias and afterwards, there is no room for any question. Numerous instances of colour remaining still on sculptures, as well as on architectural details, are to be seen in museums. The subject, however, is too exten-

sive in its relations and too controversial to be treated fully in
this place. It may be remarked, however, that what is spoken
of as colouring was, from all accounts by Plato, Pausanias, Pliny,
and Quintilian, as well as the modern writers M. Quatremère de
Quincy, M. Emeric David, and M. Hittorff, not painting with
an opaque colour, but a sort of staining of the surface by thin,
transparent colouring matter. Pausanias says of a statue of
Bacchus at Phigalia, partly clothed with ivy leaves and laurels,
that those parts which are visible shine from being rubbed over
with Cinnabar * (vermilion) (lib. viii. c. 29, Taylor's translation).
This might be done by means of a " medium," such as is invented
for painting in order to obtain transparent colour, formed of
wax and oil. By this mode of applying it the fine surface of
the marble worked by the sculptor would not be injured, and
would show through with a kind of lustre and richness like the
glow of life in the living body. The term " circumlitio," used
by Pliny, seems to be a process of rubbing in, and we may
conclude that the colouring was to some extent transient, as it
was repeated on the recurrence of festivals. Had it been a
" painting," Pliny would have used the word "pingo" in some
form.

Those instances of statues in terra-cotta found with a coat
of vermilion on them give no proof that they were painted
of that colour alone, as they appear now; vermilion remains
undecomposed by long action of oxygen and light, while any
modifying colour derived from vegetable or animal sources which
may have been mixed with it has been destroyed. M. De
Quincy states that the fine preservation of the surface of some
antique statues, such as the Apollo Belvedere, Hercules of
Glycon, and Venus de' Medici, is attributable to the use of wax

* Nicias, an encaustic painter, is said by Pliny to have been preferred
by Praxiteles to put this colour or tint upon his statues (lib. xxxv. c. 11.)
This colour was probably mixed with wax, and applied melted under heat,
or made liquid with oil and then rubbed off somewhat until the surface
became polished. Gibson, the eminent sculptor, made the experiment
with his statue of Venus and some others, carrying the colouring so far as
to tint the hair, the eyes, and the eyebrows, with some of the accessories.
The effect, however, was not generally approved at the time (1862,
International Exhibition) by the critics.

colouring. The ivory statues were certainly often soaked with oil and water to prevent cracking from dryness, for which purpose a vessel to contain oil was placed near the statue.

Stones of various colours were employed to represent different parts of the figure. Thus a helmet of Minerva is seen made of black basalt or marble, the face and neck of white marble, and the ægis and gorgon's head of green and red. In Roman busts of the emperors the dress is frequently of coloured marble, while the flesh is of white. These combinations were rarely if ever chosen by the great Greek masters, but the artifice was a favourite one during the decadence of taste in Roman times, and afterwards in the Renaissance and later styles, when a sensational effect was frequently produced by such methods, as in representing negroes in black marble, with eyes of white marble and gilded ornaments.

Bronze with marble.—The accessories of marble statues are often made of bronze, such as wreaths round the head, weapons, the thyrsus of Bacchus, the talaria and the caduceus of Mercury, the sandals, helmet, armour, lyre, and other ornaments. These were freely employed by the greatest masters, as seen in the Parthenon sculptures, in which the holes for affixing the bronze bits and bridles of the horses still remain.

Gilt bronze.—That the ancients were accomplished in the art of gilding metal is seen in the large equestrian statue of Marcus Aurelius in the piazza of the Capitol at Rome, which still retains some of the gold, and in a colossal statue of Hercules, in the Vatican, discovered a few years ago, on which much of the gold remains in brilliant condition. The bronze horses of antique work over the door of St. Mark's, Venice, are gilt. Many other smaller examples are in existence. According to Muratori, there were once twenty-eight gilt colossal equestrian statues in Rome, and eight horses gilt. There are also many examples of silver being inlaid into the bronze to mark the features, such as in the eyes, the lips, the eyebrows. It is not within the limits of this volume to go further into the subject of the use of gold in ancient statuary, neither would it be of any practical utility. That gold was used to cast statues is admitted, also that it was employed in plates hammered into shape; but beyond small objects of personal ornament no example has been found. Those who are curious upon the point will find it fully considered in the work of M. Quatremère de Quincy.

DIFFERENT MARBLES USED BY ANCIENT SCULPTORS.

Many varieties of fine marbles were plentiful in Greece and Asia Minor; they take names from the mountains where they were quarried.

SOFT MARBLES—sedimentary rocks of limestone.

Pentelic marble, from Mount Pentelicus in the neighbourhood of Athens, is found white, with a fine fracture, brilliant and sparkling, obtaining with exposure, after having received the surface polish from the hand of the sculptor, a beautiful warm tone comparable to ivory. This effect is seen in the Parthenon and other temples in Athens built of this marble, which have an extraordinary richness in their golden tint, especially under bright sunlight and seen against a blue sky. The yellow colour is said to be caused by oxydation of some salt of iron contained in the marble. The statues in Athens are also of the same marble, and many others now in various museums.

Parian is the marble from the island of Paros. The marble usually called Parian has a coarse sparkling grain, which, however, takes a high finish : but there is reason to suppose that the true Parian marble was of extremely fine grain, easy to work, and of a creamy white.

Luna—a white marble : the quarries near Florence which were worked in the time of the Emperor Augustus.

Carrara—abundant in the quarries near Florence. This is the marble principally used by sculptors, on account of its pure whiteness, though sometimes it has serious blemishes and dark veins.*

Phigalian—a grey marble, seen in the bas-reliefs from Phigalia.

Æginetan—a greyish marble, seen in the statues of the pediment of the Temple of Athene, now in the museum of Munich.

---

* As the Italian quarries were not worked till about the middle of the 1st century B.C., the marble, if identified as such, affords a test for the date of any work.

Black marble—found at Cape Tenaros.

Verde antico—found at Taygetos.

Corallitic.—Mentioned by Pliny as found in Asia, like ivory in tone—" Candore proximo Ebori."

Alabaster.—Much used by the Egyptians. It was found at Alabastron, on the Nile, whence its name.

HARD MARBLES—from igneous rocks, once in a state of fusion *Porphyry. Granite. Rosso antico* (red), *nero antico* (black). *Black and green basalt, Sienite,* a dark stone, so called from Syene, the town in Egypt near which it was found ; and others. These were principally used by the Egyptian sculptors ; there are however several large statues in the Vatican and Capitol museums made of *Rosso antico.*

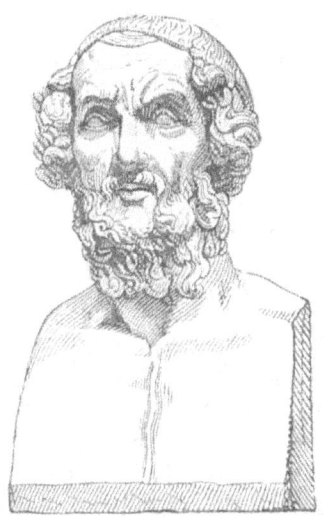

FIG. 41.—HOMER.

SECTION II.—ÆSTHETIC.

IT will have been gathered, from what has been said of
sculpture in general, of the high technical skill necessary
to the various forms of carved and modelled work, and especially
of the admirable examples of antique and renaissance work
in glyptics, that although sculpture is essentially founded on an
imitation of nature more close and palpable than the painter
can attain, yet it tends away from exact imitation towards the
realization of a certain complete beauty of form that is not to be
found in any one example of nature.

Notwithstanding that the great sculptors place before us a
figure so exactly modelled that it seems to want only the
breath of life to be another creation of the human form, yet it
is not this palpable reality of the figure that strikes the mind
so much as the suggestion that there is something more—that
the statue must have some being of its own, some supernatural

A.S.

endowment within.* The very wonder felt that a figure of bronze or marble should stand, and look, and be as if about to move, encourages this idea. Thus with all its reality of form that we can examine, and measure, and see all round on every side, the statue, according as it fulfils the lofty aim of sculpture, is more removed from the senses than a picture is. We yield to the illusion of a picture, knowing that it is not what it appears to be. But the statue does not strike us as an illusion ; it takes at once a presence, so to speak, a kind of personality, and this the more impressive because of its form being so like, and yet so unlike, the natural figure. There is the strong resemblance, yet it is impossible to conceive anything more unlike flesh than marble or bronze. It is recorded that the Huns and the Goths fled at the sight of the colossal statue of Athena Promachus on the Acropolis at Athens ; the figure of Zeus seated on his throne in the temple so impressed beholders with a sense of reality that they trembled as they thought how, were the god to rise, he would carry away the roof above his head. No *picture* of the god, however gigantic, would have produced the same sense of awe. The Egyptians, had they chosen, could have painted colossal figures, but they knew that the statue would be as the god himself. Their Glyphographic pictures they employed upon the walls of the temple, to be read like a book describing great deeds of heroes. All ancient art seems to have relied upon sculpture, as though it were an admitted truth that pictures however imposing in their size and splendour soon cease to be noticed, while the statue asserts its presence constantly. All people, ancient and modern, demand statues as monuments of great men, great deeds, and great events of history ; they seem to feel that this is in some sense to immortalize their heroes in perpetual bronze.

* Mrs. Jameson says, referring to Coleridge's definition of a picture as " a something between a thought and a thing," that " sculpture is a *thought* and a *thing*." 'George Eliot,' the eminent novelist, speaks of the statues in the Vatican as those " white forms whose marble eyes seemed to hold the light of an alien world." Such a feeling led Pygmalion to fancy his statue lived, and Donatello to call upon his " St. George " to " march."

The employment of the colossal as an expression of the ideal of superhuman almighty power, even when, as in the Egyptian statues, not associated with great beauty, has something of the sublime in it. But when Pheidias united beauty with this imposing majesty of gigantic proportions, and added the colour of the living flesh and the lifelike look of the eye, as in the ivory and gold-draped Athene and Zeus, sculpture was brought to the highest pitch of grandeur, so far as this form of art could attain it.

Apart, however, from the religious ideal which inspired the great Greek sculptor, and regarding merely the perfection of beauty of form and symmetrical unity of proportion in the figure, the colossal in size cannot be allowed to surpass the beautiful as we see it in such statues as the Theseus, the Ilyssus, and some other works of the Parthenon. What would be thought now of a colossus so closely resembling life as the great statue of Zeus by Pheidias must have done it is impossible to pronounce. The principle, however, must remain, that beauty in sculpture does not reside in colossal size. The converse may be shown to be true by the experiment of magnifying a fine antique intaglio, when the minute figure appears in perfect proportion and detail, on a scale which, compared with the actual work, is more than colossal. But though sculpture takes so much of the real and materialistic, and, moreover, confers ideal beauty upon the forms of nature, it reaches further than this in creating beings that have no existence.

The Egyptian sphinx, the Greek centaur and minotaur, those marvellous creations, are so admirable in adaptation, so instinct with life and nature, and so strong in the verisimilitude that art gives, that we could fancy they may have been among the extinct animals of creation. Although derivable from the symbolic forms of the earliest hieratic art,—the sphinx and other animal-headed figures of Egypt, the winged human-headed bulls and eagle-headed men with wings of Assyria,—yet they were made beautiful by the feeling of the artist for beauty, and the poetic conception founded on his belief in the myth. The primitive centaur was a very mechanically-put-together creature * (Fig. 42). In this the

* Pausanias says, that on the chest of Kypselos Chiron was represented with the fore-legs like a man (lib. v. c. 19).

symbolic was the aim of the design, beauty not being contemplated; as in the Centaur (Fig. 44). The predominance of the symbolic was already depressing to the development of art, as we see in later times in the productions of the debased Greek work of the Byzantine sculptors, representing the evangelists as men with the heads of the ox, the eagle, and the lion.* Still, it should

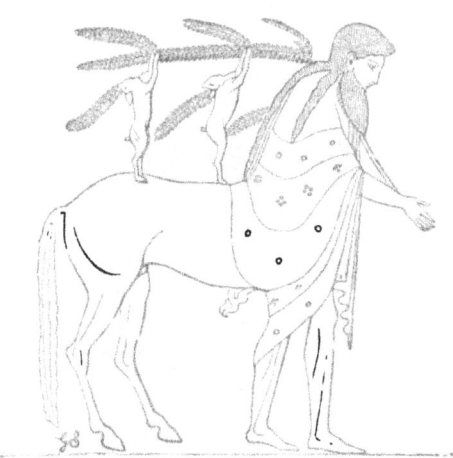

FIG. 42.--THE CENTAUR CHIRON.

From a painted vase.

be understood that the symbolic when properly subordinated, as in all the great works, plays an important part, and fills up the measure of beauty in the design. It was reserved for after ages, when nations were beginning to enjoy works of art as art and not as the idols of a religion, and when intellectual enlightenment was springing forth in literature, to render beauty paramount.

Heroes had lived among mankind, and poets had celebrated their deeds of glory. When these deeds were acted over again in tragedy, with overpowering force of action and language, and all the influence that the stage could lend, we may see how literature and the drama conspired to prompt the aspirations and the conceptions of the sculptor's art. The sculptor then became the poet in his turn,—the designer; he was no longer the servant and workman. Inspired by his art, he was called upon by the nation to mould the gods as he in his art conceived them, as the supernatural, avenging, favouring, and protecting powers. His art made the gods like men of more than mortal mould, and conferred

---

* Two bas-reliefs in the porch' of the Baptistery at Aquileja have St. Luke with the ox head and St. John with the eagle head. Mrs. Jameson remarks that the Assyrian Nisroch with his eagle head and wings is not unlike the early figures of St. John, if we substitute the book and the pen for the basket and the pine-cone ('Sacred and Leg. Art,' vol. i. p. 106).

upon the heroes born of the gods godlike beauty. Thus beauty and nobleness of form in heroes and deities supplanted the mere colossal proportions and the dry symbolic representations of an unalterable sacred type in those ancient days; as it did afterwards in the Renaissance when culminating in the grand works of Michelangelo and Raffaello. Mere characteristic representations, even of religious subjects, with a profusion of attributes and symbols, gave place to beauty, and art ruled rather as a secular, intellectual, poetic manifestation than a religious influence. Whether, then, we look to the great works of Greek art with their ideal of superhuman beauty and passionless power and majesty, or to those of the Renaissance which express an ideal of human emotion and Divine suffering and sympathy, we see the same universal and innate love of · the beautiful ever springing up in the mind. The sources of this instinctive love are presented to mankind primarily in every aspect of Nature; they are found concentrated in the beauty of the human form, and supplemented and enlarged in the abstract beauty of humanity in all its intellectual development.

That the human form should have assumed its rightful place as the epitome and summit of all nature—the cosmos of cosmos—was one of the things inevitable, long before art had pretended to represent the form Divine. But the sculptor, mindful that he had to trace the godlike gift of intellect and all that he knew of the soul of man, never ceased in his aim to mould out of the dust of the earth his Adam. At first he strove to imitate what he saw before him, but in his best successes he was humbled by the constant presence of superior beauty. He held the mirror up to Nature. Seeing where he failed, and admiring with an eye growing more and more sensitive, and a mind longing more ardently for the beauty of which he caught only imperfect glimpses in observing natural forms, he was led under the teaching of Nature to conceive an ideal of supernatural beauty. This, of course, is only what passes in the growth and culture of all art faculty; but it is necessary to state it in this place, because sculpture is more strictly bound up with the purity and truth of beauty than any other form of art work. It was in sculpture that the beautiful in art, as we are considering it, was first revealed. So beautiful was the ideal conceived from admiration of the human figure, that only the nude form was taken by the sculptor as his essay, and this was the lesson that he set himself.*

In the statue he felt that he had to mould a form that must bear the light of day on every side, that should be beautiful in every contour. There could be no illusions and no allurements of light and colour, no distance to lend enchantment, as in a picture. No deformities could be glossed over by giving the charm of human life, feeling, and sympathetic expression in the countenance. All this is denied the sculptor. His muse is a silent one. As Bulwer so beautifully said of Learning, "the marble image warms into life not at the toil of the chisel, but the worship of the sculptor; the mechanical workman finds but the voiceless stone." Or, as George Eliot has said of the Cleopatra (or Ariadne) of the Vatican, "There lies antique beauty not corpse-like even in death, but arrested in the complete contentment of its sensuous perfection." Michelangelo said, "A me soleva parere che la scultura fosse la lanterna della pittura" ('Lett. Pitt. Bottari,' vol. i. p. 7). "The ancient Greek sculptors," Sir Charles Bell remarks, "seemed to be perpetually moved by the aim at some beauty higher than anything around them."

Since then the sculptor has to rely on beauty of form alone, he has first to satisfy himself as to what is beautiful in the human form, not what is merely characteristic and natural. Thus Raffaello himself, as he has said with such profound insight in his well-known letter to Baldassare Castiglione, found

* Drapery, though designed with such consummate mastery as we see in the Parthenon figures, was comparatively an afterthought. It must be borne in mind, however, that the deities were not represented nude, not even the Aphrodite, at the finest period of Greek art. The famous Venus of Milo is a half-draped statue; so is the Dione and Venus of Capua. The goddess was not represented nude till Praxiteles set the example in his Venus of Knidos. The celebrated Venus dei Medici is a nude, but of later date.

The heroes were always represented nude—Theseus, Hercules, Perseus, Castor and Pollux. Apollo as the destroyer is nude, and as the youthful Sauroctonos. Mercury is nude, as the messenger of the gods.

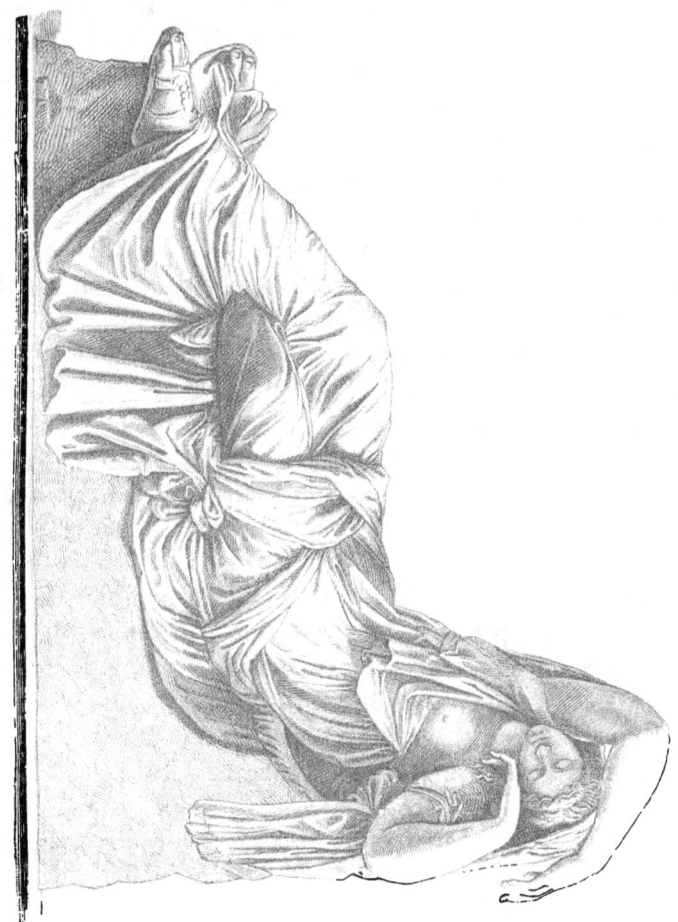

FIG. 43.—THE ARIADNE OF THE VATICAN.

it necessary to see a great number of beautiful forms before he knew what beauty was; he could not see it all in one figure, but a certain ideal came up in his mind (" Io mi servo di certa idea che mi viene alla mente ") from looking at these many beauties, and he strove to realize this in his pictures. But the sculptor, as we have seen, is bound by severer laws and works even more abstractedly from the ideal in his mind. He has to generalize and conceive this high ideal which is his type of the beautiful; and in endeavouring to realize it in his work he has to avoid and shun all that would weaken his representation or detract from the impressiveness of his figure. "The sculptor must ever bear in mind that truth is to be united with beauty, or even rejected whenever its adoption would involve a sacrifice of beauty . . . All violent expression is clearly out of the province of the sculptor . . . Complicated action is naturally unfit for sculpture."[*] His study throughout is to refine,— to reject the unessential, and select that which is essential to the true and the beautiful. With the peculiarities of individual examples he has nothing to do, except in the domain of portraiture, and even here he cannot wholly forget the typical, as, for example, when he studies the countenance of a Homer, a Sophokles or a Demosthenes, a Perikles or an Alexander, a Hadrian or a Nero. And those portraits, it will be admitted, are accepted as the truest which, besides recording the idiosyncratic and the personal, tell, by some mysterious virtue, some subtle response of intellect and hand, something of the part played and the figure made in the world by the person represented. The heroic representations of great men by the ancient sculptors were creations of art springing from the enthusiastic admiration of the characters of those personages, and not from the mere desire to preserve the lineaments of their countenances in bronze and marble. They were monumental for all time in exalting and refining the characteristics of the personages, and not mere puppets, like those waxen images of the deceased carried at funerals. Those noble heads of Homer, Sophokles, and Demosthenes are not likenesses of the men any more than the head of the Pheidian Zeus is a portrait of the god. If we

* Guizot, 'The Fine Arts, their Nature and Relations,' 1853.

want to see practically how much refinement sculpture demands we have only to look at any cast from the life to perceive at once how almost repulsive that kind of exact imitation is. A mask taken in this way, accurate as it must be, wants so much that belongs to the aminated countenance that it is scarcely recognizable as the face of our friend. Even a hand appears unlike the familiar one in this cold inanimate shape ; it seems petrified as it were. This is not wholly due to the dull opaque material, for if it were possible to carve the marble so accurately the result would be almost equally unpleasing and untrue to the cultivated eye, however it might surprise a savage.

It will be seen, then, how it is that sculpture, so eclectic in its nature, has justly been regarded as the classical in art. It is so because it begins by abstracting typical beauty out of the infinite variety of character in the human form. Thus a symmetrical whole is conceived conformable to an ideal, so to speak, of supernatural beauty. It proceeds by a comprehension of relative proportion between the parts and the whole, as we have seen in the discovery of the canon, not only in the human form but in that of all creation. Mastering this kind of symmetry, which is not merely a matter of exact measurement, like geometrical proportion, but involves a harmony of form resulting from modulations and gentle gradations and changes in the movement of the lines too subtle for any formula, the sculptor, guided by certain principles of beauty, becomes a creator.

But higher ground lies before him on those summits where the noblest intellects meet. Here he may take his place if he be worthy of it. Here are those immortal works of his art which by one voice of poetry, philosophy, and science are pronounced sublime. Here his art has surpassed the technic condition and become " phonetic." The sculptor is then a thinker and an expressionist of the highest order.

How has the sculptor accomplished this ? By compelling with his technic skill the most inanimate matter of the earth —that upon which fire has spent its utmost destructive force, the metals and the rocks—to take the shape of beauty and live again another life. By his higher art uniting the real with the unreal, the abstract with the concrete, in a manner more striking and impressive perhaps than the words of the poet or the pictures of the painter. Nothing, indeed, that we can contemplate in all the marvellous revelations of science is more wonderful than the transmutation of matter in such miracles as those worked by the hand of Pheidias and Michelangelo. In some sense, indeed, the sculptor shows us the immutable and the eternal in those stupendous colossi of Egyptian art; although they impress us by that material element of grandeur contained in immense proportions. Life, as we recognize it in living forms, being inseparable from the changes of birth, maturity, and death, these giants, created by the breath of art, calm in repose and meditation, asserted their immortality. Unlike the modern monumental effigy that sleeps in death upon the tomb, they transfigured the mortal body, and favoured the belief in an eternal life of immortal happiness. Say that the whole of the ancient Egyptian and Greek religious belief and mythology—antique religion, so to speak—was of this mythical nature; still, there it remains an unquestionable evidence of human thought, life, and history that cannot for a moment be ignored. It is however beyond our province to follow out the relations and influence of this anthropomorphic religion of antiquity in other directions than the domain of sculptural art, which is perhaps as wide and significant in its records as that of letters, and certainly as closely allied with the beautiful.

It is necessary to have full sympathy with the ancient religious beliefs, if we are to appreciate ancient art; and if anything could lead us to regard the religious belief of the Egyptians and Greeks with respect and tolerance, it should be those wondrous embodiments of it which their art achieved. What were the intellectual aspirations of such a people is to be learnt in the records of their literature, which stand as the classics of their kind along with those works of sculpture which have remained unapproached in beauty and grandeur throughout the course of more than two thousand years of civilization, and the very fragments of which are treasured in our museums as the highest examples of the grand and the beautiful in art. We hear sometimes the partisans of what is called Christian art in opposition to Pagan art, reviling classic sculpture as the product of everything unvirtuous, ignoble, and immoral even to bestiality. Its beauty they admit to a certain extent, but only as a cold inanimate expression of a renounced belief disgraceful to the human race.   We see, for example, at once how entirely Mr. Ruskin is preoccupied in his opinion when he says (p. 37, ' Modern Painters ')—" The utmost glory of the human body is a mean subject of contemplation compared to the emotion, exertion, and character of that which animates it; the lustre of the limbs of the Aphrodite is faint beside the brow of the Madonna, and the divine form of the Greek god, except as it is the incarnation and expression of divine mind, is degraded beside the passion and the prophecy of the vaults of the Sistine." That one kind of religion has been superseded, it is true, and that it has been supplanted by one far more human and more kindred to the best part of our nature—the emotions and the affections; but archaic Paganism inclosed, at any rate, the germ of that which grew out of it, and which was one of the inevitable conditions of human progress and development.

And as to antique art, so profoundly is it rooted in the sound principles of beauty, that it remains as it was, the fountain to which all students must come, and return as often as to Nature herself to refresh their art and keep it vigorous and healthy.   The greatest masters of modern art have worshipped at the shrine, and taken their teaching from the beauty of the antique.   The young student of to-day, impelled with active instinct, starts on the same path, not that he is made to do so, but that he sees in it the highest lessons of which art is capable.

. The value of these lessons has been eloquently enforced by a critic of high distinction—M. Ernest Renan—in referring to the absence of feeling for the perfect beauty of the human form to be observed in mediæval art—" L'Antiquité seule pouvait révéler aux nations modernes le secret d'un art, qui ne sacrifiât jamais la beauté à l'expression et s'arrétât toujours devant la difformité." *

Nothing is more remarkable in classic art, next to the grandeur

* ' Revue des Deux Mondes,' 1862.

of its conceptions of the godlike form, than those creations of
beings impossible to the fauna of Nature, by which are im-
personated all the instincts of sensuality inseparable from the
lower nature of the noblest animal—man.   It would have been
against all feeling for the amenities, if classic art had represented
the evil deities of the vices as hideous monsters analogous to the
demons and arch-fiends and great Satan himself, as we see them
in the works of Christian art.   The terrors of the damned were
not quite so awful perhaps in the heathen view of the future.
The ancient Egyptian judgment day is simply sculptured as a
judge weighing the departed and the condemned ones being
changed into pigs.   No torturing demons and fiends were employed, and the cruelest vengeance wreaked by the gods was the
perpetual gnawing of the sinner's liver by the bird of Jove.   The
three sister Furies sprung from the blood of Uranus, *Alecto* the
unceasing, *Megaera* the envious, and *Tisiphone* the blood-avenger,
though their hair was entwined with serpents and their faces
were terrific, were not loathsome monsters such as are represented
in the Inferno of mediæval art.   As the *Eumenides*, they were
termed gracious by the Athenians.   The Harpies, with heads of
women and bodies of birds, were loathsome and filthy, but they
are rarely seen in ancient art work.   The Harpy tomb in the Brit.
Mus. is a remarkable instance (*see* Fig. 60).   In these, however,
the heads are quite comely.   Greek art dealt beautifully even
with the bestial side of human nature, inventing the Minotaurs
and the Centaurs,* those strange wild forms so admirably conceived, who are subdued by heroic defenders of women.   Then
there was Pan, with his goatlike head and shanks, as the
personification of the spirit of wild nature.   And all the world
of Satyrs like him, the natives of the woods ; the Fauns, with
their more human form, but with their pointed ears and flattened
noses and slanting eyes, sometimes with budding horns, and
tails springing from their backs.   But none of all the great
woodland family of the Dryads and Hamadryads, of the Naiads

---

* The Centaur was derived from the expert horsemen of Greece,
Thessalonian tribes chiefly, who hunted the bull. The name means " bull-
hunter " or killer, from κεντω, to prick as with a dart, and ταυρος, bull.
They were, in fact, the originals of the modern bull-fighter.

and Nereids of the rivers and ocean,* of fabulous existence was ever devoid of a certain beauty of form compatible with the ideal intended, though so wholly opposite to that portrayed in the gods and heroes. There is a wide difference between these creations of an art which was entirely engaged in the pursuit of beauty, and those of the Egyptians, who were not so much artist sculptors as they were the exponents of a system for enforcing religious belief and exercising priestly control over the people. The Egyptian or Assyrian representation had no artistic meaning, except in so far as it was decorative in treatment; it was simply a union of distinctive brute qualities, fiercer and more unrelenting than man, with the intellectual supremacy of man; and the characteristic parts chosen were grafted on to the human form in the most direct and absolute manner, with scarcely a thought of adaptation or modification of the brute character. The heads and the wings and the bodies of the brutes were employed as accessories and symbols, while in the Greek sculptor's work the human head and torso of the Centaur (Fig. 44) are adapted to the body of the horse with a fitness that is amazing in its seemliness and wild grace of strength and ferocity.

We may reasonably conclude that the very ancient notion of metempsychosis which is frequently represented in the Egyptian hieroglyphic pictures, and the belief in metamorphoses held by all primitive people, laid the foundation for representations of this kind, and led to their being always accepted and taken advantage of by art. It was natural that such creations of the fancy should take a strong hold upon ancient art, and it is remarkable that Jewish and Christian art † not only did not renounce these

* How Shakespeare felt the beauty of these ancient myths may be observed in those lines of exquisite fancy—

"Ye elves of hills, brooks, standing lakes and groves,
And ye that on the sands with printless foot
Do chase the ebbing Neptune, and do fly him
When he comes back."—*Tempest.*

† The 'Bible abounds with allusions of the kind, and in the New Testament, the Book of Revelations, by John, is especially noticeable for descriptions of mythological animals. In fact, we may apply the term *Christian mythology* in this connection as appositely as to the myths of the Pagans.

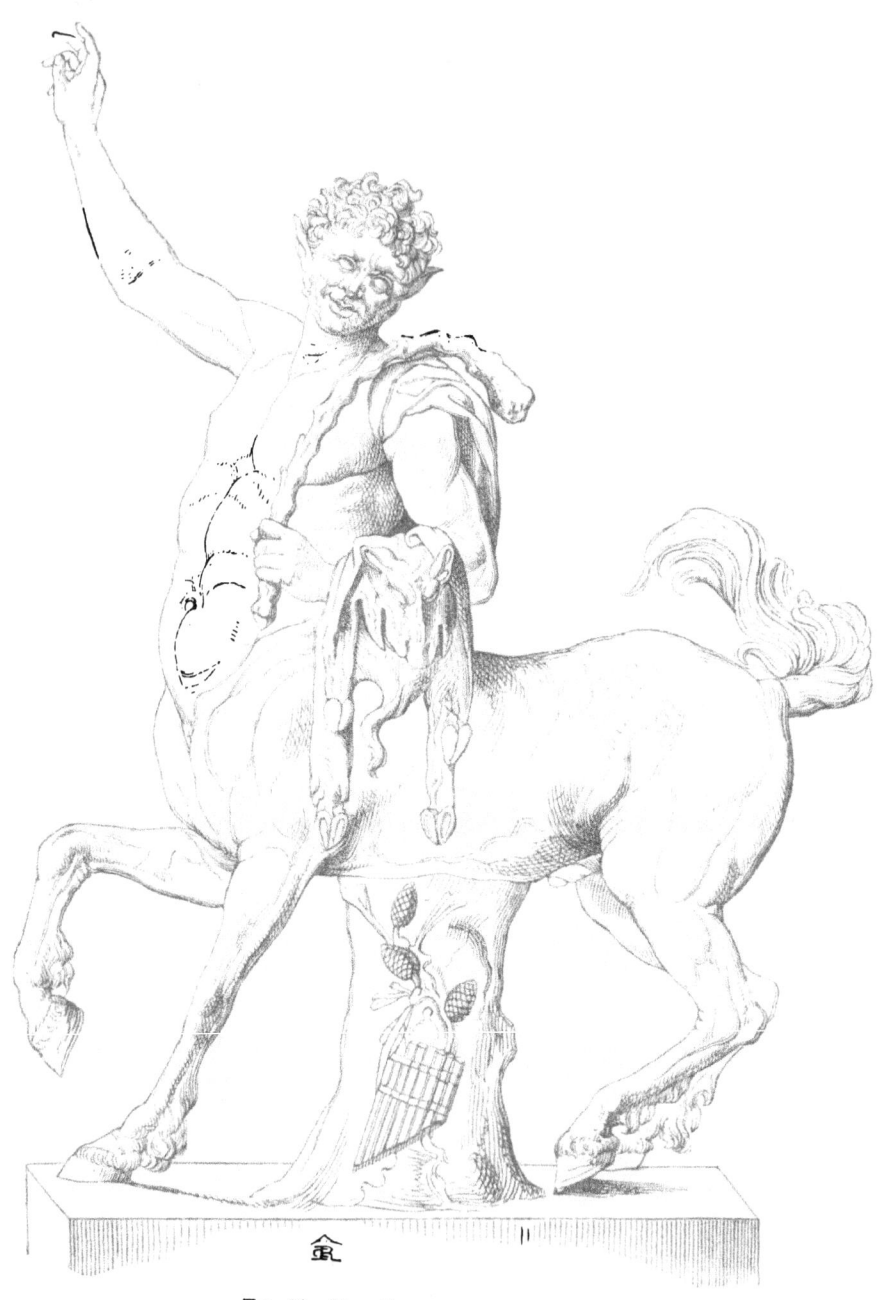

FIG. 44.—THE CENTAUR OF THE CAPITOL.
From Aphrodisias in Asia Minor. In Bigio ; a coloured marble.

heathen fancies, but took to them and employed them constantly. The winged cherubim and seraphim of the ark, the winged angels, Lucifer with the fallen angels, the demons with eagles' talons, the great serpent—the Apollyon with his scaly form, and horned head and feet and hands like claws—are all significant of the same imaginings. The unicorn was frequently employed as the animal emblem of maidenhood and virgin martyrdom. The arabesques so largely employed in ornamental work were borrowed, as the name implies, from the ancient East, and are as profusely adopted for works of Christian art as they were in the decorations of the baths of Titus and the temples and houses of the Romans at Herculaneum and Pompeii. The connection of the symbolic in Christian art with that of Paganism, and with the earlier symbolism of the Egyptians and Assyrians, is obviously too wide a subject to be more than alluded to in this place.

It is necessary, however, to understand what are the distinctive characteristics of the Egyptian, the Assyrian, the Greek, and the Roman styles. The point of highest interest that will more and more appear in the consideration of Greek art is that here alone arose the association of beauty of form with the representation of imaginary beings of superhuman nature—deities.

Egyptian.—The Egyptians made their colossal Sphinx all powerful in its lion body, and mysterious in the profound wisdom of its human head, but without a thought of beauty. Their human colossi are portrait statues of regal high priests, armed with the weapons of supreme authority and punishment. Anything of an ideal nature beyond this was conveyed in the imposing size and in the unmoved countenance, supremely self-possessed, happy and content, in an attitude of solemn calm repose never to be disturbed. The very mechanical lines * which would govern

---

* It should be understood that a line expresses movement only in proportion as it departs from the straight. The perpendicular line upon the horizontal does not express motion, variety, or change. Let the vertical line be inclined to the horizontal, and it looks tumbling down, as we say. If a vertical line be converted into a number of successive inclined points, as in a spiral—that is to say, turned round a centre instead of being prolonged to any given length—it expresses movement. If a horizontal line is converted into a series of progressive curves the form is

such figures are those which represent eternal stability—the perpendicular and the horizontal—and this is remarkably in accordance with the architecture of which these figures formed so singularly expressive an adjunct. It is remarkable that they never showed any feeling for the changing beauty of form observable in barbaric ornament; neither the spiral in any form nor the star is ever seen in their work. Neither did they ever think of the inclined form of a pediment as a feature in their architecture, although they invented the pyramid as an improvement on the tumulus. Not remarkable for their own beauty of bodily form, they were not prompted to admire human symmetry; they were not given to athletic games as the Greeks and Romans, nor were they a demonstrative and expressive people, but rather sad, submissive, and reflective. Their avoidance of expression of the emotions differed from that of the Greeks in motive: with them it disturbed repose and solemnity, with the Greeks it interfered with perfect beauty as well as with the repose and dignity of their ideal. It is well, however, to observe that the principles of repose, severe symmetry, and the imposing suggestion of the supernatural, are common to Egyptian and to Greek art. The colossal in size was also common to both, but with the important distinction of beauty added in the Greek style.

As regards accuracy of imitation of natural forms the Egyptian style is also allied with the Greek in the disregard of detail and the representation of generalities in preference to individualities.

said to be "serpentine," because it seems to creep. The curve, and the spiral, which is only a succession of curves, are forms of vegetable growth, and of the lower forms of animal life, and the whole beauty of living form is made up of curves more or less complex, changing, and irregular. Now it is remarkable that in Greek architecture the vertical and horizontal lines of columns and entablatures were not straight, but very delicate curves. This refinement is thought to have been adopted to correct the apparent error of horizontal lines in architecture due to optical illusion dependent on the spherical forms of the retina and the lens of the eye. It is well known that a tie-bar, which holds the ends of the girders of an iron roof, looks as if it sank down in the middle. Greek art succeeded in correcting this deformity inevitable to mechanical construction and irremediable by it. The discovery of the curves in the architectural forms of the Parthenon is due to the eminent architect, Mr. Penrose, whose great work (*Principles of Athenian Architecture*, 1851) is the one authority.

A conventional uniformity rules everywhere—a sort of rhythm of form. The Egyptian figure is a kind of automaton to make signs, while the Greek sculptor always gave it life and action. Thus if a procession is to be sculptured, it is done by carving each figure exactly like the rest, but slightly in advance, and in precisely the same attitude, and often the figures in this way have not their complement of legs, the sculptor only caring to suggest movement by a successive repetition of the same forms. The eye, being regarded as the evidence of life and thought, is universally represented open, and though the head is shown in profile, the eye is sculptured most carefully in full, and generally with a curious enforcing of its shape by a sort of band carved in relief round the eyelids. This subjection to symbolic meaning and representation according to formulæ laid down by authority, and adhered to with a singular and admirable regularity of workmanship, is not without its beauty, and it gives to Egyptian sculpture the distinction and dignity of a style.

Assyrian.—Little is to be said of Assyrian sculpture beyond what we shall have occasion to say of it in treating of the history. So far as it has any claim to be a style, its characteristics are an intense and vigorous spirit of closely imitative representation without the least reference to ideal beauty. Thus, so that the sculpture showed violent action where it was wanted, as in battles and lion-hunting; so that it could show the capture of a city by swimming a river and storming the walls; so that the human-headed bulls with eagles' wings were unmistakable in their attributes of power and swiftness, the Nineveh sculptor had done all that was required of him and all that he knew. It was at any rate immensely graphic, though as intensely rude in its imitative power as any barbaric art; always excepting the ornament, which has some fair claim to possess invention, and is more symmetrical though less ingenious and complex than the carvings of the New Zealanders. (See Figs. 50, 54, 55.)

We may sum up Assyrian sculpture with the opinion of M. Charles Blanc :

" Inferieur au style égyptien, l'art de Ninive et de Persepolis est plus réel sans être plus vrai, plus violent sans être plus terrible. Il est puissant, il est énergique, mais il a moins de grandeur : il est chargé d'ornements inutiles, et il n'atteint ni au

A.8.

sublime par le calme, ni à la beauté par le mouvement"
('Grammaire des arts du Dessin').

Greek.—The dawn of Greek art is eloquently alluded to by
Mr. Gladstone. "But if we may judge from the testimony of such
remains as are now accessible, there were two great schools with
which Phœnician artists must have been in relation, alike from
their political and their geographical connections : the Egyptian
and the Assyrian. It is not, I suppose, too much to say, that
we perceive in a portion at least of the actual remains of these
schools the attainment of high excellence in intention and
design with no inconsiderable progress in execution. They seem,
however, to me to represent different principles : the Assyrian
appears to embody the principle of life and motion ; the
Egyptian the principle of repose. . . In any case it would
really seem probable, from the vivid and stirring descriptions of
Homer, that these Phœnician importations supplied patterns and
suggested ideas which might well in process of time become the
nucleus of the first great efforts of Greek art. When that
nucleus was once supplied, and when the new life began to grow,
then the Olympian system of religion provided it, through the
union of the divine nature to the human form, with that lofty
aim which braced it to a perpetual effort upwards, and so
conveyed to it the pledge and the talisman of all transcendent
excellence. . . Thus Greek art was a perpetual untiring pursuit
of the highest standard of the ideal, while it seems to have had
for its starting-point foreign models which, though not similarly
inspired, were of such high merit as to suggest to Homer that
imitation might run no unsuccessful race with nature. This
happy union of the most fundamental conditions of design and
execution was seconded by the lights of a fine climate, by the
possession of the purest marbles, and by the corporal perfection
of a race abounding in the noblest models. We cannot wonder
that, with these advantages, Greece, within her limits of knowledge and experience, should have held down to our own day
the throne of art" ('Juventus Mundi,' p. 525).

The Greek style, as it was developed by Pheidias and the great
sculptors of his time, as we shall see in tracing its history,
derived some of its characteristics from the Egyptian and some
from the Assyrian. The ideal of sublime impassionate existence,

as we see it portrayed in the countenance and attitude of Zeus, of Athene, of Apollo, Artemis, and Hera, seems to be kindred to the Egyptian ideal. The strong feeling for action, and the vigorous naturalism of living men and animals characteristic of all archaic Greek work—the fierce death-struggles of the Lapithae with the Centaurs, of the Amazons with men, of the Gods with the Titans—show much of the feeling of the Assyrians. The connection of these styles will be further understood in tracing the advance of sculpture historically.

Sufficient has perhaps been said to denote the general principles upon which sculpture is based. More than can be said in words remains to be found out in presence of the great examples, especially those of Athenian art at its highest—those grand fragments of the Parthenon, of which, as Montaigne said of Ancient Rome : " La ruine même est glorieuse ; et encore retient elle, au tombeau, les marques et l'image de l'empire." The surpassing beauty of these will be noticed in the descriptive references to them. There are many points of great and inexhaustible interest on this side of our subject which will occur to the student, but these may only be hinted at within the limits at our disposal.

As to the remarkable development of beauty in plastic form, and the refinement of style that characterize ancient Greek art, it may be remarked, that the Hellenic race was naturally gifted with a finer sense of beauty of form and its expression than the Asiatic race. The admirable grace of line as well as precision of execution to be observed in some of the earlier ceramic paintings show this ; and it is more particularly to be noticed in those instances where the ceramic painter has left his work in the preparatory stage of outline. There is in the British Museum a small patera, with the outline in this state, which is quite marvellous in its freedom and beauty of line, as well as excellent in knowledge of the figure. Such beautiful art work seems to have been quite common, as there is scarcely a name of the ancient Greek potters recorded, unless it be that of Dibutades, of whom the pretty legend of the lover's portrait is told—but there is no mention of any one great master, the head of a school of potters and vase painters. We must conclude, therefore, that these were artists of the simplest native growth ; they seem to have sprung from the soil and never to have had any centre of teaching or study formed around any distinguished man of their craft, as the bronze workers and marble sculptors had. If we compare the fictile and painted work of the Egyptian and the Assyrian, more especially of the latter, with the Greek vase paintings, the great superiority of the Greek artist will be strikingly seen. Yet it is remarkable that this superiority was attained while they derived the rudiments of their art from the more ancient workers, as is seen in those Greek vase paintings which obviously resemble the Egyptian and Assyrian figures.

As to the mutual reaction of literature and sculptural art and the general temperament of mind in those ancient days, a vast field of deep interest is to be traversed in the elaborate writings of the great historians and essayists, which sculptors and all art students would do well to explore. It is from reading in this direction the modern artist may learn that—"The value of vigour and passion, of vividness of all kinds, was at least as amply recognized in theory and exemplified in practice by the artistic genius of that age as by that of any other; but its larger view never lost sight of the supremacy of measure and harmony, the powers whose gracious influence was present in every great effort of the Hellenic mind." *

In the written drama and in the acted tragedy there was a mutual reaction of the poetic, the plastic, and the pictorial arts. Upon this the following interesting suggestions are made in a series of learned papers by Mr. W. Watkiss Lloyd (in 'The Portfolio,' March, April, May, 1885). "The most astonishing developments were those of sculpture and the drama at the hands of Pheidias and Æschylus.

"There is full reason to believe that if we were in possession of specimens of the drama as composed and represented anterior to those of Æschylus we should be conscious of a transition as amazing as that from Myron and Onatas to Pheidias in sculpture. Æschylus was the first to apply the resources of free invention to theatrical costume, and to enforce it for the enhancement not only of dignity, but of every phase of

* 'Æschylus,' in 'Hellenica Essays'; by Ernest Myers, M.A., 1880. See also Mr. Gladstone's elaborate exposition of the worship of Nature-power and the development of anthropomorphism in the Olympian system, with the ethics and polity of the heroic age ('Juventus Mundi').

characteristic expression. . . . To Pheidias on his part appears due the relief of the nude in sculpture by drapery, which, while rigid archaism was rejected, became perfectly natural only to be treated with a refinement transcending nature. . . . The invariable use of masks, especially for the chief actors, the very personages who had most occasion to give visible expression to fluctuations of passion. . . . . How far a great genius like Æschylus, for a realization of his conceptions, stimulated the artists who provided his characters with appropriate masks, and how far he was himself under obligations to the characteristic ideals which painting and sculpture had already embodied." . . . That there is "much of the sculptural in the art of Æschylus, and how essentially some of the most elaborate works of Pheidias are dramatic, as in the conflict of Athene and Poseidon in the pediment of the Parthenon."

What is certainly to be observed in regarding the mutual reaction of sculptural art and the drama at these early times, is that it led to a sympathetic and simultaneous effort to render expression in the two congenial forms respectively. Thus Æschylus * portrayed in his characters the heroic style, which has its analogue in the severe archaic types of sculpture without emotional expression. Sophokles, who followed his model, went away from this more towards direct human feeling, so as to play upon the passions and sentiments of his audience by passionate words, to touch them with the pathetic. Then came his contemporary Euripides, who sought still more to affect his audience with the sympathy for human character and emotion, and impel the actor to be more histrionic. He indeed has been called infidel from his want of faith in an Almighty Deity, and his entirely secular view of life and morality. All this constant portraying of the emotional on the stage could not be without its influence upon the art of the time in changing, softening, not to say weakening, its aim and aspirations.

The change gradually arising in sculpture when Skopas and Praxiteles divided the honours, was attributable to the spirit of the times, which tended away from the severity and implicit belief of the age of Pheidias, who of all sculptors was the first and the

* Æschylus was born 525 B.C., died 456. Sophokles, b. 485, d. 406. Euripides, b. 480, d. 406 B.C. Aristophanes, b. 444, d. 380 (about).

only one who had worthily represented Zeus and Athene. The inclination of opinion, led as it was by the schools of philosophy, was antagonistic to the ancient religious belief. The universal questioning and doubt which had arisen with the intellectual culture of Athens under Perikles, was like the beginning of that eclipse of faith which has been observed in our own times.

The dawn of a materialistic and searching spirit of inquiry was shown in the philosophy of Thales (about 550 B.C.) and his followers of the Ionian school, which may be regarded also as the origin of speculative philosophy. Euclid and the Megaric school followed, and further developed the logical method. At Athens, Socrates, who was bred a sculptor,—his group of the Graces clothed in the Acropolis is mentioned by Pausanias (lib. ix. c. 35),—was in the fifth century (about 406 B.C.) accused of despising the tutelary deities of the State and of putting others in their place. He believed himself inspired by a divine voice within him (his " demon " or " genius "), obviously the first germ of the doctrine of Conscience in opposition to that of the Spirit of Nature—*Kosmos.* Out of his teachings came Plato, a greater master of thought, who expanded and advanced his view, and after him Aristotle, the father of investigative or experimental and observative philosophy, to which has since been accorded the name of Science. Diogenes and the Cynics may be noticed as conspiring with the other Greek philosophers to aid the general tendency towards the sweeping away of the ancient theogony and mythology as a religious faith, although the poetry and the art proved indestructible, both having survived to be renovated, revived, and revered as a faith by all worshippers of the beautiful.

Nothing in history is more remarkable than the spell of beauty which has hung for ages over the ruined master-pieces of ancient art, whether in Egypt, Assyria, Greece, or Rome. Had it not been for this protective influence and charm of beauty how much would never have been known! Countless works of art have been sought for and recovered at great expenditure of national treasure, and amazing personal enterprise and study. These relics, preserved like the fossils of prehistoric life buried for ages in the earth, or built into the walls of ancient castles, though the art and the artists are alike extinct, are yet accepted as the test and model of a civilization which has scarce any other sympathy with them. More than this, the long-buried seed brought to the light of day has fructified, in producing not like beauties unfortunately, for that would seem impossible, but other beauties in the creation of the art of painting. Raffaello and Michelangelo—were they not the pupils of Pheidias, of Alkamenes, of Polykleitos, and of Myron? The inspiration, if not the laws of beauty, they first learnt from the works of those masters. That which followed the Italian Renaissance was a repetition in its kind of the movement in favour of emotional and sentimental expression, of which Skopas and Praxiteles were the leaders. The sculptors, amid the general seeking for new things and more soul-stirring efforts of art, were influenced and encouraged to attempt works of over-refinement; they strained their art for new creations with more of living beauty, energy of movement, and emotional display, both in the countenance and the muscular action of the figures. The Niobe and the Laocoon groups are examples. With this came the feeling for that mode of beauty which we call "grace"— suavity of expression, representing the beauty of humanity in preference to the gravity and sublimity of the divine as conceived by Pheidias. We notice this in the Venus de' Medici, the Diana of the Louvre, and the Apollo Belvedere. The change is further observable in the altered character of the statues of Bacchus, from the bearded to the youthful head and form; of Venus Aphrodite as in the statue of Melos and the Venus de' Medici; of the Eros of the Parthenon frieze and the Cupid and Psyche of the Capitol (see *Examples*), and in many other instances.

Thus Greek art passed from the primitive condition of archaism and the hieratic form, through much tentative work, to its perfect development under Pheidias; then after a brief period of glory, fell away into repetition and borrowing from past great works, followed by the change of style under Skopas and Praxiteles, and gradually declined in power, till copying, portraiture, and the manufacturing of art work without any sense and enjoyment of beauty completed the general degradation.

Something must here be said upon what might perhaps be called the Æsthetic of Physiology—those effects upon the living

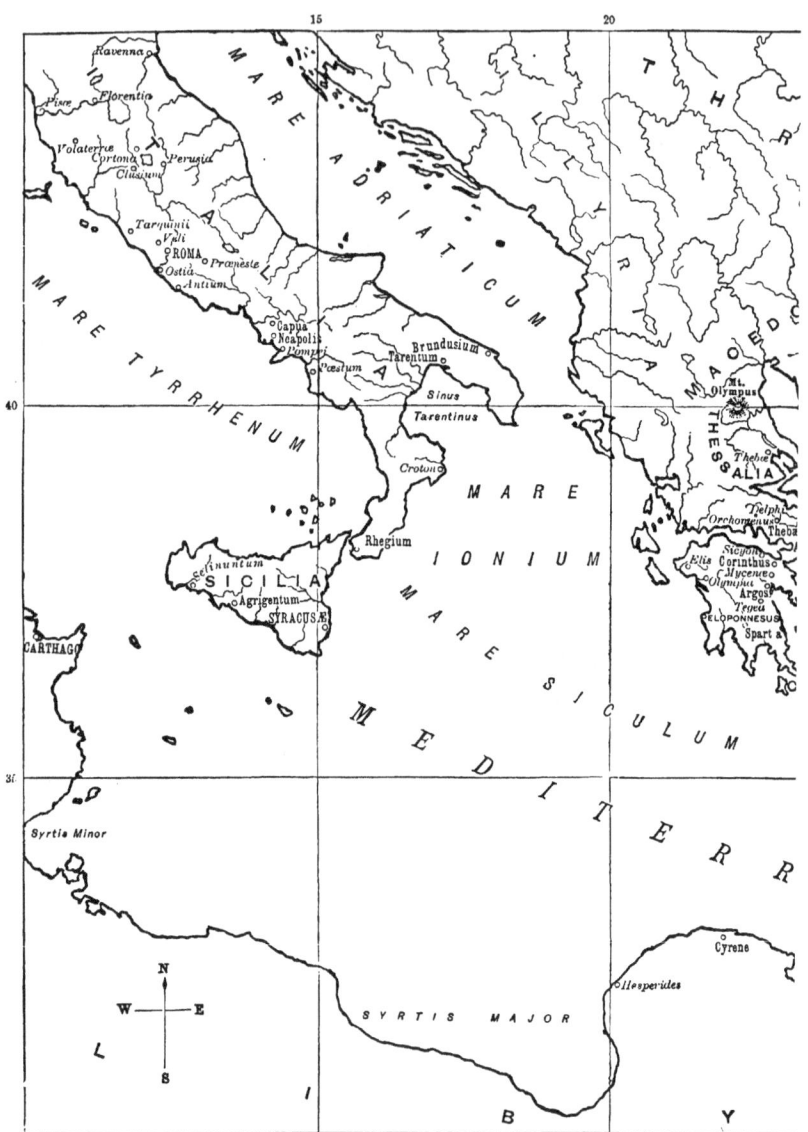

FIG. 42.—MAP OF ANCIENT GREECE.

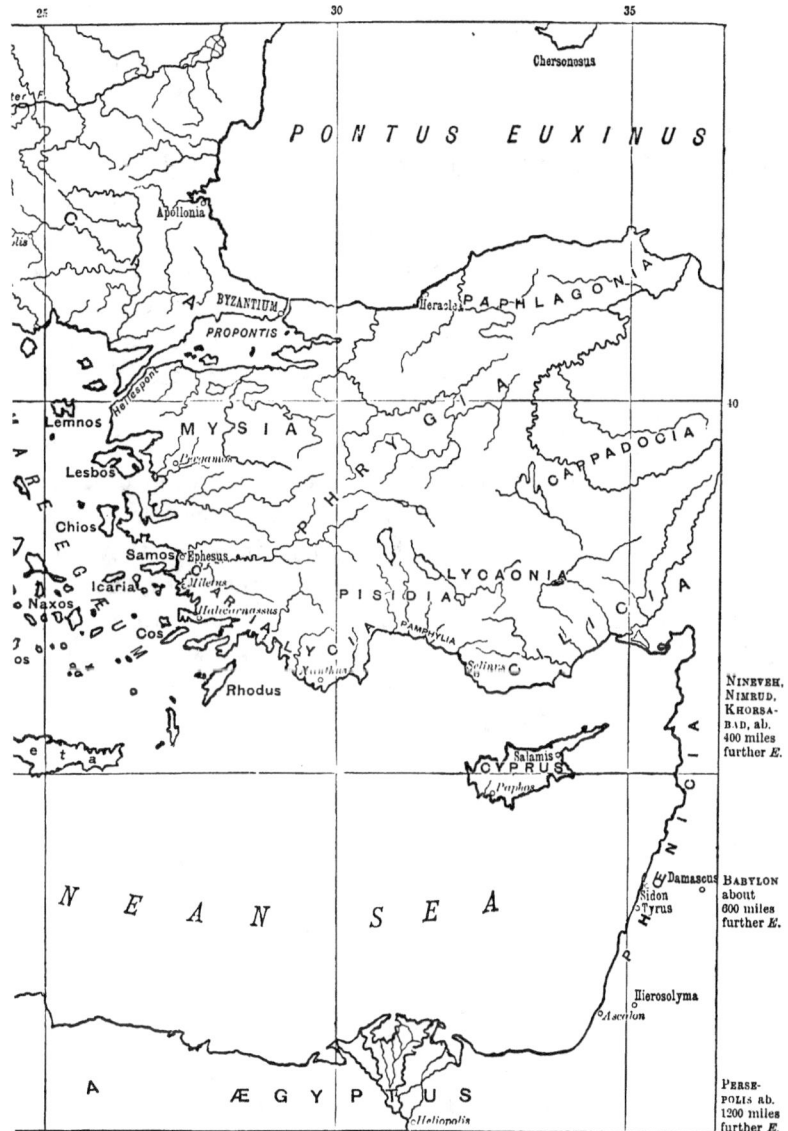

PONTUS   EUXINUS

Chersonesus

Apollonia

BYZANTIUM

PROPONTIS

Heraclea   PAPHLAGONIA

PHRYGIA

CAPPADOCIA

Lemnos

MYSIA

Lesbos

Chios

Samos Ephesus

Icaria

Naxos

os

Cos

Rhodus

Miletus

Halicarnassus

PISIDIA

LYCAONIA

PAMPHYLIA

Xanthus

Selinus

LYCIA

CILICIA

NINEVEH,
NIMRUD,
KHORSA-
BAD, ab.
400 miles
further *E*.

Salamis
CYPRUS
Paphus

NEAN   SEA

PHŒNICIA

Damascus
Sidon
Tyrus

BABYLON
about
600 miles
further *E*.

Hierosolyma
Ascalon

PERSE-
POLIS ab.
1200 miles
further *E*.

A

ÆGYPTUS

Heliopolis

MEMPHIS ab. 10 miles; LUXOR, KARNAK, THEBES, ab. 300 miles further *S*.—all on banks of the Nile.

form which are the result of brain and nerve force, and which produce action, attitude, gesture, facial expression of the countenance, and intonation of the voice, chiefly involuntary.

No writer upon the expression of the human form, whether from the artist's point of view or from that of the ordinary scientific observer, has gone so completely to the root of the matter as Sir Charles Bell, who was an excellent artist, in his great work.* As a physiologist he will for ever hold a high place as the discoverer of the distinct functions of the nerve centres and the nerve branches, and of the mode in which certain actions of the muscles are produced involuntarily, those which have the most marked effect in giving expression to the face as well as to the limbs and the attitude of the body—to all in fact that comes under the definition of " action " in the figure. A few quotations from his invaluable book will throw more light on the subject than all that could be taken from the lectures of professed Sculptors and Painters. " Anatomy, in its relations to the arts of design, is in truth the grammar of that language in which they address us. The expressions, attitudes, and movements of the human figure are the characters of this language, adapted to convey the effect of historical narration, as well as to show the working of human passions, and to give the most striking and lively indications of intellectual power and energy."

Alluding to the notion of Winckelman and other writers that " supreme beauty resides in God,—that the idea of human beauty becomes more and more perfect in proportion to its conformity and its harmony with the Supreme Being,"—Bell says we must deal with what " stands materially before us, to be seen, touched, and measured." " With what *Divine* essence," he asks, " is the comparison to be made ? The idea of representing Deity is palpably absurd ; we know nothing of form but from the contemplation of man. The only interpretation of Divinity in the human figure as represented by the ancient sculptors is that the artists avoided individuality ; that they studied to keep free of resemblance to any individual ; giving no indication of the spirit or of the sentiments or affections ; conceiving that all these movements

* 'The Anatomy and Philosophy of Expression' (1844), 6th ed. 1872. Bell's beautiful anatomical drawings from his dissections were bequeathed to the University College, London, and are to be seen in the Museum.

destroy the unity of the features, and are foreign to beauty in the abstract." "Whatever is peculiar to the human countenance as distinguishing it from the brute is enhanced." "Not only is the forehead expanded and projecting, and the facial line more perpendicular, but every feature is modelled on the same principle. The mouth, the teeth, the lips are not the mere instruments of mastication, but of speech and human expression. So of every part; whatever would lead to the resemblance of the brute is omitted or diminished." "Human sentiment prevailing in the expression of a face will always make it agreeable or lovely. Expression is even of more consequence than shape; it will light up features otherwise heavy; it will make us forget all but the quality of the mind."

While referring to bas-relief in the previous section, it was reserved to say something of its more æsthetic relations. The beauty of form in sculpture is told by emphasizing the contour of the figure; even in the round the sculptor criticizes his work by observing closely the profile, so to speak, at any and every side. He is not satisfied till he has succeeded in giving to his figure or group the utmost that he can conceive it capable of, in the composition or arrangement governing the attitudes. The flow of line must be harmonious, graceful, noble or full in the forms, not angular, sudden, abrupt, or opposed in one line or form to another near it, unless the expression demands this. But there are parts in the human figure, where Nature especially enforces the beauty and grace of form in almost pure line, where she shows to a certain extent the profile. These are to be observed only where there are cavities, and it is remarkable that these are reserved almost entirely for the head, and especially for the face or "countenance," as it is so finely called in one expressive word. The eye is the most noticeable of these, the mouth the next so, then the nostrils and the ears; all the avenues of the senses but the one of touch, which has for its prime minister the hand—an organ only second in its expressive power to the countenance.

Through the eye, as "the window of the soul," the rays of thought and feeling pass in and out. Therefore the form of the eyelid is sharply cut and brought out against the dark, shadowy, impenetrable depth of the pupil—the opening into the *camera obscura* so marvellously constructed by organic life. No curves are more beautiful and more exquisitely modulated than those of the eyelids ; and in the iris alone, with its containing sphere the eyeball, do we find the perfect form of a circle. But the eye, itself so marked, is helped by the brow, which Nature marks not only with the sharp lines of the hair forming the eyebrow, but by the projection of this brow, forming the orbit in such a way as to show the form of the forehead. In the finest heads of Greek statues it will be seen that the hairs of the eyebrow are not carved, the sharply-defined line of the brow alone is preferred by the sculptor. And how beautiful this line is may be seen especially in the Venus of Milo, the Ludovisi Juno, the Apollo Belvedere, and remarkably in the fine bronze head of Artemis in the British Museum (frontispiece).

To render more clear what is meant, it may be said that this enforcement of line to show beauty of form in Nature, is analogous to the profile of a cornice taken by the architect as the essence of his ornament, or indeed the section of any surface form.

The mouth is made out, so to speak, both with colour and form in the sharpness of line in the lips. The exquisite curved lines of the lips are relieved partly by contrast of form and colour against the teeth, but chiefly against the cavity of the mouth, as in speaking.

The ear is brought out in its beautiful shell-like, complex form by the most elaborate conjunctions of curves, made to tell by relief against the hair and the smooth parts of the cheek and neck. The shadow from the projecting parts of the ear enforces its wonderfully beautiful form, and the opening of the " meatus " contributes forcibly to this effect.

The nostril, though not of so much importance, is nevertheless of considerable value in relieving the forms against the opening to the nose, and it displays the very nicest delicacy of modelling, especially in giving the expression of the living pliant feature, as when dilated and moving with the excitement of attention, astonishment, fear, anger, or all violent emotion, when all the muscles of the face pull together, as it were, by the action of the nerves concerned in expression apart from the control of the will, as Sir C. Bell was the first to explain.

The beautiful effect of profile is often very remarkable in heads which seen in full or three-quarters are not so beautiful. This is frequently to be observed in the heads of Angels and Saints by some of the earlier Italian masters : in the works of Giotto and Fra Angelico especially. Profile seems to belong to the severer style, and that in which technical mastery has not been attained. It is therefore almost universal in Greek vase painting. It was necessarily founded on the *bas-relief* of the sculptors, and is therefore sculpturesque. The *intaglio* affords another example of the value of the relief obtained by sharply cutting the profile of a figure at the surface of a plane.

Much valuable matter upon bas-relief will be found in ' Contributions to the Literature of the Fine Arts ' (vol. i. p. 116) by Sir C. Eastlake, P.R.A., in which is pointed out the " principle of suppressing the relief within the extreme contour which, with the strong marking of the outline itself, mainly constitutes the style of basso-relievo." It follows, as will readily be seen, that since " foreshortening " is the representation of the hiding, or absorption, as it were, of parts further from the eye by those which are nearer, it cannot be employed properly in bas-relief. It is therefore never found in antique sculpture.

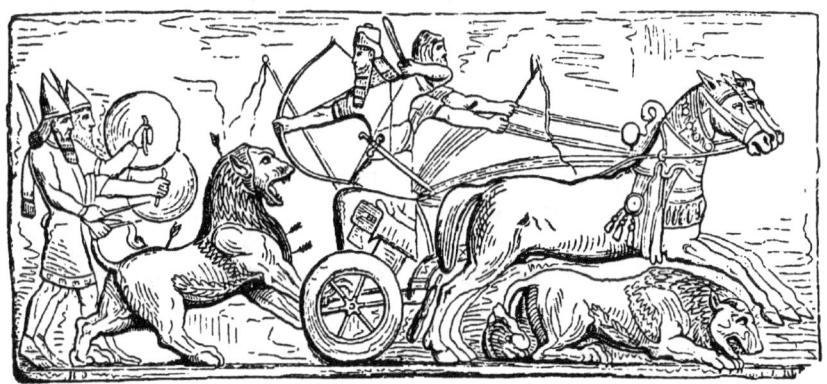

Fig. 45a.—Lion Hunt: Part of an Assyrian Bas-relief.
From Nimroud.

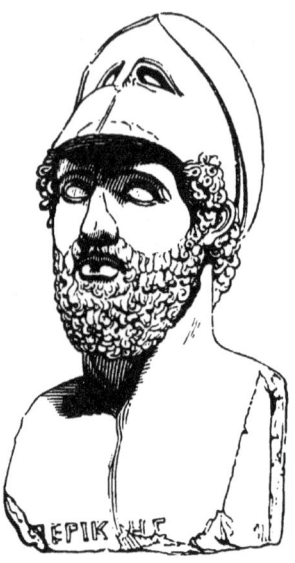

FIG. 46.—PERIKLES.

SECTION III.—HISTORIC AND DESCRIPTIVE.

IT has already been shown that history refers abundantly to primitive works in wood, clay, and stone as the original sources of the plastic art. To go further into any descriptive account of these would be foreign to our purpose in considering sculpture as a branch of art of the highest aim in the expression of ideal beauty and the representation of natural beauty of form. It is interesting, however, to observe the great similarity amongst all objects of primitive design—whether works of barbaric ornament or attempts to imitate the human and brute form, although they may be the productions of widely different nations and ages. In the work even of savages is to be found a certain innate feeling for some elementary forms of material beauty; but no effort to render the human, or even the brute figure, as beautiful as it is in nature, is to be seen in these barbaric attempts. Although in ornament the true principles of beauty were touched, yet these primitive carvers and moulders failed utterly before the figure. The rude images of Phœnician plastic work are clumsy, monstrous, grotesque, without any idea of proportion, and they are so similar to those found in ancient Peru and Mexico that they might easily be mistaken for them. The archaic figures discovered in Cyprus by Mr. Lang and others, before Cesnola's important researches there, show this strong inter-resemblance (Fig. 64). And of those dug up deep in the buried ruins of the supposed Troy by Dr. Schliemann it may be said the same family likeness is observable, while Mr. Newton assures us that these are of the same character as many found at Ialysos. There are numerous examples of Etruscan work which show similar archaic character (Fig. 58). The heads have the same naturalistic, imitative, rude portrait-like character —often the same smile peculiar to Egyptian statues made ages before and preserved afterwards in the later and much more artistic sculpture of Selinus (Fig. 68) and Ægina (Fig. 74). The bodies were thick, and the limbs were clumsy, without any perception of the rule of proportion which had been long before settled and acted upon by the Egyptian sculptors with far finer results, and followed by the greatest masters ever since.

Leaving Etruscan sculpture, of which something more has to be said as to its characteristics in the examples still in existence, a glance may be taken over those regions which were outside the great centres of civilization of ancient times—Egypt, Assyria, and perhaps other parts of Asia. It may be conjectured that as population went on radiating in every direction, towards the shores of the Mediterranean, where the sea for a time would offer some obstacles, and into the vast Continents of the East and the South, such powerful settlements would be formed as those which developed into the nations of the Medes, the Chaldæans, the Phœnicians, the Persians. The Chinese seem to have been content to wander off without ever thinking of returning to plunder their neighbours; but their records, if we are to credit them with the antiquity they claim, show that they were a factor in ancient civilization, though their sculptural and architectural art is speedily summed up without finding a trace of feeling for beauty. Had they ever mingled in the ambitious game of war and heroic enterprise that led to so much power in other peoples; had they even felt a spark of chivalric feeling, they might perhaps have had an intellectual form of art. But of them, as of all Asiatics in regard to art, it is to be said, that their bodily organization and temperament, their food and climate, led them to spend their efforts in the luxurious development of ornamental forms and the beauties of colour; all of which refer to the gratification of the senses and not the intellect. Though they perceived by instinct the influence of colossal size, they failed in the proportions of their figures and the symmetry of their buildings, and relied upon a profusion of symbols and detail of curiously-beautiful ornaments, often worked in costly material. Beyond this they never advanced. It must be borne in mind, moreover, that the best ornamental art-work of China, Japan, India, and Persia is comparatively modern, and that those monuments, of figure sculpture especially, which are ancient are barbaric in character, with no feeling for ideal and but little of material beauty.

In endeavouring, therefore, to take any comprehensive view of the development of sculpture, we arrive at the conclusion that the period of the barbaric in sculpture was common to all nations, and that art in that barbaric form was simply indigenous; but that while some nations advanced to certain degrees of improvement and there stopped, others endowed with a superior organization went on developing their art in proportion to their intellectual advancement, and step by step with their cultivation of literature.

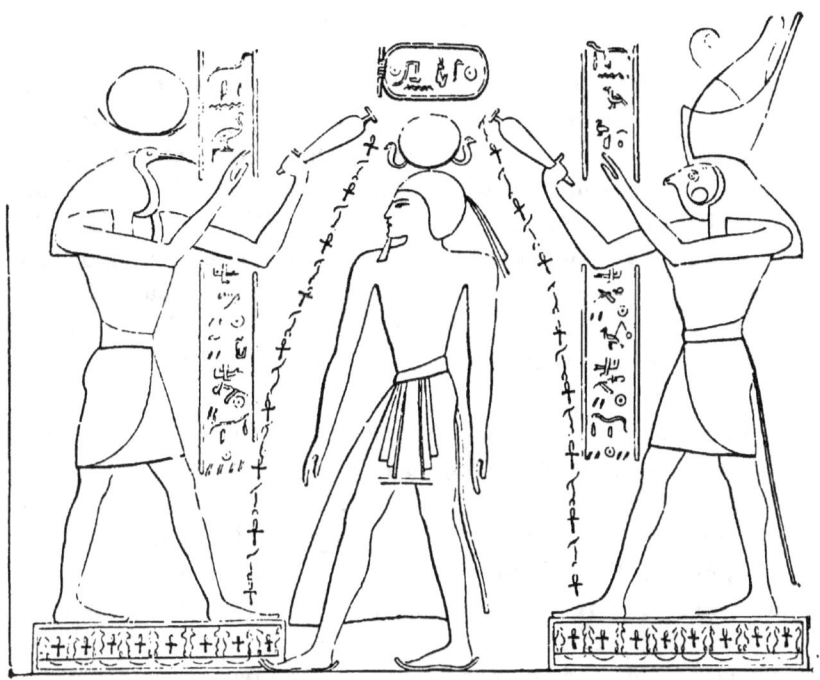

Fig. 47.—Cavo-relievo. Rhamses III. with the Gods Thoth and Horus
pouring over him the symbols of power, purity, stability,
and the keys of eternal life.

From an Alabastron. Found at Luxor.

EGYPTIAN SCULPTURE.

The Egyptians, inhabiting a flat uniform country of pure
and salubrious climate, working as sculptors before a written
language was invented, carved their colossal Sphinx almost
entirely out of the living rock; an amazing example of symbolic sculptural representation, combining the human with the
brute form of the lion.* The date of this first great work is
probably earlier than that of the earliest of the pyramids—that
built by Chofo king of Memphis, the Cheops of Herodotus, and
the larger one by Nef Chofo his son. M. Renan, speaking for
M. Mariette, states that a tablet was found by him recording

* The Sphinx is 180 feet long. There are several kinds of Egyptian
Sphinxes—the man-headed, the woman-headed, the ram-headed. The
Greek Sphinx had sometimes the man's, sometimes the woman's head,
with the body of lion or dog, and often wings.

A. S.

that Nef Chofo did certain repairs to the Sphinx ; so that since it required repairs, it must already have existed for a considerable time.* All small barbaric or archaic work of the ancient Egyptians in sculpture has perished in the vast lapse of time. But this one monument, raised at least 4000 years before the Christian era, stands to prove with its companion pyramids, the wonderful power of conception, the energy and practical skill, which characterized the early Egyptians. What they lacked in ideas of beauty, they made up for by the simple grandeur of colossal size and perfection of execution (Fig. 48).

The intention of producing a monument to last for ever was shown in an equally striking manner in the construction of the pyramids, and with an exercise of science and skill even more remarkable. Following the chronology of Mr. Sharpe in his ' History of Egypt,' Egyptian art in the form of architecture was, after the pyramids of Ghizeh, further developed about 1650 B.C. under Osirtesen I., who built the oldest of the temples at Thebes. Columns and obelisks were then invented, and the *cavi relievi* were largely used. Statuary, however, did not advance until after the Phœnician Shepherd Kings—a body of wandering Arabs, so called, who conquered Upper Egypt for a time— were driven out by Amosis, king of Thebes, about 1450 B.C.

Passing over Amunothph I. and his successor Thothmosis I., of whom there is a fine statue in the Turin Museum, we come to Thothmosis II., whose reign marks a period of vast development, as he married Nitocris, the last queen of Memphis, capital of Lower Egypt, and thus united the two kingdoms, about 1340 B.C. The great avenue of Sphinxes leading to the temple of Karnak was made in his reign, and there is a statue of Thothmosis II., a seated figure 7 ft. 9 in. high, in good proportions, of about seven heads high, the fingers and toes straight, not showing the knuckles, and the legs sharply chiselled at the shins, not showing the small bone on the outside of the leg, as in statues of the later time of Amunothph III. (about 1260 B.C.). The statue of this latter king,† brought to England by Belzoni, should be studied as showing the conventional style followed by

* ' Revue des deux Mondes,' 1865, p. 675.
† No. 21, British Museum.

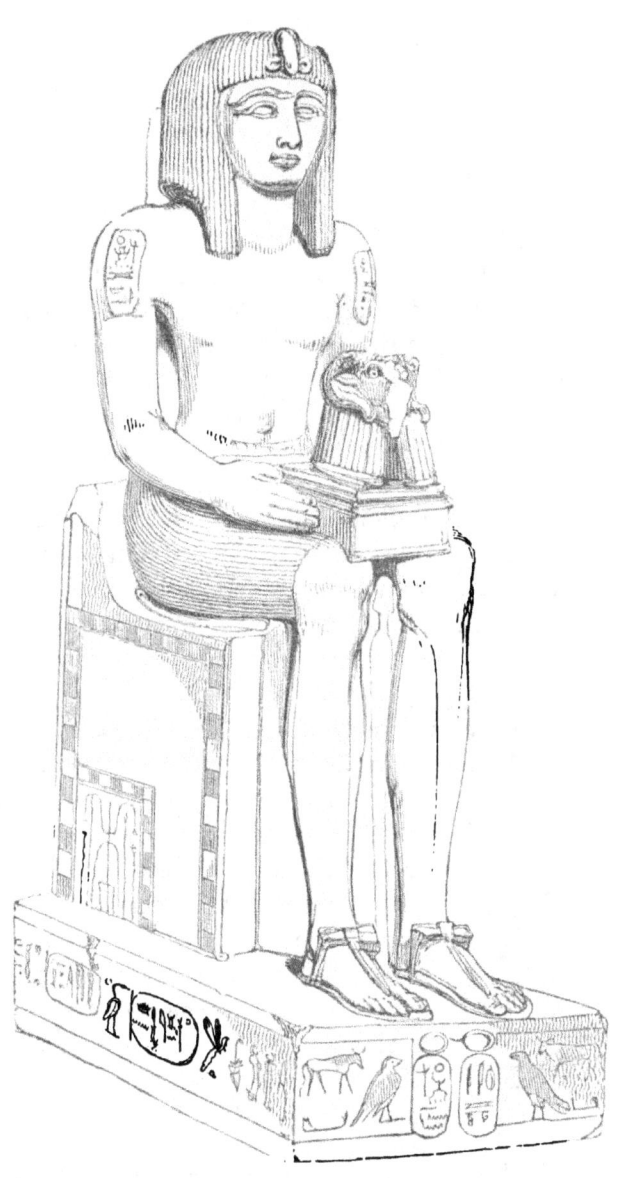

Fig. 48.—Egyptian Statue [showing fine style of work and good proportions].
the head of the refined Coptic features, the lips not thick, and the
nose not flat nor turned up, as in the Ethiopic type.

In black basalt, heroic size.   British Museum.

these mechanical workers, in the representation of the knee-cap (patella) as well as the small bone of the leg. The patella especially is wrong anatomically; instead of being broader at the upper part and narrow at the lower, it is equally large at the top and bottom. The famous colossus, called the musical Memnon, one of the two still standing in the desert near Thebes, more than 50 ft. high, is of this period. These statues are not in good proportion, being too short in the waist. The two fine lions carved in red granite, belonging to this time, which Lord Prudhoe brought over and presented to the British Museum, are remarkable as examples of fine typical treatment of the lion. They show much grandeur of feeling, and, compared with the modern naturalistic sculpture of lions—for example, in the Papa Rezzonico monument in St. Peter's, Rome, by Canova—they are superior as examples of monumental art.

In 1170 B.C. reigned Ramses II., the greatest of the Egyptian kings, under whom was invented all the wonderful adaptation of the lotus and papyrus plant to the design of columns, as seen in the famous colonnade of the hall of Karnak. His statue in the Turin Museum is in the finest style of ancient Theban art;

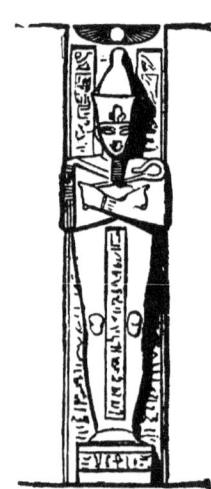

FIG. 49.—COLOSSAL STATUE OF RAMSES AS OSIRIS. At Thebes. 47 feet high.

it is a seated figure carved out of a block of black granite, but is not colossal, being only 5 ft. 7 in. high. The point to be noticed in this statue is the effort at action, which is not seen in earlier works. The right hand is raised to the breast holding the short sort of crosier of the god Osiris; the left hand, strongly clenched, resting on the knee. The colossal statue of Ramses as Osiris (Fig. 49) with that of the Memnon in the British Museum may be taken as examples of the sculpture of this time. The large Sphinx in the Louvre bears the name of Ramses II. The four seated colossi, carved out of the living rock at the entrance of the great temple of Abou Simbel in Ethiopia, represent the same king. They are between 60 and 70ft. high, and wonderfully well sculptured, but the proportions are not so good as in some smaller statues, as they are six heads only in height, and short in the waist and thick in the limbs, showing no attempt at any close or correct imitation of nature. They look straight before them with a calm smile of confident power and contentment. These statues and others which are to be seen in museums are not equal to those of the time of Amunothph III., previously referred to; they are not so well carved, and the features are heavy, with thick noses and lips, while the limbs are clumsy, and without any attempt at accurate modelling.

It will be observed, therefore, that Egyptian sculpture may be classed broadly into three styles. 1. The Egyptian proper, reaching its finest period in the reign of Amunothph III. 2. The Ethiopic Egyptian. 3. The later Egyptian, leading to the decline of that style of sculpture. Of the first it should be noticed that the general proportions of the figure were more accurately considered than the relative proportions of hands and feet to the limbs, which re generally incorrect. There are, however, some examples of excellent proportion, as in a colossal arm, and a fist, in the British Museum. This arm belonged to a statue of Thothmes III., and came from Memphis. The fist, which belonged to a still larger statue, also came from Memphis, and measures 4ft. across. The heads of statues of this period are of the pure Coptic type, with a nose somewhat aquiline, and the lips comparatively thin. The eyes, however, were always carved in full in profile represent-

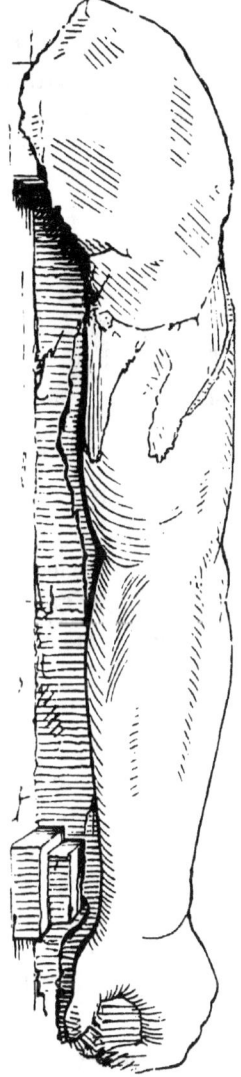

FIG. 49a.—COLOSSAL ARM ABOUT 10 FEET LONG. *In the British Museum.*

ations; the feet, one in advance of the other on the same plane. The details of form at the knuckles and legs are well indicated.

In the Ethiopic-Egyptian statues, general proportion is lost sight of; the figures become dumpy, being only six heads high; the limbs are clumsy and wanting in modelling; the hands and feet stiff and not marked by details at the joints; nor do they show the small bone of the leg. The heads are more of the Negro type, with turned-up noses and thick lips.

In the later Egyptian it is remarkable that with more attempt to imitate nature in the modelling of the muscles, the forms of the trunk and limbs became unnaturally puffed. More is added in symbolic attributes; heads of the cat, the hawk, and the ape are placed on the human body; the dress is more elaborate, that of the head especially, on which a disc for the sun was often placed, as on the god Osiris (Fig. 17). From the fall of Thebes, about 1000 B.C., to the conquest of Egypt by the Persians, 523 B.C., the sculpture became more and more degraded, and soon lost its original style of simplicity and grandeur of form.

" Egyptian sculptors of the best time (Amunothph III.) gave the character of the nation to their statues. The serious gloomy Egyptian aimed at an expression not valued by the more gay and active Greeks. Plato saw nothing but ugliness in an Egyptian statue. The Egyptian, however, had learned the superiority of rest over action in representing the sublime." (*Sharpe.*)

After some two centuries of rule, the Persians were conquered by Alexander the Great, 332 B.C., but there are no statues of Greek style of this date found in Egypt; and under the Ptolemies, his successors for 300 years, new temples of inferior but still Egyptian style were built, such as those at Phile, Edfou, and Denderah, and many statues were made, but nearly all have been destroyed, and there is not one of any king or queen of the Ptolemies.

After Egypt became a Roman province, in 38 B.C., Egyptian sculpture in a debased form was still continued in the decoration of the temples, but the statues were then in the hands of Greek artists. Still later, there is the well-known statue of Antinous as an Egyptian, the work of a Greek sculptor of the time of the Emperor Hadrian (A.D. 117—138).

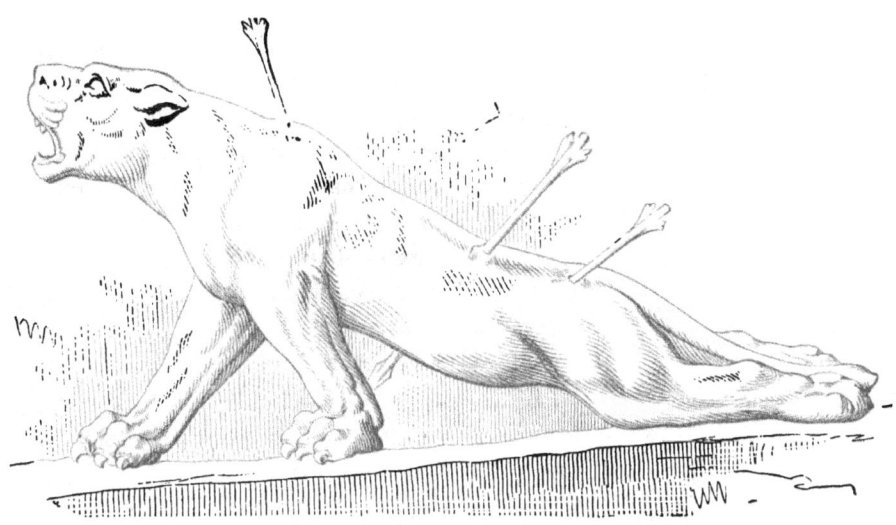

FIG. 50 —ASSYRIAN. *British Museum.*

ASSYRIAN SCULPTURE.

ASSYRIAN sculpture is a discovery of recent times, first made in 1842-3 by M. Botta, the French consul at Mosul on the banks of the Tigris, and almost simultaneously by Mr. Layard, who though he had seen the ruins of Nineveh in 1840 did not get permission to examine and excavate till 1845. The sculptures differ widely from any in Egypt in being nearly all in bas-relief and high relief. There are very few statues, carved in the round, that stand either with a support practically or on the legs. There are no colossi nearly approaching in size the Egyptian and Greek colossal statues, none being higher than 18 ft., while as we have seen 60ft. was a moderate height for an Egyptian or Greek colossal figure, and some were higher. The colossal human-headed bulls and lions with wings, at the portals of the king's palace, are in high relief on huge slabs, one on each side, facing outwards, and one on each side on the wall, with the head turned to look to the front. It does not appear that any principal figure was set up in an interior, either of these compound animals, or of any deity or king. There is the headless seated statue of Shalmaneser in black basalt, found by Layard in the great mound of Kalah Shergat, the primitive capital of Assyria, now in the British Museum, which is life-size, and resembles the Egyptian figure; and a statue of a Priest, larger than life (Fig. 51), also in the Museum.   How these were placed is not

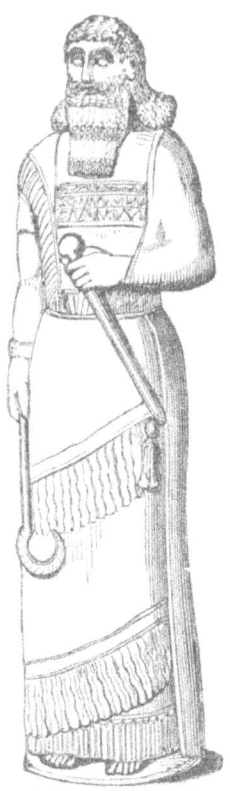

known.   No colossal seated figures like the Egyptian statues have been found.   The standing figures carved in relief differ entirely in the expression of the countenance and motive of the figure from the Egyptian. They have all some action; the king grasps a captured lion, or as chief priest he walks with his staff which he holds firmly, while the left hand rests on the hilt of his sword. It is true that the legs are on one plane, and the feet in a position that could not support the body; still the intention to show action and life is there.   There is none of the desire to express majestic, calm, eternal repose and content which is so characteristic of Egyptian sculptured statues. Throughout the great number of slabs in the British Museum and in the Louvre there is a very vigorous descriptive power displayed in carving figures of men, horses, chariots, battles, sieges of cities, hunting scenes, processions, rivers with men swimming on inflated skins, with fish and boats;

FIG. 51.—STATUE OF A   implements, weapons, chairs, baskets, trees,
PRIEST.   birds, buildings, with a close resemblance
In the British Museum.   to the real objects that is very distinctive
of the Assyrian style (Fig. 53).   The quadrupeds and birds are much better done than the human figures: the character of the bulls, the horses, and the mules is faithfully given, and there is much feeling for nature in some of the lions in the hunting-scenes.   There is no doubt, also, that this naturalistic realism was carried further by painting the sculptures.   In none of these painted reliefs, however, is there anything of the careful carving and delicate delineation seen in the Egyptian *cavi relievi*. They are all boldly done, and with a good deal of skill, but by

hands that would seem to have been self-taught, and at liberty
to represent as they pleased so that the conventional attributes
and symbolic objects were duly made clear.   There is scarcely
any regulated use of typical forms; and in the proportions of
the figures especially there is no rule.   The principal figures are
about 6½ heads high, and in others the heads are often larger,
while the arms and legs are out of all proportion gigantic, the
muscles being exaggerated into masses at the calf and knee, and
the shin-bone absurdly prominent.   All truth seems to have
been sacrificed for the sake of conveying a violent look of
immense strength.   The battle-scenes remind us of some of the
puerile representations by mediæval workmen of a poor style, or
the debased Roman work seen on sarcophaguses.   The Assyrians,
unlike the Egyptians, were "mighty hunters," consequently
horses were favourites with the Assyrian carvers, as they were
with the Greek sculptors afterwards; they seldom have more
than one fore-leg and one hind one, but their heads are carefully
carved, and all the trappings show the same intention to obtain
exact resemblance as is displayed in the dress and ornaments of
the kings and other figures (Fig. 52).   It is important to observe
that these sculptures are very equal in merit; there is no sign
of improvement, and little of falling off.   As to the date of these
sculptures, they are much later than all the Egyptian work of
the finer style.   According to Mr. Fergusson, who was guided by
Gutschmidt's reading of the text of Berosus,* the Medes conquered the Chaldæans 2458 B.C., and were driven out again by
the Chaldæans, probably under Nimrod, about 2235 B.C.   After
700 years they were invaded again from the West (possibly by
the Egyptians of the eighteenth dynasty), and soon afterwards
arose the Assyrians, founding the kingdom of Nineveh about
1273 B.C. ; while the Chaldæans were under this Western power.
The Assyrians, in turn, were conquered by the Chaldæans about
652 (the second Chaldæan kingdom), and then a century after
came the Persian conquest under Cyrus in 538 B.C.   The sculptures recovered from Nimroud, Koyunjik, and Khorsabad belong
to the period from 1290 B.C. onwards to some later date before

* Rheinischer Museum, vol. viii. p. 252.

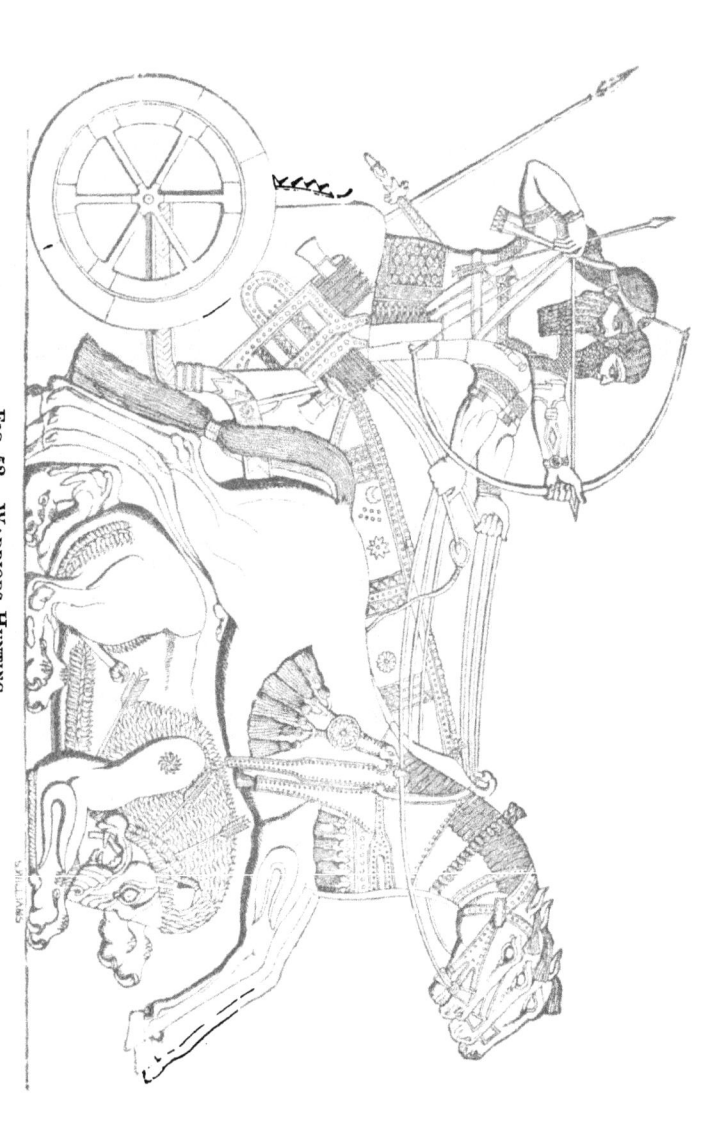

FIG. 52.—WARRIORS HUNTING.

Assyrian Bas-relief in the British Museum. Considered to be the finest hitherto discovered.

the total destruction of Nineveh in 538 B.C.* Therefore it is important to remember that the great works in sculpture due to the old civilization of Egypt belong to an age that had passed away long before the dawn of history in Babylonia. The earliest date we have of Assyrian history is 2458 B.C., the earliest in Egyptian may be taken as 4000 'B.C. As we have seen, all the great statues of Egypt were made many centuries before 1200 B.C., while the Assyrian sculptures are placed at the earliest after 1290 B.C. as a beginning.

It may be concluded that the Assyrian palaces, with their sculptured walls, took a much shorter time to build than the Egyptian, as they were built of sun-baked bricks, with ornamental slabs below, and wooden beams and columns above, all which structures have perished leaving only the stone slabs. The dates of the reigns of the Assyrian kings have been so clearly determined by Sir Henry Rawlinson, that we know that a period of about three centuries sufficed for all that was done during the high prosperity of Assyria. The soft nature of the stone, which is a kind of grey alabaster, extremely suited to carving in the manner employed, afforded the facility that influenced the style and enabled the carvers to indulge their inclination for realistic detail. They do not appear to have sought for fine coloured hard stones as the Egyptians did, nor do they show the same desire to make their work monumental and enduring. There is only one example of hard stone being used, and that is in the kind of obelisk of black marble in the British Museum, known as the obelisk of Divanubara, which bears sculptures and arrow-headed inscriptions referring to Assyrian kings named in the Bible, and the date of which has been fixed as 885 B.C.

Assyrian sculpture was always archaic, though at the same time more vigorous in what might be called graphic sculpture, and truer in imitation of nature than Egyptian, which rarely attempted action in the figure or facial expression. There is, however, no alliance between the two styles, and there was never likely to be, as the Assyrians were not a people of poetic

* According to Dr. S. Birch, "The monuments from Kouyunjik may, with due allowance for the uncertainty of Assyrian chronology, be placed between 721 B.C. and 625 B.C. (British Museum 'Guide-book').

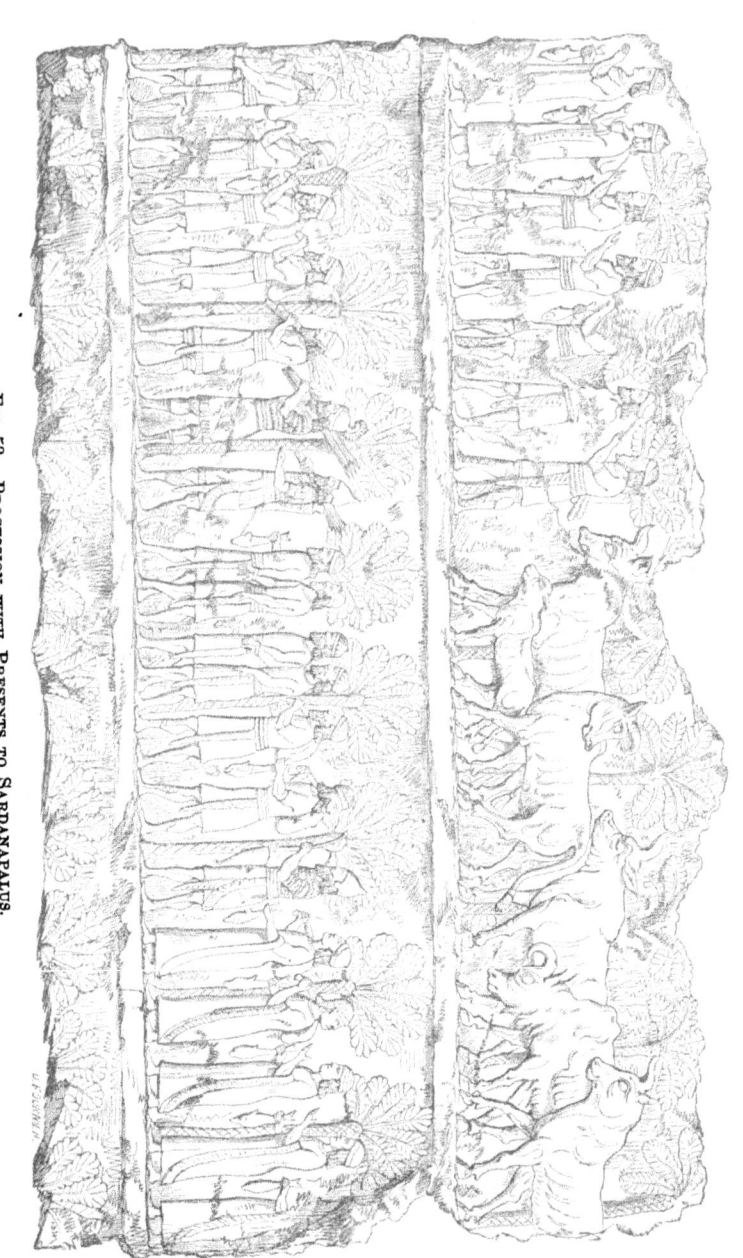

FIG. 53.—PROCESSION WITH PRESENTS TO SARDANAPALUS.

In the Louvre.

and abstract ideas, but of facts, circumstances, and action. They thought of the present glory, and did not trouble themselves about the future. The same characteristics will partly account for the absence of any kind of reference to a future state. The tree of life with the priest ministering before it and holding fruit is to be seen ; but it is remarkable that no sepulchral monuments

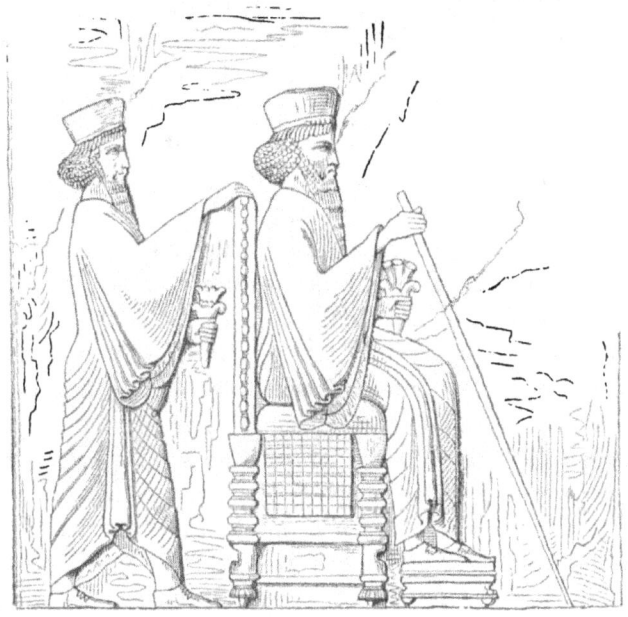

FIG. 54 — KING AND ATTENDANT.
BAS-RELIEF, SHOWING THE PROFILE STYLE, AND THE CONVENTIONAL FOLDS
OF DRAPERY PECULIAR ALSO TO ARCHAIC GREEK SCULPTURE.
From Persepolis.

have been found ; no tomb or mark of regard in any shape for the welfare of the dead hereafter has been discovered.*

It is remarkable that neither in Assyrian nor Persepolitan sculpture is the female figure to be found.† Thus we can readily see

* The tomb of Darius, at Naksh i Rustam, given in Fergusson's 'Architecture,' is an exception, but it only proves that the people were not a tomb-regarding people; it contains no monumental effigies, and is simply of an architectural character.

† And in this respect there is a similarity to the Egyptian, in which women are rarely represented, and then only as subordinates, never as a Goddess till the later times.

how it happened that the Assyrians never had any high ideal, such as distinguishes the art of the Egyptians and Greeks. Like the Hindoo, they saw that nature was infinite in power and mystery, but they never perceived her beauty. Bearing in mind that the Assyrians were never a statue-making people, and never attempted to follow the example of the Egyptians—do we find them influencing the sculptural art of any other people in work like that of the Assyrians? This question is answered at once by the remains found at Persepolis, where there are to be seen similar winged and human-headed lions and bulls, and sculptured slabs, but no statues either in the round or in alto-relievo.

The ruins of the palaces of Cambyses, Darius, and Xerxes, the date of which is from 560 B.C. to the conquests of Alexander the Great (331 B.C.), show only sculptural remains left after all the soft brick walls and the wooden beams and rafters have long perished. Persian sculptural art since those days never advanced to the dignity of statuary, but like its Assyrian predecessor stopped short where Greek art began to develope. The same is to be observed of that ramification of the Assyrian arts which is to be traced in the building of the temple of Jerusalem under Solomon, which, however, was some five centuries before the time of Cambyses, and about the same length of time after the settling of the Israelites in the Delta of the Nile (1550 B.C.). The law of Moses was sufficient to prevent any sculpture in the likeness of living things; but the cherubim, with their wings, seem to have been borrowed from the Assyrians. The temple was, no doubt, built of stone and cedar-wood after the manner of the Assyrians, and with a profusion of ornament in carving of valuable marbles, wood, and embossed work in precious metals.

The colossal sculptures in the rock-cut temples of India, whether taken as derived from the Assyrian centre or not, may be classed with that style as semi-barbaric and naturalistic, with a superadded symbolism which only led to the most extravagant deformities of the human figure * to express the power and attributes of a deity. Statuary proper never existed in any

---

* See the statues in the Elephanta cave (Fig. 54a).

shape of beauty like the human form, throughout Persia, India, and China, and there is no sign of any disposition amongst the Asiatics to learn the art from their European conquerors ; it is not in their nature.

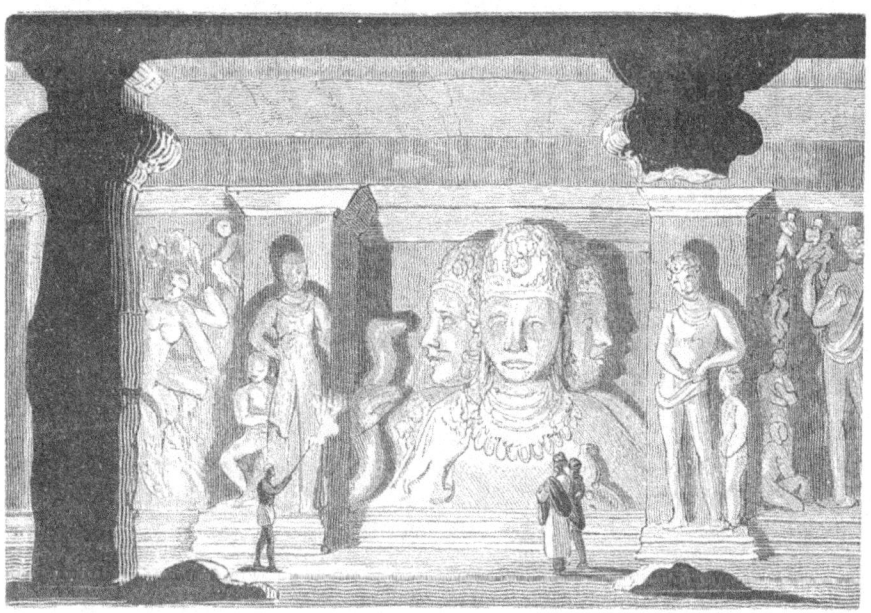

Fig. 547.—Colossal rock-cut sculptures in the Caves of Elephanta.
On a small Island in the Bay of Bombay.

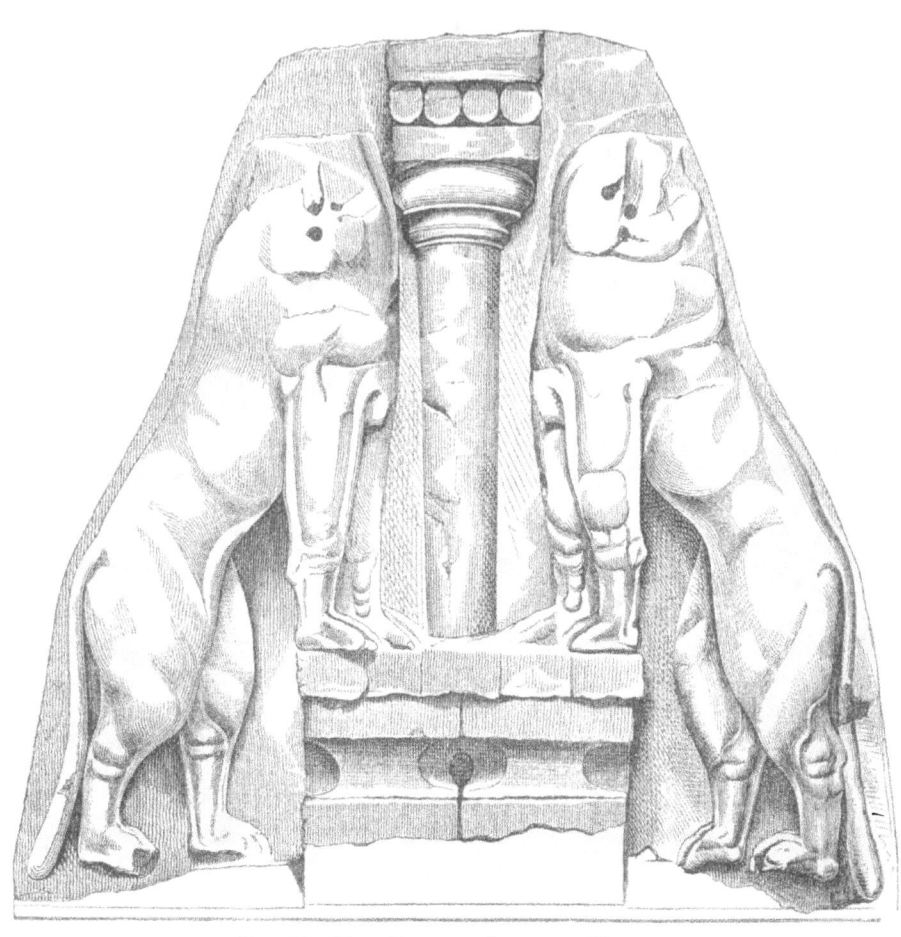

FIG. 55.—THE GATE OF LIONS AT MYCENÆ.
10 feet high and 15 feet wide; of greenish limestone.

GREEK SCULPTURE.

BUT while no advance in the art of sculpture is to be observed
in the direction of Eastern civilization—and while Egyptian
sculpture was losing its individuality of style—a new world of
art had been gradually growing amongst those people who had
been for centuries pushing their way in conquest and commerce
Northward and to the West, in every direction along the shores
and amid the islands of the Mediterranean (*see* Map, pp. 88, 89).
The history of this period is necessarily obscure, and for the
most part legendary, but it is very generally agreed that the

earliest migrations under leaders whose names are handed down in the early history of Greece are traceable to Egypt.

Thus Inachus came with his followers at the expulsion of the Shepherd Kings in the seventeenth and eighteenth dynasties—about 1830 B.C. He was the leader of a Libyan colony, the first king and most ancient hero of Argos.—Kekrops, a Pelasgic hero, whose name sounds Egyptian, was king of Attica, and while he reigned, it is said, occurred the contest between Poseidon and Athene, long afterwards represented in the sculptures of the pediment of the Parthenon. Attica was called Kekropia after him. His period is supposed to have been about 1556 B.C. Danaus, whose name was applied by the poets to all the Greeks, is said to have been the brother of Sesostris, and his migration is placed at the accession of the nineteenth dynasty, 1436 B.C.— Kadmus, who is generally considered to be of Phœnician origin, is said to have come from ancient Thebes, and the tradition of his inventing letters would connect him with Phœnicia * and Egypt about 1312 B.C. But it is also maintained that he was a Pelasgic deity. It is remarkable, however, that the Greek city of Thebes, the founding of which is traditionally attributed to him, should bear the name of the Egyptian city.—Pelops, whose name was given to the southern peninsula of Greece, Peloponnesus, is said to have been a native king, though the name resembles those of Egyptian kings. It is of interest to remember that under him, as king of Elis and Olympia, about 1261 B.C., were established the great national games which made Olympia one of the chief centres of Greek art. Statues of the victors in the Olympic games were set up year after year at that place.

* Mr. Gladstone points out what he aptly terms " the three great appellatives in the Homeric Poems—1. Danaoi, 2. Argeioi, 3. Achaioi— as used interchangeably and synonymously " ('Juventus Mundi,' p. 33). All this subject of Phœnician influence is set out with the utmost research and searching reflection. He notices the four national and tribal names applied in the Homeric poems—1. Pelasgoi, 2. Hellenes, 3. Phoinikes (Phœnicians), 4. Aiolidai. With Phœnician he blends Egyptian, remarking that the name Aiguptios is the only positive trace of it in Greece. The Greeks of the Homeric age were completely dependent on the Phœnicians for their ordinary intercourse with the outer world, . . . and with respect to fine arts the evidence is ample in favour of a Phœnician source (see 'Juventus Mundi,' p. 133).

A.S.

These references may suffice to show briefly that the origin of
the arts of Greece has been generally ascribed by her own early
records and traditions to Egyptian and Egypto-Phœnician influences. The evidence derived from the style of art followed
at this early period tends to confirm tradition. The earliest
coins of Greek work with the head of Athene show a striking
resemblance to the heads of Isis.*

There are many examples of vases, painted with figures representing in the most primitive forms the oldest mythological
heroes and deities, which closely resemble the Egyptian *cavi
relievi* and paintings ; they are always in profile with the eye
full, and the feet often turned both in the same direction, or

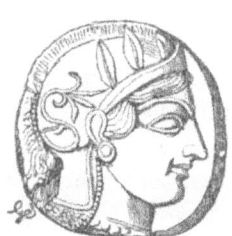

FIG. 56.—EARLY COIN OF ATHENS,
HEAD OF ATHENE ; THE EYE FULL,
AS IN EGYPTIAN RELIEFS.

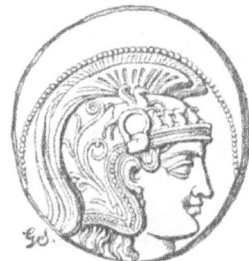

FIG. 57.—COIN OF ATHENS AFTER
THE TIME OF PHEIDIAS. WITH
THE HELMET INTRODUCED
BY PHEIDIAS.

when the figure is full-face as in some bas-reliefs (Fig. 68,
Selinus), the feet are in the impossible position of profile, and
both on the same plane. In painting, the absence of all attempt
to represent shadowing, either in the forms or in the cast shadow,
and the use of a strong black outline, sometimes incised and
having the colour filled in as a flat tint, are other points of
affinity between the early Greek work and the Egyptian.

Etruscan bears a strong resemblance, in many respects, to
archaic Greek art. But strictly the term Etruscan should be
applied to that only which belongs to Etruria, not in Greece
but a wide tract extending from the western shores of Italy
towards the Apennines. The origin of Etruscan art is also
traced from Egypt; through the followers of Tarchon who came

* Overbeck, 'Geschichte der Greichischen Plastik.'

from Lydia, and who was of the Pelasgic race.   There is much
obscurity as to the Hellenes, Pelasgi, and Etrusci, but there is
little as to the art-work to which the general term Etruscan is
applied.   It is all similar in its primitive and naturalistic
character.   What is of importance to bear in mind is, that not
only the shores of Sicily and the south of Italy were so occupied

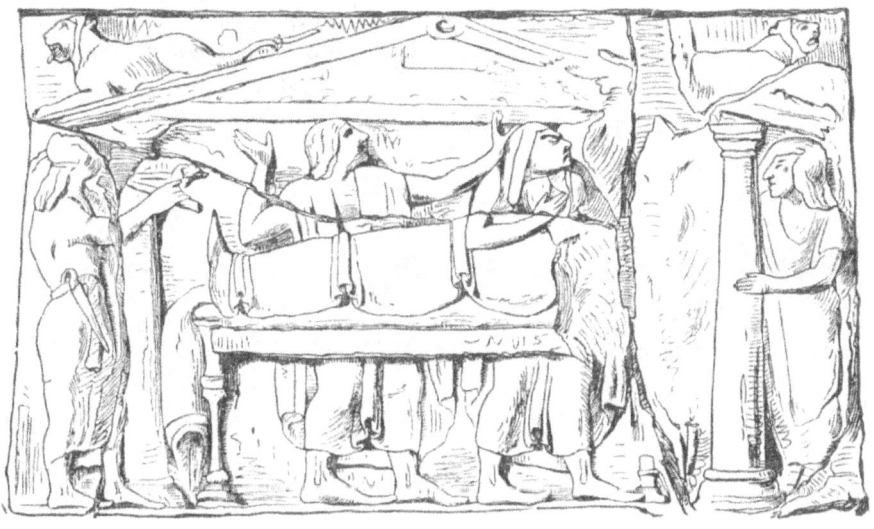

FIG. 58.—ETRUSCAN BAS-RELIEF. A TOMB WITH FUNERAL CEREMONIES.

by immigrants from Greece, that the region got the name of
' Magna Græcia,' but that " Italy was the common asylum for all
the fugitives of the ancient world ; and if we are to accept the
arguments of Micali (' Storia degli ántichi popoli Italiani'), it
would be to Egypt that Etruria, whose art is so widely seen in
Italy, owed her religion, her arts, and her sacerdotal government "
(Duruy, ' Hist. des Romains,' 1879).   Further, that early Roman
art has its style and history bound up with the advance of the
Etruscans towards the great centre of national power which
Rome became under the Tarquins.   All the temples, monuments,
and statues of Rome were Etruscan, and not only different in
style from contemporary works in the cities of Greece, but
entirely distinct by being of bronze, terra-cotta, and stone covered
with stucco-work instead of marble.   The same art prevailed

naturally in all the neighbouring cities round Rome, as the remains abundantly testify, in every direction, and further into the region which as 'Tuscany' almost retains its ancient name.

The museums of Italy contain many examples of Etruscan art, one of the most interesting being the she-wolf suckling the infants Romulus and Remus (Fig. 58a), preserved in the Capitol at Rome. The two children are considered to have been added in later times. Several examples of early Etruscan art are in the archaic room of the British Museum; among the most remarkable are No. 50, a large sepulchral cist in terra-cotta,

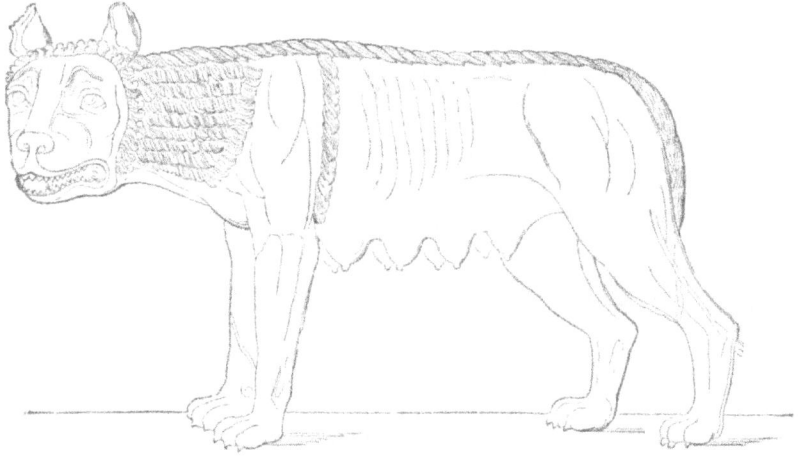

FIG. 58a.—THE SHE-WOLF OF THE CAPITOL, ROME.
Ancient Etruscan. Bronze. Life size.

with two figures modelled in the round, having the hair and eyes painted, found at Cervetri; and No. 51, a small figure from a tomb near Vulci.

But it is important to bear in mind, in a historical consideration of the question, that it was in Ionia that the arts were promoted long before Athens had begun to show any advance; and all the names, handed down by the traditions taken up by Diodorus Siculus, Pausanias, Pliny, and the late Greek writers, are those of sculptors working in the islands near the Asiatic shore and in the towns upon the mainland. Thus in the objects found by Cesnola in Cyprus, consisting of statues and other sculptures, incised gems, and metal-work of the hammered-out or *repoussée* kind, the resemblance to the art of Assyria is remarkable. Mr. Newton has pointed out that certain *repousée* circular metal plates are found equally at Nimroud, Cyprus, Palestrina, Cervetri, and Perugia, all having a decided family likeness.

But besides the workmanship there is more decisive evidence in the choice and treatment of the subjects; these tend to confirm the same view.

The bas-reliefs upon the Harpy tomb* (Fig. 59), as it is called, which was discovered in 1838 by Sir C. Fellows, were at first supposed by Gibson, the great sculptor and student of classic

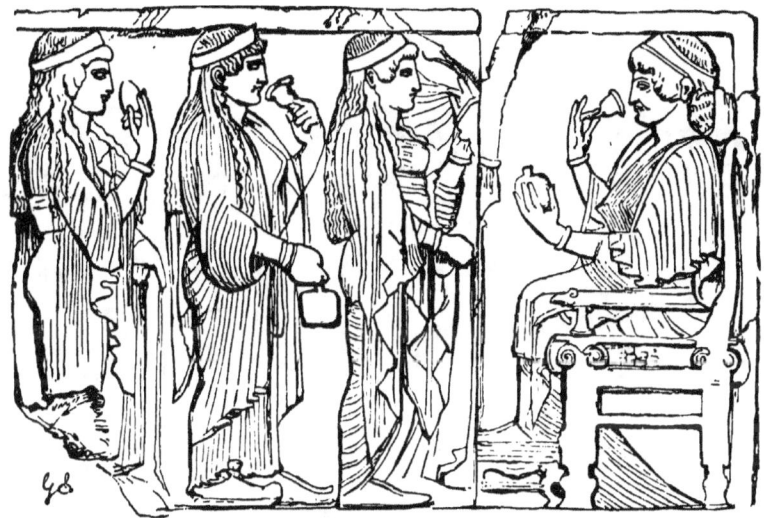

FIG. 59.—BAS-RELIEF ON THE HARPY TOMB. THE FIGURES IN PROFILE, AND WITH THE PRIMITIVE DRAPERIES.

In the British Museum.

sculpture, to have for their subject the Harpies flying away with the daughters of king Pandarus, as related by Homer (' Odys.' lib. xx.). Pandarus was king of Lycia. But archæologists are not agreed upon the point : more recent opinions conjecture that

* They were found at Xanthus, on the river of that name, in ancient Lycia, a town some two days' journey inland from Smyrna, and so are often spoken of as the Xanthian sculptures. The Harpy tomb is in the archaic room ; the other sculptures, some of which are of later date, are in the New Lycian Room.

the subject is simply funereal, and the Harpies emblematic of untimely death are bearing off the souls of mortals. The Harpy figures are more especially Assyrian in the character of the work. The date of these Lycian sculptures is not later than 500 B.C. In the other reliefs which are now on the walls of the New Lycian room, in the British Museum, there are sieges, chariots, processions, and many figures in the energetic action so remarkable in the Nineveh sculptures. The two lions sculptured in the round resemble the Assyrian lions in style. The subject was supposed by Fellows to be the siege of Xanthus under Harpagus, of whom is related the strange story of his being

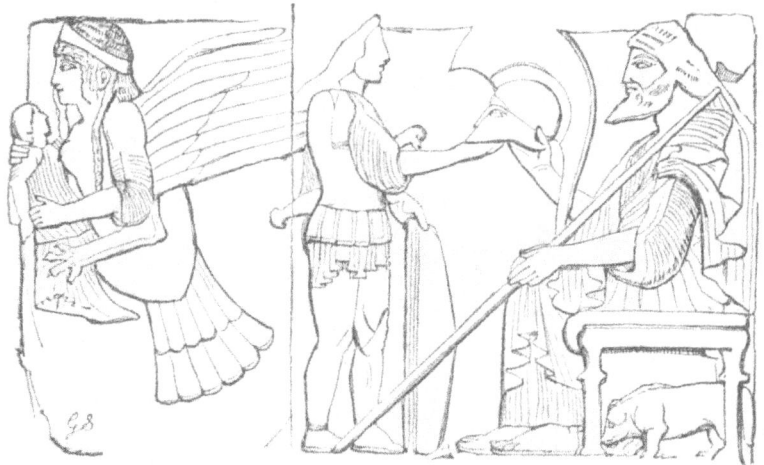

FIG. 60.—BAS-RELIEFS ON THE HARPY TOMB.

In the British Museum.

tricked by Astyages king of Persia into eating his own son, served up as food to the father, as a punishment for Harpagus having preserved the young Cyrus, foretold as the supplanter of his father the king, and consequently ordered to be slain. It was in revenge that Harpagus aided Cyrus, and afterwards as his general conquered Lycia. The Xanthians refused to·yield, and after sacrificing their wives and children, died to a man fighting to the last. All this is told in the same graphic manner as on the Nineveh slabs, and it is most interesting to compare these two series of sculptures in the British

Museum.*   It will be observed that most of the figures are in profile, and that the eyes are nevertheless shown in full ; the same peculiar smile prevails in all, which is a distinguishing feature in Etruscan works and in the Æginetan and other sculptures we shall have to notice.   This is also seen in the coins of the time, and is a feature which has, of course, some similarity to the Egyptian, but more to the Assyrian style.   The long, straight folds and zigzag edges of the draperies are also archaic forms which belong to these Lycian sculptures, as well as the sculptures found at Selinus in Sicily ; and to a draped figure found on the Acropolis at Athens in the ruins of temples and

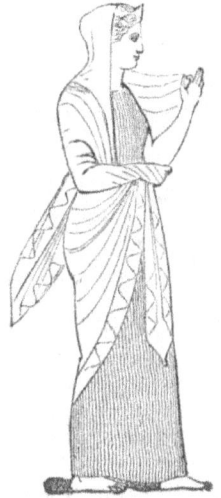

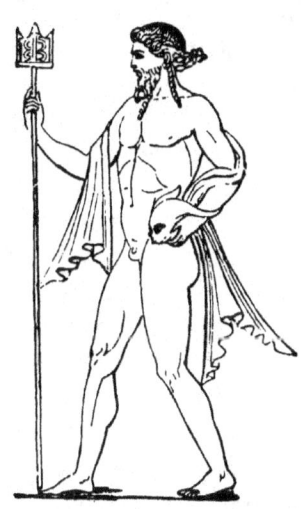

FIG. 61.—JUNO.   FIG. 62.—NEPTUNE, FROM THE RELIEF ON
                        THE PUTEAL IN THE CAPITOL, ROME.

Pseudo-Archaic Drapery.

buildings which were erected there before the Parthenon.† These were destroyed by the Persians in the early battles of the Athenians against their old enemy.   Their date is considered to be about 560—490 B.C., when Pisistratus was ruler at Athens,

* Recent authorities suppose the Ionic monument in the new Lycian room to have been erected in the first half of the fourth century B.C., in honour of the Satrap Perikles, who captured the town of Telmessus.

† Such as the ancient temple of Athene, called the Hekatompedon (100 feet in length by 100 feet in width).

Crœsus at Sardis, Tarquin at Rome, Amasis in Egypt, and Cyrus in Persia.

The archaic Artemis of the Naples Museum in bronze (Fig. 63) shows the zigzag form of drapery, which is also seen on a similar figure in the Dresden collection. The false archaic drapery of the Macedonian period is shown in Figs. 61, 62.

It has been said these archaic statues are Egyptian in style, yet it is difficult to see this character in them beyond the general rigidity and the calm smiling look of the features. But in this respect they are equally like the Assyrian, and for the simple reason that to give any expression to the countenance requires a higher exercise of art, and this these sculptors were not sufficiently skilled to do. The Egyptians could perhaps have done it, but it was not in keeping with their intention and the genius of their art. The Assyrians were very rough expressionists, rather vulgar and puerile in their imitative sculpture, but, as we have observed, inventive, and with more feeling for design than the Egyptians in their ornament.* Seeking for other signs of Egyptian teaching in early Greek sculpture, it is remarkable that not a single example can be pointed out of *cavo-relievo*, such as the Egyptians adopted so universally. Though effective, durable beyond all other forms, and capable of carrying colour, yet it never was employed by Greek carvers or architects early or late; nor, as has been pointed out, was the *cavo-relievo* ever employed in the Assyrian reliefs.

Turning next to the statues—the seated and standing figures carved universally with some supporting part of the work at the back and not in the round—the examples of similar statues in Greece are extremely rare. There are as yet only the headless seated Athene in the Museum at Athens,† and ten draped seated

---

* So also in their metal work, of which many fine specimens of ornament are to be seen in the British Museum, Layard Collection. Here we are met with the similarity to some forms of Greek ornament. The ornament known as the Greek honeysuckle, found so profusely employed upon the fictile vases, which are called Etruscan, is much more beautiful than the similar ornament seen in Assyrian work. Whether it is derived from Asiatic art or is native to Etruria is a question of great interest. The resemblance between the two is too remarkable to be lost sight of.

† See Overbeck, ‘ Geschichte,’ &c., figure No. 24.

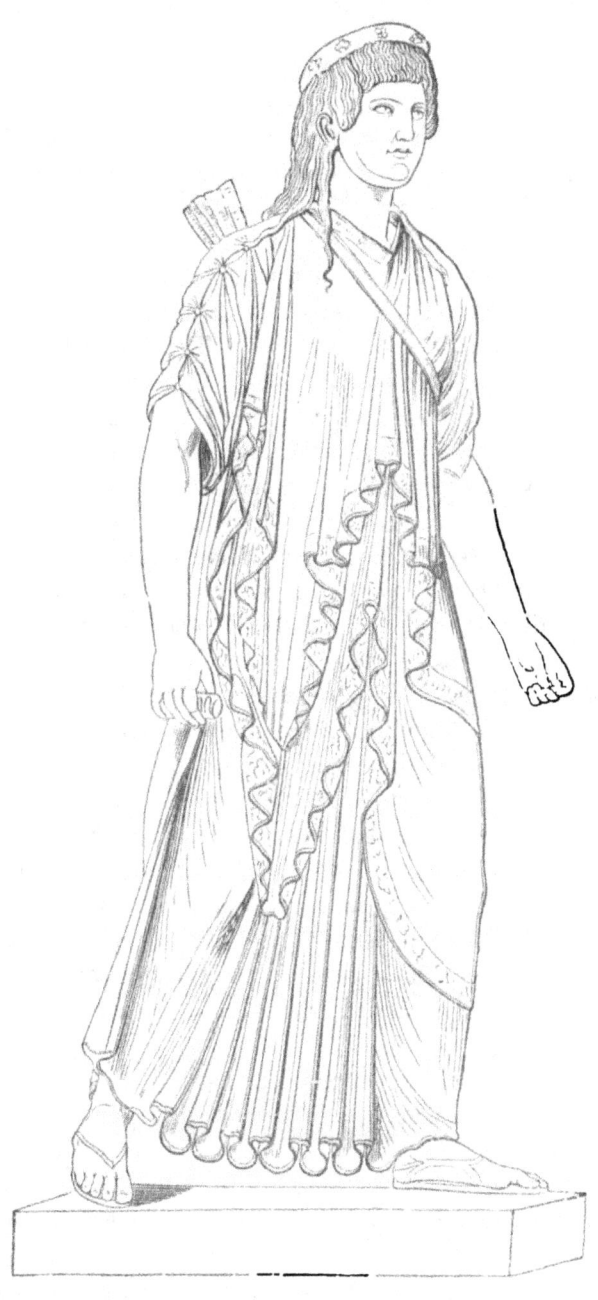

FIG. 63.—ARTEMIS, FOUND AT POMPEII. BRONZE.

Showing the archaic style of drapery folds.

In the Naples Museum.

statues found in 1858, by Mr. Newton, at Miletus on the Asiatic shore of the Ægean, all headless but one ; * of which it will be remarked that they are equally like the Assyrian seated figure found by Layard at Kalah Shergat.† They formed a sort of avenue leading from the harbour to the Temple of Apollo. The date assigned to the Miletus or Branchidæ statues and the two lions is 580—520 B.C. An inscription on the chair of one— " I am Chares," &c.—decides the date, and marks this as the oldest portrait statue in Greek art. These seated statues are of the heroic size, not colossal.

It may be observed that amongst the small objects found in Greece there are not any of those miniature figures of Deities precisely like the large Egyptian statues, which abound in Egypt. To these some importance must have been attached, since they are found in every mummy-case, often rolled up with the cere-cloths, and probably intended as amulets or guardians of the dead.

From all that we learn of the Egyptians, through such exhaustive researches as those of Sir G. Wilkinson, it would seem that the sculptors and the carvers of hieroglyphics were a distinct class or caste, descending from father to son, and always under the close control of the priestly rule. It is not likely that they would ever become colonists and travel away from their city. Those who did wander off with Kekrops and Kadmus were not any of them sculptors, or we should have found some trace of their work. The Egyptians were a religious, not a commercial, people, and not colonisers. They devoted themselves to a life of ease and luxurious repose; they were dreamers over the abstract, and only entered into wars to defend themselves and their territory.

The Phœnicians are sometimes spoken of as teachers; but they never developed any art in the direction either of beauty of form or energy of expression. As the earliest and most expert metal-workers, they taught their neighbours, and carried the materials both along the coast and to the islands of the Ægean. In Cyprus abundant examples have been found in the discoveries of General Cesnola of Phœnician and Græco-Phœnician work.

* British Museum, Archaic Room, No. 2—13.   † British Museum.

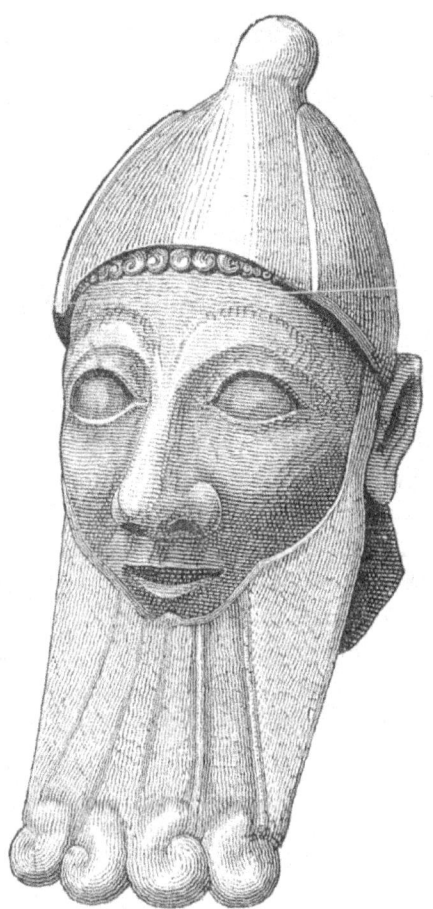

Fig. 64.—Colossal, 34 inches high.

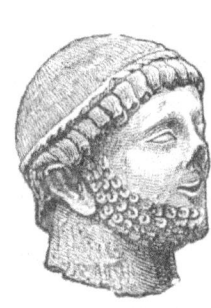

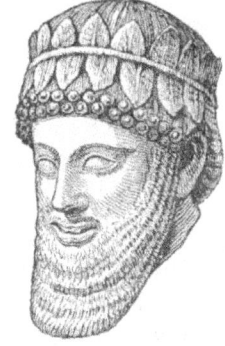

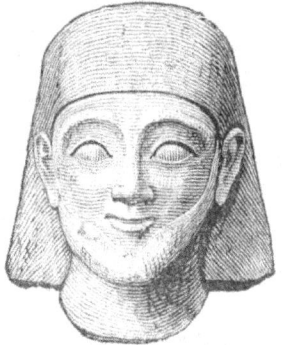

Fig. 65.—Stone, 9½ in.   Fig. 66.—Stone, 12 in.   Fig. 67.—Stone, 14 in.
HIGH.   HIGH.   HIGH.

Heads found by Cesnola in the Temple of Golgoi, Cyprus.

Let us endeavour to trace in other monuments that remain, the influence of Egyptian and Assyrian art, as shown in the work of the Pelasgi and Etrusci. Those which are simply barbaric, as we have already pointed out, have no value for sculptural art in helping us to identify any foreign influence, since they belong to no individual style. Neither is much to be learnt from sepulchral structures such as the tumuli common to the plains of Troy and the far west of Europe, as well as the far east of India; nor from the underground structures known as 'treasuries.' Sculptural art did not take its great spring in advance from any of these, as no statues of any value in art have ever been found in them.

At Mykenæ, once perhaps in the days of Homer (850—800? B.C.) the most important city of Greece, there are sculptural works in the remains of two lions over the entrance-gate (Fig. 55), which are examples of Pelasgic art. The height of these is about 10 ft., and the width 15 ft.* The stone is a greenish limestone. The holes show where the metal pins held the heads, long since decayed. Fragments as they are, they show an Assyrian rather than an Egyptian influence in the strong marking of the muscles and joints, softened though it is by decay, and in the erect attitude, which denotes action, such as is not seen in Egyptian art of this kind. Whether it is a column they support or an altar is doubtful; but the four round projections above the capital resemble the wood structure of the Lycian tombs. The peculiar tail of the lions, with the knob at the tip, is exactly such as we see in the Assyrian lions. These lions should be compared also with the wounded lion in the British Museum, Nineveh collection (Fig. 52). Of this 'gate of the lions,' which has long been known as a most ancient work of early Greek sculpture, it must be noticed that it is not in the round but only in high relief. And this is the case with all the earliest works, just as it is with the Assyrian sculptures. They tend to show therefore that the Greek sculptor had not

* In the Dilettanti Society's work they are given as height 9 feet 8½ in. by 11 feet 6 in. in width. Mr. Simpson, the well-known artist-traveller, tells me he examined these lions closely and drew them, and that they seemed to him to have had heads of metal, perhaps gold, and gold plates over the whole bodies.

yet learnt to model and carve in the round in marble and stone.

There are early records of statuary being made in marble. Pliny says the first of all distinguished for marble carving were Dipoenus and Skyllis, who worked together at Sikyon.

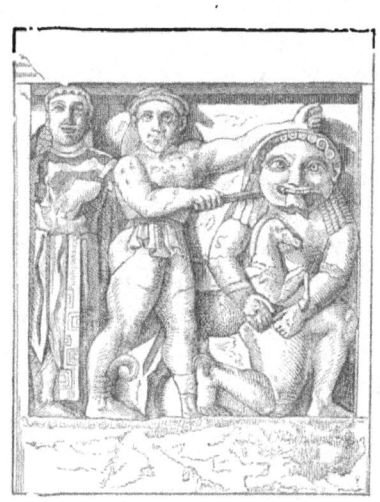

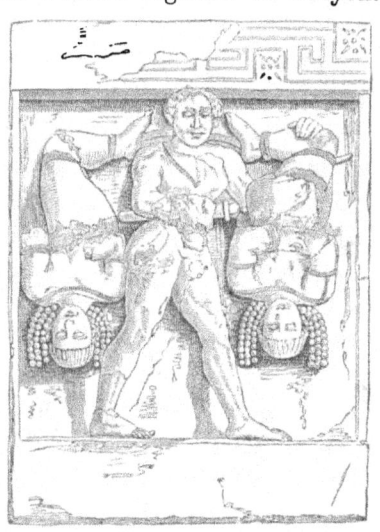

FIG. 68. –PERSEUS KILLING MEDUSA.
SELINUS METOPE.
In the Museum at Palermo.
Cast in the British Museum.

FIG. 69.—HERCULES CARRYING OFF
THE CECROPES (*Robbers*).
SELINUS METOPE.
Cast in the British Museum.

They were born in the island of Crete during the existence of the empire of the Medes, before Cyrus began his reign in Persia, about the fiftieth Olympiad (Plin. lib. xxxvi. c. 5). As the Olympiad reckoning began from the victory of Koroibos in the foot-race at the games in the year 776 B.C., this would be about 580 B.C. Pausanias says (lib. ii. p. iii. 9), they were pupils or followers of Daedalus. They are named also by Clemens of Alexandria as the sculptors of statues of Castor and Pollux at Argos, of Hercules at Tiryns, and Diana at Sikyon. It is also related by Cedrenus, that in the time of the Emperor Theodosius at Byzantium, was to be seen a statue of Minerva Lindia * of 'smaragdus' stone (verde antique?) four cubits

* Lindus was a town in the island of Rhodes. Angelion and Tectaeus are two sculptors named by Pausanias as learning from Dipoenus and Skyllis, and the makers of the wood statue of the Delian Apollo.

high, the works of Skyllis and Dipoenus, which had formerly been sent by Sesostris, the Egyptian tyrannus, to Kleobulus of Lindus. These references are so far interesting and important as showing with fair probability that these statues were sculptures in the round. There is no doubt the Phœnicians at Tyre and Sidon produced much work in bronze and other metals of an ornamental character, like the shield of Achilles described by Homer, before this time ; but no statues are known, and neither Homer nor Hesiod ever mentions such works. Many names of sculptors in these early times are mentioned by Pausanias and Pliny, but it is impossible to discover precisely what their works were, and as most of them are said to be disciples of Daedalus, it may be concluded that their works were of the very primitive character previously described. Those who are curious upon this point will find full references in the great work of Junius. Numerous examples of archaic sculpture in bronze and marble, some of hammered-out work, are to be seen in all the museums, a large proportion of which are bas-reliefs representing the figure in profile. Good examples are Figs. 70, 71, which show a general resemblance to the Assyrian sculptures rather than Egyptian, as well as those found at Selinus (Fig. 68). But the examples in the archaic room, at the British Museum, must be studied in order to come to any clear understanding of the characteristics. Particularly should be studied, the casts of the Selinus reliefs (Nos. 16—19), and No. 27, a relief found at the Acropolis, Athens. No. 28, the Leucothea relief in the Villa Albani, Rome, should be compared with the Harpy tomb reliefs. Nos. 30 and 31, small nude statues of Apollo, without the legs ; very stiff, and showing the muscles of the abdomen and chest divided into square regular masses, the edges of the rib cartilages being marked with straight lines at an acute angle to the median line, and the hips narrow in proportion to the trunk. The sharp features with the turned-up nose and smiling mouth, and the short, crisp, formal curls at the forehead, are also characteristic of archaic Greek work, and are seen again in the small full-length Apollo represented in Fig. 72, where we also notice the stiff attitude with one leg slightly advanced. Similar statues are the bronze Apollo in the Louvre, which has

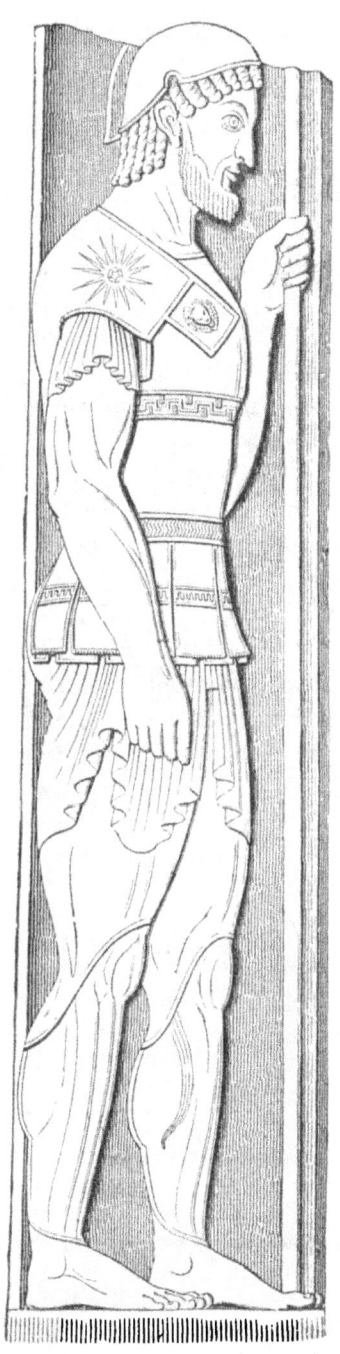

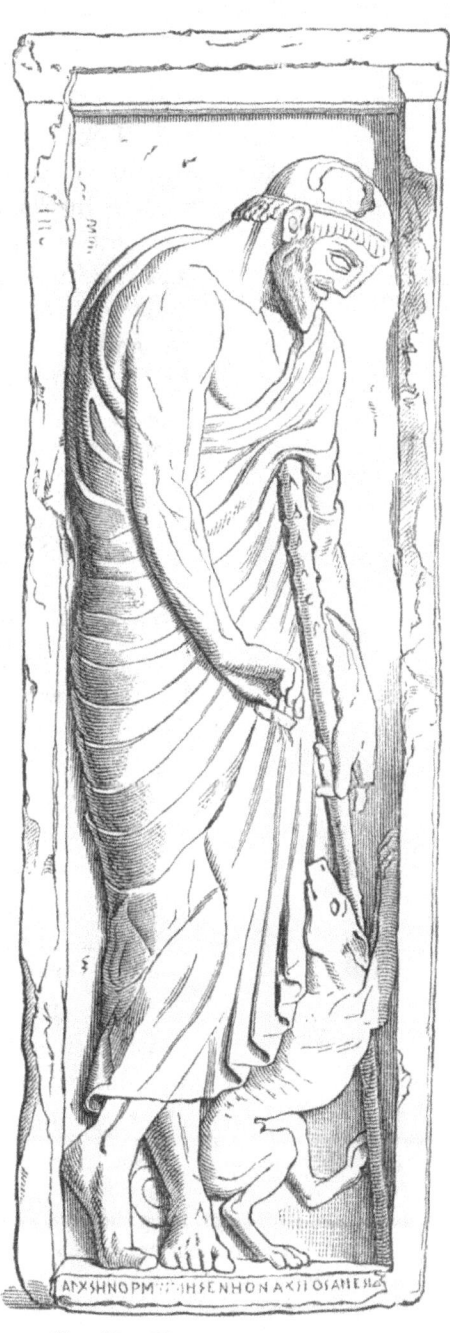

FIG. 70.—WARRIOR OF MARATHON.
Inscribed εργον Αριστοκλες.
Found in Attica.
In Athens Museum.

FIG. 71.—ULYSSES (?) MARBLE.
Inscribed in Oscan Characters.
In Naples Museum.

the left foot advanced, and on it incised the words AΘANA : A ΔEKATAN ; also the small marble figure called the Strangford Apollo in the British Museum, which has lost the arms and legs.

Among the remains found by General Cesnola in Cyprus, are numerous representations in bas-reliefs and in incised gems * of

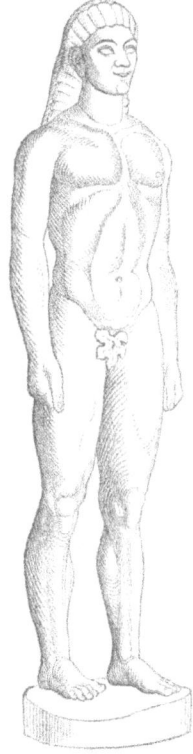

the most ancient Greek heroes, such as Perseus and Hercules, and of the deities, Athene, Hera, and Aphrodite. This representation of the ancient Greek myths which is universally found in Etruria also, in paintings on the oldest terra-cotta vases, in bas-reliefs and bronze figures, is remarkable ; and it must not be overlooked that this is peculiar to those parts through which the people we call Pelasgi, Etrusci, and Hellenes traversed and settled. Nothing of the kind has been found in the Assyrian sculptures. Whatever may have been the primitive art of the people of Etruria before the arrival of Demaratus with his colonisers from Corinth, in 664 B.C., it took from that time the Greek style of the archaic form then practised, and adopted the Greek subjects. How far the mythology is derivable from the Egyptian theogony is another question, too wide to be entered into here.

The instances are rare of any of the statues in bronze by the early masters of Greek art before Pheidias and his school, having been satisfactorily identified with the marble reproductions which have from time to time been discovered. Pausanias actually saw and described many of

FIG. 72.—APOLLO OF TENEA.

Munich Museum.

* Many were found in the Treasury of Kourium in Cyprus, of which Mr. King says, they are " a true revelation of the history of the Glyptic art in its rise and progress from the earliest times down to the beginning of the fifth century before our era." The subject of one of the finest of these archaic Greek intaglii is Boreas carrying off Orithya, daughter of Erectheus, from the banks of the Ilissus, a very ancient myth, which is also represented on the famous coffer of Kypselus, a work two centuries older at least. ('Cyprus,' by Gen. Cesnola, p. 378, Appendix.)

them on the very spot where they were originally placed, and he wrote towards the end of the second century A.D. He speaks of two statues of Harmodios and Aristogeiton the tyrannicides * in 510 B.C., made in their honour by Antenor (lib. i. 8, 5). They were, he says, near the Temple of

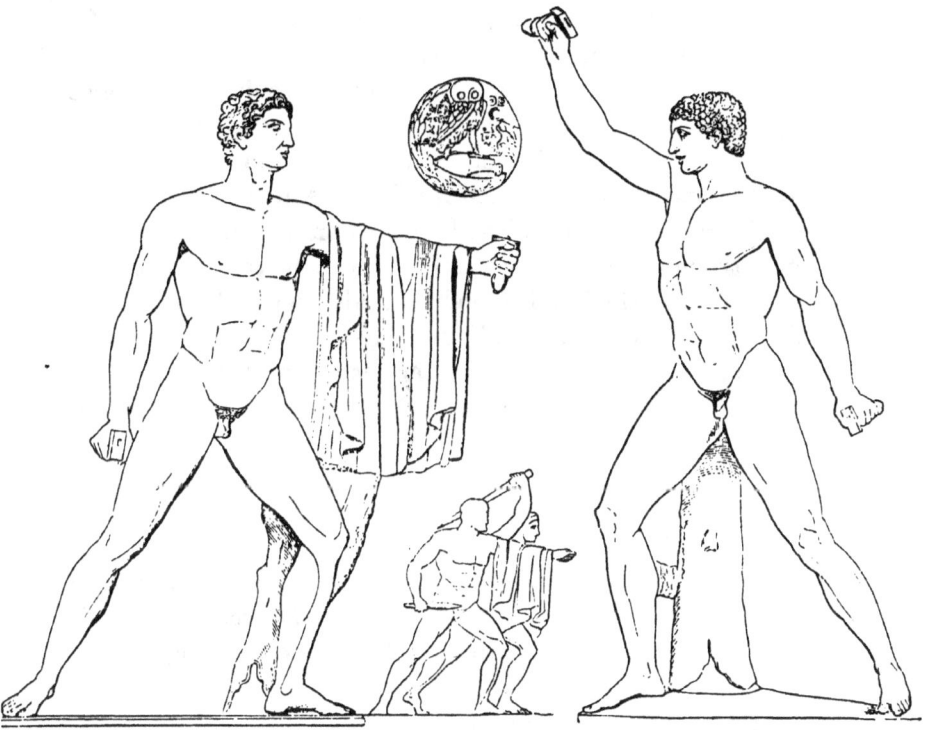

FIG. 72a.—STATUES OF HARMODIOS AND ARISTOGEITON, BY KRITIOS AND NESIOTES. *Marble.* *Naples Museum. The small outline shows the conjectured form of the group by Antenor, as seen in a relief on a marble chair in Athens Museum, and upon a prize vase, as well as a coin of Athens. The coin shown above is the tetradrachm referred to which bears the group, and the names Mentor and Moschion, magistrates probably of the time.*

Mars (Athens) with other statues named, the older ones being by Antenor and the later by Kritias, and that they were

* The story of these two friends who assassinated the tyrant Hipparchos will be found in the Biographical Dictionaries and in Grote's History.

carried off by Xerxes, but afterwards restored to the Athenians by Antiochos.* Lucian also speaks of these statues—ἐν οἱς καὶ τὰ Κριτιου του Νησιώτου πλασματα ἔσηκεν, ὁι τυραννοκτόνοι. After some fifty years of research it is now considered that the marble reproductions of these statues are the statues in the Naples Museum (Fig. 72a), and this is supported by a bas-relief of them as a group upon a marble chair in the Museum of Athens (shown in Fig. 72a), and still further by a coin (also in Fig. 72a) found at Athens bearing a rude representation of the group, and the names of the magistrates Mentor and Moschion. The same group is seen on a painted vase. It is known that when Xerxes took away the statues by Antenor, copies of them were made by Kritios and Nesiotes† to replace them. All, however, are lost. The Naples statues are singularly fine in the action of the figures, though the arms are restorations, and the head of the younger figure, which is Harmodios, is also new. But the head of the Aristogeiton is true antique, and shows the severe style of the archaic though modified by the feeling of the later artist. If these statues were placed together as a group they would closely resemble the relief on the marble chair.

The important point to bear in mind is the general archaic condition of sculpture prevailing at a time extending from the first Olympiad 776 B.C. to the middle of the sixth century B.C.; examples of which, all more or less resembling each other, have been found at Mycenae, Xanthus, Miletus, Ephesus, the islands of Cyprus and Rhodes on the Asiatic side of the Ægean; at

---

* Arrianus, the accurate historian of Alexander's Anabasis, says it was he, Alexander, who returned those statues. He wrote about the middle of the second century A.D., and his great work is still extant.

† There was long a question as to the name of Nesiotes, as Pliny has it Nestocles, and Pausanias does not mention him. But Lucian's reference is more precise, and leads to the conclusion that there were two sculptors— Kritios (Kritias) and Nesiotes, the latter a pupil perhaps of the first-named, who was distinguished as a master. Pausanias speaks of a statue of a runner Epicharinos (lib. i. 23, 11) ; and the base of this statue has been found at Athens bearing the names of Kritios and Nesiotes, besides two others having their names inscribed. The interesting questions as to these statues are ably examined by Mr. A. S. Murray in his ' History of Greek Sculpture,' 1880.

Selinus in Sicily, and throughout Magna Graecia; in Italy at Palestrina, Perugia, Cervetri, as well as in all Etruria far up on the west coast of Italy; in Greece proper, in the Peloponnesus at Sparta, Sikyon and Argos, Athens, and Ægina—then an independent island and always possessing a very vigorous school of sculpture, in bronze especially, though destined to yield the palm when Athens rose to her high state.

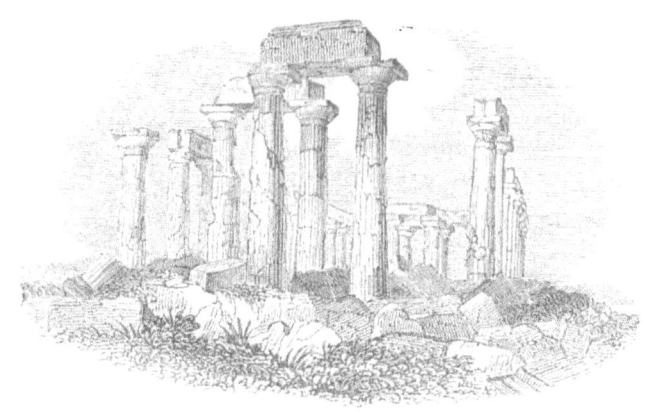

FIG. 73.—TEMPLE OF ATHENE AT ÆGINA.

THE ÆGINETAN STYLE.

In Ægina a temple of Athene was begun about B.C. 480—478;* therefore, about 26 years before the Parthenon was begun at Athens, and about the same time as the victories of the Greeks over the Persians at Plataea and Mycale, and the battles of Thermopylae and Salamis. It was also about the time when the poet Æschylus wrote. The ruins of this temple were explored by the late Mr. Cockerell, R.A., the distinguished architect, in 1811. The temple, and with it the statues, had been all thrown down by an earthquake long before. Baron Haller, MM. Linkh, Stackelberg, Forster, and Brönsted assisted in the discovery of the broken statues which had belonged to the pediments. The temple was built of sandstone, and coated with stucco, in a method resembling that employed in the temple at Selinus in Sicily. These statues, and those of the Parthenon, are the only examples as yet found of a complete pediment series, as they were designed to fill the architectural space. The Niobe figures in the Florence Museum are supposed to have formed a similar composition; but this is not yet a settled point, though they have been placed in this form. These Æginetan statues (Fig. 74)

* According to Mr. Newton.

are of marble, and were purchased by the late King Ludwig of Bavaria, and placed in the Glyptothek at Munich, after having been very much restored by Thorwaldsen at Rome. (Casts are in the British Museum arranged in the pedimental form.) The western pediment is that given in our illustration; and the subject, formerly thought to be the contest for the body of Patroklus, is now thought to be the fight of Greeks and Trojans around the body of Achilles, who lies at the feet of Athene.* These eleven figures are in better preservation than those of the eastern pediment, which was so far destroyed that only five could be put together. Those of the east pediment are rather larger. They represent either Hercules and his companions fighting over the body of Laomedon, or an incident of the expedition of Hercules and Telamon against Troy. Athene is represented closely after the hieratic type, considerably larger than the other figures, with her feet turned sideways, but her face to the front; while the mortal combatants are placed in various attitudes of strong action, but

* It may be remarked in favour of the subject being the death of Achilles, as first pointed out by German writers, that the kneeling figure with the Phrygian cap and close Asiatic armour may be Paris, who shot the arrow that hit the only vulnerable part of Achilles. But the subjects represented and the personages are still undetermined.

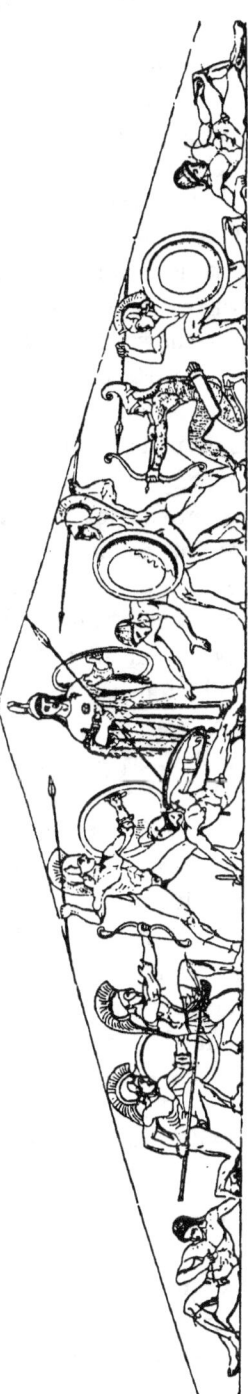

FIG. 74.—WEST PEDIMENT OF THE TEMPLE OF ATHENE AT ÆGINA. Munich Museum. [Height of Athena, 5 ft. 6¼ in.]

with most of the heads in profile. These statues are all carved
in the round, and are, consequently, most interesting as showing
the great step in advance that had been made in technic capa-
bilities. The study of the figure will be noticed as singularly
accurate, even to the veins and tendons, and the anatomy of the
joints. This vigorous naturalism is carried out also in the
spirited attitudes, and in the fallen and falling combatants.
Still greater realism was obtained by making the weapons—spears
and bows—(shown as replaced by modern ones in the cut) as
well as other parts of the details, of bronze. On some of the
figures of the eastern pediment the hair of the beards was finished
with curls of metal wire attached; while the eyes were painted,
and the bloody wounds were also coloured. This may have
been an improvement of a later taste, but, whenever applied,
portions of the colour remain still to be seen. The figures of
sturdy, robust, and gladiatorial forms, are short in the proportions and are under the size of life. The heads are
particularly significant of the art of the time, carved with artistic
skill, but all of one type, and having no other expression than
the same complacent smile. Whether attacking to the death, or
whether in the last agony, there is the same smile. This was so
probably because the sculptor did not allow himself to depart
from the received type of the heroic countenance. It was not
that he was incapable, or how could he have modelled the body
so exactly with an accuracy that perhaps even approaches to
dryness? Still, it was not the portrayal of beauty that was the
aim, but a forcible representation of a scene of historic interest,
with all the accentuation and emphasis that exact imitation could
give without the expression of the countenance. As to the
sculptor of these remarkable statues, two names are recorded as
celebrated by Quintilian—Kallon (Καλλων), and Hegesias; but
whether both were engaged upon them, as if one did the
eastern and the other the western pediment, it is not related.
All that Quintilian has to say is: " Duriora et Tuscanicis
proxima, Calon atque Egesias; jam minus rigida, Calamis;
molliora adhuc supra dictis, Myron fecit diligentia acdecor in
Polycleto supra cæteros " (Quin. lib. xii. cap. 10). It is interesting to observe that the style is so well distinguished as

" harder, and like the Tuscan;" and the mention of Kalamis as " less stiff;" and of Myron, the sculptor of the Discobolus, as a still softer modeller.

Two small statues of draped female figures showing the archaic form of drapery, which were found with the Ægina statues, are thought to have stood one on each side of the apex of the pediment. For further illustration of the style of this period the bas-reliefs in the Museum at Athens, the Charioteer and others, casts of which are in the British Museum, should be noticed. The remarkable style in which the athletic points of the figures are displayed by the sculptor, has been attributed to the knowledge of the figure which he gained when he witnessed the Olympic games, the victors in which were honoured by having statues made of them, often at the expense of their city or state, to be placed in the groves of the temples.

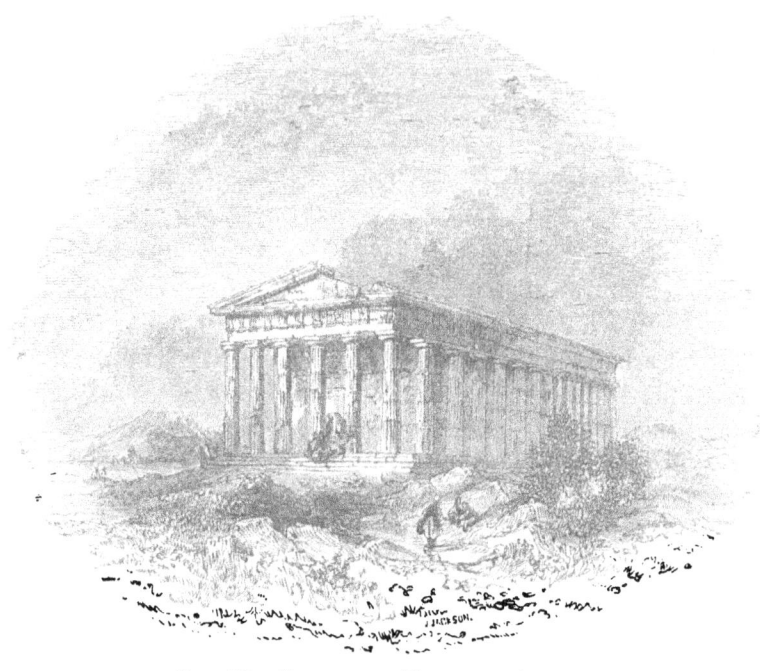

Fig. 75.—Temple of Theseus, Athens.

THE ATHENIAN STYLE.

At Athens we have already seen what the style of sculpture during the time of Pisistratos and his successors (560—490 B.C.) was in the stiffness and archaic forms of the draperies, and we have noted the absence of any sculpture in the round in marble, at least so far as discovery has hitherto gone. But art and especially architecture had advanced ; the *Hekatompedon* had been raised upon the Akropolis, though doomed with other buildings to speedy destruction by the Persians. This, however, only led to greater efforts to mark the national power when they had conquered their invaders. When the bones of Theseus were found in Skyros, one of the islands of the Ægean, by Kimon in 469 B.C., the oracle directed that Athens should be their guardian ; and the temple called the Theseium (Fig. 75) was built to do honour to the great hero and king of Athens. The pediment of this temple, which is of Pentelic marble, contained statues ; but they have been destroyed. Some of the metopes, and the sculptured friezes in high relief at the east and west ends, are still in their ancient position. Figs. 76 to 79 show some of them, and casts of the whole series are in the British Museum. The subjects of the frieze are, at the east end, the battle of the gods and the giants, and at the west Theseus fighting with the Centaurs. Theseus, it will be remembered, killed the Minotaur, conquered the Amazons, and subdued the Centaurs at Thebes. Referring to the illustrations it will be observed what an extra-

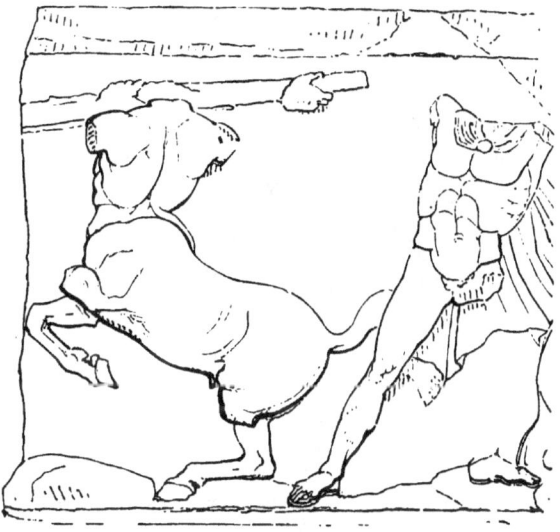

FIG. 76.—METOPE; FROM THE TEMPLE OF THESEUS, 29 IN. HIGH.

ordinary advance there is in these figures from the style of the Æginetan statues ; the forms are well-proportioned, the head not too large, and the muscles displayed in the swelling, life-like movement of muscles in action. The one figure in which the sculptor evidently intended to show his knowledge of the anatomy of the back, perhaps the most difficult of any, is most remarkable (Fig. 79). There is nothing finer than this throughout the Parthenon frieze. Indeed, it will be admitted on comparing these Theseium sculptures with those of the Parthenon, that the former are of such excellence as to have been well worthy of being examples to the sculptors who, a few years afterwards, were engaged under Pheidias. Mr. Scharf * remarks upon "the silence of writers, with the exception of Dodwell, upon their merits;" pointing out, also, how completely they anticipated the Parthenon sculptures in the original conception of the Centaur, which till then had been represented in the most archaic fashion as an animal with a complete human form, and only the body and hind quarters of the horse, as Chiron is seen upon painted vases (Fig. 42). In the drapery also, "instead of folds encircling motionless limbs, or hanging straight down, they

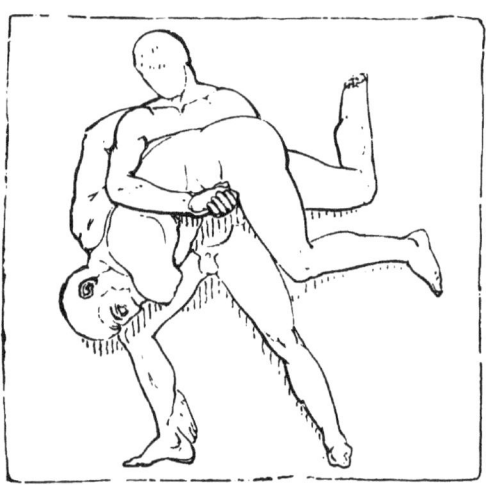

FIG. 77.—METOPE; THESEUS OVERCOMING THE WRESTLER KERKYON.

are made to flow and assume every variety of direction in accordance with the subject, and by their arrangement to set off the figure to the greatest advantage."

It is, therefore, important to understand that these sculptures of the Theseium must have been studied by Pheidias and his contemporaries, and that they must have raised the art to a very high standard, such as would inspire the loftiest ambition in those who were afterwards entrusted with the works of the Parthenon. It is not known whether Ageladas the master of Pheidias was the sculptor who designed these fine works; but if he were, we might imagine that some of these figures are to be ascribed

* 'Handbook to the Greek Court in 1855, Crystal Palace,' p. 26.

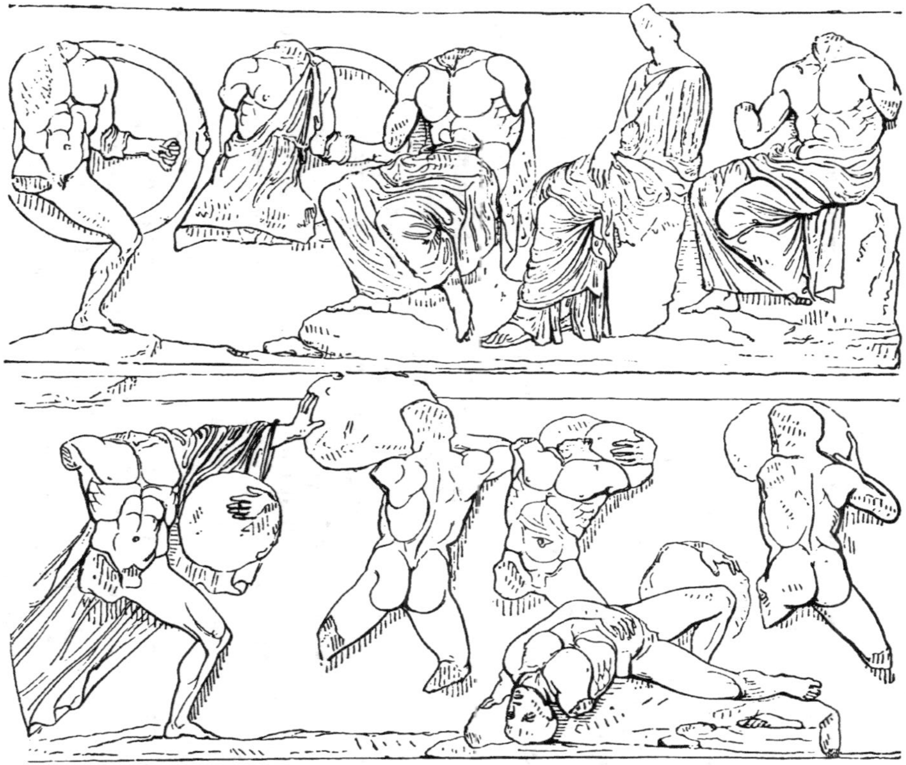

Figs. 78, 79.—Temple of Theseus Frieze. I. The Gods watching the Battle. II. The Battle of the Gods and Giants.

to his pupil, destined to become the master famous for ever as the greatest in classic sculpture. Other able sculptors of the time were Myron, Onatas of Ægina, and Kalamis, whose name is associated with bronze work, and who is distinguished as the sculptor of the Apollo Alexicacus.

It is known that Pheidias finished his great statue in ivory and gold in the Parthenon in the third year of the 85th Olympiad, 438 B.C., when he must have been about 58 or 60 years old,* if born as presumed between the 70th and 72nd Olympiads (Raoul Rochette, Lectures) ; therefore it is quite possible that he might have been engaged upon the sculptures of the Theseium as a young man. That he must have acquired the reputation of being the first sculptor in Athens at the time the ·Parthenon was determined upon by Perikles, is only what is to be concluded ; otherwise, such an important work would not have been placed in his hands. The strong action of many of the figures in the Theseium sculptures, and especially the cast of the flying draperies, would seem to be not unlike the first great work of a young sculptor in the full vigour and flush of genius. The gravity and reserve of power so distinctive of the Parthenon pediment figures, and the perfect grace and dignity of the motives, would mark the work of an accomplished master well assured of his power and working well within his resources. The question whether Pheidias had any hand in the Theseium sculptures is one that is full of the deepest interest, and it has not hitherto received the attention it calls for. It will be admitted, at any rate, that some great innovator was at work upon the sculptures of the Theseium.† All the archaisms we have before noticed were cast aside in favour of a direct study of nature—and this not only in

---

* In the figures fighting the Amazons, sculptured on the shield of Athena, alleged by his enemies to be portraits of Pericles and himself, and for which he was accused—Pheidias was represented as a bald oldish man.

† Myron has been named as the sculptor, but Mr. A. S. Murray ('Hist. of Greek Sculpture,' 1880, p. 252) says this "cannot well be supposed. They may have his faults and his, peculiarities, but not the style of so great a master. A pupil could have executed them, and it may reasonably be doubted if any but a pupil of his could." But then to this opinion there is the obvious corollary that Pheidias was the fellow-pupil of Myron, and unquestionably the greater master.

representing the figure in strong action with great beauty and truth, but remarkably so in the draperies. " The sculptures of the Theseium display a wonderful advance beyond all previous attempts. No period during the whole course of Greek art affords so striking an instance of sudden progress" (Scharf, *loc. cit.*). It remains to be said that some doubt has been raised by German archæologists as to the date of the Theseium, and whether it was not later than the Parthenon.

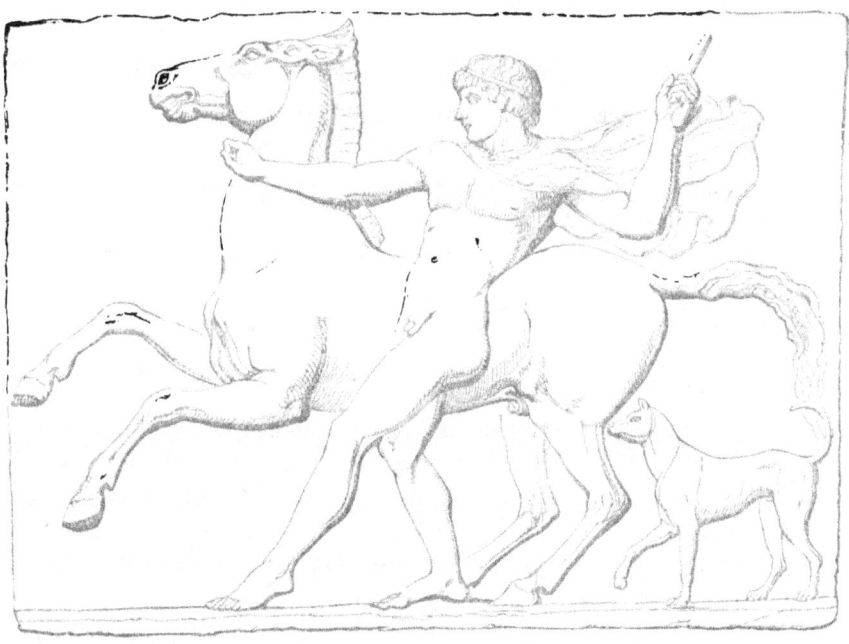

Fig. 79*a*.—Castor. Bas-relief in British Museum.
Said to be Archaic.

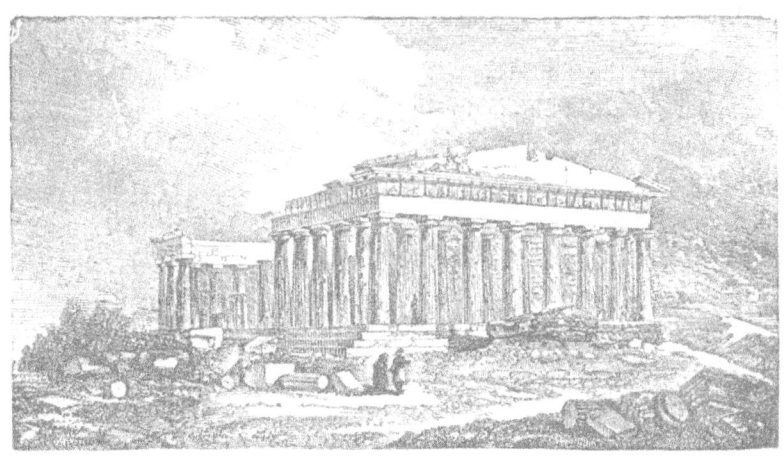

FIG. 80.—THE PARTHENON. TEMPLE OF ATHENE AT ATHENS.

DEVELOPMENT OF THE GRAND STYLE.

WE have arrived now at a period in ancient art when at Athens, the centre of the civilization of the world, the Parthenon, the most beautiful example of architecture, adorned with the grandest works of sculpture, was created. Pheidias was entrusted by Perikles with the general design and direction of this great national work (454—438 B.C.), while two architects, Iktinos and Kallikrates, are also recorded as the practical builders and probably the designers, with Pheidias, of the temple. The whole world of art, ancient and modern, has always with one voice extolled the architecture and the sculpture. It has been pronounced " of all the great temples the best and most celebrated ; the only octa-style Doric temple in Greece, and in its own class undoubtedly the most beautiful building in the world. It is true it has neither the dimensions nor the wondrous expression of power and eternity inherent in Egyptian temples, nor has it the variety and poetry of the Gothic cathedral, but for intellectual beauty, for perfection of proportion, for beauty of detail, and for the exquisite perception of the highest and most recondite principles of art ever applied to architecture, it stands utterly and entirely alone and unrivalled—the glory of Greece." *

* Fergusson's 'History of Architecture,' 1865.

Pausanias is the great historian of art to whom we owe the most authentic description of the temple, its sculptures in the pediments and the frieze, and of the colossal statue of Athene in ivory and gold which stood within. Plutarch, writing in the second century of our era, described it as retaining all the freshness of youth.

It is not within our limits to enter fully into the architectural details of the temple; but it is necessary to say that in plan it was, as the ruined edifice shows to this day, a regular parallelogram of 228ft. long by 101 wide (Fig. 81), giving the proportion of a little more than twice the width for the length. Upon this base stood 8 columns 34¼ft. high, at each end, and showing 17 at each side, forming a colonnade all round, or

S

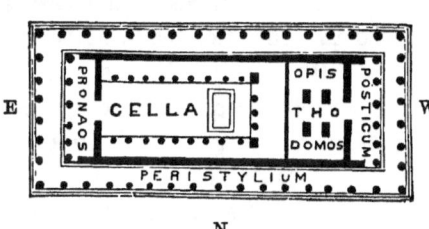

N

FIG. 81.—PLAN OF THE PARTHENON.

peristylium. These columns supported the roof and pediments: and the frieze in which the *metopes* (Fig. 87), sculptured in high relief, occupied spaces between the *triglyphs* all round the building. The interior of the temple, called the *cella,* in which stood the altar (see plan), was 15ft. distant from the columns on each side. The very beautiful and celebrated frieze, sculptured in rather flat relief, occupied the upper part of the outer wall of the cella close up to the ceiling. This frieze was therefore seen from below, by the light coming in between the columns and reflected from the pavement and other surfaces around. It ran all round—525ft. in length— and represented the Panathenaic Procession to sacrifice at the shrine of Athene, and offer to her a new veil (*peplos*) on her birthday, which was celebrated every fifth year (Fig. 85). Of this frieze 335ft. still remain, nearly all of the Western sculptures being still in position on the temple. Casts of these are arranged in order on the walls of the Parthenon-room in the British Museum, together with some original slabs, and casts of those which are in the Museum at Athens, and the Louvre, and part of one in the Vatican, with other fragments obtained from private collectors who had become possessed of them; so that the whole work is there to be studied.

The temple was in early Byzantine times converted into a Christian church; and afterwards, when the Turks were masters at Athens, 1455-6, it was turned into a mosque, with little alteration of the Basilica form given to it by the Christians. A plan made by Fanelli in 1687, given in the great work of De Quincy,* shows that a semi-circular apse had been made at the east end, and the inner row of six columns, which formed the front of the *pronaos*, removed; the east end being thus entirely closed, and the entrance made at the west,† according to Christian usage. But the Christians, requiring light in the apse, made an aperture by breaking through the pediment, and thus displaced and left to destruction the noble group of statues which, occupied its centre. The most serious and extensive damage which has ever befallen the Parthenon was done during the siege of Athens by the Venetians in 1687, when a bomb-shell fell and exploded a powder-magazine within the temple.‡ After the siege the victorious general Morosini § tried to carry

* 'Restitution des Frontons du Temple de Minerva.' 1825.

† For a length of time it had been concluded that the entrance was at the west front, at the Propylæa; although Pausanias had stated clearly that the temple was entered from the east, and that above the *pronaos* was the sculpture depicting the birth of Athene; and the great statue within faced the worshipper on entering.

‡ The state of the Parthenon sculptures previous to the siege of 1687 is shown in the drawings of Jacques Carrey, in the Louvre Library. They are drawings of the frieze, the metopes, and the pediments, done by Carrey for the Marquis Ollier de Nointel in 1674. Copies of some of these drawings of the actual size will be found in the works of James Barry, R.A., 1809.

§ Morosini did succeed in carrying off a large marble lion, which is to be seen still in the arsenal at Venice. This fine work is considered by Mr. Newton to resemble the lion of Knidos in the British Museum, which is the largest hitherto found in Greece. ('Essays,' 1880.)

off the statues of the western pediment, which were still comparatively uninjured; and in the process of removal many of these were allowed to fall from the pediment, and were broken to pieces.   The fragments were utilized by a builder, who burned them to make mortar.   Those which remained on the pediment were among the sculptures removed by Lord Elgin in 1803, which in 1816 came into the possession of the Trustees of the British Museum, by purchase from Lord Elgin for £35,000.

The subject of the Parthenon sculptures has received an immense amount of learned investigation, particularly by the German archæologists, and especially by Michaelis,* who may be said to have almost exhausted the materials.   It would be impossible, within any practical limits, to place before the reader the arguments as to the identification of the various figures.   We shall therefore content ourselves with a brief statement of the conclusions arrived at, and for further information reference can now be made to the new 'Guide' to these sculptures just published by the authorities of the British Museum, which affords the indispensable advantage of being compared with the sculptures themselves.   In this Mr. Newton, the accomplished director of the Department, has with the utmost perspicuity and completeness set before us all that can at present be told; giving also the tabular statement arranged by Michaelis of the various opinions which have been held as to the personages represented in the east and west pediments and the frieze, from the time of Spon, 1678, to Brunn, in 1874.   All the slabs of the frieze, the metopes, and the statues of the pediments in the British Museum being numbered, the student is now enabled to follow out the course of the Procession, and to understand the whole design in all its amazing beauty of work and intellectual meaning.

THE FRIEZE. It should be understood that the frieze as it is viewed on the walls of the Museum is seen in the reverse position to that it occupied on the cella of the temple, where it was placed outside.   The effect of the lighting from above is also different from that intended by the Greek sculptor.   It should be borne in mind also, that the bronze trappings, arms,

* 'Der Parthenon,' Leipzig, 1871.

A.S.

and ornaments, some of which were probably gilt, are gone;
and that colour was probably employed upon the plain surfaces
and some parts of the figures.

 "On the birthday of the Goddess the Procession which
conveyed the *peplos* to her temple assembled in the outer
Kerameikos (quarter of the modellers), and passed through the
lower city round the Acropolis, which it ascended through the
Propylæa.   During its passage through the Kerameikos the

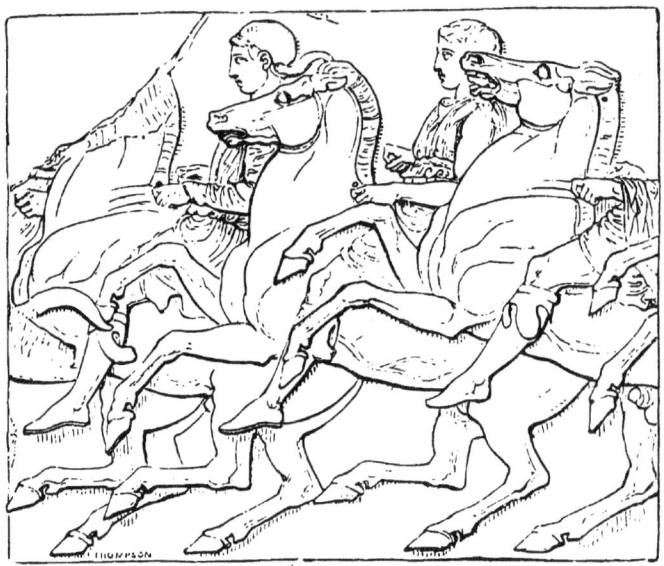

FIG. 82.—From the Frieze of the Parthenon (47½ in. high
without the architrave and cornice, 52½ with them).

peplos was displayed on the mast of the ship which was pro-
pelled on rollers.   On the eastern frieze the delivery of the
peplos is represented in the presence of certain deities (Fig. 85).
Towards this central point converge two lines of procession,
which, starting from the west side of the temple, proceed along
its northern and southern sides towards the centre of the
eastern front." *   Beginning with the western frieze, the start
of the horsemen under the direction of one of the marshals,
and the figures of men in various attitudes of mounting and
riding, display the wonderful power of the ancient Greek

* 'British Museum Guide to Sculptures of Parthenon,' 1880.

sculptor in representing the horse and his rider (Fig. 82). Nothing can be finer in composition than many of these groups of complex forms, or more striking than the effect given with such very low relief. Along the northern frieze the horsemen are continued in crowded though admirably composed throngs. Amazing inventive faculty is shown in the variety of attitude and unflagging spirit and life-like energy characterizing the figures. As Mr. Newton remarks—" In the 125 mounted figures in this cavalcade we do not find one single monotonous

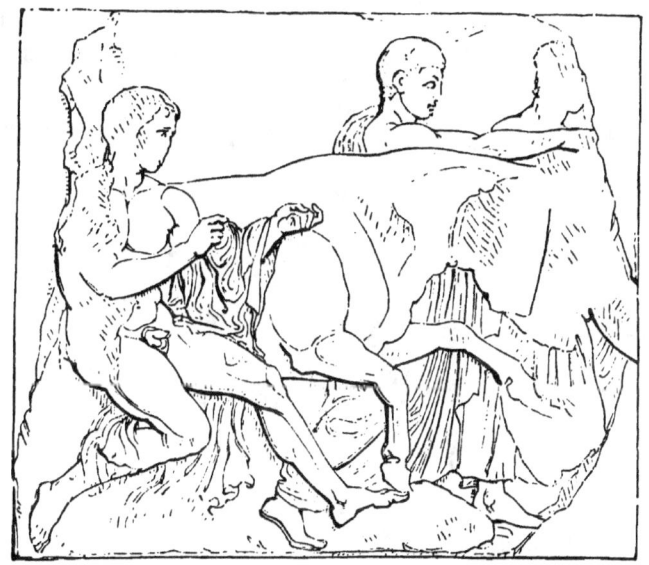

FIG. 83.—PART OF THE SOUTHERN FRIEZE OF THE PARTHENON.

repetition . . . A rhythmical effect is produced by the contrast of the impetuous horses and their calm steadfast riders " (Fig. 86). Slabs ix. and x. should be noticed for the figures of elderly citizens bearing olive-branches (*thallophori*), who are preceded by four flute-players, *auletæ,* and four lyre-players, *kitharistæ.* Several figures carrying vases, others with trays holding offerings of cakes, and others leading the cows to be sacrificed, are remarkable for freedom and naturalness (Fig. 83). These last were the offerings contributed by the colonies to the great festival. On the eastern frieze we see the two great lines

of the Procession meeting over the entrance, where a group of
magistrates receive the advancing procession on either side.

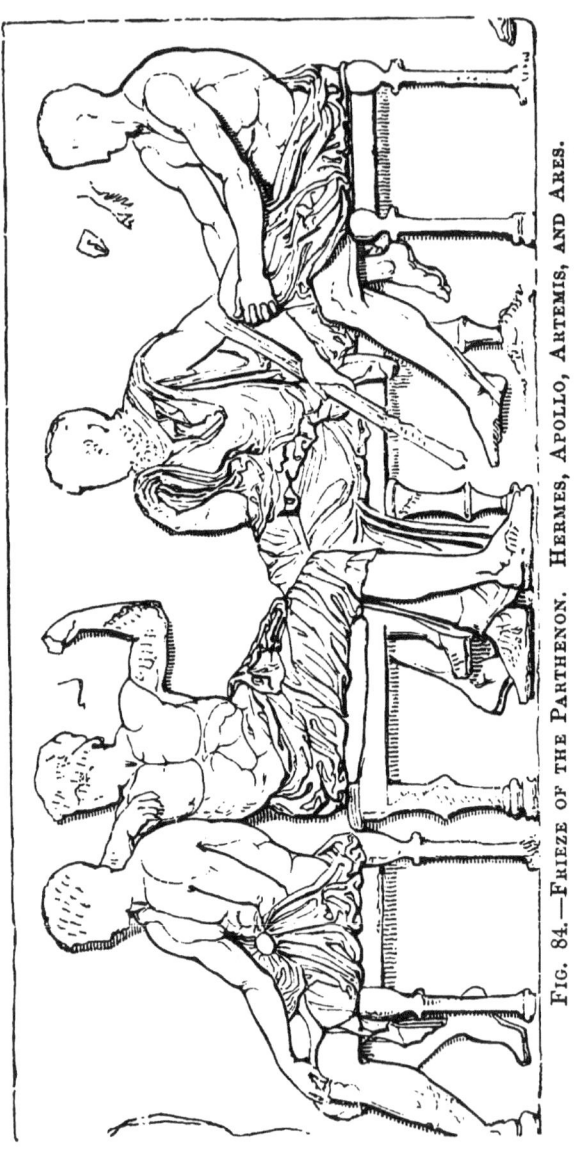

FIG. 84.—FRIEZE OF THE PARTHENON. HERMES, APOLLO, ARTEMIS, AND ARES.

Here are two groups
of twelve seated male
and female figures
in pairs, six on one
side and six on the
other. Between
these are five stand-
ing figures (Fig.
85), representing
the offering of the
peplos. The beauti-
ful maidens of
Athens, draped and
carrying jugs
(*oinochoe*), are noble
figures in graceful
and stately atti-
tudes.

The central por-
tion of the eastern
frieze has been the
subject of much dis-
cussion, but, the
faces as well as the
attributes and other
indications by
which they could
be identified having
suffered much in-
jury, it is very diffi-
cult to judge the
true interpretation.
The explanation of
Michaelis is accepted
by Mr. Newton with certain changes suggested by Flasch, in his
recent memoir ('Zum Parthenon Fries,' Wurzburg, 1877). In

the group the bearded figure (No. 29, B. M.) is Zeus, the goddess at his side is Hera his consort, and the youthful figure is probably Iris or Nikè from the outline of a wing seen on the marble. Opposite Zeus, the seated goddess (No. 35 in the British Museum) is assumed to be Athene, and the remains of her *Ægis*, not worn on her breast but crumpled on her knee, with one of the serpents of the fringe curling round her arm, are to be seen, while some rivet holes show where the spear once was. Next her (No. 36, British Museum) is Hephaistos, then Poseidon, Dianysos (or Apollo), Eros and Aphrodite pointing to the advancing procession (No. 40), and Demeter (or Peitho) next to Dyonysos. The seated male figure to the left of the cut 84 is un-

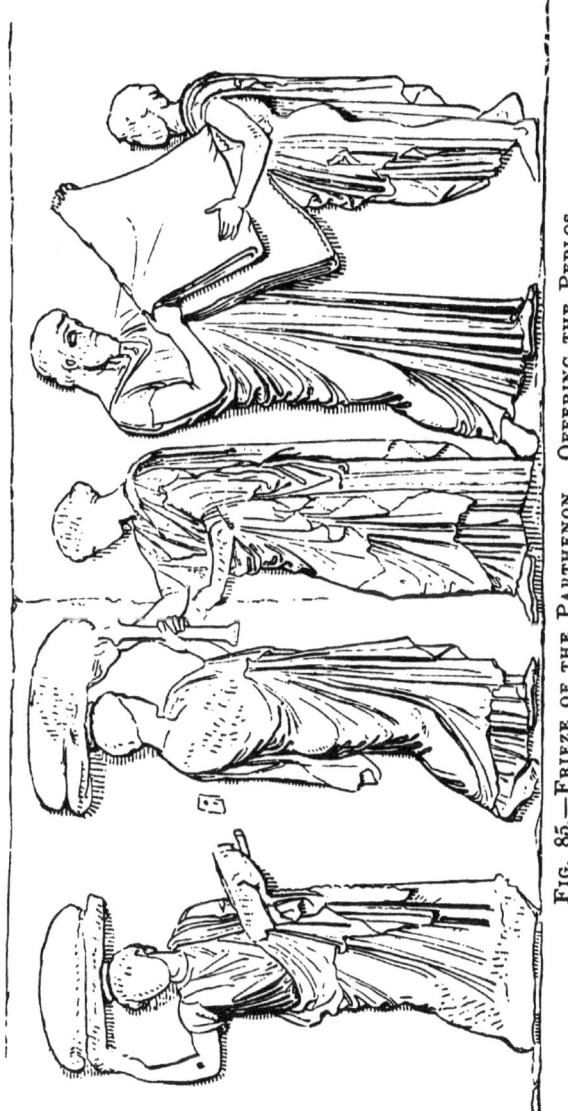

FIG. 85.—FRIEZE OF THE PARTHENON. OFFERING THE PEPLOS.

doubtedly Hermes, wearing the high boots (*endromides*) and having the *petasus* on his knee; a hole in the hand shows

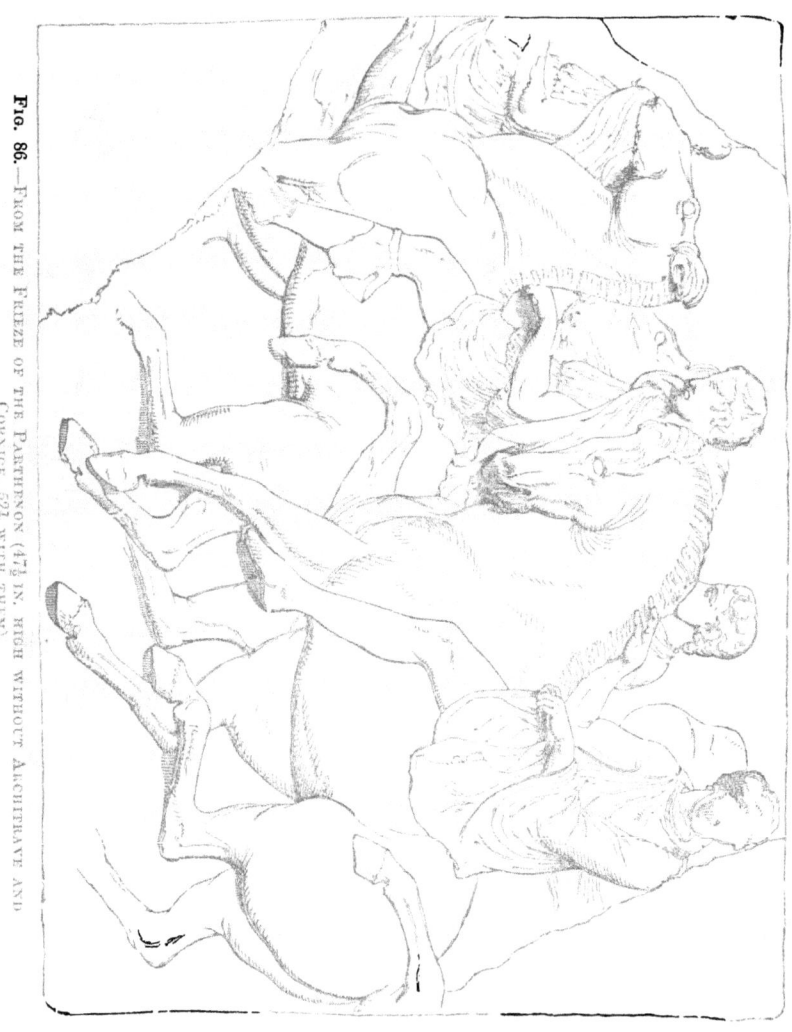

Fig. 86.—From the Frieze of the Parthenon ($47\frac{1}{2}$ in. high without Architrave and Cornice, $52\frac{3}{4}$ with them).

where the *caduceus* was once placed. The figure leaning on his shoulder, called Dionysos by Michaelis, has his knees placed as if clasping those of the female deity. Flasch believes these two figures to represent Apollo and Artemis, and Mr. Newton remarks that the "singular interlacing of their limbs would thus be a symbol of their twin birth, while the torch (held by Artemis) is an attribute as fitting for Artemis as for Demeter." The youthful seated figure on the left of Artemis is probably Ares. Mr. Newton considers that "on the whole the scheme of Flasch presents the fewest difficulties, and it may be admitted that he has brought this most difficult problem nearer to solution than any of his learned predecessors." In confirmation it may be added that the attitude of the figure last referred to (Ares) has long been observed to be similar to that of a well-known statue of Ares, called "the Ludovisi Mars" (Fig. 137, p. 247). As a seated figure thus made equal to the other deities of Olympus, it could not with propriety be Triptolemos, who is generally represented as a youth standing (Fig. 105, p. 192).

Another most interesting portion of the frieze is that group of five—three women and two men (Fig. 85)—which relates to the offering of the *peplos* (Nos. 30 to 34, B. M.). It is not clear whether the elder figure is receiving the *peplos* from or handing it to the youth, or whether they are engaged in folding it; but evidently this represents the important object of the procession, and the bearded figure is either the chief Archon or one of the treasurers of the sacred property of Athene. The meaning of the three female figures is yet unexplained. The two with the *peplos* "stand in the centre of the eastern front under the apex of the pediment and over the door of the *cella*. Such a position would be peculiarly appropriate to this group if intended to represent that solemn ceremony which was the crowning act of the festival, and consequently the key to the whole composition of the frieze" (Newton). The grand female figure next the bearded man is probably the priestess of Athene, who takes from the head of the maiden the cushioned stool, *diphros*, another being borne on the head of the other figure, who holds in her hand some object too much broken to be made out. The legs of the sacred *diphros* have been lost, but a hole in the arm shows where they were fixed, and they may have been of bronze. The lower stature of the two bearers indicates probably their subordinate rank. Other interesting details will be understood on seeing the frieze with the aid of the Museum ' Guide Book.' It is of additional interest, however, to note that in the figure No. 17, the right foot and leg as high as the calf, and No. 16, the left leg and foot, have been acquired recently by the Museum, having belonged to the late sculptor, M. Steinhauser, and these fragments were not known by Michaelis when his work was published. The group No. 27 should be noticed as being similar to the two celebrated colossal statues of men with horses on the Monte Cavallo, so-called after them, at Rome. Here, too, should be observed an instance of the recovery of a portion of the original marble in a fragment adjusted to the cast. This, like others since acquired by the Museum, was brought ·from Athens many years ago and presented to the nation by the owner. No. 97, head bound with a diadem, was formerly in the Pourtales Collection, and was purchased in 1865 at the sale, to be inserted in its place here. Another fragment (slab xxxii. No. 75) was preserved by the Dilettanti Society, and presented to the Royal Academy, from whom it passed to the British Museum in 1817. Another fragment (in slab xxxv. 85) was discovered in the Marbury Hall Collection, in Cheshire, and was presented by Mr. J. Smith Barry. There are some spaces left for missing slabs, and some yet unappropriated ones.

The southern frieze is occupied with the chariots and the sacrificial cows and sheep, the offerings of the colonies, with numerous figures of drovers and others in every beautiful variety of attitude (Fig. 83). In Carrey's drawing there are eight chariots, three only of which have been identified by Michaelis, and there should be nine according to Mr. Newton. Each charioteer is accompanied by an armed warrior either in the chariot or at its side, not as in the northern frieze stepping into it. The horsemen on this south side are in more regular order, and not in a tumultuous throng as on the opposite side, and therefore it has been supposed they are the trained cavalry of Athens (*Hippeis*). This part of the frieze is much injured.

Some small parts have been added since the work of Michaelis appeared, in which the frieze will be found engraved in consecutive order according to Carrey's invaluable though rough drawings, which show, in many places, the now missing portions. It is encouraging to learn that there are still fragments preserved in the stores of the Museum of which some have been recognized after long study, and added to the frieze as well as other parts of the Parthenon sculptures. Of the metope No. 3, B. M., it should be observed that the heads of both figures and the right arm of the Centaur are casts from the original fragments in the Copenhagen Museum, which were carried off from Athens at the time of the siege in 1687 by a Captain Hartmand, who served under Count Königsmark in Morosini's army. In the same museum there are a Centaur, foot, and lower part of a leg which, according to Michaelis, belong to a group seen perfect in Carrey's drawing. No. 9, B. M., is a cast from the slab in the Louvre. No. 10, B. M., a cast from the one in the Athens Museum, the marble foot of the right leg being kept in the wall case C, being too heavy to be attached. Some fragments are also in the British Museum belonging to other thirteen metopes shown in Carrey's drawing of the same subject, and of eight more, the subject of which is not known, though supposed, from the parts of draped female figures, to refer to the ritual of Demeter and other Attic divinities.

THE METOPES. These are the blocks sculptured with groups partly in high relief and partly in the round, which occupy the spaces, *metopæ*, between the ornaments called, from the parallel vertical channels cut in them causing three projecting lines, *triglyphi*. They were on the outside of the temple, above the architrave, and were continued all round, 92 in number, viz. 14 at each end beneath the pediments and 32 at each side. Fifteen of them, brought from Athens by Lord Elgin, are on the walls of the Parthenon Room, while one other was obtained by M. Choiseul Gouffier, the contemporary French ambassador at Constantinople, and is preserved in the Louvre. All these sixteen are from the south side of the temple; some of the others remain in such a very ruined condition on the building that they can scarcely be understood, while many are destroyed and are only known by the drawings of Carrey. Of the 32 on the north side only 12 remain in their original position, and three of these cannot be made out. The explosion of the bombshell and powder magazine in 1687 destroyed 20, leaving only a few fragments. A model in the British Museum shows the state of ruin produced.

The metopes on the south side have for their subject the contest of the Centaurs and Lapithæ at the marriage feast of Peirithoos. The twenty-eighth metope in the original series (No. 13, B. M.) is pointed out specially by Mr. Newton—"for dramatic power in the conception and truth in the modelling of the forms this metope is unrivalled" (Fig. 87).

The metopes of the north side are so much damaged that their subjects cannot be made out, but it is conjectured by Michaelis that they may have represented a scene from the taking of Troy; while Mr. Newton suggests they may have been a continuation of the series of combats of Centaurs and Lapithæ. A cast of the only one sufficiently perfect is the last in the series at the north-west angle of the temple. It represents a draped female figure seated on a rock with another advancing, remarkable for fine treatment of the drapery. It is No. 18, B. M., Parthenon Room.

Of the metopes on the west front, all except two remain in position, but are too much injured to be made out : the subject appears to refer to the battles of Greeks with Amazons. (No. 19, B. M., is a cast from one of them.)

The metopes of the east front are all in position on the temple, though much injured. The subject, however, is known to be the battle of the gods and giants, the *Gigantimachia*.

To follow out the design of these metopes, discussing each as to its composition and particular treatment of the figure, would be impossible without the fullest illustration by those that remain, which is entirely beyond the scope of the present volume. The student should however avail himself of the ample descriptions now to be had, which with the original marbles and the casts in the British Museum will enable him to master the subject. It may be remarked of the technical qualities of the metopes, that as examples of inventive power in design and

variety in the treatment and grouping of the figures they are of
the highest order. The placing of the metopes in contrast with
the straight lines of the entablature of the Parthenon and the
triglyphs, showed a perfect perception of what could be most
effective in sculpture. Statues in the round would have been
out of place and well-nigh impossible from the amount of projection required; while bas-relief and even mezzo-relievo would
have been scarcely forcible enough when coming immediately

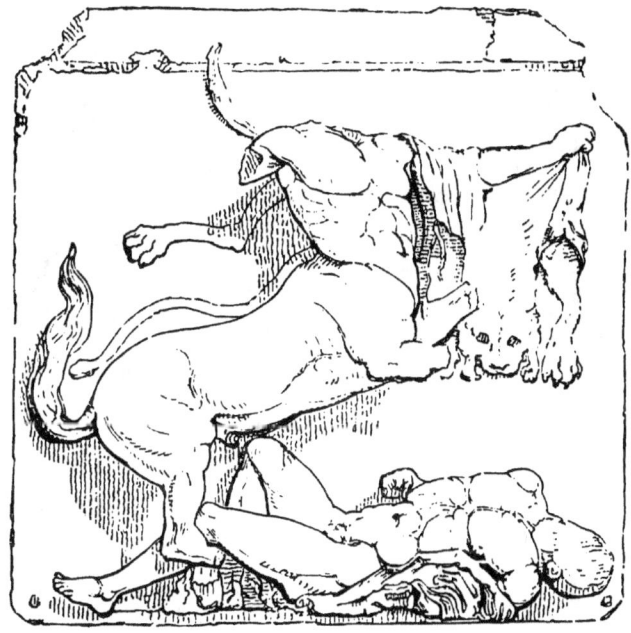

Fig. 87.--Contest between the Centaurs and the Lapithæ.
One of the Metopes of the Parthenon.

into comparison with the strong work of the pediments. The
metopes being a sort of compromise between the round and the
alto-relievo—the figures in each being partly in complete relief,
and quite in the round in the salient members of the group—
keep their importance with the pedimental figures, and at the
same time gain in vigour from the quiet and reposing lines of
the architectural parts near them. The filling of the small
spaces with groups of such extraordinary vigour of action,

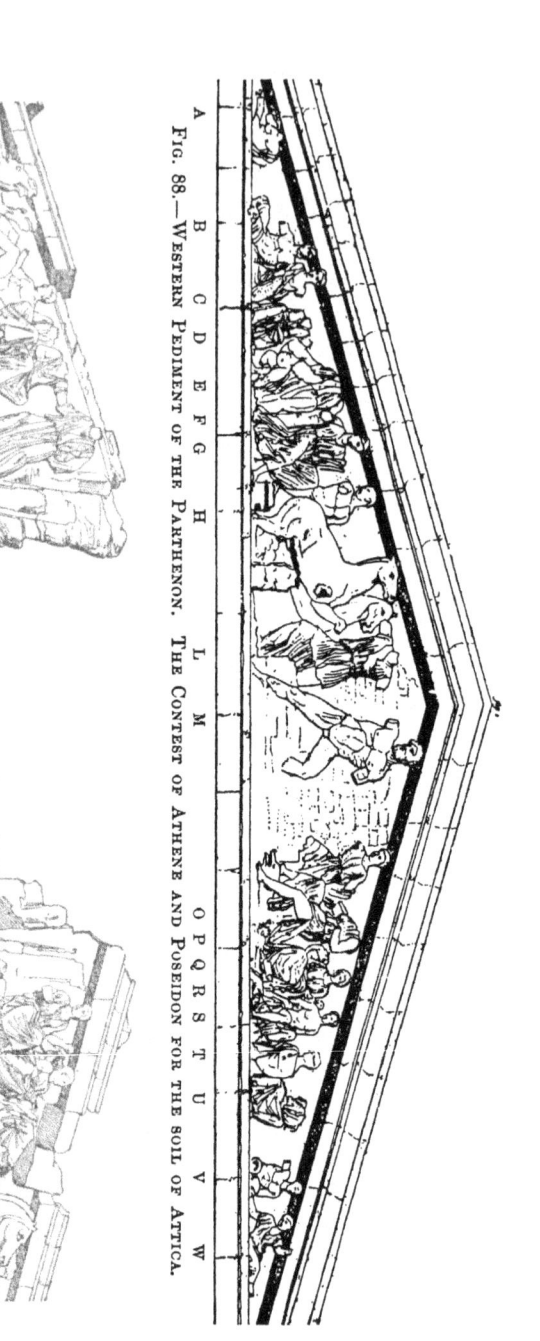

A   B   C   D   E   F   G   H   L   M   O P Q R S T U V W

FIG. 88.—WESTERN PEDIMENT OF THE PARTHENON. THE CONTEST OF ATHENE AND POSEIDON FOR THE SOIL OF ATTICA.

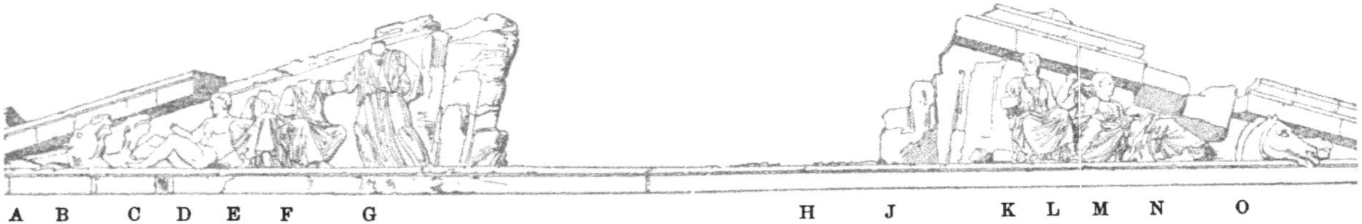

A   B   C   D   E   F   G   H   J   K   L   M   N   O

FIG. 89.—EASTERN PEDIMENT. THE BIRTH OF ATHENE.

The gap was filled by the lost group of the Birth of Athene; the composition of which is unknown. The suggestion of M. de Quincy taken from an ancient bronze Etruscan engraved patera will be seen in Fig. 95.

Copied from the drawings by Jacques Carrey made in 1674, now in the Louvre, Paris.

N.B.—The letters refer to the statues as they are marked in the British Museum, and in the description in these pages.

displayed in combats of two figures only, without one instance of feebleness or anything approaching repetition, are points of the greatest importance for study, as examples of striking power of conception and composition, and knowledge of the form displayed in the work of the figures. It is not known who was the sculptor of the metopes, and from the inferiority of some of them, it does not appear probable that they were all done by the same hand; but it has been thought by Mr. Newton, and so suggested by him in his recent valuable lectures upon Greek art, that the style of Myron is recognizable in some of the groups.

THE SCULPTURES OF THE PEDIMENTS (Figs. 88, 89) represented, as Pausanias describes, over the eastern end, above the entrance to the temple, the birth of Athene, and over the western end the contest of Athene and Poseidon for the soil of Attica. But there are no detailed descriptions by the ancient writers of the groups that filled the pediments. Vitruvius tells us of a volume written by Iktinos and Karpion upon the Doric Temple of Minerva on the Acropolis; Polemo and Heliodorus are also said to have written upon the subject, but these treasures are lost. The broken statues and fragmentary parts are preserved in the British Museum, and are all marked for identification.

The group which still remains on the pediment at Athens is considered to be that of Kekrops and Aglaurus. The heads are gone. These are the statues once supposed by Dr. Spon and Sir G. Wheeler to be Hadrian and Sabina his empress, a mistake that was followed by Stuart and Fauvel, who was fifteen years at Athens, and who pronounced them to be of different work.

The identification of each of the figures of the pediment sculptures must still be a matter of discussion; and as we cannot pretend to give a statement of the various opinions that have been given, we must refer the reader to the writers who have devoted so much attention to the subject. The drawings by Carrey afford, after all, the only trustworthy evidence as to the position of the statues; which are to be seen in their fragmentary condition in the British Museum arranged as far as possible according to these drawings.

THE EASTERN PEDIMENT.

The names given to the broken statues above mentioned are those which were proposed by the archæologist Visconti in 1816 in the memoir he read to the Institute of France at the time when the Parthenon marbles were acquired by the British Museum. The various conjectures which have since that time been made

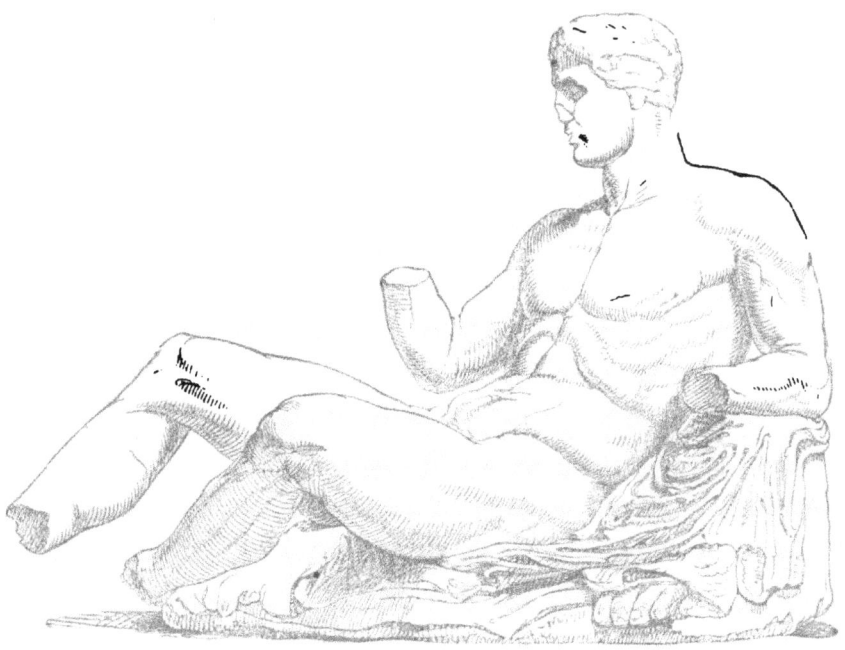

Fig. 90.—The Theseus, sometimes called the Idaean Hercules.

are shown in the tabulated form by Michaelis, to be found in the 'New Guide Book' of the British Museum, with the addition of the opinions of Petersen, published in 1873, and Brunn in 1874.

It will be observed that nearly all agree with Visconti as to the figures in the angles of the pediment, only that instead of the name *Hyperion* (A.) * Helios is proposed as that of the Sun-god

* Hyperion was a Titan born of Uranus and Ge (the Heaven and the Earth), father of Helios, Selene and Eos (the Sun, the Moon, and the Dawn).

rising from the ocean, and this is adopted by Mr. Newton, with that of Selene or Night, which had not been discovered in Visconti's time, though he had rightly conjectured that the beautiful horse's head (O. in British Museum, one of the two of which the other remains on the pediment) belonged to the car of Night descending into the sea.

The grand figure commonly called the *Theseus* (D. British

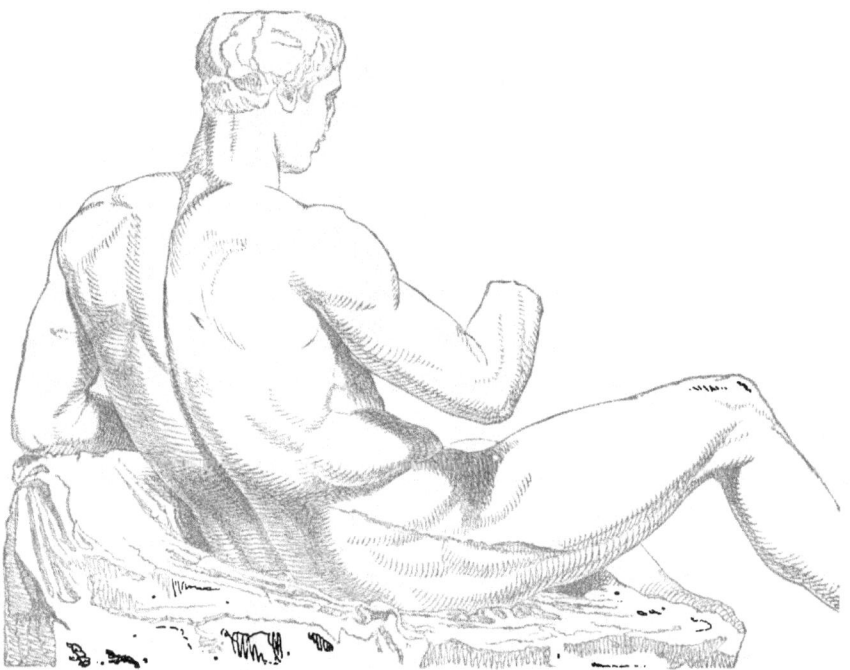

FIG. 91.—THE THESEUS OR IDAEAN HERCULES.

Museum), facing the horses of Helios, which Visconti named Herakles from a resemblance to that hero as on the coins of Kroton, is still by several authorities thought to be rightly named. But Mr. Newton remarks that the skin on which he reclines seems more like that of a panther, and therefore it has been thought to be Dionysos (Bacchus), as there is a figure (Fig. 112) similar to it in the frieze of the Monument of Lysikrates. A better suggestion is made by Bröndsted that it is Kephalos, constantly associated with Aurora, and in the ancient myth carried off by her. A very striking and most poetic interpretation of this fine figure as Mount Olympus, receiving the first rays of the rising sun, has been recently (1874) given by Brunn. From the grandeur of the form and the imposing attitude of sublime repose, it had before been compared by Mr. G. F.

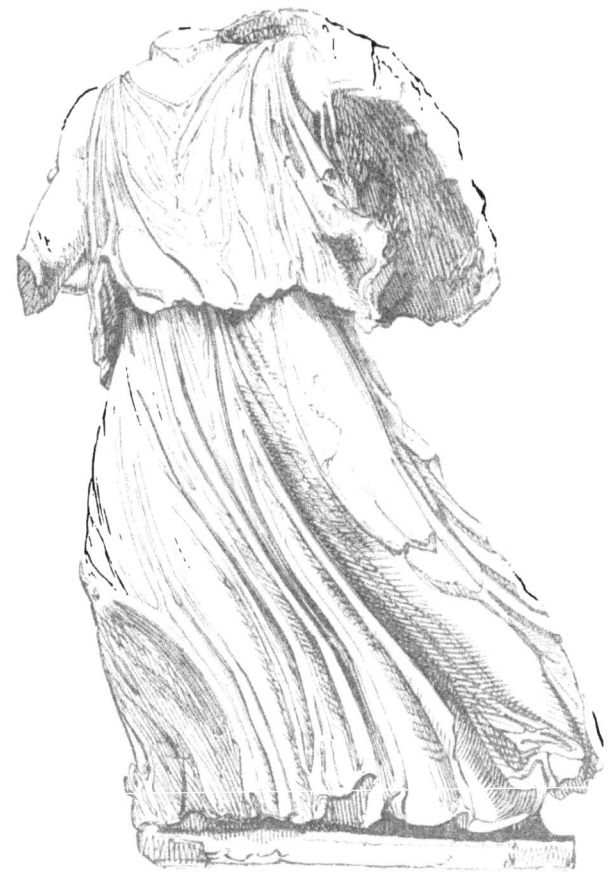

FIG. 92.—IRIS. ON THE EASTERN PEDIMENT OF THE PARTHENON.

Watts, R.A., to the beautiful form of a mountain. Kekrops and Pan are other suggestions.

The *Ceres* and *Proserpine* of Visconti (E. F.) are called the Horæ (Hours) by Brunn; Thallo and Auxo (Two Seasons) by Millingen and Overbeck; simply two goddesses by Müller.

That they are closely related as mother and daughter or two sisters, in accordance with Visconti and most writers after him, is evident; of which Mr. Newton remarks, "this attribution would be strengthened if the reclining nude figure could be identified with Dionysos;" and on the assumption of Bröndsted that they are the Horæ who guarded the gates of Olympus, the position of Iris next to them would represent her as on the point of passing to the outer world to announce the birth of Athene (Newton).

As to the *Iris* (G.) (Fig. 94), all agree with Visconti except Brunn, who proposes that it may be Hebe, and he also suggests

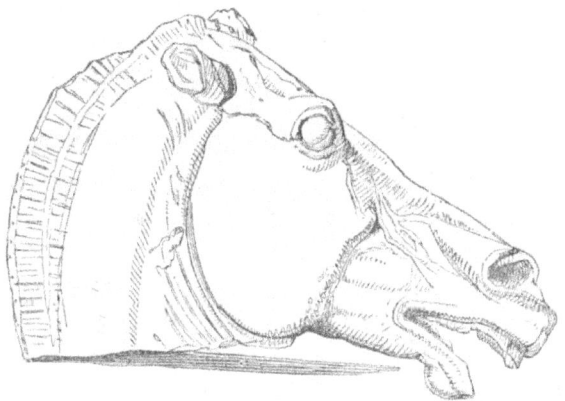

FIG. 93.—THE HORSE'S HEAD. CAR OF SELENE.

that the whole subject was the moment before the birth of Athene. To this it must be an obvious objection that the figure displays the action of rapid movement upwards and away from the central group. Hebe as the daughter of Zeus and Hera would not be an appropriate personage at the birth of Athene, while Iris as the messenger of the god has a most significant part, and fills up the fine poetic conception of the subject.

The Horse's head. (O. British Museum.) Of the two heads of the horses belonging to the car of Selene (N.), this has fortunately been preserved in much of its original beauty. The other, which remains on the pediment, is described as now a mere shapeless mass; though as it was hidden behind the head now in the

A.S.

British Museum which is seen in Carrey's drawing it may never have been so highly wrought as its fellow. Some interesting points are to be noticed in this grand head. It is inclined downwards, as in the descent of the departing Night before the advancing horses of the Day at the opposite angle, whose fiery heads are tossed as they spring into the air out of the waves. "In the whole range of ancient art there is perhaps no work in marble in which the sculptor has shown such complete mastery over his material. The nostrils 'drink the air' as if animated with the breath of life" (*Newton*). It was highly praised by Goethe. It is a remarkable example of the genius of Greek art in uniting exact imitation of nature with the higher beauty of an ideal type, or in the words of Goethe, "seems the revelation of a prototype; it combines real truth with the highest poetical conception." This head, as seen in Carrey's drawing, projected in front of the cornice, and the marble has been cut away to allow of this. There are also some drill-holes behind the ears and on the nose, showing that a metal bridle was originally fitted to it, and the crest of the hogmane has holes which served to fasten some ornament.

The three Fates. (K. L. M. British Museum.) Though headless now, two of them are seen in Carrey's drawing with their heads, the one nearest the angle turned towards the horses of Selene, the other towards the central group. The right arms of two were then only partially injured, but are now lost. These three figures correspond with the triad at the other side, of Theseus, Demeter, and Persephone, and the reclining figures, Theseus and the draped female (N.) next the horses, appear to be similarly inattentive to the great event, while the figures nearest the centre are as it were listening (*Newton*).

To the view of Visconti it is now objected that if the three grandly-posed draped figures were intended to be the Fates they would have been placed in the central part of the composition. Several authorities agree with Visconti, but "on the other hand the plan of this triad in immediate succession to Selene would point to some mythical connection between these figures and the goddess of Night" (Newton). Hence they are named by

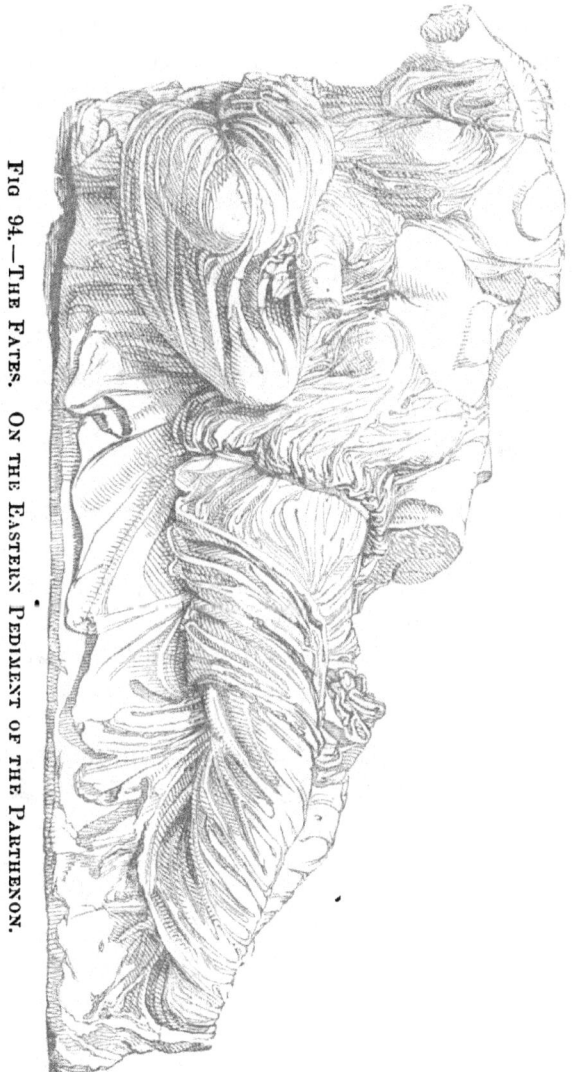

Fig 94.—The Fates. On the Eastern Pediment of the Parthenon.

Welcker (1845) the three daughters of Kekrops—Aglauros or Agraulos, Herse and Pandrosos ; and Overbeck (1857) adopts this view ; while Dr. Brunn, also connecting them with Selene, thinks they are personifications of the Clouds.   These daughters of Kekrops held an important place in Attic mythology, had their festivals and sacrifices, and Pandrosos, "the all-bedewing" or "refreshing," was worshipped at Athens with Thallo, having a sanctuary near the temple of Athene Polias.

It may perhaps be worthy of remark, in reference to this point, that although the Fates were believed to be present at the birth of mortals as holding the destiny and duration of human life, it is not altogether appropriate that they should play any similar part at the birth of an immortal goddess over whom they held no influence.   Still, they were divinities, and may be taken to represent the eternal power presiding over all birth, the spinning of the thread at the beginning of life, and controlling the destiny of the newly-born.   In this view they would hold a place of more dignity and solemnity than as secondary attendants upon Selene.   And this would seem to be indicated by the surpassing grandeur of the forms so large with majestic grace and nobleness of character, and seated upon a rock.   As the daughters of Zeus they take the corresponding place to Demeter his sister, and Persephone his daughter, with Herakles the son of Zeus.*

The Nikè, Victory.   This figure, not in Carrey's drawing, was found lying on the ground below the pediment, and Visconti naturally concluded it had stood as "Victory" present at the birth of Athene.   From its resemblance to the figure (N. British Museum) in the western pediment drawn by Carrey and Dalton, it was thought that it was wrongly placed by Visconti, but Mr. Newton points out that a "Victory" associated with the defeat of Poseidon would be inconsistent, and that the subject of the east pediment would be incomplete if Nikè were not present to

* Herakles, the son of Zeus by Alcmene, is to be distinguished as the Theban Hercules from the more ancient hero, the Idæan Herakles, who protected Zeus when in his infancy, and aided the god in clearing the earth of monsters in the Gigantimacchia.   This statue may, as Visconti remarks, be intended for the Idæan Hercules.

welcome Athene, concluding that the probability is that this torso belongs to the east pediment as assigned by Visconti.

Some most interesting discoveries have been made amongst the fragments brought with the Parthenon marbles by Lord Elgin. In 1860 Mr. Watkiss Lloyd identified the thigh of this Nikè, and in 1875 the knee was recognised, and these have since been added to the statue. Wings of marble were attached to the shoulders, where are to be seen the deep sinking for their attachment with holes for metal dowels. The position of the Nikè in the pediment would depend on these wings; as if they were much raised it must have stood nearer the centre than it is placed in the Museum.

Prometheus or *Hephaestos* (H. British Museum, a cast). A torso in the Museum at Athens, which was found on the east side of the Parthenon in 1836 and was unknown to Visconti.

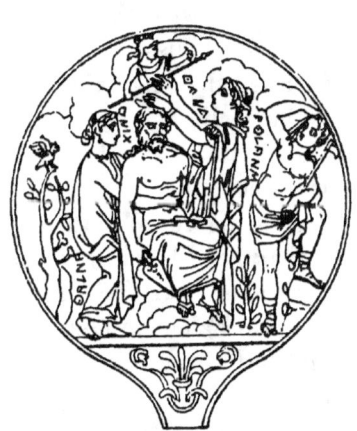

FIG. 95.—BIRTH OF ATHENE, ON A PATERA.

" The action of the shoulders and muscles of the back suggests the notion of a figure about to strike with both arms lifted above the head " (*Newton*). It is considered to be either that of Hephaestos, who according to the ancient myth cleaved the head of Zeus with his axe to accomplish the birth of Athene, —as represented on the patera (Fig. 95), showing him standing near holding his axe—or Prometheus, to whom Attic tradition preferred to attribute the deed. De Quincy proposed that this patera might be taken as an authority for the destroyed central group of the pediment, and he gives a restoration taken from it in his great work above referred to, from which this patera is taken.

THE WESTERN PEDIMENT.

The mutilated statues of the western pediment as seen in Carrey's drawing (Fig. 88), are sufficiently complete to indicate the subject; but they were reduced to mere fragments and torsos before Stuart saw the Parthenon (A.D. 1751). By referring to the engravings (Figs. 91, 92), which have never before been given in this convenient form, the reader will be enabled to understand the arrangement of the statues as far as it can be made out.

In the centre were Athene and Poseidon, with her chariot and horses driven by a figure Nikè (Victory), the blank space being filled, it is presumed, on the other side near Poseidon by his chariot and horses driven by Amphitrite (O. British Museum) (Newton). The central group was no doubt composed in this manner, with the olive tree which sprang up as Athene struck the soil with her spear, and perhaps some representation of the salt spring that Poseidon caused to rise at the spot he struck with his trident.

The angle on the left of Athene was filled with the beautiful nude reclining figure, commonly known as the Ilissos (A. British Museum), but now called Kephissos after the small river near Athens; in the angle on the right, the reclining female figure (W.) is thought to represent the fountain Kallirrhoe. The kneeling figure (V.) next is Ilissos the river-god.

Between the Poseidon and the female figure (W.) there are nine figures in Carrey's drawing, the charioteer Amphitrite being the best identified; the others being variously named as a group of the marine deity Leukothea and her son Palaimon Melikertes, Thalassa (the sea) with Aphrodite in her lap as sea-born, and next a female sea-deity not identified.

Between the horses of Athene and the reclining figure Kephissos in the opposite angle, are seven figures in Carrey's drawing. These are named in the order from the Chariot—1. Ares (Mars) (H. British Museum), or Hermes, or one of the Attic heroes Erictheus, Ericthonios, or Kekrops: 2. Nikè as the charioteer. 3. 4. 5. Two female figures and a boy may be Demeter and Korè with Iakchos (D. E. F. British Museum). 6. 7. May be Asklepios and Hygieia. The coil of a serpent found has suggested its belonging to a group of Asklepios and Hygieia; or Kekrops and one of his daughters, with his son the young Erysichthon (Newton).

The general conclusion come to, first by De Quincy and Visconti, is that the composition of this pediment was arranged as if embraced between the two rivers of Athens—the Ilissos and Kephissos—the figures on the left hand side of Athene being Attic deities or heroes, while those on the side of Poseidon are marine deities, his allies as ruler of the ocean. The various opinions as to the different personages may be seen in Michaelis's table in the 'British Museum Guide Book.'

The numerous fragments collected in 1833, after many years' neglect, were placed in a magazine on the Acropolis, and casts of them are to be seen in the Parthenon-room of the British Museum. In 1835, in clearing the ground, parts of the horses of the chariots, let fall under Morosini's attempt to lower them, and the crouching figure (V. Fig. 88) were found.

The Athene (L. British Museum). The torso as described above has had added to it a cast of the fragment of the lower part of the neck found on the Akropolis, which shows that the head was turned towards the Poseidon. The portion of a head which Visconti considered to belong to the Athene is not adjusted to the neck, and is still to be seen lying on the pedestal upon which the torso is mounted in the British Museum. This is so because, although it is of the same scale as the torso and was found built into the wall of a Turkish house at the west front of the Parthenon, it has been pronounced by Michaelis a doubtful fragment. It is of whiter marble than the other pieces and highly polished in the flesh part, with some traces of red colour in the hair; while it is considered to be hard and conventional in the work.

The Poseidon (M. British Museum). To this torso has been added a cast of the fragment preserved at Athens found since Lord Elgin's removal of the marbles, and a smaller portion of the lower part of the body. A left foot also at Athens may, it is thought, belong to this figure. As an example of grand sculpture of colossal proportions and noble form, conceived in the spirit of Homer's description of the vast chest of Poseidon—Στερνον δε Ποσειδωνος ('Iliad,' 6. 2. v. 479)—and extremely noble in the forms, this torso is remarkable.

Amphitrite (O. British Museum). A draped torso without the head, arms, and legs, except the upper part of the left thigh.

The attitude is full of spirit and that of holding the reins in
driving, not that of a Victory without wings as Visconti supposed.
Mr. Newton directs attention to the attitude as that of standing,
and not as Carrey's drawing shows it seated, and compares it to
a similar charioteer in the north frieze (No. xii. 33).

Leukothea (?) (Q. British Museum). The lower limbs only of
a seated female figure; the lap and legs to the ancles. The outline of the legs of the youth (P.), seen in Carrey's drawing, is
traceable on the marble. Traces of three fingers of the boy at
her side in Carrey's drawing are on the right knee of Leukothea.
Next to this is a draped figure (T.), with a nude female figure on
the knees (S.), and a boy (R.). This group is supposed to be
Aphrodite in the lap of Thalassa with Eros by her side. The
only remnant of the draped figure Thalassa is a part of the right
thigh. No part of the next draped figure (U.) in the drawing
has been found.

Ilissos and *Kallirrhoe*. These are still at Athens, casts being
in the British Museum (V. and W. British Museum). The male
torso was found on the Akropolis in 1833, the lower half of
the other is still on the pediment; both were unknown to
Visconti. The fragments correspond to the figures in the corner
of the pediment in Carrey's drawing. The association of the
two is taken to support the view that they represent the river-
god and the celebrated fountain. Under the right leg of the
Ilissos a wavy line indicates water. All that remains of the
Kallirrhoe is the right side from below the arm to a little below
the right hip, and part of the leg below the knee. On the pediment beyond the feet of this figure is a round hole in which it
is conjectured a bronze hydria may have been placed.

Kephissos (A. British Museum). This fine, nearly nude
figure, reclining on a rock, so well-known as the Ilissos, is much
as it was when Carrey drew it, although it had been thrown down
from the pediment when removed by Lord Elgin. It has long
been a study for sculptors[1] and all artists, especially for the
natural modelling of the trunk in the sway of the flexible parts
of the abdomen and the fine treatment of the details of the
body in the ribs and muscles of the chest. It is remarkable also
that the back is so carefully sculptured, and that the polish

of the work is still retained.   The space between this and the
next group (B. C. British Museum) Mr. Newton suggests may
have been filled with a crouching water nymph and a river-god
corresponding with the group on the opposite side.   It should
be added to this description that "a drawing by Pars, taken
during his visit to Athens in 1765-66, shows part of the right
fore-arm not shown in Carrey's drawing, and the outline of the
four fingers of the left hand overlapping the edge of the
pediment" (Newton).

Kekrops and *Pandrosos* (B. C. British Museum)   These are
still on the pediment though much decayed ; casts being in the
British Museum.   It is stated that in 1802 these figures still
had the heads on, and the drawing by Pars in the print-room of
the British Museum shows them turned towards the central
group.   The fragment of a snake in the Elgin collection was
found to fit into the remaining part between the two figures
on the pediment.

The figures D. E. F. seen in Carrey's drawing are only now
known by a single fragment at Athens, identified as the left knee
of a seated figure with the hand of a boy resting on it.   A cast
of this is in the wall-case S. British Museum.

The Charioteer—Nikè—(G. British Museum).   "The only
remains that can be attributed with any probability to this figure
are the head formerly brought from Venice by Count de Laborde,
and a fragment of a draped arm now at Athens" (Newton) ;
casts of both being in the wall-case S. British Museum.

Hermes (?) (H. British Museum).   The torso only of this figure
in Carrey's drawing, between the horses and the charioteer, is in
the Parthenon room.   The hole on the left clavicle and one
between the two collar-bones show that a *chlamys* was fastened
here and passed round the arm in a manner characteristic of
Hermes.   A cast of a fragment in the collection at Athens has
been adjusted to the left shoulder.

Of the fragment in which Visconti recognized the feet of
Athene and the stump of the olive tree it is now said, "There is
no sure evidence as to where this fragment was found nor whether
it belonged to either pediment.   It is of Pentelic marble, and
was removed from the Akropolis with the rest of the Elgin.

collection" (Newton, ' British Museum Guide Book '). It has also been assigned to the male figure H. (Hermes.)

There are eleven fragments in the British Museum of limbs and parts of limbs, and drapery, which have not yet been assigned positively to any figures, though certain conjectures have been made as to their place. There are also no less than fifty-five casts from fragments of the pedimental sculptures at Athens in the wall-cases. One of the most interesting of these is a female head which was formerly built into the staircase of a house at Venice of the San Gallo family, one of whom, Felice San Gallo, was secretary to Morosini. This has been thought to belong to the Victory G., as above stated, but there is no certainty of this. Of the horses there are forty-four casts of fragments.

Marble fragments of the Metopes yet unassigned, to the number of twelve, are in the wall-case C. ; and casts of fragments of the Metopes preserved at Athens are in the wall-cases A. to F.

A marble fragment of the frieze, the head of a youth, is in wall-case D., recently acquired from Mr. Steinhauser of Karlsruhe.

Many casts from fragments of the frieze are in wall-cases G. H. and K., to which as yet only conjectural places have been proposed, amongst which is one of the upper part of two horse-men and a horse's head and neck, the original marble being in the possession of the Archduke Karl of Austria, and formerly belonged to the late Duke of Modena.

It remains to be said of these wonderful sculptures of the Parthenon, that it is impossible they could all have been by the hand of Pheidias ; or, that they could have been done in the time of certainly not more than sixteen years, by any one man. Then the question arises whether Pheidias only modelled the statues of the pediments which are admitted to be the finest, and left the marble to be carved by sculptors employed under him. The same would apply also to the Metopes and the frieze. It would appear to be quite beyond the bodily powers of any ordinary man even to design by drawings and to model in clay such a number of important works, especially when at the same time he must have been engaged upon the colossal work ·of the statue of Athene for the temple. Pheidias, it must be borne in mind also, was 56 years old when he began the work on the Parthenon, about 62 when he finished, and 68 * when he died at Elis, after having completed the Jupiter. There may be some doubt as to the birth-date of Pheidias and of his death, and M. de Quincy states that he was more than 80 when he died; but this would not affect the question above set forth.

A very decided opinion is given by M. Rochette: " These sculptures which emanated from the mind of Pheidias, and were most certainly executed under his eye and in his school, are not the works of his hand. Pheidias himself disdained or worked but little in marble. His most skilful pupils were Alkamenes and Agorakritos, and it was most probably the latter who executed the sculptures in alto-relievo in the two pediments. And those were artists without name but certainly not without merit, who produced from the designs of Pheidias the bas-reliefs of the frieze." As to Pheidias not working in marble, M. Visconti remarks: "If it were imagined that Pheidias devoted himself exclusively to the *toreutic* art, and that he employed in his works only ivory and metals, this opinion would be confuted by Aristotle, who distinguishes this 'great artist by the appellation of σοφος λίθουργος, i. e. *a skilful sculptor of marble*, in opposition to Polykletos, whom he calls simply a statuary, ἀνδριαντοποιον, since this latter artist scarcely ever employed his talents except in bronze ('Ethic Nicom.' lib. 6, c. 7). It must be remembered, however, that 'Statuarius' was the term applied to the higher rank, and 'Sculptor,' with 'Scalptor,' 'Fictor,' 'Faber,' 'Mechanicus' and 'Plasta' to artists engaged upon smaller work.

It is in vain to attempt to pronounce as to which of the beautiful fragments of the Parthenon statues is by the hand of Pheidias; but by the common consent of critics the Theseus, the Ilissos or Kephissos of the nude figures, the Fates and Demeter and Persephone of the draped figures, are acknowledged to be the grandest examples of sculpture ever achieved. That Alkamenes, who was taught by Pheidias, must have been

---

* Michaelangelo was a most extraordinary instance of working power. He began the Sistine ceiling when he was 36, and finished it in two years. The *Last Judgment*, on the east wall, 60 feet high and 30 feet wide, he began in his sixtieth year, and finished it in eight years (1533—1541).

esteemed a great man, is shown by his having contended with Pheidias in a competition for a statue of Athene. He competed also with Agorakritos for a statue of Venus; and his work was preferred—" non opere sed suffragiis civitatis contra peregrinum suo faventis" (*Pliny*, lib. xxxvi.)—"not for the work, but by the votes of the city, preferring its own man to a foreigner." His Venus, which was called " Venus of the Garden" ('Αφροδίτη ἐν κήποις), was his most celebrated work; but it was so because it was known that Pheidias had given a finishing touch to it, " Huic summam manum ipse Pheidias imposuisse dicitur" (*Pliny*). Pausanias also mentions the statues of Juno, Mars, Bacchus of ivory and gold, Hecate tricorpor, Aesculapius, Hercules, and a Centaur, all by Alkamenes (lib. i. p. 33). Agorakritos, another pupil of Pheidias, was almost equally esteemed. He was of Paros, and for this reason the Athenians would not accept his statue in preference to that of Alkamenes; so he sold it and called it " Nemesis." It was at Rhamnus, and is extolled by M. Varro (Pliny, lib xxxvi.); and Strabo says that though some declared it to be the work of Agorakritos and others of Diodotos, it was most excellent in grandeur and elegance, and not inferior to the works of Pheidias (" et mole et elegantia præstantissimum, neque Pheidiæ operibus cedens"— Strabo, lib. ix. p. 396). The frieze of the Parthenon is universally acknowledged to be the grandest example of bas-relief, and as regards some of the highest points of excellence in art— such as composition, variety and truth of action in the numerous figures, and in the horses grouped together with such extraordinary beauty, it is quite equal in many of its groups to the sculptures of the pediments. There are no records which refer to any sculptor of the frieze. It has been conjectured that as Kalamis was so famous for his horses that he was engaged upon the frieze. He was celebrated at Ægina before the Parthenon was begun. It is, however, impossible to pronounce when it is so well known that the ancient sculptors all prided themselves upon their ability to represent the horse and the Centaur. The heads of the horses of the pediments are, however, the finest of any, and this has led to these being attributed to the hand of Pheidias.

It is evident, therefore, that Alkamenes and Agorakritos were considered in their day to be second only to Pheidias, and they are well worthy to share with the great master the renown of the Parthenon sculptures.   Mr. Newton thinks that the style of Alkamenes is to be seen in them and in the sculptures of the Nikè-Apteros (Wingless Victory).

We have next to notice the other great works of Pheidias, which, though utterly destroyed, were fortunately seen by Pausanias, whose descriptions of them remain.   There were three great statues of Athene on the Akropolis.   1. The bronze colossal statue known as Athene Promachus, which stood between the Propylæa and the Parthenon; it was between 50 and 60ft. high, and probably gilt, and it was cast from the spoils of Marathon. The crest of the helmet and the point of the spear could be seen far out at sea.   The shield of the goddess was carved by Mys from the designs of Parrhasius the great painter.   It was still erect in 395 A.D., and is said to have struck terror into the barbarian soldiers of Alaric.   It is to be seen on the coins of Athens, and it was probably copied by the sculptors of the well-known statues, the Minerva or Pallas of Velletri, in the Louvre, and the Giustiniani Minerva.   Demosthenes spoke of it in his orations.   2. A bronze known as the Lemnian because it was made at the cost of the people of Lemnos; this Pausanias and Lucian describe as the most beautiful, and on this Pheidias inscribed his name : it is not stated to have been colossal. 3. The one of ivory and gold in the Parthenon, about 37ft. high not including the pedestal, which was about 10ft.

The Parthenon statue was seen by Pausanias, and is described by him as erect with a garment reaching to her feet. Her helmet has a sphinx on the cone and two griffins; she holds a spear, and a shield is at her feet with a dragon.   In her hand stands a Victory of four cubits (5ft. 9in.) in height.   A Head of Medusa in ivory is on her breast.   On the base is the Birth of Pandora, who, according to Hesiod, was the first woman.   Plato speaks of this statue, and Thukydides tells the value of the gold ; Perikles also counted it in the resources of the state, to be used if required and returned to the Temple.   This gold mantle was carried off afterwards by Lachares,* 296 B.C. (about), in the time of Demetrius Phalereus, and was never restored. The head of Gorgon in gold was also carried off by one Philorgos before this time, and its place supplied by the one of ivory which Pausanias saw. From other accounts it is known that on the front of the helmet was a group of four galloping horses. On the shield the combats of the Gods and Giants in the inside, and the Athenians with the Amazons on the outside. It was on this part that Pheidias carved his own portrait with that of Perikles as fighting an Amazon with his arm raised to conceal his face. He represented himself as a bald-headed man lifting a stone. In a treatise attributed to Aristotle it is related that this head of Pheidias was so fixed in the shield that it could not be removed without letting the whole work fall into separate pieces, as if it were a sort of keystone. It was for placing his portrait on the shield of the Goddess that he was accused on the ground of a sacrilegious act (see p. 140). A statuette in marble was recently discovered on the Akropolis, which corresponds with the descriptions of the great statue, but has a support to the arm holding the Victory which would not be required in the Chryselephantine statue. This is, however, a work of very coarse and poor art of Roman time, intended as a votive offering. ᵢ

The still more famous colossal statue by Pheidias, the Zeus at Olympia in Elis, was his last great work. It was made between B.C. 438, the date of the consecration of the Parthenon statue, and B.C. 432, the year of his death, at Elis.

This was a seated statue (Fig. 16), of ivory and gold, 55ft. high including the throne. Strabo remarks, that "if the god had risen he would have carried away the roof," and the height of the interior was about 55ft. ; the temple being built on the model of the Parthenon at Athens, which was 64ft. to the point of the pediment. Pausanias (lib. v.) has given a minute description of this renowned statue, from which we learn what an extraordinary amount of sculptured work was bestowed as accessory

* Pausanias says of him, " he was of all men the most savage in his manners and the most impious towards the gods "—" he carried away the golden shield and all such ornaments of Athene as could be removed." (lib. i. c. xxiv.)

to the statue. "There are also many statues, amongst which are four Victories in a dancing posture at each foot of the throne; two others near the sandals of the god, and near the foot of the throne Theban infants torn away by Sphinxes, under which are Apollo and Diana shooting the children of Niobe. On the fillets there are. seven statues, the eighth being lost; they represent gymnastic exercises; the rest are adorned with the heroes that accompanied Hercules against the Amazons, in which Theseus is distinguishable." The base was painted by Panænus, the brother of Pheidias, with Atlas, Hercules, and other subjects named by Pausanias, and "upon the top of the throne over the head of the statue Pheidias has introduced three Graces on one side, and three Horæ on the other. On the base are golden lions, and the battle of Theseus and the Amazons; and on the plinth supporting the whole mass, the Sun mounting his car in gold.

Pausanias is particular to say that Pheidias put his name to the Jupiter of Olympia : " Καὶ ἐπίγραμμα ἐστιν ἐς μαρτυρίαν ὑπὸ τοῦ Διὸς γεγραμμένον τοῖς ποσί, Φειδίας Χαρμίδου υἱὸς Ἀθηναίος μ' ἐποίησε." " And there is for a witness this inscription written below the feet of Zeus, ' Pheidias, the son of Charmides, the Athenian, made me.' " *

The statue was also seen in its temple by Paulus Aemilius in the second century B.C., who has left his impressions in the words, " Jovem velut præsentem intuens motus animo est." Epictetus says, alluding to the pilgrimages made to Olympia to behold the famous Jupiter, that " it was considered a misfortune for any one to die without having seen the masterpiece

* The date of the work at Elis is decisively settled, as M. Emeric David shows, by the youth Pantarces, a favourite of Pheidias and victor in the Olympic games, being carved on the base of the statue. Pantarces was crowned victor in the 86th Olympiad, B.C. 436-433.

Pheidias is said by Nazianzenus (Carmin. Iam. xviii.) to have inscribed the name Pantarces on the finger of his statue of Athene, and Clemeus Alexandrinus and Arnobius said that he carved the words ' Pantarces Pulcher' on the finger of the Zeus. This Pantarces is spoken of by Pausanias as ' the lover of Pheidias!' The whole tradition seems questionable. It is, however, brought forward by Emeric David, though he does not say the inscription was on the finger. At any rate the figure of Pantarces was carved by Pheidias in the reliefs upon the base of the statue.

of Pheidias." In the time of Julian the Apostate (A.D. 361 —363) " it continued to receive the homage of Greece in spite of every kind of attack which the convert zeal of Constantine had made against Polytheism, its temples and its idols." (Rochette.) This is the last notice we possess giving authentic information of this grand statue. " It has been said, however, by some Byzantine writers, and repeated on the authority of Winckelmann, that the Jupiter of Olympia, the Venus of Knidos, and the Juno of Samos were to be admired at Constantinople * in the eleventh century, and only perished in the taking of the town by the Crusaders A.D. 1204. From more creditable accounts the greater number of these works were destroyed in the burning of the Palace of Lausus, about 475 A.D., under the Emperor Basilicus, but there is nothing to prove that the Jupiter was ever transported to Constantinople." " Such a mass could never have resisted the risks of the voyage, when so many passions against the ancient worship conspired to complete its ruin. Everything leads us to believe that the Jupiter of Pheidias was destroyed on the spot where it was placed by the great sculptor, in those ages of decline when fanaticism broke or mutilated the ancient idols, when the necessities of religious worship and the state claimed the materials, when individual cupidity in concert with general superstition shared the fragments " (Rochette, ' Lectures '). Pheidias is said to have executed many other statues. Thirteen in bronze from the booty of Marathon, and consecrated at Delphi under Kimon—statues of Apollo, Athene, Miltiades with those ten heroes, Eponymi, or those who had given their names to the ten Athenian tribes.

---

* It is also stated in Smith's ' Dictionary of Antiquities,' under *Pheidias*, that the statue of Zeus had been removed to Constantinople by Theodosius I. and destroyed in a fire in 475 A.D., but this cannot be accepted. Theodosius suppressed the Olympic Games which had been kept up from the first Olympiad, 777 B.C., to his time, A.D. 394. Very little is known of this period as regards the statues, which numbered, according to Pausanias, 3000, some being large equestrian groups. He gives a list of more than 300, mostly of bronze. But the Christians in all probability destroyed and carried off all valuable statues in gold, silver, and bronze. Any that remained were afterwards taken by the Goths under Alaric in the following year, A.D. 395.

An Athene for the city of Pellene in gold and ivory; another for the Platæans, of the spoils of the battle of Platæa, made of wood gilt, with the head, feet, and hands of Pentelic marble; a statue in marble of Nemesis, elaborately described by Pausanias (lib. i. c. xxxiii.). "These," says Rochette, "may be considered the productions of his youth." For further interesting details as to dates and the supposed death of Pheidias in prison, see note, p. 214.

WE may now notice some examples of sculpture of the time of Pheidias and of the later Athenian style about the middle of the 5th century B.C., which have been discovered at Olympia on the west side of the Morea (*see* map) within the last few years in the researches made under the direction and at the expense of the German Government. Olympia, it was known by the history of Pausanias, had its Temple of Zeus, the pediments of which were filled with statues by Alkamenes, who was a pupil of Pheidias, and by Paeonios,* and some of these pediment statues have been recovered in a very broken state and put together. The most important discoveries, however, next to the inscribed stones found, are the heroic statue of Hermes carrying the infant Dionysus by Praxiteles (Fig. 96), and a Victory, the head and arms of which are lost, the work of Paeonios.†

The subjects of the sculptures in the pediments of this temple are described by Pausanias. In the eastern pediment the Contest between Pelops and Oenomaus was by Paeonios, whose name has now been discovered carved in the marble; and in the western pediment the Battle between the Centaurs and Lapithae was by Alkamenes. These works have been

* This sculptor, though contemporary with the architect of Ephesus, must not be mistaken for him.

† Discovered by Dr. Hirschfeld in 1878. Casts of both the *Hermes* and *Victory* are in the British Museum, obtained from Berlin. The originals of all found are preserved by the Greek Government in the Museum at Athens. The base of the great statue of Zeus by Pheidias was also found *in situ*, made of black limestone (marble?) about 21ft. wide by 31ft. deep. This was in 1880, when many parts of the architectural ornament and pavement of the temple were also discovered.

A.S.

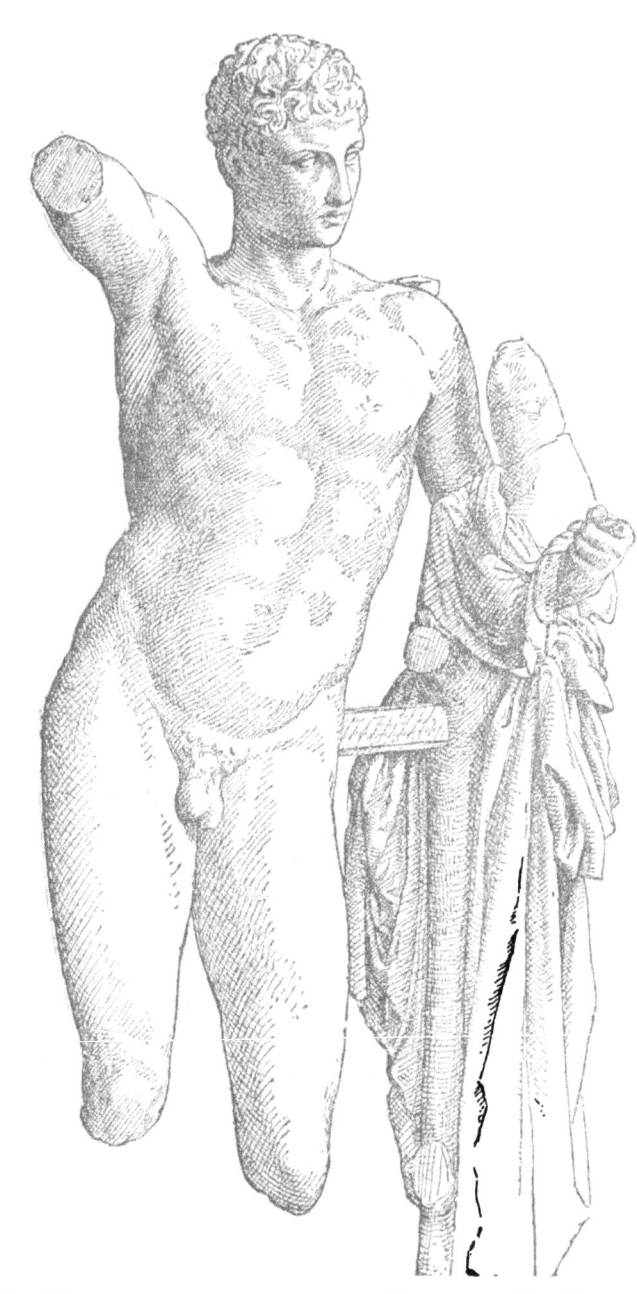

FIG. 96.—HERMES CARRYING THE INFANT DIONYSOS. BY PRAXITELES.
Recently discovered at Olympia. A cast is in the British Museum.

critically described by Mr. Newton in a valuable lecture before
the Royal Academy (Feb. 1880).   Of the Victory, Mr. Newton
said that "the flying drapery was well expressed, though dry and
meagre in parts, yet showing the influence of Pheidias.   The
pedimental sculptures by him (Paeonios) are inferior.   Those by
Alkamenes are better preserved, but though bold and original,
and fine in design, yet bordering on the extravagant and wanting
in harmony.   In both the same shortcomings in the execution
are observable ; the draperies turgid with bloated folds, and the
forms of the figures not understood.   The two great sculptors,
he thinks, left them to be executed by half-trained local sculptors
who ʻscampedʼ their work.   The Metopes found are of a better
school, but austere as Peloponnesian art is generally."

The Hermes with the infant Dionysos was in the Heraeum
(Temple of Juno), according to Pausanias, who speaks of it as the
work of Praxiteles.   Mr. Newton says "all the finer and more
delicate traits which distinguished the style of Praxiteles, that
play of passing emotion in the features, that robustness tempered
by grace, the consummate technical skill, concealed, not vaunt-
ingly displayed, which ancient critics state to have been the
special excellence of Praxiteles, are apparent in this statue."
The legs have not been found, neither have the right arm
and both hands, but the head is perfect.   The young Dionysos
resting on the arm is much injured, and a part of the drapery
over the arm, which is carried in a manner similar to that in the
Vatican *Hermes*, which fine statue this resembles in style, as it
does also the Hermes in the Græco-Roman Room No. 3 in the
British Museum, known as the Farnese Mercury.

It should be stated that it was Winckelmann who induced the
French Government to explore Olympia.   So far back as 1820
some fragments were then found and deposited in the Louvre.   But
the recent recovery of the Hermes and the pediment statues by
Alkamenes and Paeonios is of far greater importance, as enabling
us to identify the work of Praxiteles, the sculptor of the famous
Venus of Knidos.   The style and works of Praxiteles, however,
will come in for consideration further on, while some other
sculptures of this period require to be here noticed.

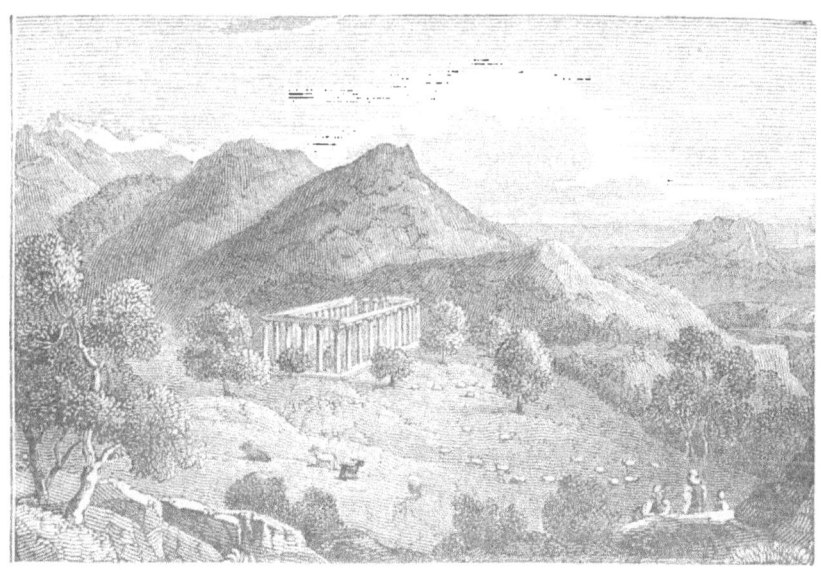

Fig. 97.—Temple of Apollo Epicurios. Phigalia.

TEMPLE OF APOLLO AT PHIGALIA.

Iktinos, the architect of the Parthenon, was employed to build a temple to Apollo Epicurios near the ancient Phigalia in Arcadia at the time after the plague in 430 B.C. (Fig. 97). The frieze of this temple is in the British Museum, placed round the walls of the room in which are the casts of the Ægina pediments, called the Hellenic Room. They decorated the interior, and the figures are in high relief, showing very strong action, with draperies much contorted and exaggerated in the curves of the folds, as if the sculptor having noticed the fine effect in the Parthenon figures had tried not only to imitate but to surpass them, and thus failed while becoming too artificial, and departing from the true forms sanctioned by Pheidias. There is, however, much power and originality in some of these works, as in Fig. 98, of the Amazon being dragged from her horse. The name of the sculptor or sculptors of these is not known. There are twenty-three slabs, eleven representing the battle between the Centaurs and Lapithae, the rest the contest of the Greeks and Amazons. This frieze was placed about 23 feet from the ground, being a little more than two feet in height. There were originally twenty-four slabs extending about a hundred feet in length, so

that one is lost. The ruins were discovered in 1812 by the late
Mr. Cockerell, R.A., Mr. Forster, and two Germans, Messrs.
Haller von Hallerstein and Linkh, to whom we owe the recovery
of the Ægina marbles. These were purchased by the English

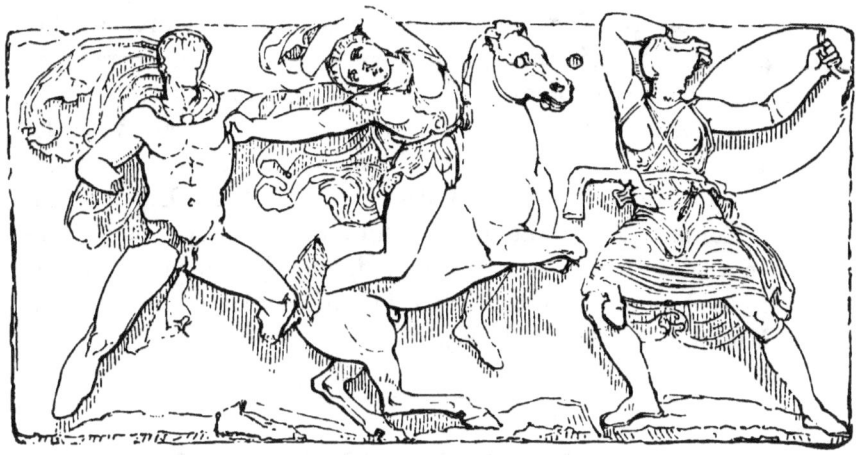

FIG. 98.—FRIEZE OF THE TEMPLE AT PHIGALIA (27¼ IN. HIGH). *Brit. Mus.*

Government for £15,000 and brought here in 1815, when they
were put together by Mr. Westmacott. Opinions of critics differ
as to the merits of these sculptures. Flaxman thought they
were of the same age as the Parthenon, but inferior in style and

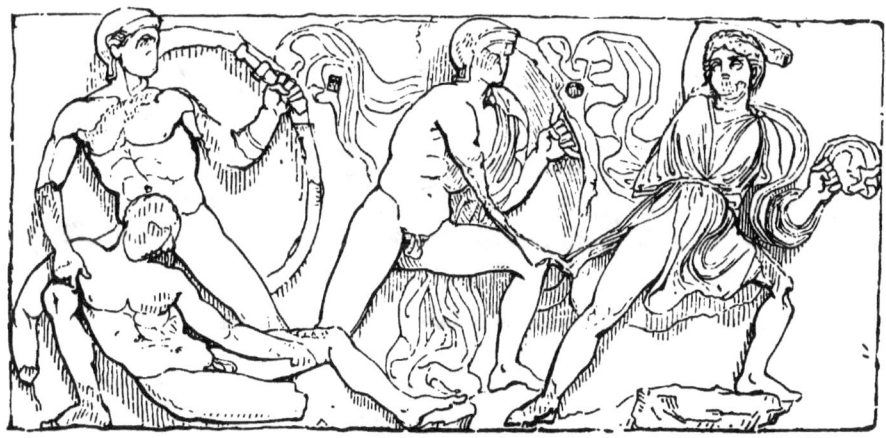

FIG. 99.—FRIEZE FROM THE TEMPLE OF PHIGALIA.

work generally, though in parts of the draperies equal to them; " but in proportions they are unequal to the Parthenon marbles, which possess truth united with form, which is the essence of sculpture." Mr. G. Scharf remarks, "There is a fatness in the forms; the attitudes of some of the figures seem to be ignorantly copied from the Temple of Theseus; and there is a remarkable degree of flourish in the drapery upon the background, introduced merely by way of ornament and to fill spaces between some of the figures. Such waving draperies are only to be seen with the same effect upon some of the Etruscan engravings on bronze mirrors and cistæ" ('Crystal Palace, Greek Court, Handbook'). Mr. Combe remarks the want of uniformity of style, as if more than one sculptor had been engaged, and that in some the legs are too short and the just proportions of the figure not preserved ('Museum Marbles,' vol. iv.).

TEMPLE OF NIKÈ-APTEROS (WINGLESS VICTORY).

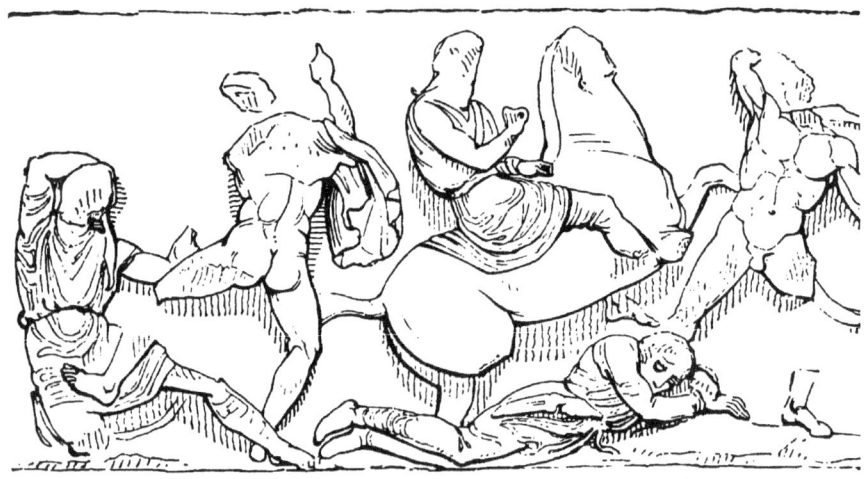

FIG. 100.—UPPER FRIEZE OF THE TEMPLE OF NIKÈ-APTEROS (48 IN. HIGH).

PORTIONS of a frieze (now in the Elgin Room of the British Museum), from the little temple of Nikè Apteros, near the Propylaea of the Acropolis at Athens, built in the time of

Kimon, B.C. 450, should be noticed as showing work of the
Pheidian period.   The drapery is larger in style than in the

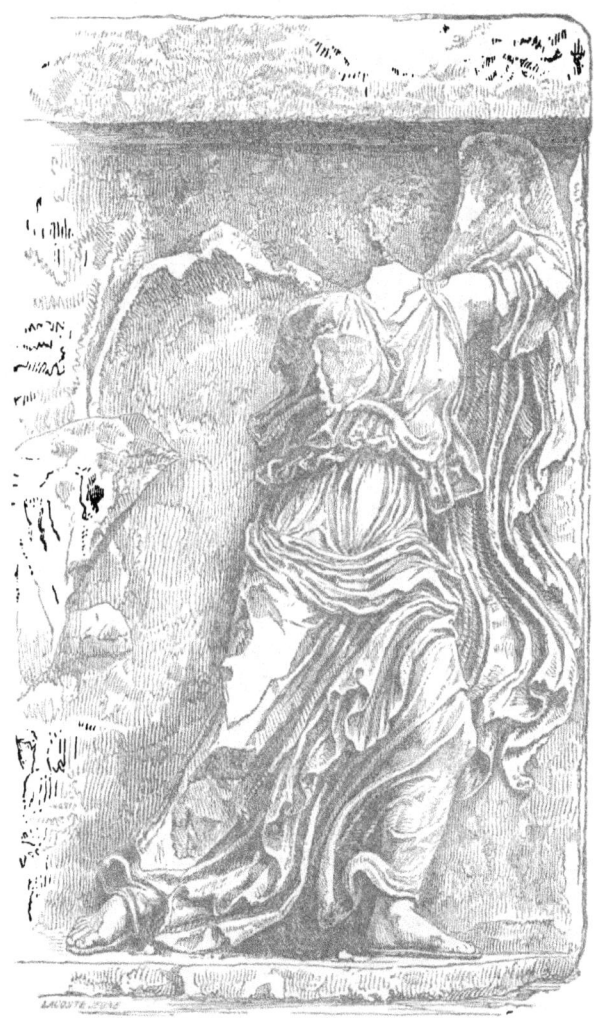

Fig. 101.—From the Frieze of the Temple of Nikè Apteros.
Victory leading a Bull.

A cast is in the British Museum.

Phigalian reliefs, which these sculptures somewhat resemble.
There is also a similarity to the Lycian sculptures.   They are

placed for comparison above the Parthenon frieze. They belong
to an upper and a lower frieze, four from the upper being the

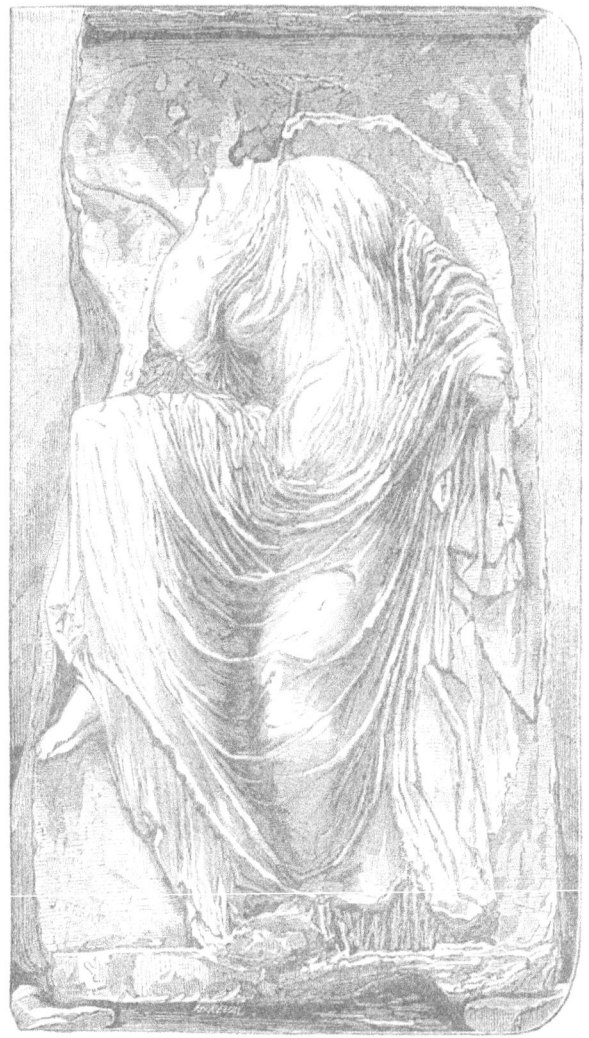

FIG. 102.—FROM THE FRIEZE OF THE TEMPLE OF NIKÈ APTEROS.

(*About* 48 *inches high.*)

original marbles, and the fifth a cast representing, in high relief,
Athenian warriors fighting with men, some in Persian, others

in Greek dress. The four casts from slabs of the lower frieze represent five figures of 'Victory,' two of which (partly seen in Fig. 101) are leading a bull to sacrifice. "These reliefs are all in the finest style" (*Newton*). The grand treatment of the draperies is especially remarkable in the beautiful figure with the one foot raised as if to tie the sandal (Fig. 102), in which the form is finely shown beneath the drapery.

THE MAUSOLEUM AT HALIKARNASSOS.

THE discovery by Mr. Newton, in the year 1857, of the ruins with sculptured figures in the round and friezes belonging to the famous tomb of Mausolos (died 353 B.C.)—which was raised to his memory by his wife Artemisia at Halikarnassos in Caria—was an event of very great interest. It brought to light the works of no less than five sculptors whose names had long been known through Pliny's account (lib. xxxvi. c. 5) of the structure which gave the name " Mausoleum " to all tombs that approached this in importance and magnificence of decoration. The Greeks called a tomb of this kind *Heroon*, and this particular one so surpassed all others that it was named amongst the seven wonders of the world. It was of Parian marble, 140ft. high, pyramidal in form of steps, supported on a peristyle of Ionic columns on a lofty basement. The whole was surmounted by a colossal group of a chariot and four horses, with Mausolos standing in it, and another figure—supposed to be either a goddess as charioteer or Artemisia herself, who died before the completion of the work. This group was the work of Pythis or Pythius, who was also the architect ; while the various statues, lions, and reliefs—of which fragments more or less broken are to be seen in the British Museum—were by Skopas, Leochares, Bryaxis, and Timotheus. The east side was the work of Skopas, the north of Bryaxis, the south of Timotheus, and the west of Leochares, as described by Pliny, who also names Pythis as the sculptor of the quadriga and figures on the summit. In style these sculptures resemble the Phigalian reliefs, having similar strong action and flying draperies (see Figs. 100, 101). All these sculptors belonged to the later Athenian school ; and it will be observed in their works, fine as they are, how far the art had already begun to decline. The head of Mausolos, Mr. Newton remarks, is "not of the Hellenic type, as he was a Carian," but it is remarkable in characteristic expression and as a portrait. The date of these works is about B.C. 352.

The sculptors were selected from those who had already distinguished themselves. Scopas was a native of Paros, and he and Praxiteles, after the time of Pheidias, were heads of the school of architecture and sculpture at Athens, which arose subsequent to the Peloponnesian war. His name is repeatedly mentioned by other ancient writers besides Pliny and Pausanias — by Cicero ('De Divin.' lib. i.) and by Horace ('Car.' b. iv. ode 8)—

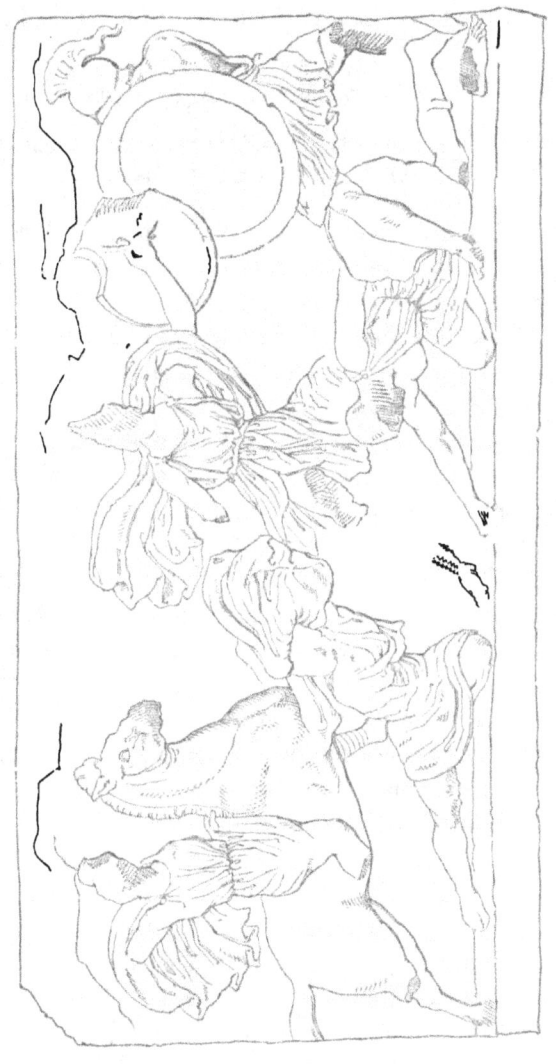

Fig. 103.—From the Frieze of the Tomb of Mausolos, Halikarnassos (29 in. high).
British Museum.

"Quas aut Parrhasius protulit aut Scopas ;
  Hic saxo, liquidis ille coloribus.
  Solers nunc hominem ponere, nunc Deum."

It is doubtful whether he or Praxiteles was the sculptor of the

Niobe Statues (Fig. 140) which were in Pliny's time in the temple of Apollo Sosianus in Rome. A Greek epigram upon the Niobe is extant in which Praxiteles is thus named:

'Εκ ζωῆς με θεοῖ τεύξαν λίθον· ἐκ δε λίθοιο
Ζωην Πραξιτέλης ἔμπαλιν εἰργάσατο.

"I am she whom the gods from life had changed into marble.
    Praxiteles by his art woke me from stone into life."

Bryaxis was of the school of Rhodes, where he made five of the smaller bronze colossal statues of the Sun God (Plin. l. xxxiv. c. 7). In Knidos he made other statues. Clemens of Alexandria says that some attributed works of Pheidias to him, while Columella includes him with such masters as Polukleitos, Lysippos, and Praxiteles.

Timotheus and Leochares appear to have been Athenians. Pausanias mentions the latter as the sculptor of several statues in bronze, and in ivory and gold. Plutarch speaks of his Rape of Ganymede as his masterpiece. Of this a copy in marble is in the Vatican collection—a fine group of a figure, nude except a mantle across the neck falling down behind, raised by the eagle through the air, while his dog looks upwards from the ground.

An interesting illustration of the way in which the discovery of one example of sculpture leads to the identification of others, may be noticed in connection with these works from Halikarnassos. When the twelve slabs sculptured with the battle of the Greeks and Amazons, which were discovered in 1846 built into the walls of the fortress of Budrum, were afterwards removed by permission of the Porte to be presented to the British Museum, they led to researches directed by Mr. Newton on the site of the Mausoleum. Here four more slabs were found. It was soon observed that these sculptures bore a close resemblance to a solitary slab which had for years been in the possession of the Marchese Serra at Genoa; it was soon decided that it belonged to the series; and the result was that this slab was purchased by the Museum Trustees, and once more placed amongst its companion sculptures from which it had been so long separated.

It will have been seen from what has been said of the works of sculpture which are known to have been executed by the sculptors contemporary with Pheidias, and by others who followed in the school which arose around him, and who formed what is spoken of as 'the later Athenian School,' that none approached the great examples of the Parthenon. Sculpture then reached the highest point in the grandest style, whether in the treatment of the statue in the round or of bas-relief as in the frieze, or alto-relievo as in the metopes. As to the Chryselephantine statues of Pheidias, it may be concluded without hesitation that though we are compelled to rely upon descriptions only, they must have been works of the great master even more beautiful than the marbles. There is every reason to conclude that although colour was applied, and the eyes perhaps even made to resemble life very closely by means of enamel of some kind, yet such was the perfection of form obtained, that these were minor adornments only adopted to give the appearance of real life and complete the illusion in the minds of the worshippers. It may be difficult to reconcile the minute execution of detail in the work of Pheidias with his grand ideal of the beautiful in simple form. But the descriptions recorded prove that he carried 'finish' to its extreme point, as Leonardo and other great artists after him have delighted in doing, as if to bestow the utmost of his art was a point of devotion and worship. Nicephorus Gregoras ('Hist. Byzant.' lib. viii.), writing in the 14th cent., said, Φειδίας ἐν Ἕλλησι μέγας ἔκ τε τῆς μελίττης, ἔκ τε τέττιγος, "Pheidias among the Greeks great at bees and grasshoppers," alluding to his having sculptured these insects in bronze with such exact resemblance.

Of the few statues that can be confidently attributed to the contemporaries of Pheidias, some are described amongst the examples, of which the engravings will afford a good general idea. The attention of the student should be given to those two important statues (Fig. 125) in the Hellenic Room in the British Museum, representing the one, an athlete of full life-size, the other a youth; each winding a fillet round his head, and considered to be copies from the celebrated statues of

Polukleitos, called the Diadumeni, mentioned by Lucian and Pliny (see Fig. 130).

Certain bas-reliefs, resembling in style the art of Pheidias,

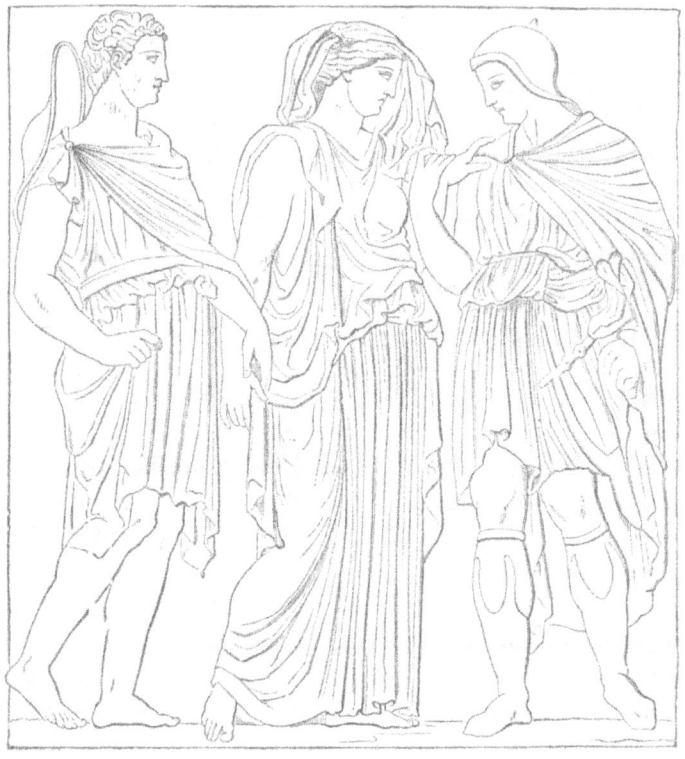

FIG. 104.—BAS-RELIEF OF HERMES, EURYDICE, ORPHEUS.
Similar to the one at Naples, which bears the inscription in sharply-cut letters.

are to be found in the museums, such as that in the Naples collection, of *Orpheus, Eurydice,* and *Hermes* (Fig. 104), in-

ΗΡΜΗΣ   ΞΥΡΥΔΙΚΗ   ΣΥΞΦϙΟ

scribed in letters of the time, two repetitions of which exist, one in the Louvre, the other in the Villa Albani; the alto-relievo of Perseus and Andromeda in the Capitol at Rome, a cast of which is in the Crystal Palace Collection; a large relief, in Pentelic marble, of two combatants and a horse, in the Villa Albani, a cast of which (No. 34) is also in the Crystal Palace.

The bas-relief of Eleusis, discovered in 1859 (Fig. 105), may perhaps also be considered to be of about this time. The names of the sculptors of these works are, however, unknown.

The influence of the sculptures of the Parthenon is seen in many directions, as has already been observed in referring to the Phigalian, the Halikarnassian, and the Olympian sculptures; but besides these, it will be seen in comparing the frieze of the monument called the Nereid monument, at Xanthus, on the walls of the New Lycian Room in the British Museum, the date of which is considered to be about 350 B.C. In some of these slabs the resemblance to the Parthenon figures is remarkable, as in Nos. 38 and 37.

In the works of the later Athenian school, at the head of which were Skopas and Praxiteles, the sublime ideal of Greek art was no longer sustained by any new creations that can be compared with those of the Pheidian school; no rivalry with those great masters seemed to be attempted. The severe and grand was beyond the comprehension, or probably uncongenial to the spirit of the age, which inclined towards the poetic, the graceful, the sentimental and romantic, as we have already observed in speaking of the æsthetic tendencies of that period. The whole range of the beautiful myths found abundant illustration in forms entirely different from the ancient archaic representations, and in these the fancy of the sculptor was allowed the freest and fullest indulgence. Nymphs, Nereids, Mænads, and Bacchantes occupied the chisel of the sculptor in every form of graceful beauty (Fig. 106).

After this epoch, to which so many of the fine statues belong —repetitions in marble of famous originals in bronze—Greek sculpture took another phase in accordance with the social life and the taste of the age, which inclined towards the feeling for display that arose with the domination of the Macedonian power brought to its height by the conquests and ambition of Alexander the Great. Lysippos, a self-taught sculptor of Sikyon, was the leading artist of his time. He was evidently a student of nature and individual character, as he was the first to become celebrated for his portraits, especially those of Alexander. He

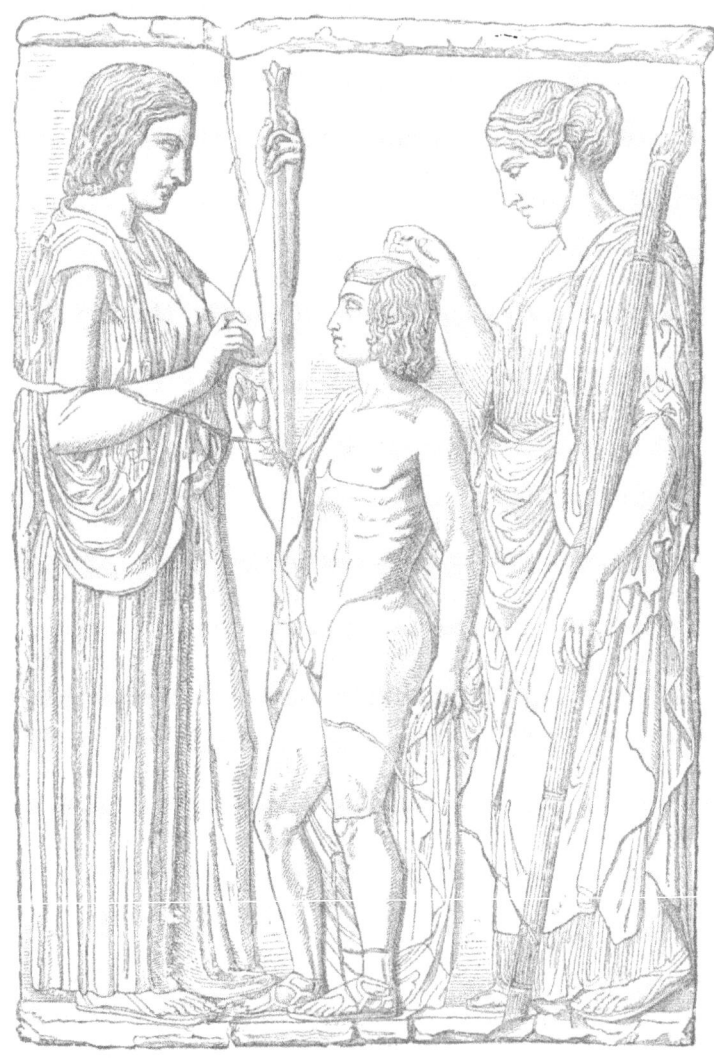

FIG. 105.—BAS-RELIEF OF ELEUSIS. CERES. TRIPTOLEMUS. PROSERPINE.

Discovered 1859. In the Museum at Athens.

departed from the severe and grand style, and in the native conceit of all self-taught men sneered at the art of Polykleitos in the well-known saying recorded of him, "Polykleitos made men as they seem to be, but I make them as they ought to be."* However this may be true or not, Cicero said, "Polycleti Doryphorum sibi Lysippus ajebat magistrum fuisse," and we know that his statue of Hephaistion was attributed to Polykleitos ('De Claris Oratoribus'). He seems to have been the first great naturalistic sculptor—"Gloria Lysippo est animosa effingere signa" (Propertius, lib. iii. El. 8). Pliny says that he made the heads of his statues smaller than the ancients, and defined the hair especially, making the bodies more slender and sinewy ('corpora graciliora siccioraque'), by which the height of the figure seemed greater. The Apoxyomenos (*see* Fig. 121) may be regarded as a good example of his work ; this however was in bronze, and so probably were all his statues. The taste for colossal statues was met by many from his hand, such as the Hercules of Tarentum, from which perhaps the well-known Farnese statue by Glykon was taken, and a colossal Zeus, besides many others, to the number of several hundreds, as related by Pliny and Pausanias.

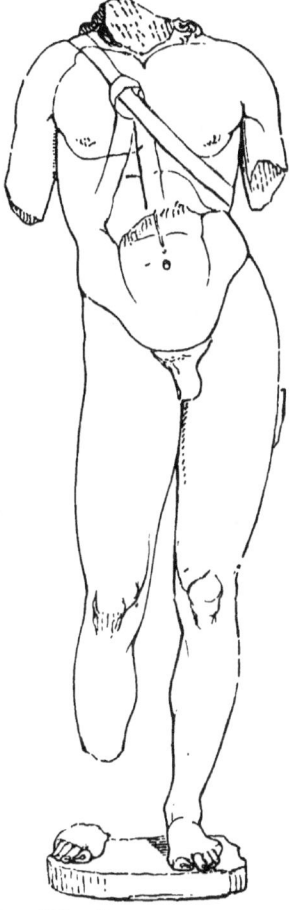

FIG. 106.—IKAROS : FORMERLY CALLED EROS.

Marble : In British Museum.

Found on the Acropolis, Athens.

In the style of Praxiteles.

* The words of Pliny are—after referring to there being no Latin word for 'Symmetria,' which Lysippus always preserved although departing from the 'quadrates veterum statuas'—"vulgoque dicebat ab illis factos, quales essent homines ; à se, quales viderentur esse," which bears a meaning that would be more in keeping with his naturalistic style of representing men as he saw them.

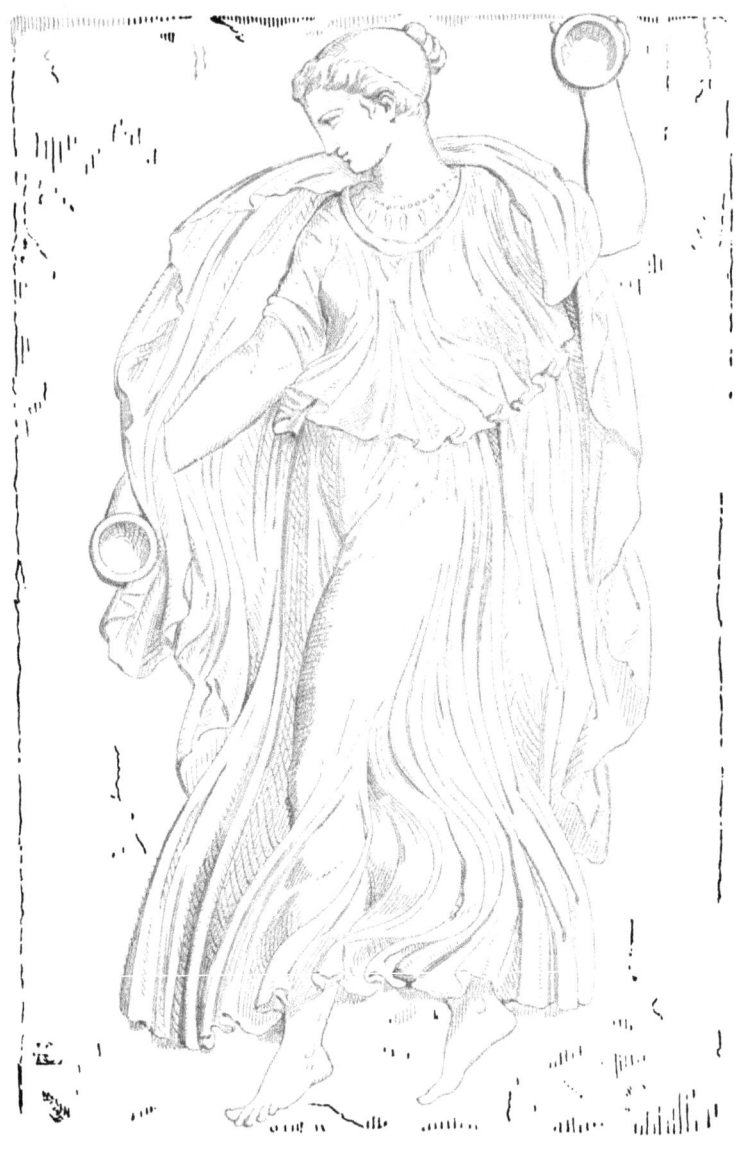

FIG. 107.—THE CYMBAL-PLAYER. A BAS-RELIEF IN THE VILLA ALBANI.
Style of Skopas.

The famous Colossus of Rhodes has been also attributed to him, though more probably it was the work of his pupil Chares. His great bronze equestrian group of Alexander and the horsemen who fell at the battle of the Granicus, was brought to Rome by Metellus (146 B.C.) to be shown in his 'triumph.' Such was the general influence of Lysippos under the high patronage of Alexander the Great, who only permitted him, Apelles the painter, and Pyrgoteles the glyptic artist to represent him, that the style which then prevailed and retained its influence until the time of Augustus has been generally called 'Macedonian.'

A peculiar treatment of the hair in two strong rising curls above the centre of the forehead is characteristic of this period. This arose from Lysippos having in his portrait busts and statues adhered so closely to this peculiarity in Alexander. It is seen in the head of him in the British Museum (Mausoleum Room) and on the coins. It was to flatter Alexander that he gave this peculiarity to all his heroic figures and to the gods ; it is seen in the head of the Colossus of Rhodes, on the coins, and again in the heads of the colossal marble figures of Castor and Pollux on Monte Cavallo, at Rome, which—though bearing the names of 'Pheidias' and 'Praxiteles,' absurdly carved upon the pedestals in letters of a kind not used before the time of Sixtus V.—are fine works, not of very high pretensions, but probably copies from bronze statues of the Macedonian period. Visconti considered them to be Roman works of the time of Nero, but Mr. G. Scharf expresses an opinion that they are copies from bronze originals of the Macedonian epoch. They were evidently copied in the Augustan Age. " The elaborate curls and horn-like projection of the hair indicate the Alexandrian period. This is further borne out by the small head, projecting brow, large eye, full neck, and violent expression of countenance. The limbs tapering down to the extremities are very different from the known works of Pheidias." * Flaxman accepted the

* These statues, complete with the horses, were cast for the Crystal Palace collection, and erected at great expense ; it is much to be regretted that they are hidden under the great orchestra, and that the difficulties and cost of removal are considered to be too serious to be undertaken. Such important and interesting examples would find a more fitting place in the British Museum, and might possibly be acquired at a merely nominal cost.

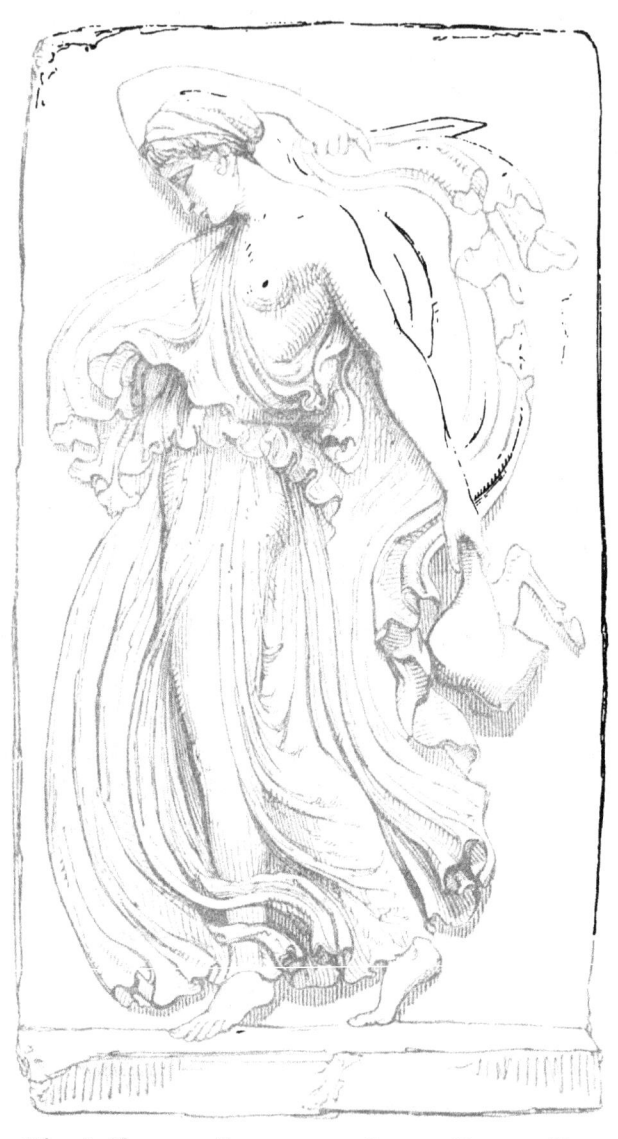

FIG. 108.—A MÆNAD. BAS-RELIEF. IN THE BRITISH MUSEUM.
Fine example of drapery. Attributed to Skopas.

names given to them on the pedestals, finding in them a resemblance to a figure in the Parthenon frieze, and "because the animated character and style of sculpture seem peculiar to the age in which those artists lived."

In the same room with the Halikarnassos marbles above referred to there is a cast of a metope, the original of which was for some time placed in the South Kensington Museum with Dr. Schliemann's collection. It is of marble, and represents the Sun God, Helios, in his four-horsed chariot (quadriga). It is a work which, though small in size—being about a quarter that of the life—shows excellent design and good work, but not of any originality; it is evidently of that borrowed style which always follows upon the great achievements of a school like that of Pheidias. This metope was found at Ilium Novum in 1872, and is said to have belonged to a Doric temple. It is the most important, in an artistic point of view, of any of the sculptures recovered by Dr. Schliemann, and as to style has been compared with the works of the school of Lysippos.

In the frieze round the Choragic monument of Lysikrates at Athens, sculptured in the year 334 B.C., the subject of which is Dionysos transforming the Tyrrhenian pirates into dolphins, a certain softness in the forms and picturesque action suggests the inquiry whether the reliefs may not be the work of Praxiteles, to whom as regards date they might be attributable. They are certainly not like the work of Lysippos (Figs. 109 and 112). The entire structure is to be seen as a cast in the Crystal Palace.

The discovery at Ephesus by Mr. Wood in 1873, of the ruins and sculptured columns of the famous temple of Diana, built B.C. 323, brought to light the "*columnæ celatæ*" described by Pliny. The lower drum of one, six feet in diameter, is now in the Elgin Room of the British Museum. Six figures on this are full life-size in mezzo-relievo, and in the Hermes and the winged Thanatos the style of Lysippos may, it is thought, be recognized (*Newton*). That Skopas sculptured one of the columns is related by Pliny, but that any of these fragments in the Museum are to be attributed to him is not at present decided. Pliny gives the number of columns as 127, each the

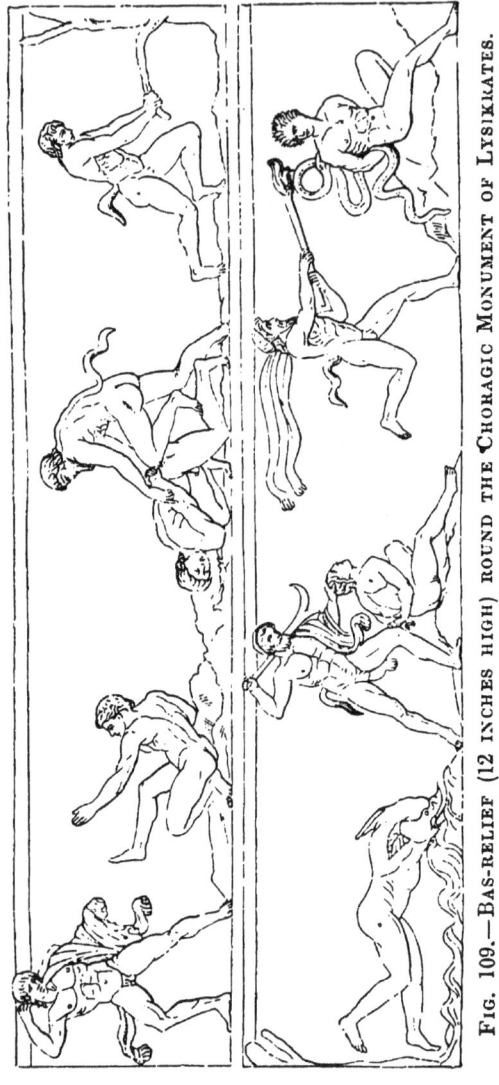

FIG. 109.—BAS-RELIEF (12 INCHES HIGH) ROUND THE CHORAGIC MONUMENT OF LYSIKRATES. *In the style of Praxiteles.*

gift of a king, and says that 36 of them were *celatæ* (sculptured in relief); their height was 60ft. Roman. Mr. Newton remarks that the surface of some of the square bases, which are sculptured in high relief, show the marks of a column having rested, and that " we thus have the combination of a richly - sculptured shaft resting on a richly - sculptured square pedestal, a combination which may have been the prototype of Trajan's and other triumphal columns." The pediments of this temple no doubt were filled with statues, as in other instances, but Mr. Wood did not succeed in finding any fragments belonging to them, if they ever existed. The temple, which, as ' The Artemisium,' was celebrated as one of the seven wonders of the ancient world, in Roman times had become the depository of an immense treasure of works of art of all kinds, none of which have been as yet discovered.* The Goths burnt and plundered the temple in A.D. 262. A comparison between the sculptures of the *columnœ celatœ* with those of the Mausoleum and the Priene Temple now in the British Museum, will show that they belong to the same school and are quite worthy of the age of Skopas (*Newton*). It may be remarked, however, that there is about the Ephesus columns, which are unique of their kind, a certain Asiatic taste which is also shown in the more ancient sculptures of the old temple dedicated to the Asiatic Artemis. She was represented in the temple statue with many rows of breasts, her robe ornamented with bees, flowers, fruit, heads of animals,

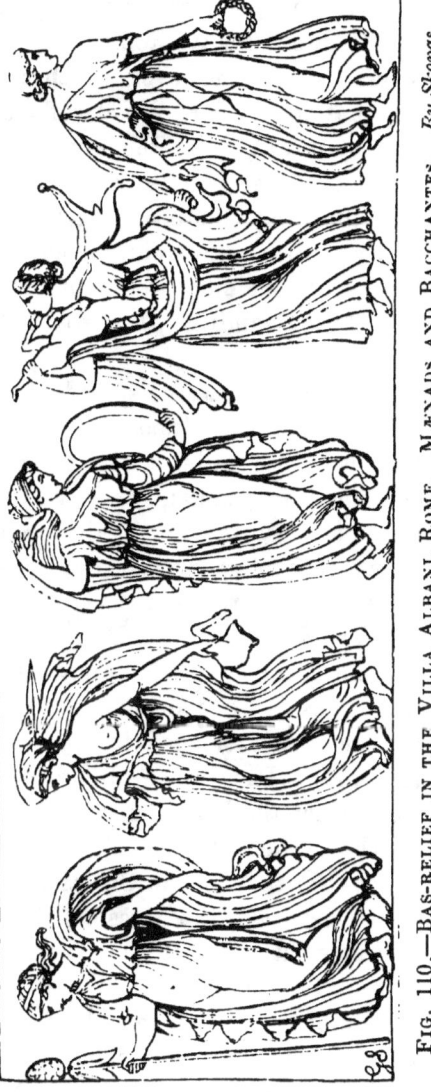

FIG. 110.—BAS-RELIEF IN THE VILLA ALBANI, ROME. MÆNADS AND BACCHANTES. *By Skopas.*

* Though Mr. Newton is compelled to ask, " When we think how much history has gained by this exploration, partial and inadequate as it has been, of the ruins of Ephesus, when we review the marvellous discoveries which have recently taken place in Cyprus and the Troad, and actually now going on at Olympia and Mycenae—why, with all the appliances, and with boundless wealth at the command of individuals, if not of governments, do we grudge for these great enterprises the money which is daily wasted on trivial and ignoble objects ? " (' Essays on Art and Archæology.')

and the modius (corn measure) for her crown, as the Mother
of all life. Many Roman repetitions of this Artemis exist.
There is now, however, in these sculptures recovered by the
explorations of Mr. Wood sufficient to enable us to judge of
the style, and it is therefore feasible to speak of the school
of Ephesus as one in which a vast amount of architectonic
sculpture was produced, together with innumerable statues in
bronze, silver, and gold, many of a votive character. These
it may be concluded were more allied to the style of Lysippos
and the Alexandrian than to the grand works of the Pheidian
school.

Connected with the spread of the naturalistic taste in sculpture, of which Lysippos was the most distinguished master, as
Skopas and Praxiteles were of the feeling for the pathetic and
emotional in general, we have to notice a singular retrograde
movement in favour of the archaic forms. This may have
arisen in protest against innovations and departure from the
austere symmetry and severe beauty of the classic Athenian
style, somewhat as the Preraphaelite painters of our day took
up the manner of the early Italian schools. This style is
known as the pseudoarchaic, in which the ancient "Hieratic
treatment is prolonged for the sake of religious associations"
(*Newton*). It is to be observed remarkably in bas-reliefs and
coins after the Macedonian period, and in some statues, as that
of the Apollo (Fig. 111), possibly a work of Roman times,
which has the hair in the stiff curls of the true Archaic Apollo
placed near it in the Museum.

Rhodes had unquestionable right to give her name to a school
of sculpture, both from the great antiquity of the origin of the
culture of the arts in the island, and from the number of more
than one hundred colossal bronze statues of the Sun God, at
the head of which stood the great Colossus by Chares, who was
the most renowned pupil of Lysippos.

The Rhodian school is also distinguished by those remarkable
examples of sculpture in marble of large groups of figures—the
Toro Farnese (Fig. 141) and the Laocoon (Fig. 136). In these
works—which are described amongst the *Examples*—there is the
same feeling for display of artistic accomplishment that has been

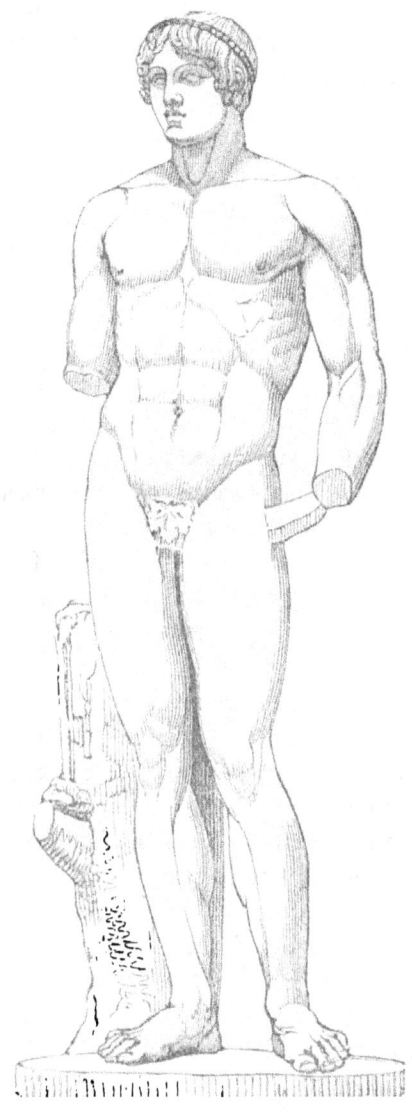

FIG. 111.—APOLLO.

Heroic size.   Marble.   British Museum.

noticed as characteristic of the Macedonian age, with that effort at the pathetic, especially in the Laocoon, which belongs to the finer style of the later schools, as displayed in the works of Skopas and Praxiteles, as seen in the Niobe figures and others.

At Pergamus, another school allied in style to that of Ephesus arose, of which the chief sculptor was Pyromachos, who, according to Pliny, flourished in the 120th Olympiad, B.C. 300—298, with Eutychides, Dahippos, Kephisodotos, called the son of Praxiteles, and Timarchos. Pliny also mentions a great work by many artists (artifices) representing the battles of Attalus against the Gauls, in which Pyromachos, Isigonos, Stratonikos, and Antigonos were engaged (lib. xxxv. c. 8). Pergamus was raised to the highest importance under Attalus (B.C. 247—197), and Eumenes II. his successor, who adorned it with many fine buildings and founded the famous library. A statue of Æsculapius by Pyromachos was a work of some note in the splendid temple at Pergamus, and is to be seen on the coins of that city. It is also conjectured that the well-known Dying Gladiator and the group of Paetus and Arria of the Villa Ludovisi are copies of bronzes by Pyromachos (Scharf). However this may be, the subjects are evidently taken from scenes that occurred at this time, and were characteristic of the Gauls, who constantly slew themselves and their wives and children rather than allow them to fall into the hands of their conquerors.

The vigorous naturalistic style of these statues, surpassing anything of preceding schools in the effort at expression, may be taken as characteristic of the school of Pergamus, then completely under Roman influence, and destined to become more so. But all question as to the nature of the sculptures was set at rest by the discovery of many large works in high relief by the German expedition at Pergamus in 1875. These are now in the Museum at Berlin. They are of almost colossal proportions, representing, as Pliny described, the wars of Attalus and the Battles with the Giants. In these the nude figures especially show the effort to display artistic ability and great energy in the action. In these points there is observable a connection with the well-known and very striking example of sculpture of

ΑΓΑΣΙΑΣ.
ΔΩΣΙΘΕΟΥ
ΕΦΕΣΙΟΣ
Ε ΠΟΙΕΙ

this order—the Fighting Gladiator, or more properly the Warrior of Agasias, who, as is certain from the inscription on his work, was an Ephesian.

The equally renowned statue of the Apollo Belvedere, finely conceived and admirably modelled as it undoubtedly is, bears the stamp of artistic display which removes it from the style of the great classic works of sculpture (see *Examples*).

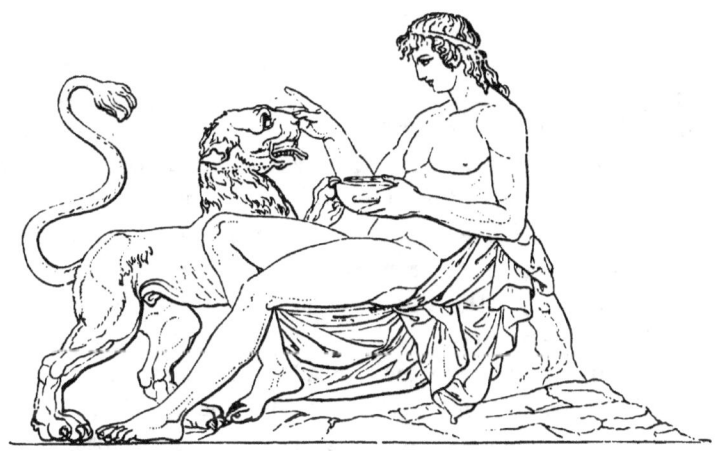

Fig. 112.—Figure on the Frieze of the Monument of Lysikrates.

Thought to resemble the Theseus of the Parthenon.

GREEK INSCRIPTIONS.

STATUES, bas-reliefs, engraved gems and cameos, coins, metal mirrors, and many other things ornamented by ancient artists and art-workmen, frequently have names of deities, heroes, kings, and places, with sometimes the name of the sculptor. Examples of this are to be seen in many of the descriptions here given of statues, bas-reliefs, coins, and gems.

The form of letter and the manner of writing changed with time; consequently, by observing these, the date of a work of art may be found approximately. In early times letters were scratched, as it were, very rudely into clay, marble, or bronze, and were thin and irregular; if painted with a brush as on vases they would be thick and perhaps blotchy. "It is probable that the custom of engraving words on stone or metal began among the Greeks soon after they became familiar with the alphabet which they borrowed from the Phœnicians. What may have been the date of those very early Greek inscriptions which Herodotus and Pausanias describe as written in Cadmeian characters, and which they believed antecedent to the first Olympiad, 776 B.C., we have no sure information" (*Newton*, Essays, 'Greek Inscriptions'). On the leg of one of the colossi at Abou Simbel is a Greek inscription in archaic letters recording the names of Greek mercenaries who served under king Psammetichus I. or II., either B.C. 611 or 589. Very ancient Greek letters may be seen on some of the statues brought from Branchidæ in the Archaic Room of the British Museum. Compared with the Abou Simbel writing these are considered to be of about the same date, between 580 and 520 B.C. In the islands of Thera, Melos, Crete, Paros, and Naxos very early inscriptions have been found "which want the four double consonants Ξ, Ψ, Φ, X, which the Greeks added to the Phœnician alphabet from some other source" (*Newton*). These are of the seventh century B.C. The lists of the treasure of the Parthenon from Pericles to the fall of Athenian supremacy, cut into slabs of marble, still exist, dating from 434 B.C. to 404 B.C.

Early Greek writing was written from left to right on one line, and from right to left on the next, in the manner which, from its resemblance to the turning of an ox in ploughing, is called the '*Boustrophedon*' (from βους, an ox, and στροφη, turning), as in the following inscription :

ΦΑΝοΔΙΚΟ   φανοδικο

which is the beginning of the celebrated Sigean inscription in the British Museum, "a genuine specimen of Greek writing in Asia Minor, contemporary or nearly so with the Branchidæ inscriptions." On coins and bas-reliefs the letters read in some words backwards, in others forwards (as in the above), which are examples of the thin kind of letter. The famous chest of Kypselos at Elis, Pausanias describes as having *boustrophedon* writing, and winding characters difficult to read. "The letters for the two long vowels *e* and *o*—H and Ω—were in use on the West Coast of Asia Minor in early times long before Simonides used them, and before the Persian war" (*Newton*). The *Kappa* (our K) is the first letter of Korinth and Kroton, and the Digamma F is the first in Elis on the coins, but they were not used in the time of Pheidias. The early forms of the letters Γ, Λ, A, N, Θ, were /\ /_ /\ /\/ ℰ. The letter H was in early writing used as an aspirate as we use it. An epitaph of 432 B.C., in the British Museum, shows this, also that the genitive *ου* is written as O, and the datives are marked by the I *adscript*. The Ω is not used.

In shape letters varied much. The M is straggling and widely spread out, the N has the first limb longer than the second and third ; the A has very short legs, the circle is very low in the stem of Φ, and the O is always small (see Fig. 26). The letters on the archaic bas-relief (Fig. 71) are in Oscan characters.

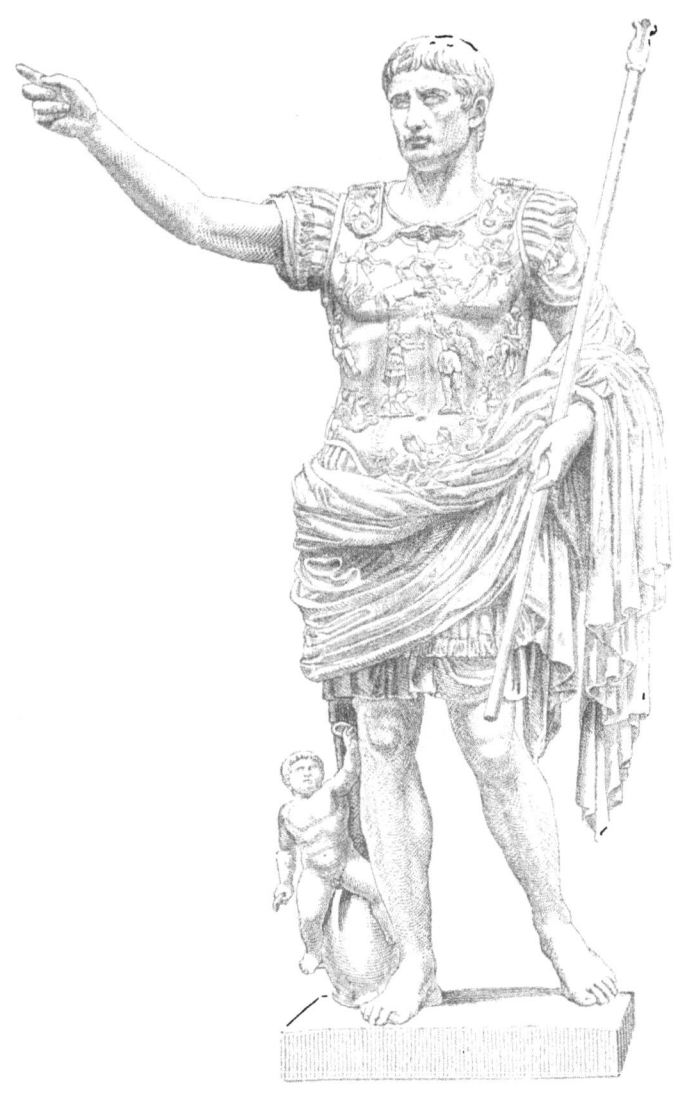

Fig. 113.—Statue of Augustus. *Marble. In the Vatican.*

ROMAN SCULPTURE.

The history of Roman sculpture is soon told. If it have any
real roots, they are to be traced in the ancient Etruscan; for all
that was really characteristic in it as art is associated with that
style. This is shown in that intense naturalism which became
developed so strikingly in the production of portrait statues

and busts, and in those great monumental works in bas-relief which are marked by the same strong feeling for descriptive representation of the most direct and realistic kind, upon their triumphal columns, arches, and Sarcophagi.

As has already been stated, early Roman sculpture, if such it can be called, was entirely the work of Etruscan artists employed by the wealth of Rome to afford the citizens that display of pomp in their worship of the gods and the triumphs of their warriors which their ambition demanded. All important works were made of colossal size. Some of the early Roman (quasi-Etruscan) statues have before been mentioned; others which are spoken of by the historians are a bronze colossus of Jupiter, made by Carvilius of the armour taken in the Samnite war—so large that as it stood on the Capitol it was seen from the Alban Hill. Pliny refers to an Etruscan bronze colossus of Apollo, 80ft. high, in the Palatine Library of the temple of Augustus. A portrait statue of an Orator in the toga, and a Chimæra, both of bronze, are in the Florence Museum.

Sculpture, from the love of it as expressing the beautiful in the ideal form of the deities, or the heroic and the pathetic of humanity, never existed as a growth of Roman civilization. The inclination of the Roman mind was towards social, municipal, and imperial system and ordering; in this direction the Romans were inventors and improvers upon that which they borrowed from the Greeks. But in art they began by hiring, and they ended by debasing the work of the hired.

They took away the bronze statues of Greece as trophies of conquest, covered them with gold, and set them up in the palaces and public places of Rome. They subsidized the sculptors of Greece who under Roman influence had fallen away from their high traditions; they did nothing for the sake of art, but simply manufactured, as it were, copies and imitations of Greek statues for their own use. Happily we have to be grateful for the fact, though we cannot honour the motive. Had it not been for this bestowal of their wealth in the gratification of their taste for luxury and display, many of the renowned statues of ancient Greek art would have been known only by the vague mention of them by Pausanias and Pliny, by the early

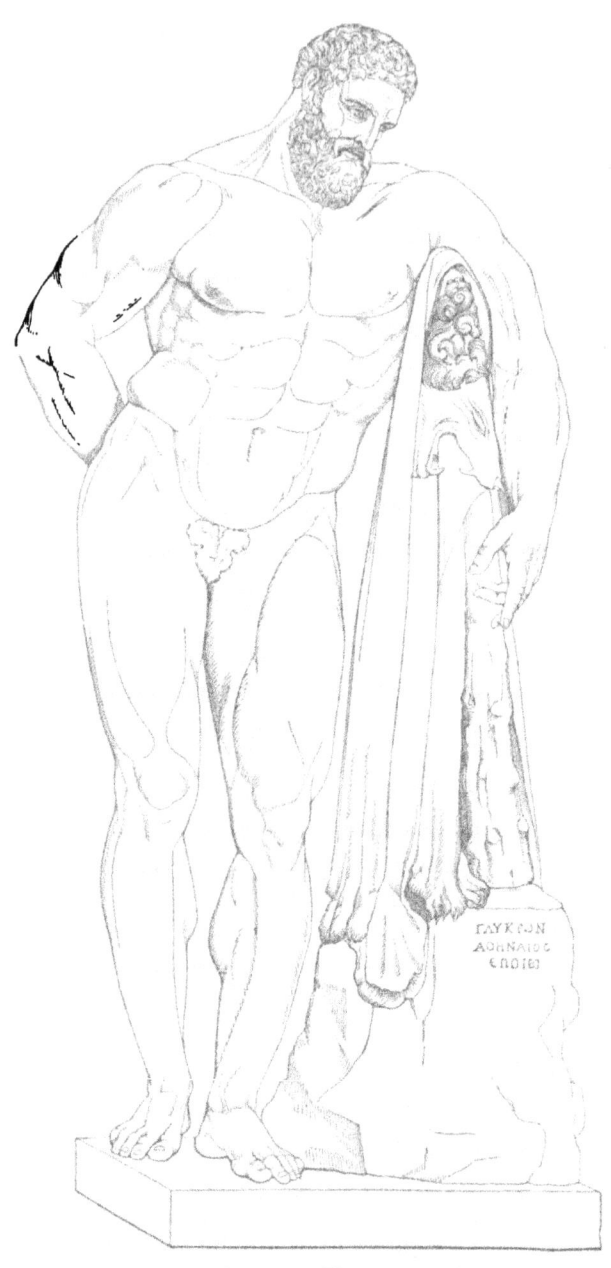

FIG. 114.—THE FARNESE HERCULES. COLOSSAL.
Grechetto Marble. Height, 12 *ft. Naples Museum.*
(Described in *Examples*.)

Christian writers of the Church, or the poetic allusions of the Greek Anthologists and the Latin Epigrammatists.

In architectonic sculpture, as well as in architecture, the Romans proved themselves real inventors, whatever may be the estimate in point of æsthetic merit. To cover with descriptive sculpture the whole of the lofty marble columns of Trajan and Marcus Aurelius Antoninus, in a continuous spiral round the shaft, was a work in every way most remarkable and most valuable, in recording great events of history; and to surmount them with colossal statues of these Emperors was another innovation, especially Roman.

The column of Trajan * was the great work of Apollodorus, the favourite architect of the Emperor, dedicated in A.D. 114. It is 10½ feet in diameter and 127 feet high, made of thirty-four blocks of white marble, twenty-three being in the shaft, nine in the base which is finally sculptured, and two in the capital and *torus*. The reliefs at the base are smaller than those towards the top, being two feet high, increasing to nearly four as they approach the summit; this was, of course, to enable the more distant subjects to be seen equally well with the others, a singular illustration of the intensely practical turn of Roman art in its application. There are about 2500 figures not counting horses, representing the battles and sieges of the Dacian war. The whole of the reliefs are engraved beautifully in the work of Pietro Santi Bartoli. The column of M. Aurelius Antoninus erected A.D. 174, is similar in height, but the sculptures, although in higher relief, are not so good. They represent the conquest of the Marcomans.

The 'triumph' of Paulus Æmilius after the conquest of the Macedonians, 168 B.C., accurately described by Plutarch, took place when Eumenes was king of Pergamus, Ptolemy of Egypt, Antiochus of Syria, and Pharnaces of Pontus; but though he brought vast treasure in gold, silver, and vessels, and jewelled cups, no statues are mentioned. In the next great 'triumph,' however, that of Metellus, 146 B.C., the famous equestrian group of Alexander and his horsemen and foot-soldiers, by Lysippos,

---

* Some of the groups on the Trajan Column were evidently studied by Raphael. A cast of the whole in two sections is in the S. K. Museum.

A.S.

was carried in the procession. Mummius, called Achaicus, as conqueror of the Achaian League at Corinth, is said to have done more in destroying and selling works of art in Greece than any of his Roman predecessors; either being entirely ignorant of art, or valuing money higher, he sold all the paintings and sculptures he had captured, many to the king of Pergamus. Polybius relates that, during the destruction of Corinth, he saw Roman soldiers playing at draughts on the far-famed picture of Dionysos, by Aristides. After this victory over Achaia, Pliny records (lib. xxxvii. c. 1, 2) how the rage for works of art of every kind arose in Rome, and he enumerates many incised gems by such great artists as Dioscorides, Apollonides, and Cronius, with statues in bronze and in gold of Minerva, Mars, and Apollo, which had been taken by the conquerors. A statue of Apollo, by Skopas, was brought by Octavius after his victory at Antium, and placed in the temple on the Palatine Hill: while Sylla despoiled Athens and Olympia; and Verres, as Cicero accused him, took many works of sculpture from Sicily and Asia Minor.

The Augustan age (B.C. 36—A.D. 14), favourable as it was to literature, only contributed to the multiplying of copies of the Greek statues, such as we see in so many instances, some of which are of great excellence, and inestimable as reliable evidence of fine Greek sculpture. These copies were sometimes varied by the sculptor in some immaterial point of detail, as is noticeable in the two statues of Apollo Sauroctonos, one in the Vatican, the other in the Louvre; in the Jason of the Munich collection, that of the Louvre, that of the Vatican which is smaller, and that at Lansdowne House. There are also five Discoboli, as many Wounded Amazons, and four of the Boy with a Goose (Fig. 115), all found in one place, showing how these were made for sale as popular works. Where the Laocoon was discovered, there were near it the pieces belonging to another group, apparently precisely of the same design.

Nero (A.D. 54—68) is said to have adorned his Golden House with a colossal statue of himself, 120ft. high, and no less than 500 statues brought from Delphi. In the Baths of Titus, still in existence (they were built on the ground of the house and gardens of Maecenas), many valuable statues have been discovered. The arch of Titus furnishes an excellent example of bas-relief of that time, in which the golden candlestick and other spoils from the temple of Jerusalem are shown.

Hadrian (A.D. 117—138) encouraged the reproduction of the Greek statues, for his famous villa at Tivoli, with great success as regards execution. And besides these are the statues of his favourite Antinous, which are the most original works of the time. That in the Capitol and that in the Naples Museum are the best, while the colossal figure having the lotus flower on the head, in the Lateran Museum, and a half-draped statue holding a thyrsus, may be named as among the best works of their kind. Hadrian's imperial and liberal promotion of sculpture, gave an immense impetus to the production of statues of every form. All the towns of Greece which he favoured made bronze portrait statues of him, which were placed in the temple of Jupiter Olympius at Athens, and the enclosure round more than half a mile in extent was filled with its many statues. He made his own tomb in the building now called the Castle of St. Angelo at Rome, and

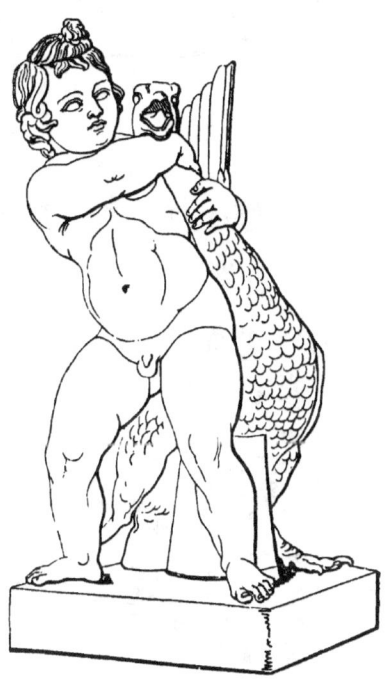

FIG. 115.—BOY WITH GOOSE.*
In the Capitoline Museum.

adorned it with many statues of men and horses, which were destroyed by the Goths. Many fine broken statues were recovered near the building, amongst them the famous heroic-size statue of a Sleeping Faun now in the Munich Museum, known as the Barberini Faun. (See *Examples.*)

Among the Greek sculptors of some eminence who were

* Probably a copy from the work of Boethus mentioned by Pliny. It was found in the Via Appia, Rome, 1789.

attracted to Rome there is mentioned by Pliny, Pasiteles, who carved an ivory statue of Jupiter for the temple of Metellus.

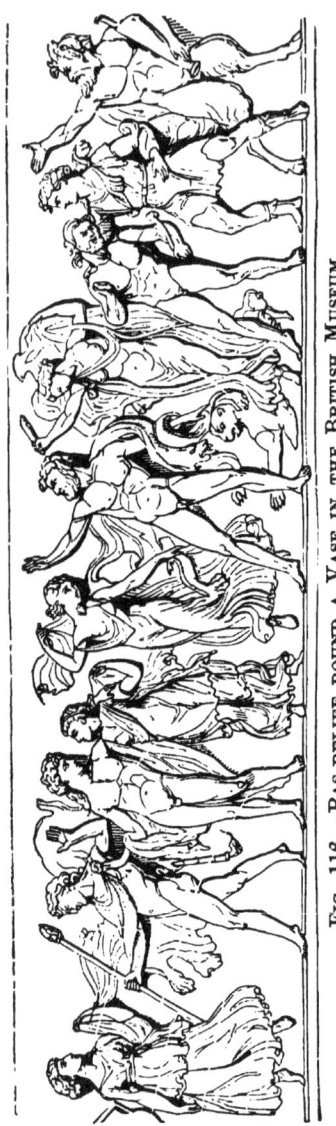

FIG. 116.—BAS-RELIEF ROUND A VASE IN THE BRITISH MUSEUM.

Colotes, mentioned by Pausanias, as a sculptor of Paros, was pupil of this Pasiteles (Plin. lib. xxxv. c. 12).

The learned Varro speaks of Arcesilaus as the sculptor of Venus Genetrix, in the forum of Cæsar, and of a beautiful marble group of Cupids playing with a lioness, some leading her, others beating her with their sandals, others offering her wine to drink from horns. Olympiosthenes is named by Pausanias as having sculptured statues of three Muses on Mount Helicon (lib. ix.). Pliny mentions Strongylion as the sculptor of an Amazon, which from the beauty of her legs was called *Eucnemon*. Pausanias speaks of a Diana and three Muses by him, and says that he sculptured horses and oxen admirably. Possibly some of those preserved in the Hall of Animals in the Vatican may be works of this sculptor.

Under the Antonines arose the outrageous fashion of representing noble Romans and their wives as deities, and this was carried so far that the men are not unfrequently nude as if heroic. The bas-reliefs on the arch of Septimus Severus at Rome, and that which goes by the name of Constantine—though made chiefly of reliefs belonging to one raised in honour of Trajan—show the poor condition of sculpture at that time. The numerous sarcophagi, some made by Greek sculptors for the Roman market, and others by those working at Rome, are other examples of the feeble style of imitators and workmen actuated by no knowledge or feeling for art. Some of these are still to be seen in the collections at Rome, sculptured with mythological subjects, the heads being left unfinished, so that the portraits of any family could be carved when required.

The rule of Constantine was however far more disastrous to art on the removal of the seat of the Empire to Byzantium. Most of the finest statues accumulated in Rome were removed there only to be lost for ever in the plundering of wars and the fanatical rage of the Christian Iconoclasts.

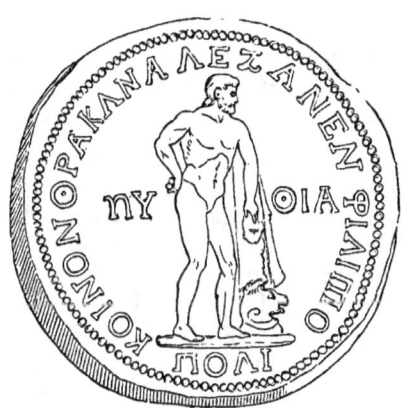

FIG. 117.—COIN OF CARACALLA.
With the Hercules of Glykon.
In the British Museum.

" The Olympic Festival though shorn of its ancient splendour was still maintained with a certain dignity during the reign of the Emperor Julian. In the year A.D. 394 the games were finally suppressed by Theodosius. Whatever remnant of pagan worship had been preserved at Olympia up to that date must have been abolished, and such sacred lands and treasures of the temples as had not been previously appropriated by Constantine the Great must have been confiscated. Christian iconoclasm, while destroying the statues of the gods, may have spared those which commemorated agonistic victors ; but we may be sure that nearly all the works in metal which the Christians spared were melted down by the barbarous hordes of Gothic invaders, who under Alaric occupied the Morea about A.D. 395." (Newton, *Essays, &c., Olympia*.)

Thus ancient sculpture died out in the complete decadence of art in late Roman times and in the coming darkness that preceded its revival. Here, however, we approach the subject of Sculpture as connected with the rise of Ecclesiastical religious art, which necessarily belongs to Byzantine, Mediæval, and Renaissance art.

NOTE ON PHEIDIAS :—SHOWING THAT THE STORY OF HIS BEING ACCUSED OF STEALING THE GOLD GIVEN OUT FOR THE STATUE OF ATHENE, OF HIS BEING CONDEMNED AND ACTUALLY DYING IN PRISON AS COMMONLY RELATED AFTER PLUTARCH, IS NOT TRUE.

There is much uncertainty as to the precise dates relating to Pheidias as well as the circumstances of his life. Dr. Smith, in his 'Classical Dictionary,' says : " He was born about the time of the battle of Marathon, B.C. 490. He began to work as a statuary about 464, and one of his first great works was the Athena Promachus, about 460. Having finished his great work at Athens, he went to Elis and Olympia. He was there engaged for about four or five years—from 437 to 434 or 433, during which time he finished his Olympian Zeus. On his return to Athens he fell a victim to the jealousy against his great patron Perikles. . . Pheidias was first accused of peculation " (stealing the gold to be used in the statue ; but the weight of this had been recorded through the caution of Perikles, and the drapery was made movable, so that it was taken off, and when weighed found to be the correct weight). " The accusers then charged Pheidias with impiety in having introduced into the battle of the Amazons, on the shield of the goddess, his own likeness and that of Perikles. On this latter charge Pheidias was thrown into prison, where he died of disease in 432." So lately as 1874, Mr. Alexander Murray of the British Museum, writing in the ' Contemporary Review,' says : " We think of Pheidias dying in prison, while fate in partial recompense has preserved the sculptures of the Parthenon." The whole subject has been completely examined by M. Emeric David (' Examem des inculpations dirigées contre Pheidias,' &c., a memoir read to the Academy of Inscriptions and Belles Lettres of the Institute of France, so long ago as 1817). " Le fait de cette accusation de sacrilége, totalement invraisemblable, n'a d'ailleurs que de témoin que Plutarch. Ni Diodore de Sicile ni Philochore, ni aucun des scholiastes d'Aristophane, qui, tous, rappellent le pretendu vol, n'en ont dit un seul mot. Il se trouve par consequent démenti." He goes on to show that Diodorus Siculus, although he related the fact of the accusation, does not say anything of any arrest or any prosecution of Pheidias or Perikles ; in fact Plutarch relates how as above stated the accusation was met and refuted. He concludes, therefore, that the sacrilege was not seriously considered, and that it could not have been, otherwise the alleged portraits would not have been allowed to remain, as they were undoubtedly, for they were seen by Apuleius six hundred years afterwards (' Vidi ipse in clypeo Minervæ oris sui similitudinem ; Apul.' ' De Mundo,' p. 74). He asserts that Pheidias did not die in the prisons of Athens, and he never was banished ; he was never even arrested ; his flight was by his own free will, and he was incapable of any crime. M. Emeric David points out how Aristophanes, who alludes to Pheidias as having left Athens, would not have spared his satire had he and Perikles deserved it. Instead of which he (' Pax,' v. 600—613) makes the villagers inquire of Mercury, why Peace has deserted them so long—to which he answers that it was the misfortune of Pheidias that was the first cause of the calamity. Pheidias was necessary to Peace ; inseparable from one another, they have disappeared together ; she herself has taken to flight—῾Ηδε δ' ἠφανίζετο :—Chorus exclaims, " What ! Then is Peace the parent of Pheidias ? Ah ! then I am not surprised that she should be so beautiful ! " (v. 614—617.) Aristophanes speaks only of a flight and disappearance, and his testimony is confirmed by that of Philochorus, who says only, that having been called to account he took to flight.

The precise date of the Olympean Zeus is proved, M. E. David says, incontestably by Pausanias having related that Pheidias executed a bronze statue of Pantarkes, a young Elean, who carried off the prize in the Olympic games, and that he represented this youth in the bas-reliefs of the throne of Zeus. Pantarkes was crowned in the 86th Olympiad (Pausanias gives this date), therefore Pheidias was engaged at this time upon the throne, i.e. between 436—432 B.C. St. Clement of Alexandria, Arnobius, and St. Gregory Nazianzus also had recognized the name of Pantarkes as traced by the hand of the master himself. " Dodwell and Heyne, obliged to adhere to the story of Plutarch (M. David says), that Pheidias died in prison at Athens, are constrained to suppose that the Zeus was finished before the Athene of the Parthenon," otherwise he could not have been in Athens at the time. This is obviously incompatible with the date of the consecration of the Parthenon statue (438 B.C.). As to the story that Pheidias committed similar theft of the gold for the Zeus at Elis, and was put to death by the Eleans, it is, M. Emeric David declares, more absurd than the other, and is clearly only an altered repetition of it, and he considers that the translation from the Scholiast is erroneous, and that instead of the passage, " he died by the Eleans," the Greek text properly rendered is, " he died amongst the Eleans "—(" il mourut chez les Eléens.") But not to dispute over an equivocal text, M. David points out the inconsistency of supposing Pheidias condemned to death in the first year of the 87th Olympiad, i.e. the first year of the Peloponnesian war, when it was in the first year of the 90th Olympiad that Aristophanes had his play ' Pax ' performed at Athens, in which he, thirteen years after the supposed crime and expiation, pronounced his eulogy of Pheidias. How could this have been if he had escaped the vengeance of the people of Athens, and suffered at the hands of the Eleans the punishment of a similar crime? Would not Aristophanes in his 'Acharnians,' played in the third year of the 88th Olympiad, 426 B.C., in which he denounced Aspasia and the women of her court in casting blame upon Perikles, having included Pheidias in the obloquy? "What a rich subject," he says, "for blackening the administration of this celebrated man—the ignominious death of the most notable of his *protégés!*" He further shows the impossibility of accepting the account of Plutarch, and those put forth by certain German biographers. Meursius ('De Archont. Athen.' lib. iii. c. 4, tom. i.); Hoffman, Moreri (au mot 'Pheidias'); Schlotzer ('Historie Universelle'), who has the cruel indifference to say Pheidias was hung as a thief! Both Boettiger and Quatremère de Quincy have expressed their dissent from this view, which M. Emeric David so ably refutes. So far from the Eleans having dishonoured Pheidias it is beyond dispute that they honoured him in every possible way. After his death they at once took charge for ever of his children, and made them the keepers of the temple of Zeus containing the statue, giving them the title of *The Phaidrontes*. Near the temple, the studio and the house of Pheidias were religiously preserved, and an altar was raised sacred to all the gods, as Pheidias had represented them all so worthily. Pausanias relates all this, and, as M. David states, all the great writers of antiquity—moralists the most rigid, satirists the most biting— are unanimous in their praises, without a single word of restriction or reserve. And even the Fathers of the Church, thundering against the idolatry and immodesty of atheistic heathens, have not a word to say about theft. Pheidias, it is true, was proved to have been falsely accused, and it is equally certain that he was never condemned and never prosecuted, and still more certainly was not poisoned in prison. The argument of M. David was confirmed by M. Rochette in his lectures to the French Academy in 1839.

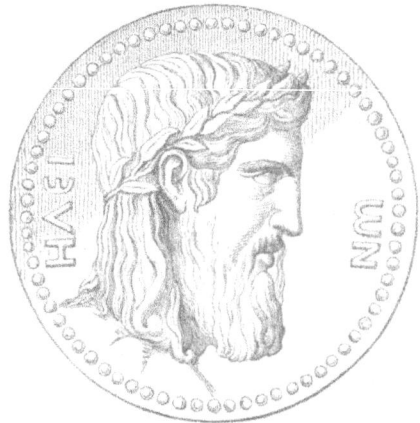

SECTION IV.—EXAMPLES.

DESCRIPTIONS OF STATUES.

ARRANGED ALPHABETICALLY.

[*Abbreviations : m., marble: b., bronze.*]

ACHILLES. The *Borghese Achilles*. Heroic, m. Parian ; ht., 6ft. 1½in. Louvre. A fine statue, nude with a helmet ; a form combining power with youthful vigour and activity ; the trunk rather turgid in the muscles, but the legs especially are finely modelled, as if to warrant the epithet of 'swift-footed' applied to him. The ring round the right ankle has been supposed as a protection to the only vulnerable part of his body. Winckelmann suggested it was the remains of a fetter, as there was a statue of Mars chained at Sparta. It may have been an ornament worn in foot-racing. The attitude is that of one about to start in the race. There was a celebrated bronze by Alkamenes, of which this may be an imitation (*Visconti*). It was formerly in the Borghese collection, which was sold by Prince Camillo Borghese to Napoleon in 1806, and sent to the Louvre in 1808, since which time the Borghese Palace has acquired another collection.

Restorations.—Left fore-arm, fingers of right hand, and tips of the toes.

ADONIS. m. Grechetto ; ht., 5ft. 8in., life-size. In the Vatican. This graceful statue is thought to have been originally an Apollo or Eros, but the arms were restored by Albacini with part of an arrow in the right hand, and it was called an Adonis. The head had been separated, but is antique ; and with the body, especially the shoulders, is very beautiful. It was found in the Via Labicana in 1780.

Restorations.—The nose, the hands and arms from the shoulders, the right leg, and left foot.

ADONIS OF CAPUA. Heroic ; Grechetto m. Ht., 7ft. 3½in. Naples Museum. A very fine example of the time of Hadrian, the body so beautifully modelled, the attitude graceful and free. Like an Apollo. Found in the amphitheatre at Capua.

Restorations.—The legs, left arm, and right hand, with accessories, by A. Coli.

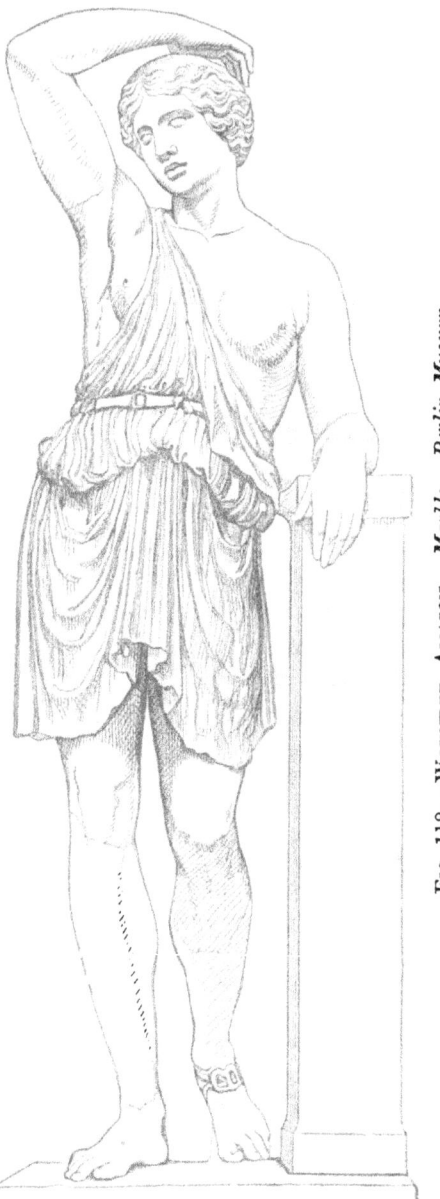

FIG. 118.—WOUNDED AMAZON. *Marble. Berlin Museum.* Much restored. Differs from the others chiefly in having no quiver, or shield, and the left arm supported on a pillar.

AMAZON, m.; 6ft. 5in. Berlin. This claims to be a copy of the bronze of Polykleitos, and one of the five made in competition for the Temple of Artemis at Ephesus, by Polykleitos, Pheidias, Ktesilas, Kydon, and Phradmon. At least seven are known besides this : two 'in the Vatican, one of which, the Mattei statue, also claims to be after that of Polykleitos ; two in the Capitol, one in the Louvre, one in Vienna Museum, and one at Petworth House. They all bear some resemblance one to the other, but are different, some being wounded. The Vatican statue (No. 265, *Mus. P. Clem.*), distinguished as the 'Mattei Amazon,' is loosening her bow, with the right hand over the head, a quiver at her left side, a shield by the right leg on the tree-trunk, the battle-axe, and a helmet at her feet. On the left ankle is a spur, as in the Berlin figure. The Mattei Amazon was in the Villa Mattei on the Cœlian Hill, Rome, for two centuries, till Clement XIII. had it placed in the

Vatican.   On the plinth was inscribed '*Translata de Schola Medicorum*'—which was the Portico built by Augustus for the Physicians.   But where the statue was found is not known. The other Amazon of the Vatican is wounded, has the right arm raised over the head, while the left falls by her side.   A very fine Head of an Amazon is No. 150, British Museum, and there is a good *torso* in the Berlin Museum, a cast of which is No. 53, Crystal Palace.

ANTINOUS.   Heroic ; m. Carrara ; ht., 6ft. 6½in.   Capitoline Museum, Rome.   This fine statue of the favourite youth of the Emperor Hadrian, who was drowned in the Nile A.D. 122, represents him as a Mercury, in the attitude adopted for the messenger of the gods.   The right hand originally held the caduceus.   The treatment of the hair also shows the intention of the sculptor. It was found in Hadrian's villa.

Restorations.—The right leg below the knee ; the left foot and left fore-arm ; two fingers of right hand.

Several other statues of Antinous are in the museums.   One at Naples, in a similar attitude, in which the iris of the eye is carved.   The arms and legs of this are, however, modern.   A cast is in the Crystal Palace collection (No. 288).   Antinous as a good genius (Agathodaimon) is a heroic st. of Parian m. in the Berlin Museum, formerly at Sans Souci.   It is an important example, as having the hands and feet perfect, except one finger of the right hand.   The hollow sockets of the eyes show that it had originally eyes of coloured glass or precious stones.   A cast is in the Crystal Palace (No. 314).

The statue called the Braschi Antinous is colossal ; in the Lateran Museum, formerly in the Braschi Palace, Rome.   It was found at the end of the last century, by Gavin Hamilton, near Palestrina.   It is a half-draped statue, holding a thyrsus or pine-cone staff in the left hand, and with the lotus flower on the head.   A cast of the bust is in the Crystal Palace (No. 347). The statue in the Vatican, called the Egyptian Antinous, from the head-dress and the loin-cloth, is 7ft. 6in. high ; m.   The arms are held straight at the sides, and the hands clenched, in the fixed attitude of Egyptian statues. It has been regarded as a standard of proportion. It was found in Hadrian's villa about the middle of the last century. A fine bas-relief is in the Villa Albani, Rome, of the upper part of the figure of Antinous, larger than life, crowned with the lotus, restored, as are also some of the fingers. This was in Hadrian's villa.

ANTINOUS Agathodaimon. Heroic; Parian m. Berlin Museum. A fine Roman statue, with the elephant trunk and serpent as emblems of a good deity; well preserved, having the eye-sockets hollowed to receive coloured stones or glass.

Restorations.—Only the finger, the rest considered to be antique.

APOLLO BELVEDERE. Heroic size; m. Carrara or Luni.* Ht., 7 ft. 2 in. Vatican. Once thought to be a repetition in marble of a bronze, by Kalamis,† but now considered to be of the time of Lysippos. If it is of Carrara or Luni marble, it was most probably executed at Rome. Formerly considered to be the most beautiful of antique statues, but since placed in an inferior rank in art. It may represent Apollo either as the destroyer of the Python and protector from evil, or, as Pausanias described the statue of Apollo by Kalamis, as the protector after the plague had left Athens, having the serpent, the emblem of the healing art, twining round the Delian olive (lib. i. p. 6, 20). Visconti took this view, while Winckelmann thought he had just discharged the arrow that killed the Python. The small snake upon the trunk, however, would not warrant the latter opinion, and evidently refers to the healing power of the god, as it does in statues of Æsculapius. A bronze statuette in Count Stroganoff's collection has the Ægis in the left hand as in the figure, No. 119.

* Visconti got certificates from many judges that the marble was not Carrara or Luni. But when the statue was in Paris Musée in 1814, where Napoleon placed it (16th Brumaire An. 9), the experts asserted that the marble was unlike any Greek marble.

† The statue of Hermes bearing a kid on his shoulders, in the Wilton House Collection, is attributed to Kalamis.

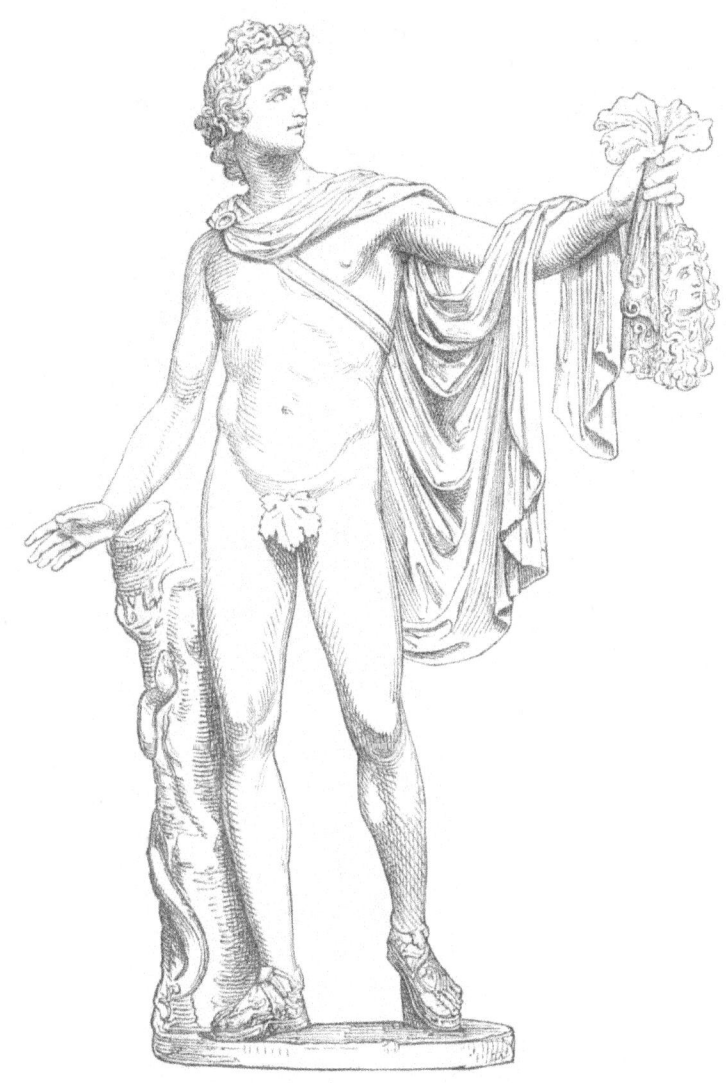

FIG. 119.—APOLLO BELVEDERE.

In the Vatican.

The left hand restored in this cut as holding the Ægis.
In the Vatican restoration part of the bow is held.

It was found at the close of the 15th century in the ruins at Antium where the Gladiator or Warrior of Agasias was, and was purchased by the Cardinal delle Rovere, afterwards Julius

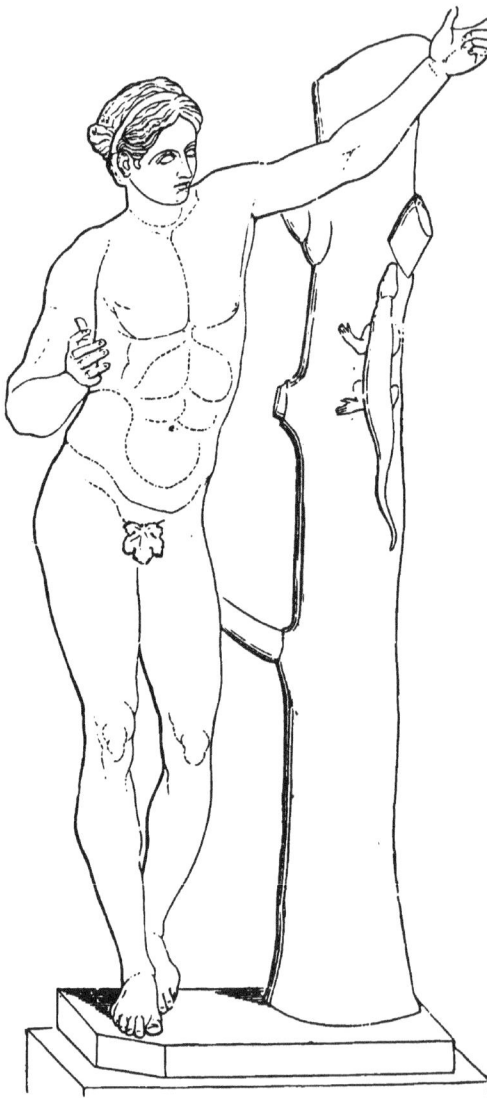

II., being one of the first works of the Vatican collection, taking the name of Belvedere from the gardens.

Restorations.—The entire right fore-arm and left hand were supplied by Montorsoli when employed by Clement VII. Marc Antonio engraved the statue (B. 133), and this shows it without the hands and the left wrist and part of the right fore-arm. Therefore it is entirely a matter of conjecture whether the original statue in bronze held a bow or the Ægis, or simply had the hand extended.

Fig. 120.—APOLLO SAUROCTONOS. *Parian Marble. In the Vatican. Copy of the bronze by Praxiteles.*

APOLLO SAUROCTONOS. Life-size ; m. Parian; ht. 4ft. 10½in. Vatican. One of the best copies from the celebrated work of Praxiteles in bronze described by Pliny : "Fecit et puberem

Apollinem subrepenti lacertæ cominus sagitta insidiantem, quem Sauroctonon vocant" (lib. xxxiv. c. 8).   The right hand held a dart.   Found in 1777 in the Villa Magnani on the Palatine Hill, Rome.   Resembles the statue in the Louvre (No. 70) from the Borghese collection, which is of Parian marble—height 4ft. 10½ in.—much restored.   The head was broken off but belongs to the statue.   The right hand with part of arm, the left arm almost entirely, the feet which were broken are cemented.   The head and tail of the lizard are modern.

Restorations.—The right arm above the elbow, left hand, part of face and neck, left leg from knee, right from the middle of the thigh, tree-trunk and lizard except the tail.   A bronze statue, 38in. high, is in the Villa Albani. Cast No. 373, Crystal Pal.

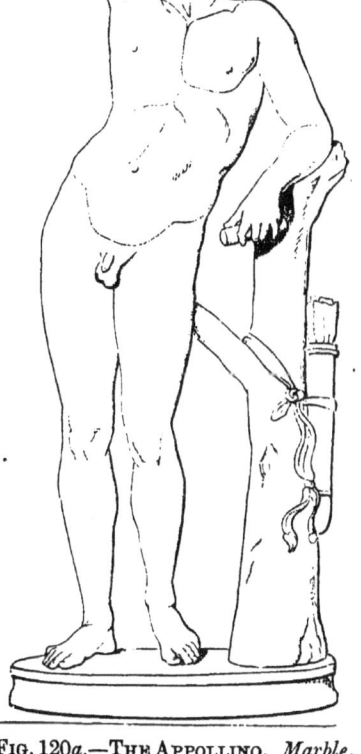

Apollo (the Lycian Apollo). Heroic; Greek m.   Ht., 6ft. 7in. Louvre.   Beautiful, graceful, and noble in character, standing in repose, the left hand probably held the bow.   Called the Lycian from the epithet λύκειος, from the old Greek word λύκη, *light.* It was once at Versailles in the Gardens.

Fig. 120a.—The Appollino. *Marble. Florence Museum.*

Restorations.—The right hand and wrist, the left fore-arm and hand with the bâton.

Apollo Musagetes.   Heroic, draped; m.   Ht., 5ft. 8in. Vatican.   Holding the lyre.   The drapery is the 'palla' worn by poets, actors, and musicians—'Pythius in longa carmina veste sonat' (Propertius). Found near Tivoli.

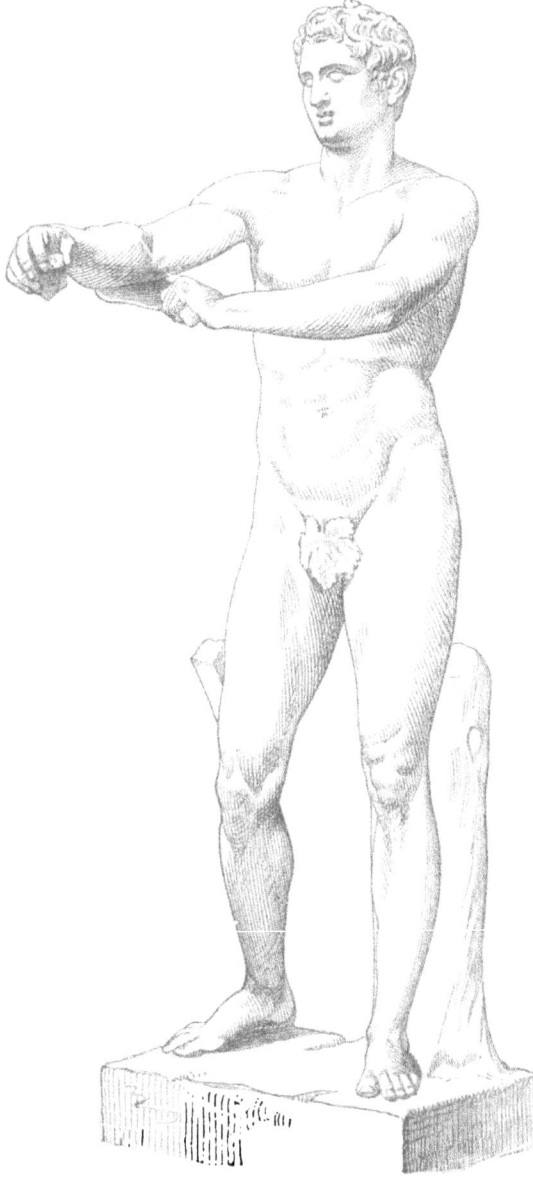

FIG. 121.—THE APOXYOMENOS. *Vatican.*
Athlete using the Strigil.

APOXYOMENOS. Heroic; m. Greek. Ht., 6ft. 5¾in. Vatican. This fine statue is an example of the school of Lysippos, and considered to be taken from the famous bronze mentioned by Pliny as removed by Tiberius from the baths of Agrippa to his own palace, and restored in consequence of the clamour of the people. It is also remarkable as representing an athlete using the *strigil*. The dice held in the right hand is an addition of the modern restorer.

This copy of the celebrated statue was found in the Viccolo della Palme in the Trastevere, Rome, in 1849, and, though in many pieces, nearly complete.

Restorations.—Part of the nose, and the fingers of the right hand with the dice.

THE APOLLINO. Small life size, m.; ht., 4ft. 8½in. Florence Museum. The young Apollo. The most beautiful and perfect statue of a youth. The forms are so graceful and soft that it has been attributed to the hand of the great sculptor, Praxiteles, and it resembles a bronze in the Villa Albani by him; but the attitude and details are the same as the Lycian Apollo worshipped at Patara, a copy of which stood in the Lyceum (Lucian Dialog. Anarcharsis). It stands with the Venus dei Medici in the tribune of the Florence Gallery, and is thought to resemble the style of that renowned statue.

It represents the god in his amiable character, the form being feminine and delicate, differing widely from the Apollo Belvedere. It is almost entirely antique, and therefore most precious. The attitude of the Lycian Apollo corresponded with this apparently—the right arm over the head, the left holding a bow, and the figure leaning against a column. The Florence statue leans on a tree. The coins show the Lycian Apollo.

Restorations.—Both hands and wrists, and the nose.

ARIADNE. Heroic; reclining, partly draped, m. Parian; ht., 5ft. 2in. by 6ft. 10in. Vatican. (Fig. 43.) This beautiful statue has been called a Cleopatra from the snake coiled round the arm; but as this was no doubt intended simply as an armlet ornament, it is also called Ariadne asleep, deserted by her lover Theseus. Statues representing eternal repose, as this does, were intended for tombs. It got the name of Cleopatra from the Latin poem written by Castiglione when it was first found. There is a similar statue in the Madrid Museum, and a smaller one in the Louvre, No. 238, formerly in the Villa Borghese.

Restorations.—The nose, mouth, right hand and wrist, and part of the left, several toes, and parts of the drapery.

Formerly ornamented a fountain at the end of a corridor in the Vatican. It was from this statue that Raphael took his Dying Cleopatra, which Marc Antonio engraved from the original drawing.

A.S.

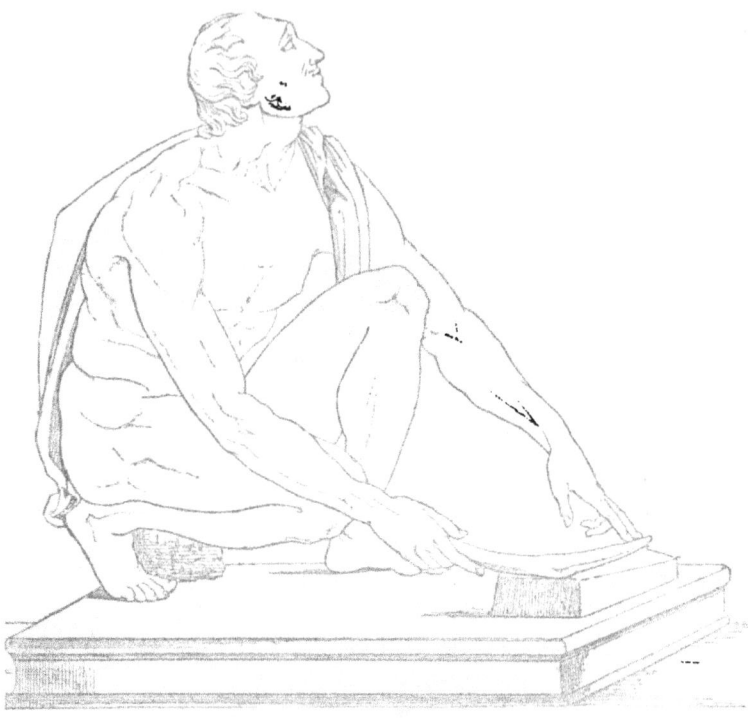

FIG. 122.—THE ARROTINO ; A SCYTHIAN, OR LISTENING SLAVE.
In the Florence Gallery.

THE ARROTINO. Life-size ; m. Ht., 37 inches. Florence.
This statue is considered to belong to a group of Marsyas about
to be flayed ; the Scythian sharpening his knife to execute the
command of Apollo. The subject is common in antique sculpture, and is seen on coins and sarcophagi. The figure is kneeling
with right knee, the other being bent only, and looking up.
Almost entirely nude, a slight drapery only over the left shoulder.
Cast No. 13, in the Crystal Palace.

Restorations.—Some of the fingers only, and part of the
knife.

ARTEMIS. *See* DIANA.

ATHENA. *See* MINERVA.

BOY AND GOOSE. (*See* Fig. 115.)

BACCHUS. Life-size; m. Naples Museum. A beautiful statue of Greek work. Crowned with grapes and vine leaves, the right hand raised holding a bunch of grapes, the left holds a cup.

Restorations.—The arms by Albaccini. The head does not seem to belong to this statue. (*Clarac.*)

SILENUS WITH INFANT BACCHUS. Heroic. Ht., 6ft. 1½in. Louvre. A work which resembles in style the Laocoon, has the same exaggerated muscular development, showing the muscles in active contraction where they would be passive and scarcely seen. It was found in the gardens of Sallust in the 16th century. A similar group is in the Glyptothek, Munich, and another in the Vatican, which was once in the Ruspoli Palace, Rome, which is 6ft. 3½in. in height.

Restorations.—The arms and hands, and right fore-arm and foot of Silenus, left leg and part of right arm of the Bacchus.

THE RICHELIEU BACCHUS (Dionysos). Gk. marble. Ht., 6ft. 2½in. Louvre. This is one of the most beautiful statues of Bacchus. The youthful rounded limbs with the lazy attitude give that voluptuous languor admired by the Romans. It was brought from the castle of Richelieu.

Restorations.—The right arm from above the elbow, the left fore-arm and hand, the lower part of left foot, the right leg from knee to ankle.

BOY EXTRACTING A THORN, *or* SPINARIO. Bronze. Ht., 2ft. 4in. Capitoline Museum. One of the finest bronzes. Considered to be a youth who has got a thorn in his foot while racing in the Stadium. It was in the Museum before 1652, as it is mentioned by Aldroandi. It was amongst the statues taken to the Louvre. A similar statue in marble is in the Florence Gallery.

Restorations.—The nose and some toes of the right foot are the only parts added.

It has been attributed to Pasiteles.

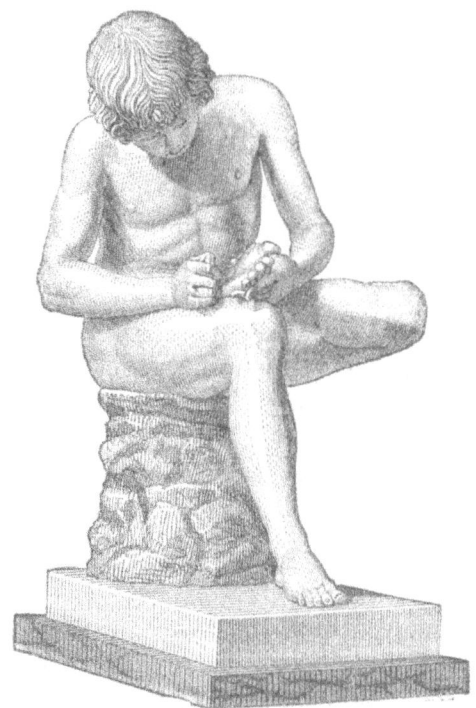

Fig. 123.—Boy Extracting a Thorn.
In the Museum of the Capitol.

Centaur of the Capitol (Fig. 44); m. Bigio Morato. Ht. 54½ in. One of the two found in Hadrian's Villa. The other is old and bearded.

Cupid and Psyche; m. Parian. Ht., 4ft. 1¼in. Capitoline Museum, Rome. Found on the Aventine. Emblematic of the union of the body and soul.

Restorations.—Nose, chin, right hand, left foot of Cupid. Psyche remarkable as being without wings.

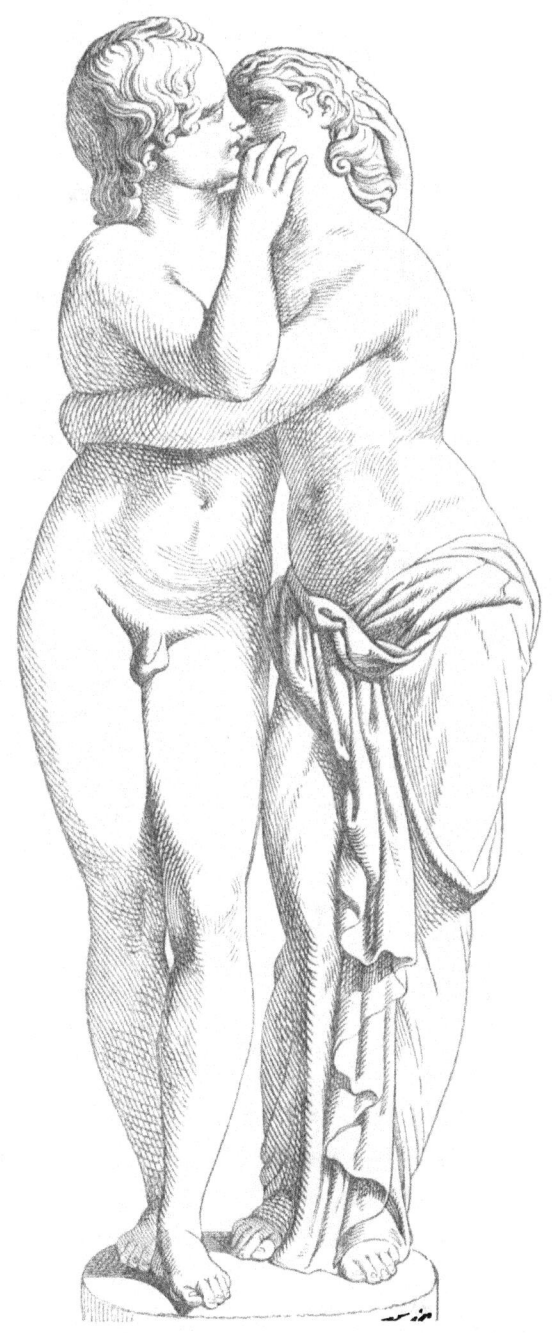

Fig. 124.—The Cupid and Psyche of the Capitol.

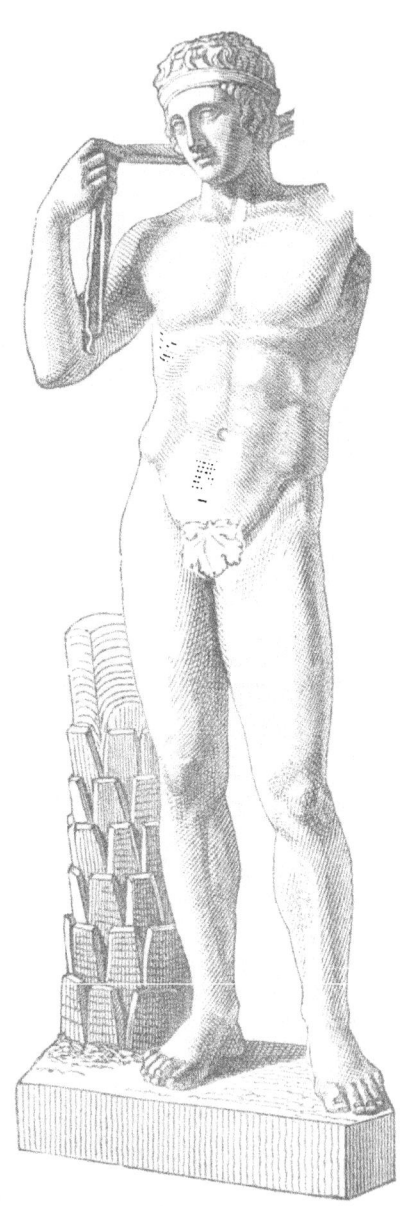

FIG. 125.—THE DIADUMENOS.—The left arm and shoulder lost.
Marble; life-size. British Museum.

DIADUMENOS. Life-size; m. There are two Diadumeni in the British Museum; this one, known as the Farnese statue, and the other as the Vaison statue, from having been found at that place in France. Both are supposed to be copies of bronze statues by Polykleitos referred to by Pliny (lib. xxxiv. c. 8), one of a young man—"*Diadumenum fecit molliter juvenem*" —the other of a youth of manly form "*idem et Doryphorum viriliter puerum.*" This Farnese statue may be the soft and graceful figure, the Vaison statue, the strong, square-built, young athlete. The last-named is also defective in the left hand and the fillet, but it has the arm entire. Both rest with one leg at ease, an attitude peculiar to Polykleitos, and seen in the Doryphorus at Naples. A small bronze is in the Bibliothèque, Paris.

DIANA *with the Stag.* Heroic, m. Parian; ht., 6ft. 7in. Louvre. It is not known where or when this statue was found; it has been in France a long time, and was probably one of the 184 that Primaticcio brought from Rome for Francis I. It was once at Versailles, hence called 'Diane de Versailles,' also 'Diane à la Biche.'

Restorations. — Barthélemy Prieur is said to have done a little too much to the surface, the feet having got something of the style of Germain Pilon and Prieur (*Clarac*). The left arm is by the sculptor Lange of Toulouse, done in the Louvre before 1809. The nose, ears, part of neck, right hand, half of fore-arm; left hand, with arm to the deltoid; right foot and upper part of leg. Stag, nearly all.

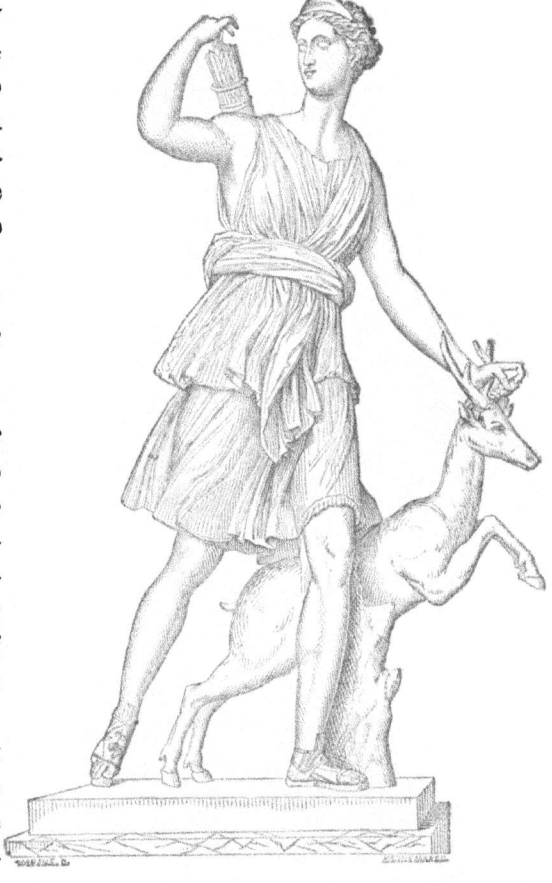

FIG. 126.—DIANA WITH THE STAG OF BRAZEN FEET (*Ceryneia.*)
In the Louvre.

A work of 1st cent. A.D., if not by the same sculptor, probably of the same period, as the Apollo Belvedere (M. Fröhner, Louvre Cat.). Many repetitions exist, one at Holkham (Lord Leicester's).

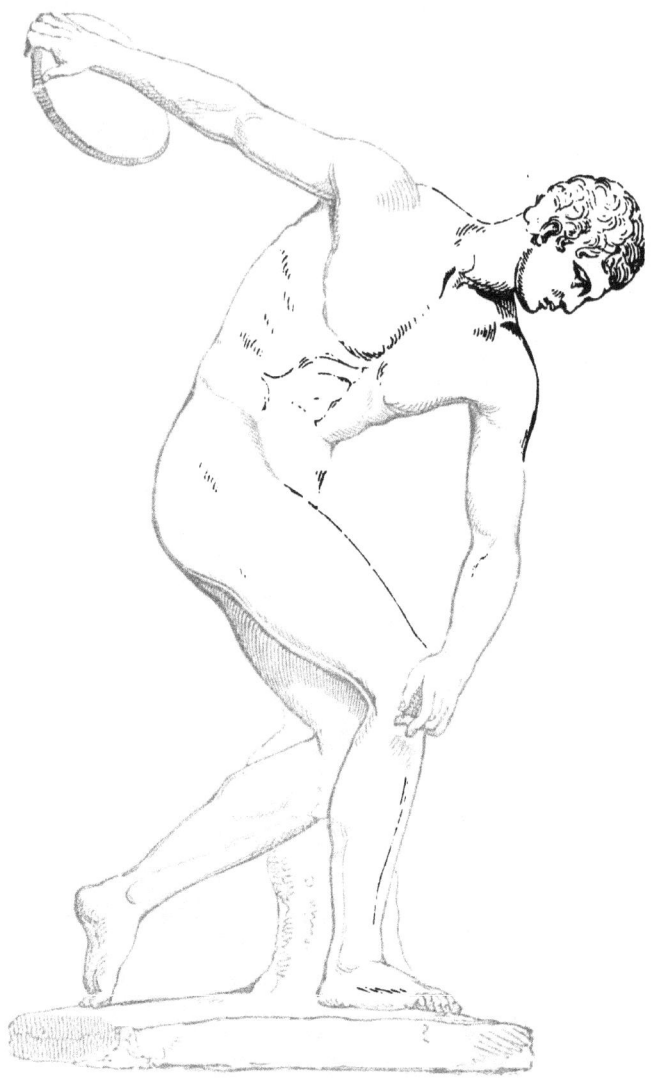

FIG. 127.—THE DISCOBOLUS. *British Museum.*

DISCOBOLUS OF MYRON.   Above life-size ; marble ; height, 5ft. 8in.   British Museum.

There are no less than five statues like this, all copies of the famous bronze by Myron, which is described by Quintilian (A.D. 40) and afterwards by Lucian (A.D. 120), and copied on to gems and coins still in existence (*see* Fig. 128). Has the head less turned back than the Vatican figure, but it does not belong to the statue, though "it seems to be antique" (*Newton*). It was found in 1791. The Vatican statue has the head, arms, and right leg modern. Another in Turin Museum, and one in Naples Museum.

The Discobolus in the Palazzo Massimi at Rome is the best preserved of any; the head, which has not been separated, in this is turned more backwards. Found in the Villa Palombaro on the Esquiline Hill in 1781. A small bronze in which the head is turned back is in the Munich Museum.

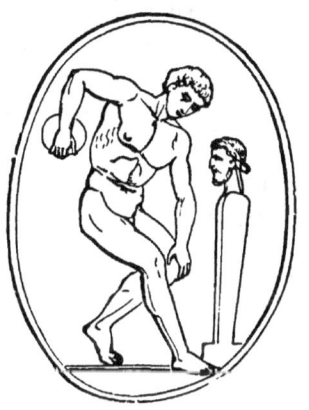

FIG. 128.—ON A GEM.
See Visconti, Vol. I. p. 120, and Tassie's Gems, No. 7967.

Myron (Μύρων) was born about 480 B.C.; he was a pupil of Ageladas of Argos and fellow-student with Polykleitos and contemporary with Pheidias. He became celebrated about 431 B.C. for his works in bronze, especially for his 'Cow lowing, with her calf,' which stood in the great square of Athens in the time of Cicero, and after being removed to Rome and placed in the Temple of Peace, was eventually destroyed or lost; and for his Ladas, a runner who fell dead as he won a race.

In the bronze the figure would not have required the tree-trunk to support it. Upon this part is sculptured a 'strigil,' used as a scraper by athletes (Fig. 121). The action and motive of the figure are readily understood, and could not be more concisely described than in the words of Lucian, who saw it at Athens. "The discus-player (δισκεύοντος) bending down as if about to throw, and looking back towards the hand that holds the discus, with one knee bent as if prepared to rise after the cast. That is the Discobolus, the work of Myron." Also praised by Quintilian. Mr. Newton thinks that the work of Myron may be recognized in the metopes of the Parthenon (Lectures on Greek Art, 1880).

DISCOBOLUS OF NAUKYDES. Life-size; m. Pentelic. Ht., 5ft. 7in. Vatican. The quoit-player in the attitude of measuring

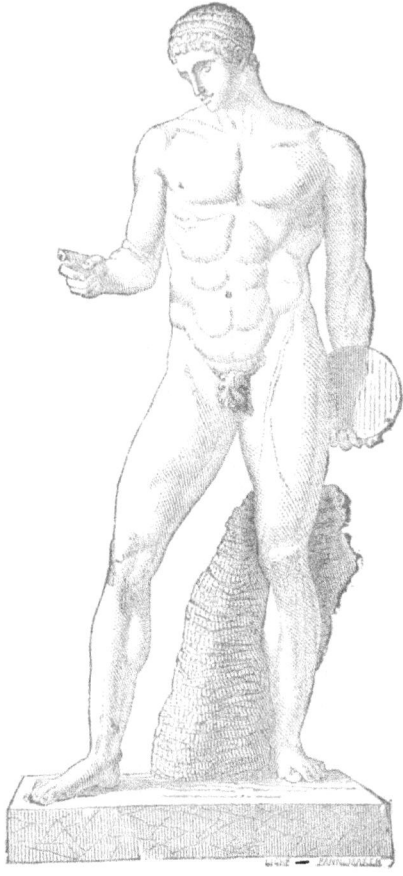

his distance before casting. Mentioned by Pliny as the work of the Argive sculptor Naukydes (B.C. 350— 326): "Naucydes Mercurio, et Discobolo, et immolante arietem censetur" (Plin. lib. xxxiv. c. 8). "Few antiques have suffered so little injury as this; it has no fracture, but the surface is corroded by damp; the tenons remain undisturbed. Were it not that the statue in many parts is unfinished we might fairly conclude this to be the actual work of Naucydes, such is its superlative excellence" (*Scharf*).

It was found at Colombaro on the Via Appia, eight miles from Rome, where the Emperor Gallienus is said to have had a villa, by Gavin Hamilton, and was placed in the Vatican by Pius VI

FIG. 129.—DISCOBOLUS OF NAUKYDES. *Vatican.*

Restorations.—None.

Another statue similar but more erect is in the Borghese Palace; and another is engraved in Cavaceppi (v. 1, pl. 42), which was then in England, and came from the Villa Montalto, and is now in Lord Faversham's collection. This Discobolus of Naukydes has recently been conjectured to be the work of Alkamenes, whose statue of an athlete is referred to by ancient writers as the Enkrinomenos.

FAUN OF THE CAPI-
TOL. Life-size; m.
Pentelic. Ht., 5ft.
7¾in. Capitol, Rome.
Often called "the
Faun (or Satyr) of
Praxiteles," being
thought to be a copy
of the famous bronze
so far famed that it
was spoken of at the
time as περιβόητος.
Many repetitions of
it were made, some
slightly varied. The
folds of the skin
sometimes erroneous-
ly called the *nebris*,
but which is that of
the panther, indicate
the sharper forms
which would be
chosen by an artist
working in bronze.
The grace of line in
the figure, amount-
ing to what would be
termed elegance, and
the expression of the
head, mark the style
as that of the later
Athenian sculptors.
The Faun of the
Vatican, which close-
ly resembles this,
also called by the

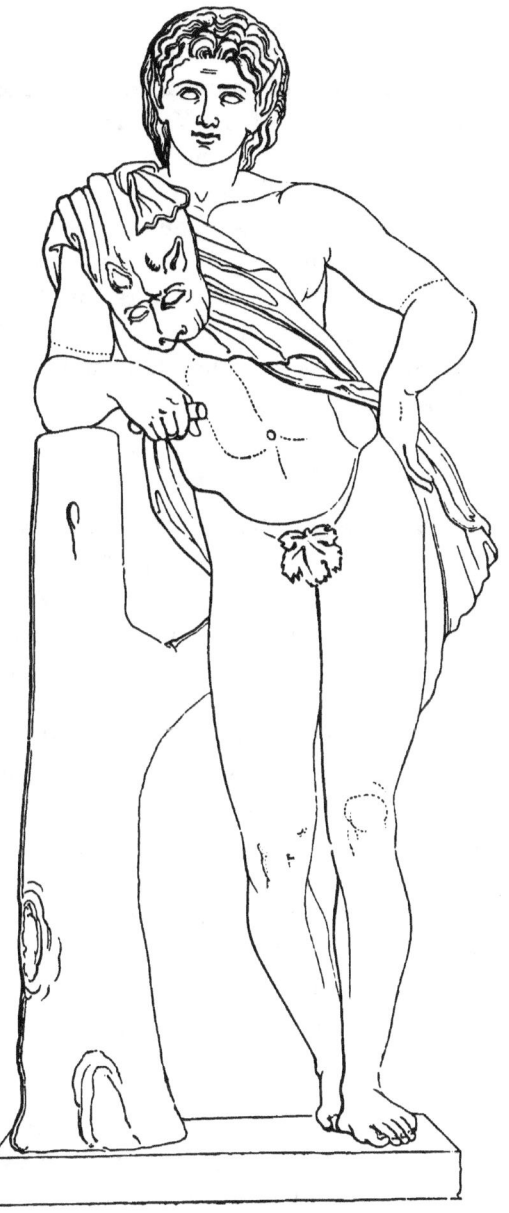

FIG. 130.—FAUN OF PRAXITELES. *Capitol, Rome.*

name of Praxiteles, differs in being higher (6ft.), having
the right foot a little more behind the left leg and more bent,

the head inclined to the right (of the figure); the right hand holds a short *pedum* or crooked stick instead of the flute, and the skin hangs down behind the left leg to the ankle. Another like this of the Vatican was in the Palazzo Ruspoli, the head of which bore a pine-branch. Winckelmann counted thirty similar statues in Rome.

It was found near Lanuvium (Avita Lavinia), a villa of Marcus Aurelius, in 1701, and was formerly in the Villa d'Este, from which it was removed to the Capitol in 1753 by Pope Benedict XIV.

Restorations.—The left arm and part of the right, and the nose.

THE SLEEPING FAUN, or Barberini Faun. Heroic ; m. Parian. Ht., 73½in. Munich Museum, formerly in the Barberini Palace, Rome. A work of the time of Skopas and Praxiteles, B.C. 392— 364. The knowledge shown of the anatomy and proportions of the figure distinguish it as the work of some master-hand, perhaps Skopas himself, as it is bolder and more robust in style than Praxiteles. It was found in the 15th century close under the castle of St. Angelo at Rome, the Mausoleum of Hadrian, which was so richly adorned with statues. It may have been amongst those which were hurled down upon the besieging Goths by order of Belisarius in the year 537 A.D. It was sold by the Prince Barberini to the Prince Royal of Bavaria for £3000 about the year 1814, when so many works of art were disposed of in Italy. Cast No. 19 in Crystal Palace.

Restorations.—The. right leg and part of the left, the right elbow and finger of right hand, the left fore-arm. These were made in stucco by Paccini at Rome in 1814 (Clarac) ; the rock upon which he reclines is also supplied.

There is another sleeping faun which differs from this in the Dresden Museum, which was found in the same place in 1623-44, and a bronze life-size statue very similar in attitude was found at Herculaneum 1756 (Tav. 40, Vol. vi. *Antich. di Ercolano*). See cast No. 372, Crystal Palace.

FAUN—torso. Life-size; m. Florence Museum. This very beautiful work is worthy of the highest art of the best style of Greek sculpture. A small tail on the back shows that it is a Faun, otherwise it might be mistaken for some heroic figure from the fine character of the head. It was formerly in the Gaddi Collection. A cast is in Crystal Palace Collection, No. 62.

THE PIPING FAUN. Small life-size; m. Ht., 4ft. Vatican, Rome. This graceful little statue, often repeated, is considered to be one of the best. It somewhat resembles the so-called Faun of Praxiteles, in having the legs crossed, but differs much in the attitude, the figure leaning with the left shoulder against a tree-trunk, upon which hangs the skin fastened over the shoulder. He holds the flute with both hands. The figure is nude except where the faun's (*nebris*) skin passes across the shoulders.

It was found in the ruins of the Villa of Lucullus in the Circæan lake.

FAUN WITH PATERA (Fig. 131).—LAUGHING FAUN (Fig. 132). These statuettes in marble are in the British Museum.

THE CLAPPING FAUN (Fig. 39). m.; life-size; Florence Museum. Has been attributed to Praxiteles. The head and arms restored by Michelangelo.

THE RONDININI FAUN, OR SATYR. M. Ht., 5ft. 9in. Brit. Mus. Restored as playing the cymbals with the arm raised. Formerly in the Rondinini Palace, Rome; purchased in 1826.

Restorations.—All the figure but the body and the right thigh, therefore of little value as an example.

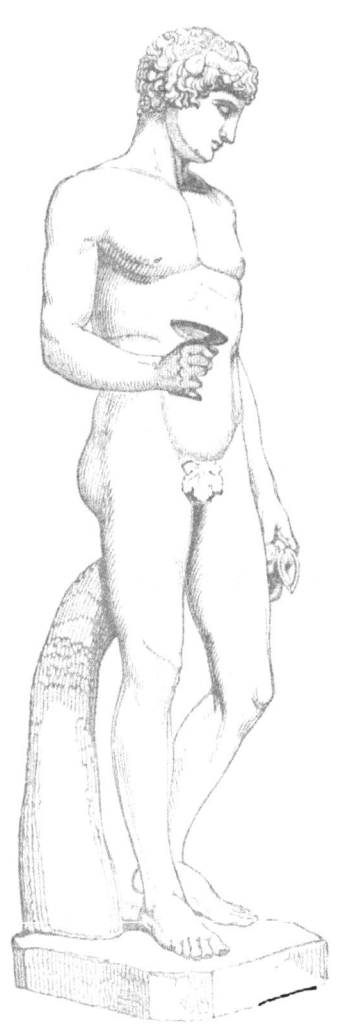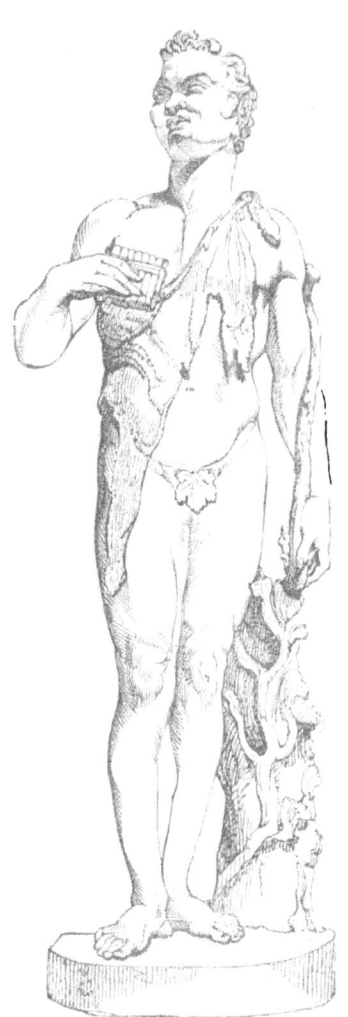

Fig. 131.—Faun with Patera.

M. Statuette. In the British Museum.

Fig. 132.—The Laughing Faun.

M. In the British Museum.

GERMANICUS. Life-size; Parian m. Ht., 5ft. 11in. Louvre. Once in the Villa Negroni, Rome, then in Versailles Gallery. The name of Germanicus is erroneous, and the head does not resemble the coins, besides being that of a middle-aged man, while Germanicus died in his 34th year. It is some personage of importance represented, as was often done, in the character of Mercury, the God of Eloquence (*Hermes logios*). Nearly nude, with the chlamys falling from the left shoulder down to the tortoise at the feet, the right arm raised in the attitude of an orator. Remarkable for the accurate study of the figure and fine work nearly all antique. It was bought for Louis XIV. under the advice of N. Poussin the painter. On the tortoise is the inscription in letters of the century before the Christian era—Κλεομένης Κλεομένους ᾿Αθεναῖος ἐποίησεν. The left hand held a caduceus.

Restorations.—Only the thumb and fore-finger of left hand.

GENIUS OF DEATH, or of Eternal Repose. Life-size ; m. Pentelic. Ht., 77½ in. Louvre, formerly in the Chateau d'Ecouen. Standing leaning against a pine-tree sacred to Cybele, the legs crossed and the arms bent over the head. Similar figures seen on sarcophagi in the Vatican, some with an inverted torch, as the emblem of the extinction of the fire of life. Similar statues are in the Vatican and Naples Museum.

THE DYING GLADIATOR. Above life-size, m. Height, 33in. ; length, 66in. In the Museum of the Capitol, Rome. Though long called 'The Dying Gladiator' to distinguish it from the 'Fighting Gladiator,' this fine statue is now more properly called a Dying Gaul, or a Gaulish Herald, who has been mortally wounded, or may have slain himself. The large horn on the ground within which he lies, as though it had slipped off his shoulders, has been considered to be that carried by heralds. The twisted ring of metal round the neck is a '*torque*' such as was worn by the Gauls. The expression of the face and the whole figure is finely portrayed, and with

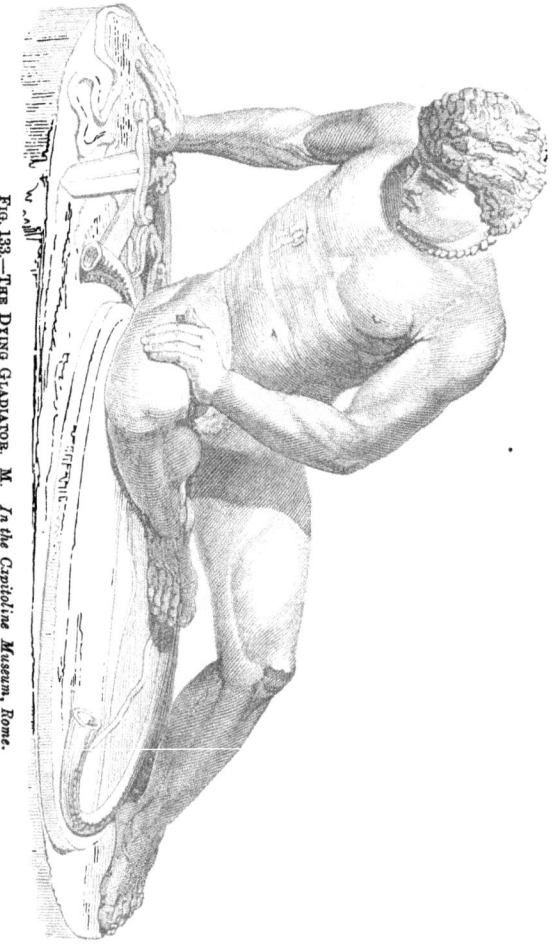

Fig. 133.—The Dying Gladiator. M. In the Capitoline Museum, Rome.

strong realistic truth, very characteristic of the Pergamus school. It was found in the ruins of the Garden of Sallust in 1770, and was once in the gallery of the Villa Ludovisi, Rome. It was purchased by Clement XII., and was taken to Paris among the spoils of Napoleon. It is considered to be a work of the time of Hadrian.

Byron alluded to this statue, and has described it with admirable 'perception of the expression, and great beauty of language—

> "He leans upon his hand—his manly brow
> Consents to death, but conquers agony."

Sir Charles Bell points out the remarkable truth of observation with which the sculptor had studied his subject: "He seeks support to his arms to fix them that their action may be transferred to the chest, and thus assist the labouring respiration." This would be the action in a strong man dying from a mortal wound.

It should be observed that the muscular action, though so thoroughly understood, is not in any degree forced, though the appearance of effort to breathe, and restrain a cry of pain, is strongly marked. The veins are prominently shown on the ankle and arms.

Restorations.—The right arm, and toes of both feet.

Pliny speaks of a bronze statue by Ctesilaus of a wounded man dying, and perfectly expressing how much life remained in him. Montfaucon and Maffei have supposed it to be a copy of that statue. There are several inferior statues of the same subject varied (*see* Duruy, 'Hist. des Romains').

THE FIGHTING GLADIATOR: The Warrior of Agasias: The Borghese Gladiator. Life-size; marble; height, from left foot to head, 5ft. 4in. By Agasias of Ephesus. Louvre.

Though commonly called The Fighting Gladiator it is more probably a hero fighting on foot against an antagonist on horseback, as the upward look of the head suggests. There is no statue of a gladiator perfectly nude. The handle or belt of the

A.S.

shield still remains on the left arm, while a sword was no doubt held with the right hand. It might therefore be an Achilles, only that the rather thin and sinewy form is not such as would be chosen for the famous hero of the Greeks.

The name of Agasias is cut on the supporting part of the marble (*see* p. 203). But Agasias is not mentioned by Pausanias nor Pliny, so that his date is probably not, as supposed, 330 B.C. The name of Heraklides, son of Agasias, is on a statue of Mars in the Louvre. This statue was formerly in the Borghese Palace at Rome, and was taken to Paris and exhibited in the Louvre, first in 1815. It was found in 1620 at Antium on the coast of Italy where the Apollo Belvedere was found, and on a spot where there was once an ancient Roman Palace. The right arm was wanting.

Restorations.—The right arm and ear.

It has been thought to be a copy from a bronze statue; and there is in the collection of the Duke de Blacas, a small antique bronze in the same attitude, but wearing a helmet, with the hair short and curly, supposed to be Deiphobus defending himself from Achilles on the night of the taking of Troy.

HERMES — MERCURY of the BELVEDERE — formerly called *Antinous* of the Vatican, *Theseus, beardless Hercules,* and *Meleager.* Heroic ; m. Parian. Ht., 6ft. 6in. Vatican. That this fine statue is in the style of Praxiteles is presumable from the discovery of the beautiful broken statue of Hermes with the infant Dionysos at Olympia, known to be by Praxiteles. The character of the head, with the short curly hair, and its inclined attitude as of obedience to the message of the gods, although without the *petasus,* suggests a Hermes. The supple, muscular limbs also denote activity without the winged heels. Visconti first named it a *Hermes,* though Winckelmann thought it a *Meleager,* and Gerhardt thought it could not be an *Antinous* as the style is superior to the time of Hadrian. The slight drapery carried round the left arm is significant of Hermes as seen in the Olympia statue.

Several statues resemble this. One in the Glyptothek, Munich ; another in the Lansdowne collection ; another in the Louvre with remains of a caduceus ; another in the Museum at Athens ; and one in the British Museum (171), might represent Mercury as god of the *palæstra*, but the hair is not that of an athlete as in a Hermes Enagonios (*Newton*).

Restorations.—None.

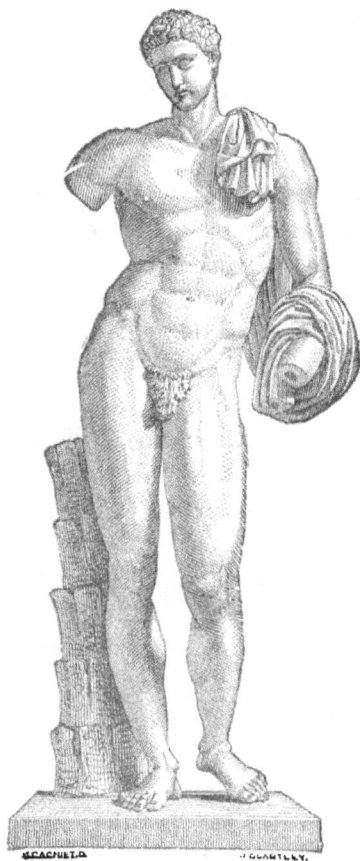

FIG. 134.—THE HERMES OF THE VATICAN.

HERCULES—the Farnese Hercules. Colossal. M. Grechetto. Naples Museum. Formerly in the Farnese coll., Rome. Found in 1540, in the baths of Caracalla, much broken and without legs, which were discovered long afterwards in 1787. (*See* Fig. 114.) A copy is in the Pitti Palace, Florence.

Restorations.—Half the forearm and hand, toes of both feet, but the hand with the apples is antique. Guglielmo della Porta supplied the legs when it was discovered, but the present legs are antique.

HERMES AND INFANT DIONYSOS, BY PRAXITELES. (*See* Fig. 96.)

JASON. Life-size, 4ft. 7in. ; m. Pentelic. The head of Grechetto m. Louvre. Formerly called Cincinnatus, from the ploughshare and one shoe at the base, but Winckelmann saw

that it was Jason, who was a farmer on the banks of the
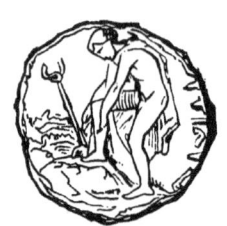
river Anaurus, and having forded the river
he tied on one sandal and forgot the
other, hurrying to assist King Pelias in
a sacrifice. The oracle had warned Pelias to
beware of a man with one shoe, and it was
this Jason who in the end slew him, though
he was sent away to get the golden fleece.

FIG. 135.—COIN.   A more acceptable fable is told by Pherikides,

Showing Jason.   that he left the plough to undertake the
Argonautic expedition at the bidding of Pelias. This has led
to the supposition that the statue was intended for a Cincinnatus.

Many varied repetitions exist—one in Munich Museum, one
smaller in the Vatican, and one in Lord Lansdowne's collection,
which is the only one having the original head. They may be
taken from a statue by Lycius, son of the famous Myron, who
is related to have sculptured one of the Argonauts.

Restorations.—The head though antique does not belong to the
figure, as is the case also with the Munich statue. The left arm,
right hand and part of arm, and the ploughshare are modern.

––––––––

THE LAOCOON.—Heroic; Grechetto marble; ht., 5ft. 10in.;
in the Vatican, Rome. This fine group was found in 1506 in
the Baths of Titus where Pliny said it was placed—not in a
vineyard on the Esquiline Hill as stated by F. di Sangallo.
This was in the pontificate of Julius II. while Michelangelo
was engaged upon his great works at the Vatican. That great
sculptor is said to have called it "a wonder of art." Pliny
speaks of its being in the palace of the Emperor Titus (lib.
xxxvi. c. v.). Michelangelo, who with Christoforo Romano was
directed to examine it, pointed out that it was not of one block,
but of three,—one for the son on the left, another for the figure
of Laocoon to the knees, and the third for the rest of the group.
It has, however, been since found to be made of six blocks.
When dug up, the right arm of Laocoon was gone as well as
the shoulder and the pectoral muscle; the right arm and foot

of the younger son, and the same parts of the elder, were also
broken off and lost.

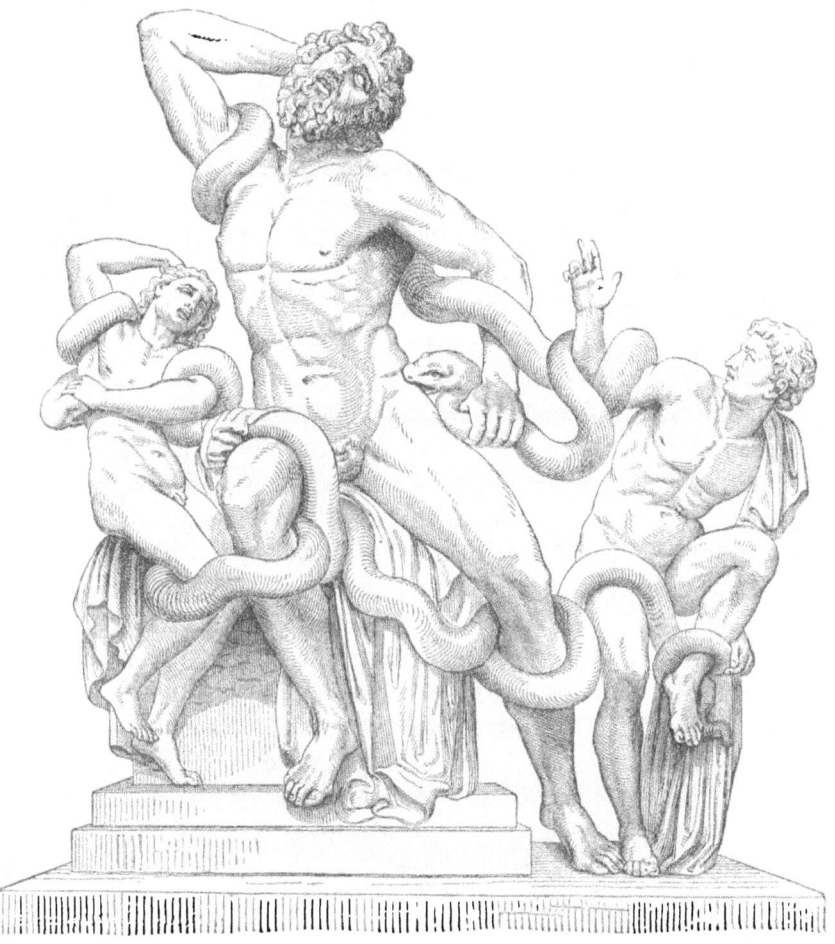

FIG. 136.—LAOCOON AND HIS SONS.

The work of the Rhodians Agesander, Athenodoros, and Polydoros.

In the Vatican. But with the arm as restored by Montorsoli.

The right arms and legs of the sons restored by Cornacchini, after designs by Bandinelli.

Restorations.—The right arm of Laocoon was supplied in
terra-cotta by Bernini, according to Winckelmann. But according to Fea ('Misc.' vol. i.) the arm at present on the Laocoon was

made by Cornacchini (see below). But Montorsoli (Giovan'
Angelo), a pupil of Michelangelo, about 1527, also designed an
arm which was left unfinished, and is still to be seen in the Vatican where it used to lie near the group. Montorsoli observing
a projecting fracture of the marble at the back of the head,
conjectured that the hand grasped the hair here, and he therefore made his arm bent back in such an attitude (*see* Fig. 136).
This is certainly a much finer conception, and more in harmony
with the composition. The existing restored arm makes the
group lean to one side, and with the hand grasping the serpent
and stretching out its long coil, the line of the arm is repeated as
no great master would have done. Canova had remarked that
this arm was wrong. Vasari relates also that Baccio Bandinelli
made an arm in wax in 1525, but this was never adapted upon
the original, although he took it in his well-known copy of the
group in the Uffizi which has the arm stretched out. Bandinelli's arm appears in Marliani's engraving of 1544, so Winckelmann cannot be right in attributing it to Bernini, who was not
born then. Marliani probably copied the copy at Florence. The
antique group had been promised to Francis I. by Leo X. at
Bologna, but he repented and ordered Bandinelli to make the
copy which he intended to present instead; but it was not
finished before his death, and was in hand during the Papacy
of Adrian VI. The copy, however, in the Florence Gallery is
not an accurate one, being varied in several of the forms. It
should be remembered also that the antique group was removed
to Paris by Napoleon with many other of his Italian art spoils;
and the catalogue of the Musée of 1815 states that the missing
parts were then supplied at Paris. " Le bras droit du père et
deux bras des enfans manquent: sans doute un jour on les
exécutera en marbre ; mais provisoirement on les a suppléés par
des bras moulés sur le groupe en plâtre, restauré par *Girardon*,*
qui se voit dans la Salle de l'Ecole de peinture."

The arms and feet of the two sons are the work of Agostino
Cornacchini of Pistoia, who is said to have simply followed the
restoration designed by Bandinelli, who was a great favourite

* François Girardon, the great French sculptor of the 17th cent. (died
1715) went to Rome to study and returned to Paris 1650.

with Pope Clement VII., and had rooms in the Belvedere while he was engaged in these restorations. It was he who designed and executed the right fore-arm and hand of the Apollo Belvedere, according to Vasari, who however in another place names Montorsoli. Clarac remarks that the head of the

Laocoon has been doubted, as the fragments of a similar group, were found in the ruins of the Palace of Titus ; but a close examination since made showed that the neck had never been broken through (Scharf, ' Crystal Palace Handbook'). A head of the Laocoon is in the Brussels Museum, considered by some to be antique, but by others as modern.

Mr. Ruskin's criticism upon the Laocoon is : " I suppose that no group has exercised so pernicious an influence on art as this."

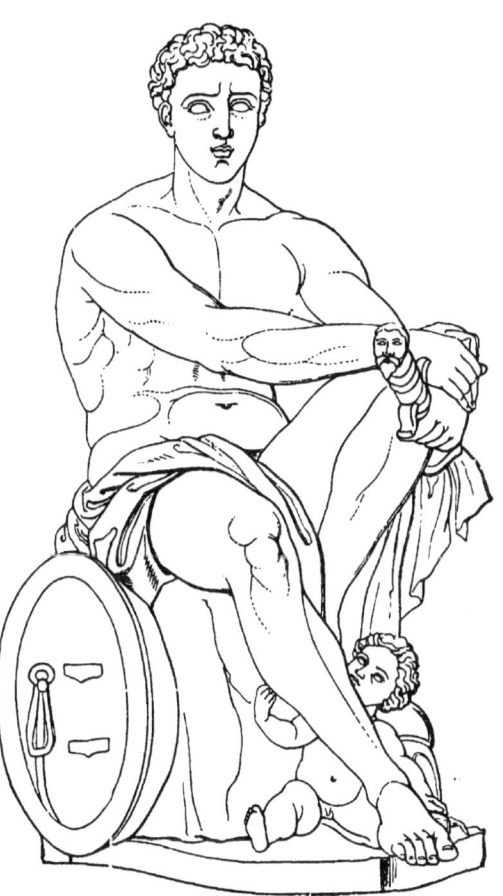

Fig. 137.—The Ludovisi Mars.
In the Villa Ludovisi, Rome.

MARS. The Ludovisi Mars. Seated statue, heroic, m. ; ht., 4ft. 10in. In the Villa Ludovisi, Rome. A warrior resting, holding his sword, with his shield lying by his side. The Cupid is a modern addition by Bernini, who restored the statue. It was found in the portico of Octavia. The attitude

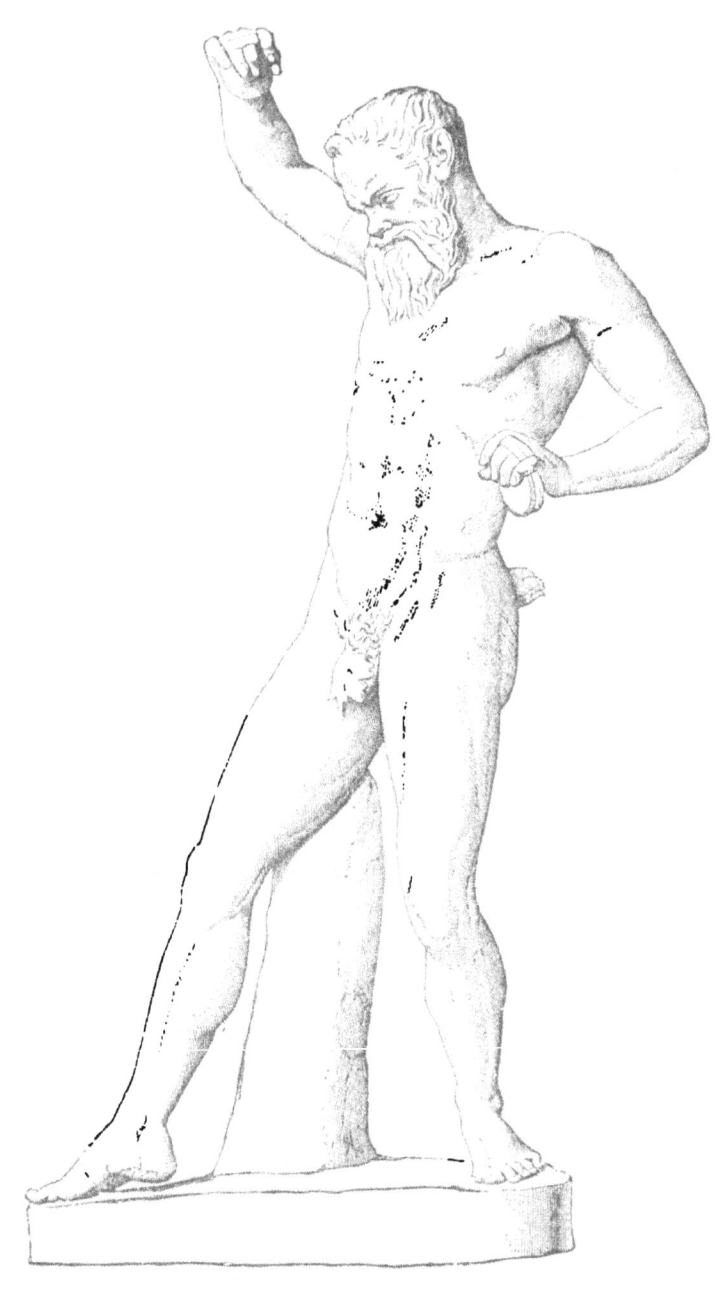

Fig. 138.—Marsyas. *Lateran Museum, Rome.*
Attributed to Myron. The arms modern.

is similar to that of Ares in the Parthenon frieze, No. 26, in the eastern frieze in the British Museum. It is no doubt taken from some fine original work, probably in bronze. The pose of the figure is strikingly grand, denoting the design of a great master. The execution of this marble is however not of high excellence.

Restorations.—Both arms and hands, and the handle of sword.

MARSYAS.—Life-size, m. Lateran Mus. The arms erroneously restored in this cut as for a dancing satyr. Probably belonged to a group of Athene and Marsyas about to seize her flutes, of which a bas-relief exists. Pausanias saw such a group in the Acropolis, Athens, and Pliny speaks of a work by Myron —" Satyrum admirantem tibias et Minervam" (xxxiv. 57). A small bronze in the Brit. Mus. with the arms is a similar figure. The attribution of this marble to Myron is at present not accepted.

MARSYAS—torso. Life-size; m. Pentelic. Berlin Museum. A very fine example, particularly of masterly technical skill. Cast in Crystal Palace, No. 73.

MELEAGER. Heroic; m. Ht., 6ft. 6in. Vatican. A noble work of its kind and remarkably perfect. It was once called Adonis, and is one of the celebrated statues in Rome. Even Michelangelo was not bold enough to model a hand for this fine figure. It has been known in Rome for at least three centuries, having been found in the 16th century, but precisely where is not settled : according to Flaminio Vacco on the Esquiline Hill, but Aldroandi says near the Porta Portese. It was in the Palazzo Pighini, and was acquired for the Vatican by Clement XIV.

MINERVA—THE PALLAS OF VELLETRI. Colossal; m. Parian; ht., 9ft. 10in. Louvre. A very noble statue, the head of severe and commanding character, though somewhat benign in expression. The goddess wears the helmet; the tunic has a belt of serpents, and has the Ægis with scales and numerous small serpents round the border, and the Medusa Mask.   The right foot is in advance, and the sandals are of the kind called Tyrrhenian, with five soles. It is a Roman copy from some famous Greek statue in bronze, and thought by M. Fröhner to be of the 1st century A.D. (Louvre Catalogue). The marble is in six blocks. It was found in 1797, in a vineyard about a mile from Velletri, the ancient Velitrae, between the road from Naples and that to Coni, where another statue of Athene was also found.   Traces of red colour are on the eyes and lips.   A bust in the Munich Museum, from the Villa Albani, resembles this.

Restorations. — Both hands, half the right foot, toes of left with part of sandal, and some small parts of the Ægis, drapery, serpents, and helmet.

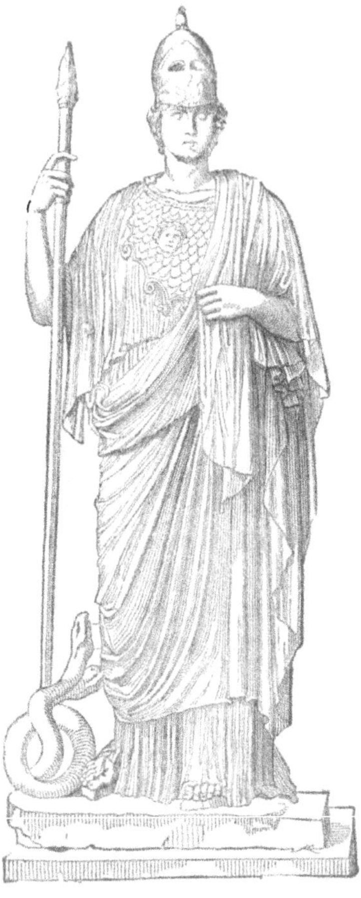

FIG. 139.—THE MINERVA OF THE VATICAN.

MINERVA, *known as* THE FARNESE MINERVA. Heroic, draped ; m. Greek ; ht., 6ft. 11in. Naples Museum. This resembles somewhat the Louvre statue, and is thought to have held a figure of Victory in the hand. The arms however are modern. It was found at Velletri. A similar statue is in the Hope collection at Deepdean, and another is engraved in Cavaceppi, called Pallas Albani.

MINERVA—THE PALLAS OF THE VATICAN.   Heroic, draped ; m. Parian ; ht., 6ft. 10in.   This statue has been restored with the attributes of 'Minerva Medica,' the serpent raising its head by her side, a spear in her right hand, the arms, the Corinthian helmet and Ægis, with mantle over the shoulders. It was found in the temple of Minerva Medica on the Esquiline, Rome.

This statue was for a long time in the possession of the Giustiniani family, and afterwards passed into the collection of Lucien Bonaparte, from whom it was eventually purchased by Pope Pius VII., and added to the Gallery of the Vatican. It represents the goddess as the beneficent protector and preserver of health by her wisdom. The drapery is an especially good example of the grave dignity given to the figure by the toga so admirably sculptured.

The form of the helmet is not that of the Athena of Pheidias, seen on the coins of Athens, but that found on the coins of Corinth.

Restorations.—Right arm and hand with spear and the serpent, emblem of health and long life, as seen in statues of Æsculapius.

THE MONTE CAVALLO COLOSSI. These two fine groups in marble of nearly nude figures each holding a prancing horse, stand on the Quirinal Hill, Rome, opposite the Palazzo Quirinale, one on each side of an obelisk, where they were placed by the architect and sculptor Fontana in the 16th century. The horses are supported by a sort of pedestal under the belly, and the figures by parts of suits of armour at the one leg. This armour is similar to that seen in ancient vase paintings and in the celebrated equestrian bronze of Alexander the Great in Naples Museum, also in other bronzes of Alexander. The treatment of the hair is similar to that on coins of his time, as has already been stated (p. 195); there are other points of resemblance to the Macedonian style of sculpture. The subject might therefore be Alexander with his horse Bucephalus, or, as has also been suggested, Bellerophon with his Pegasus, or, according to later views, the Dioscuri, Castor and Pollux. There are three Roman coins on which groups like these are seen— one struck in the time of Nero, another of Hadrian, and the third of Commodus. Visconti states that Flaminius Vacca relates a tradition that these statues were found in the ruins of the baths of Constantine on the Quirinal, and that he had them brought from the vestibule of the Palace of Nero, also that some architectural fragments found with them correspond with those found on the Palatine Hill. Visconti thought they were the work of sculptors of the time of Nero, such as those semi-colossal figures of the Nile and the Tiber in the Vatican. He suggests they may be copied from bronze works of Hegesias, which Pliny relates stood before the Temple of Jupiter Tonans in the Capitol. He also points out a resemblance in style between these figures and the well-known 'Warrior,' or Fighting Gladiator, by Agasias, whose name he thinks may be the same as ' Hegesias,' changed in the dialect of the Ephesians. This however, is very conjectural. As regards execution, these figures are rather roughly done, and the hind-quarters of the horses seem as if not intended to be shown, which would confirm the opinion that they stood close to a building. Flaxman accepted the opinion that they were the works of Pheidias and Praxiteles, according to the inscriptions on the pedestals, and from a resemblance to a figure managing a horse on the Parthenon frieze, but it is sufficient to observe that the style is not that of either of those great sculptors.

The Niobe group—14 figures. Life-size ; m. Florence Gallery. A very celebrated group of statues, which once adorned the temple of Apollo Sosianus at Rome. They were referred to both by Horace and Pliny as the work either of Skopas or Praxiteles.

Probably none of the original figures remain ; those that are at Florence are only a part of the copies made, for some do not belong to the subject and have merely been supplied to make up the number. The Pedagogue and Son are not at Florence, but in the Louvre, and are a very inferior group found at Soissons in France.

The head of Niobe is proverbial almost as an example of the

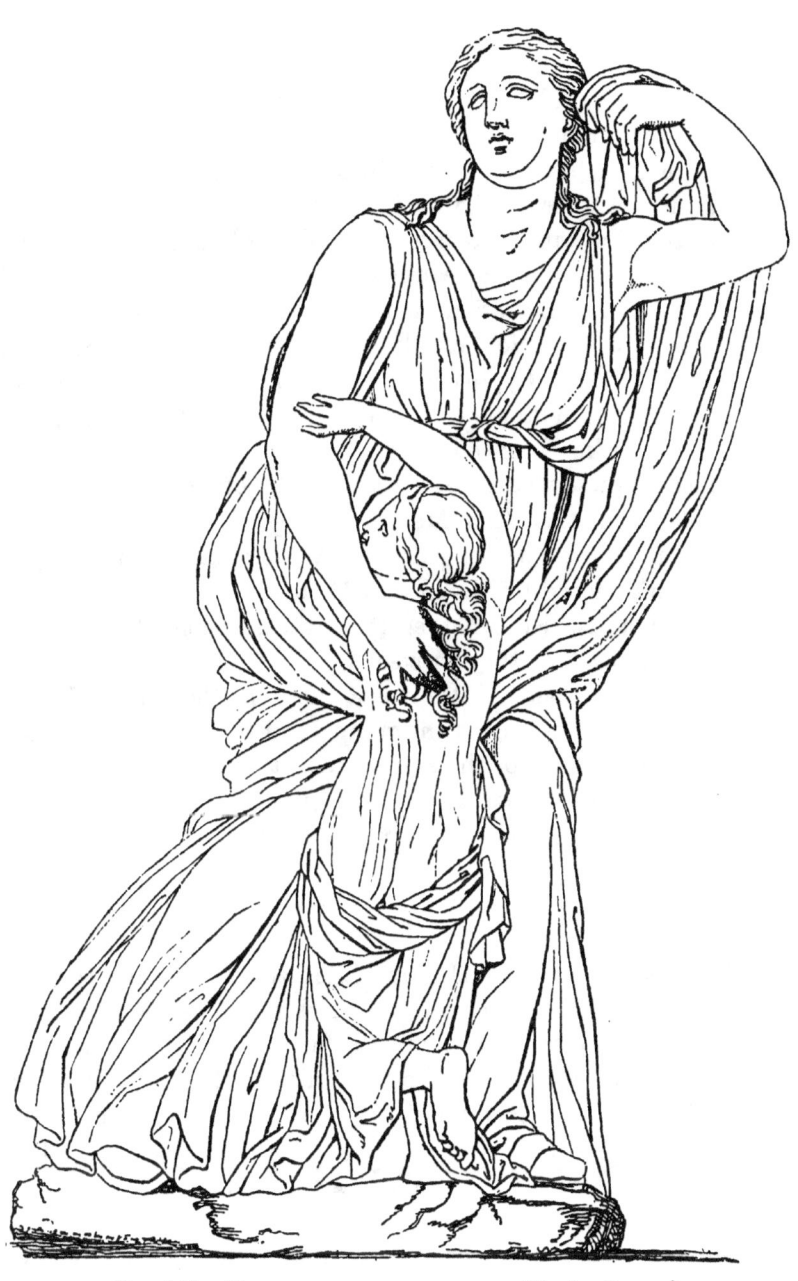

FIG. 140.—NIOBE AND HER CHILDREN. (Centre Group.)
Now in the Florence Gallery.

pathetic (Fig. 140). It was the favourite study of Guido, as is seen in his pictures.

There is a head of Niobe in Lord Yarborough's collection which is considered to be finer than that of the statue.

In the Vatican there are two 'Daughters of Niobe' from another group. In the Munich Museum is a very fine nude kneeling figure in Parian marble much injured, the arms and head lost, of the Son of Niobe looking up, which is called 'Ilioneus' (125, Glyptothek Cat.). There is also one of the sons lying on the ground. In the Capitol Museum, Rome, there is one of the kneeling sons.

Most of these statues were discovered before 1583, at Rome, and placed in the Villa Medici, having been obtained by the Medici family, in whose palace they were, till Pierre Leopold had them removed to Florence in 1776.

It is not decided whether the statues belong to the same group and whether they formed a pedimental or merely a semicircular arrangement. Also it is a question whether Apollo and Artemis did not belong to the group; and there is in the British Museum a bas-relief of the subject with those deities.

Restorations.—These are so very numerous in arms, hands, feet, and some legs that it is impossible to name them all.

SOMNUS (Hypnos)—reclining. Life-size; m. Vienna Imperial Museum. A boy sleeping on a lion's skin upon a rock, the right hand resting on the left shoulder, and the head upon the arm, the hair gathered into the knot peculiar to the antique Genius and Harpokrates. Several other statues like this are in various collections—in the Vatican, and in British Museum and in Dresden Museum. Clarac calls this a Cupid Asleep.

Restorations.—The right foot below the instep.

Somnus was a different god from Morpheus, his son, who presided over dreams, moulding the forms of them, as his name implies (Μορφη = form). A lizard is often represented near the figure of Somnus, and he often holds poppies, as the plant producing opium. Sometimes he has wings, at the shoulders and temples, and these are sometimes like those of a bird, in others like the butterfly. He is of all ages, from a boy to old age,[*] naked or loaded with clothes, or with the chlamys only. Sleep and Death were brothers in the Homeric poems, represented as young, holding the inverted torch and sometimes the poppy.

TORO FARNESE. Colossal group; m. Grechetto; ht., 12ft. 4in., on square base.   Naples Museum.   By Apollonius and Tauriscus of Rhodes. This is the group described by Pliny, representing Dirké being tied to a bull by Amphion and Zethus, the sons of Antiope, who thus revenged the insult of their mother, whose husband, Lykus king of Thebes, had forsaken her for Dirké. Antiope, according to some versions of the story, interposed to save her rival, but according to others Dirké was dragged about by the bull till she was dead, and was then thrown into a well, which to this day is called "the well of Dirké."

So much that is expressive in the heads and figures not being due to the ancient sculptor, but to the restorer Bianchi under the direction of Michelangelo, the group is chiefly valuable as an example of the ambitious style of colossal work which characterized the later Rhodian school after the time of Lysippos, when it was brought to the extreme by Chares in his Colossus. The lyre hung upon the tree and the Pandean pipes are in allusion to Amphion's skill in music: "Movit Amphion lapides canendo" (Hor. Car. III. xi.). The wild animals, with sheep and oxen carved on the base, describe the pastoral life led by the sons of Lykus on Mount Cithæron when expelled by him with their mother.

Pliny tells us (lib. xxxvi. c. v.) this grand work was brought from Rhodes to Rome, and that it was cut out of a single block of Greek marble, and that Asinius Pollio purchased it in the time of Augustus. It was much broken, and some parts entirely gone—as the head of the bull, for example. It was placed in the court of the Farnese Palace, where Michelangelo superintended

---

[*] The old man on some funereal sculptures was probably the Etruscan Charon waiting for the soul.

the restorations by Giov. Battista Bianchi. In 1786 it was removed to Naples and suffered further injuries in the transport, which had to be restored; it was then placed in the Villa Reale,

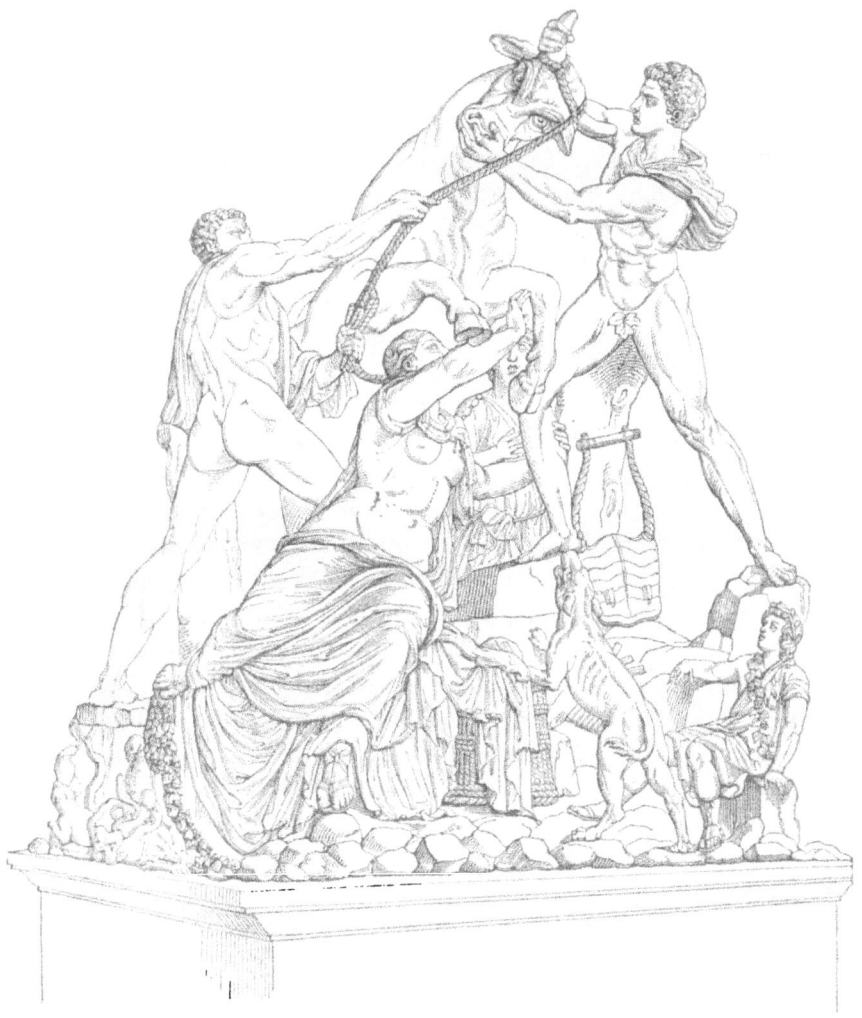

FIG. 141.—TORO FARNESE.
In the Naples Museum.

and after remaining exposed to the weather for many years it was removed to the Royal Museum by order of Francis I.

It was found at Rome in the Baths of Caracalla, with the

Hercules of Glykon (Fig. 117), during the Pontificate of Paul III.

Restorations.—All of Dirké above the waist; the head and neck of Amphion, the arms, part of hands, the legs to above the knees, only three toes being antique. The head of Zethus, the left leg from foot to thigh at the tree, right knee and part of leg, right arm between wrist and shoulder, left fore-arm with drapery, hand, and cords. Head and neck of Antiope, arms, hands, and parts of leg. The bacchanal boy's head less restored, but arms, legs, and goat skins, &c. modern. The head of the bull. The dog is new all but one paw, and the base is much restored by Bianchi.

A cast of this fine work is in the Crystal Palace.

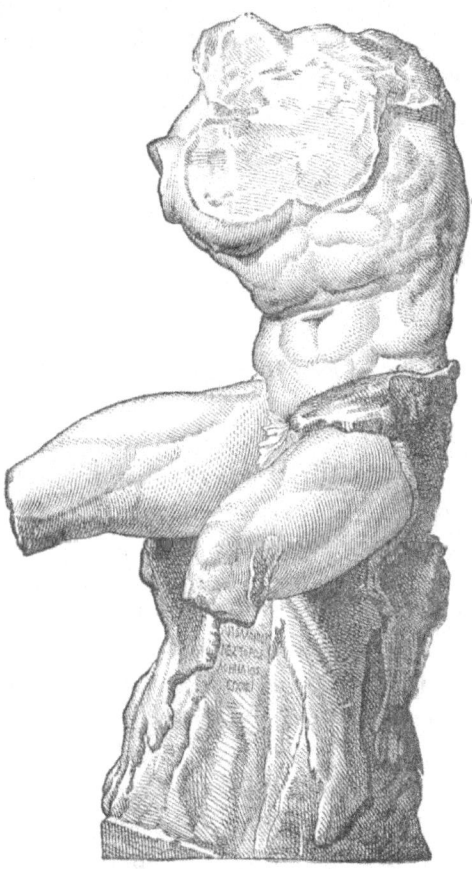

FIG. 142.—THE TORSO BELVEDERE.
In the Vatican.

THE TORSO BELVE-DERE. Heroic; m. Pentelic; ht., 5ft. 1½in. Vatican. By Apollonios about 336 B.C. The celebrated torso often called after Michelangelo because he studied it so profoundly, and made it his great example for sculptors. Flaxman borrowed it for one of his compositions of the Apotheosis of Hercules. That it is a Hercules is shown by the remains of the Nemæan lion's skin on the thigh and the rock. On the rock is cut the

A.S.

name of the sculptor—ΑΠΟΛΛΩΝΙΟΣ ΝΕΣΤΟΡΟΣ ΑΘΗΝΑΙΟΣ ΕΠΟΙΕΙ—who was careful to show he was an Athenian. He was not the Apollonios who with Tauriscus made the *Toro Farnese*.

It was found in the Campo dei Fiori, near the theatre of Pompey, at the end of the 15th century.

It is remarkable that so fine a work should not be mentioned by Pliny or any of the ancient writers. There is another fine torso in Naples Museum (*described below*), known as the Farnese Torso, which is sometimes spoken of as a rival of this one, but being a Bacchus it is different in character, yet it may fairly be compared. There is also a colossal torso in the Naples Museum which is a fine work, though the forms are somewhat fleshy. It is a Bacchus, from the fillets on the shoulders.

Torso, *known as the* Farnese Torso. Life-size; m. Greek. Naples Museum. This beautiful *torso** of a seated figure is almost as celebrated as that of the Vatican collection—the Torso Belvedere. It is remarkable for the full and noble form, and the grand style of the treatment of the figure. It has been thought to be a Narcissus, or more probably Bacchus from the curling hair falling on the neck, and the fillets of the vine (*vittæ*). The head was turned away towards the left, the inclination of the figure being to the right. The neck is firmly set on, a portion of the right arm remains, and part of the thighs. There are indications of a staff (*thyrsus*) upon the thigh and belly. It was removed from the Farnese Palace in Rome to the collection at Naples. Poussin the French painter is said to have especially admired and studied this statue. Engraved in Clarac Musée, pl. 683. This is not to be confounded with the other torso in the Naples Museum which is colossal in size, and perhaps a Bacchus, but of inferior style. Casts of both may be compared in the Crystal Palace, Nos. 188 and 193, the Farnese Torso.

Theseus of the Parthenon. (*See* Fig. 91.)

* *Torso* means the trunk from which the head and limbs have been torn off.

VENUS. Life-size; m. Florence Gallery. A half-draped standing figure, holding the drapery with the left hand, the other being raised and touching a lock of hair. A diadem on the head showing traces of red and gold, with holes for jewels, and the ears are pierced. A bracelet is carved on the right arm.

VENUS OF ARLES. Heroic; m. Greek, of Hymettus. Ht., 6ft. 5½in. Louvre. This statue resembles the Venus (Fig. 147), having the drapery round the hips and over the left arm, her right arm raised as if to dress the hair which is bound into a fillet, the head turning as if towards a mirror or flask held in the other hand. The mirror and the apple with the arms and hands are, however, modern. It has been considered by some to be a Venus Victrix, but M. Fröhner does not admit this. He thinks it and the Towneley Venus in Brit. Mus. belong to the school of Praxiteles, and are from the same original.

It was found in 1651 at Arles in France, where the worship of Venus was especially followed; *Julia Arelatensis*, the name of the town, referring to the descent of the family of *Julia* from Venus and Anchises. It was found in sinking a well in the ruins of the ancient theatre, and was placed in the Great Gallery at Versailles in 1685, after having been brought to Paris in the care of Jean Dedieu, a sculptor of Arles and pupil of Puget.

Restorations.—The head was broken off the neck, but part only of the fillet is new. The right arm, the left fore-arm, the two hands with the apple and mirror handle, and many parts of the drapery, were done by Fr. Girardon in 1684.

VENUS. Colossal bust. This beautiful work, in Parian marble, was found at Arles. It belonged to a statue. It is in the Museum of that town, and was presented by the Duc de Luynes. It is considered to be of the same school as the Venus of Melos, and may be regarded as of the Praxitelean style.

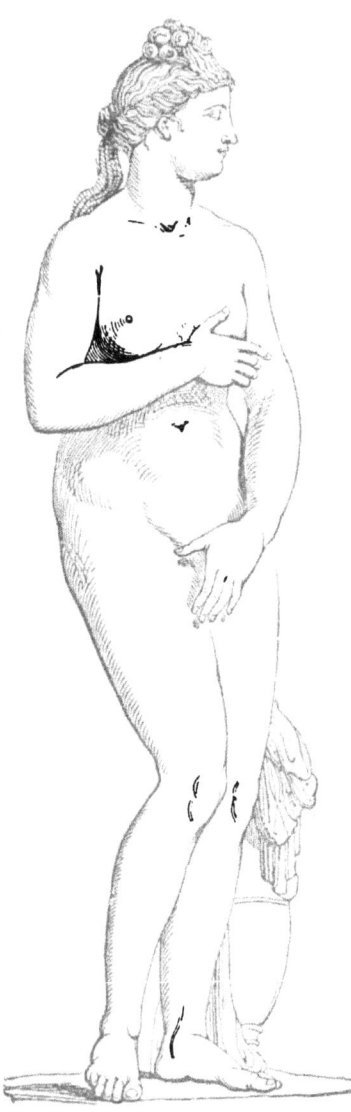

FIG. 143.—VENUS.

Resembling the Statue in the Capitoline Museum, Rome.   British Museum.

VENUS OF THE CAPITOL. Heroic; m. Parian. Ht. 6.$\frac{2}{10}$ft. This statue has a nobler character in the form and is altogether a more complete work than the Medici Venus, than which it is much larger. It has the special interest of being nearly as perfect as the ancient sculptor left it. Flaxman said, " an example of more dignified and less insinuating beauty than the Venus dei Medici, and certainly a copy from one of the three enumerated by Pliny among the works of Praxiteles." It has, from the form of the hair in a knot on the top of the head, been thought to be an Artemis.

Restorations. — Only the tip of the nose and two of the fingers.

It was found at Rome towards the end of the 18th century near the " Suburra di monti."

The statue (Fig. 143), British Museum, is very similar but inferior. Another is in the Louvre (152), one of the Borghese statues. The height of this, however, differs from the Capitol Venus, being 6ft. 9in., and it is much restored—right arm from elbow, left fore-arm, right foot and ankle, heel and half of left foot. Several other copies exist. " All are probably repetitions of the Knidian Venus of Praxiteles, modified to please Roman taste " (*Newton*).

VENUS OF CAPUA. Heroic; m. Greek. Ht., 6ft. 7in. Naples Museum. Half-draped, similar attitude to the Venus of Milo, Venus of Arles, and Towneley Venus, but having a tiara or front-let on the head. It is a fine statue taken probably from a Greek original of the type *Venus Victrix*.

Restorations.—The arms have been supplied by wooden ones, and a Cupid in plaster added, as some traces of small feet are seen on the plinth.

VENUS or Dione. Heroic; m. Greek. Ht., 6ft. 7in. British Museum. This fine statue is commonly spoken of as the Towneley Venus from the name of the collector from whom it was acquired. It is nude to the waist. The right arm is raised gracefully while the left holds the drapery, but as this is a restoration it is doubtful " whether the left hand held up a mirror, a diadem, or a small flask, *alabastron*, containing unguent. It may possibly be a work of the Macedonian period, though it may with more probability be referred to the Augustan age " (*Newton*). It is in two pieces of marble joined at the drapery. It was found in the ruins of the baths of the Emperor Claudius at Ostia, 1776.

Restorations.—The left arm, right fore-arm, tip of nose, and parts of drapery.

VENUS GENITRIX. Life-size; m. Parian. Ht., 5ft. 4½in. Louvre. This is a standing draped statue of Venus as the mother of the Romans (Genitrix) as on the medals. She holds the apple; the drapery is very thin, without girdle or sleeves, showing the figure; the ears are pierced, and she wears sandals. Flaxman thought it copied from the draped Venus of Cos by Praxiteles which the people bought of him. Similar statues are in the Naples Museum, and one at Holkham (Lord Leicester's), holding a vase, which is modern, in the left hand.

Restorations.—The head fixed on : the left hand and apple in the right, with the part of the drapery held in it, are modern.

VENUS DE' MEDICI.   Life-size; m. Parian.   Ht., 4ft. 11⅓in.
Florence, in the Tribune of the Uffizi; by Kleomenes of
Athens.

In allusion to the birth of the goddess from the foam of the
sea, is the Dolphin, on whose back are sporting the two boy
deities, Eros and Himeros.   The hair is bound up as the Horæ
were said to have done it.   The ears are pierced and no doubt
once had ear-rings, and on the left arm is the mark of an
armlet.

It was found in the Forum of Octavia or Hadrian's Villa at
Tivoli about 1680, with other beautiful statues, amongst which
was the knife-sharpener 'L'Arrotino.'   (Fig. 122.)

It was brought to Florence in the Pontificate of Innocent XI.,
in the reign of Cosmo III. di Medici, and placed in the gardens
of the Medici in the 16th century, and was placed in the
gallery of the Uffizi in 1680.

Restorations.—It was broken into thirteen pieces; the head
was off, the trunk injured, the thighs broken, the feet, the arms,
and hands almost entirely gone.   Fortunately the fractures were
so regular that the pieces were easily joined with the exception
of some parts in the trunk.   The right arm and hand and the
left from the elbow were lost, and these, it is said, were supplied by Bernini.   This accounts for some of the affectation
shown in the position of · the arms and hands.   These are
not at all of the antique character, and the statue is much
grander without them, as indeed it should always be when
studied from.   The plinth is also modern, the ancient one
having been too much broken to be used, but the Greek
inscription was accurately copied, which translated reads (*see*
Fig. 144)—

" Kleomenes, son of Apollodoros the Athenian, did it."   He
is spoken of by Pliny as a sculptor of the highest repute for his
female figures.   The son of this sculptor is thought to be him
whose name is cut upon the tortoise at the foot of the statue
called Germanicus in the Louvre, No. 184.

It is thought to bear some resemblance to the famous
Venus of Praxiteles, the first representing the goddess nude,
of which some idea is obtained from the coins of the time

of Caracalla and Plautilla
(*see* Fig. 146). Old copies
in marble of the Venus of
Knidos are in the Vatican
(Fig. 145), and an especially
good one in the Glyptothek
at Munich. An antique
marble copy of the Medici
Venus in the Louvre (156)
has the arms, which are
modern, slightly different
from Bernini's in the Florence statue. The left foot
and some toes of the right
are also new. This be-
longed to the Campana Collection, and was found at
Porto d'Anzio (Antium).

A statue in the Dresden
Museum closely resembles
the Medici Venus, the legs
however being lost from
about half of the thighs. A
small bronze in the Brit.
Mus. is in this attitude.

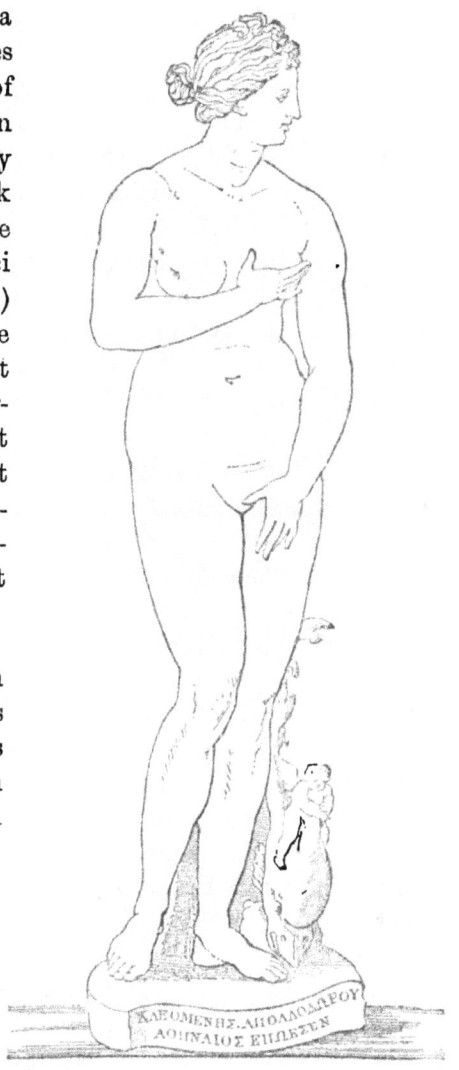

FIG. 144.—VENUS DE' MEDICI.
In the Tribune of the Uffizi Gallery.

ΚΛΕΟΜΕΝΗΣΑΠΟΛΛΟΔΩΡΟΥ
ΑΘΗΝΑΙΟΣ . ΕΠΩΕΣΕΝ

VENUS OF KNIDOS. Heroic; m. Greek. Ht., 6ft. 8in. Vatican. Presumed to be a copy of the famous Venus of Praxiteles, described by Pliny (lib. xxxvi. c. 5), made of Parian marble, standing in a little temple open on all sides, so that it could be seen all round. Lucian describes the mouth as open and smiling, admires the beauty of the hair, the well-pencilled eyebrows and swimming softness and vivacity of the eyes (ὀφθαλμων το ὑγρον ἁμα τῷ φαιδρῷ). The original was destroyed in the burning of the Lausium Palace at Constantinople in 475 A.D. Imperial medals struck at Knidos have Caracalla and Plautilla, and on reverse this Venus. The position is reversed in the figure taken from the engraving by Episcopus (or Bischop, 17th cent.), which is not very accurate. The statue in the Vatican has a modern stucco drapery from the loins, put on by order of the Pope, with which it has been ignorantly engraved in the Museo Pio Clementino.

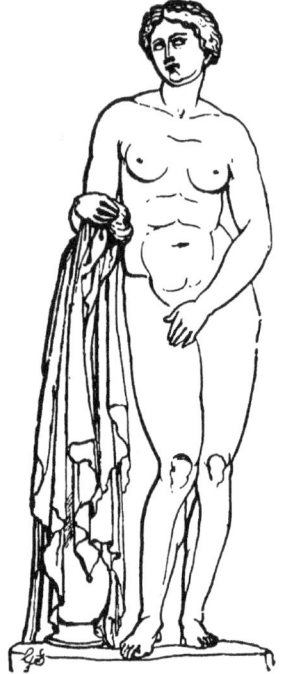

FIG. 145.
THE VENUS OF KNIDOS.
Vatican.

Another statue, considered to be much finer, is in the Glyptothek, Munich, which is life-size and of stone; found in a vineyard at Rome at the end of last century.

A bronze statue of the celebrated Venus was made by Praxiteles, destroyed in the reign of Claudius by a fire at Rome. ('Hist. Nat.' lib. xxxiv. c. 8.)

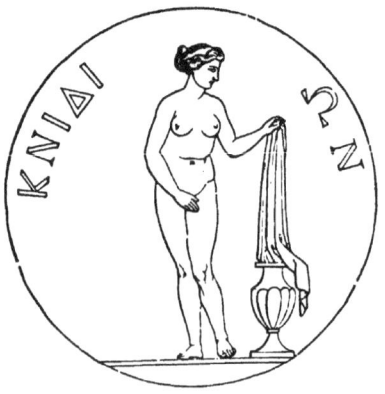

FIG. 143.—COIN OF KNIDOS. VENUS.

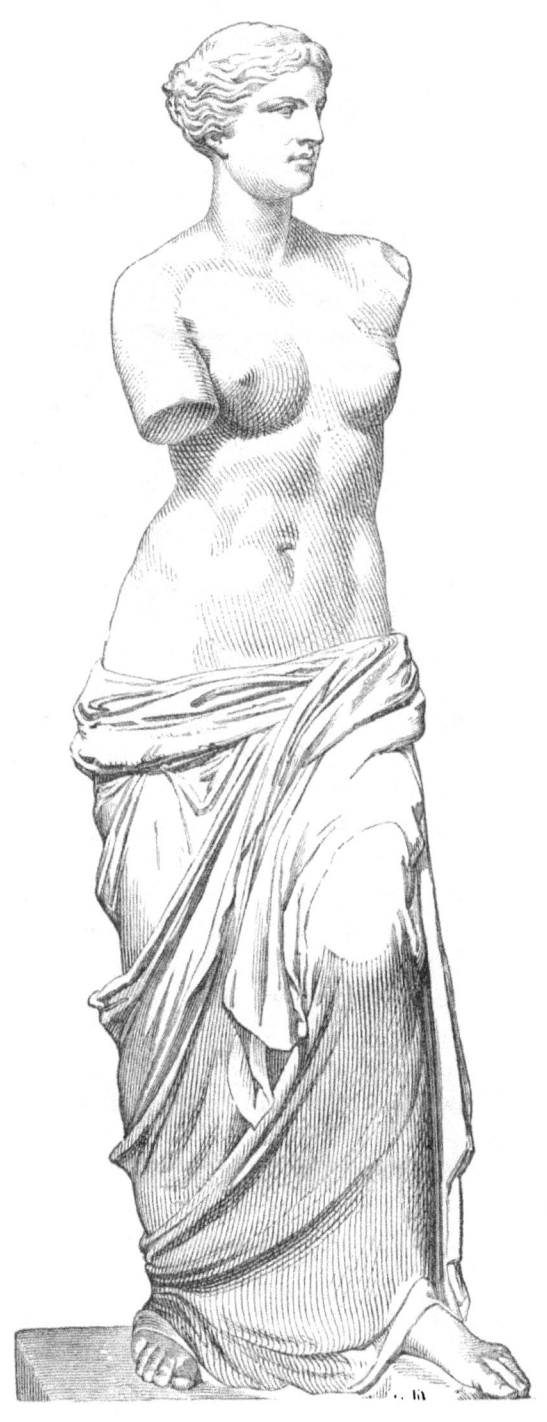

FIG. 147.—VENUS OF MELOS. *In the Louvre. The left foot added.*

VENUS OF MILO *or* MELOS, the name of the island in which
it was found. (Venus Victrix.) A half-draped heroic-size
statue, the arms and left foot broken off. Marble. Height, 6ft.
8in. In the Louvre; No. 136. Corallitic marble, like ivory in
colour, and very close in the grain.

The name of the sculptor is not known, but this beautiful
statue is considered by Clarac to be of the school of Praxiteles.
But being partly draped some think it to be of an earlier time.
Others have attributed it to Alcamenes and to Agesandros. By
Overbeck it ·is considered to be of so late a time as that of
Augustus. Mr. Newton would place it about 250 B.C. It was
found in 1820 by a Greek peasant in getting up the roots of a
tree, when the whole fell through into a hollow place which
proved to be a tomb in the rock. The bust was first found, and
then the trunk in two parts, separated where the drapery
begins, at the hips; but the head was not separate, being
perfect with the exception of the nose; the left foot was quite
lost. A hand holding an apple was found, and a fragment of
a plinth was also found near the statue, inscribed with the last
letters of a name, . . . ΑΝΔΡΟΣ, supposed to be part of the
name Ἀγησανδρος, and the rest of the inscription Μηνιδου (Ἀντ)
ιοχευς ἀπὸ Μαιάνδρου ἐποίησεν (*Clarac* Inscrip. pl. 54). "The
son of Menides of Antioch near the river Maeander has done it,"
all in letters of the best period. This fragment, according to
M. Clarac, fitted the broken plinth on which the statue stood.
The statue was purchased by the Count Marcellus (the friend
and secretary of Chateaubriand when he was in London), and
presented by him to the French nation.

Restorations.—The nose, and the left foot. The plinth has
been let into a new block of marble, and until within the last
ten years the figure had an inclination out of the perpendicular
caused by the lower part of the plinth not being quite true.
This has been rectified, and the statue is much improved by it,
but in all the old casts the defect will be noticed.

It may be noticed that the attitude suggests that some object
was held resting on the knee, such as a shield. A bronze statue
in a somewhat similar attitude, now in the Louvre, is a winged
figure of Victory holding a shield, and inscribing it, which was

found at Brescia about twenty years ago. There is also a resemblance in attitude to the Venus of Capua in the Naples Museum. M. Fröhner is of opinion that the left hand with apple belongs to this statue, but the right hand held the drapery. M. Claudius Tarral, sculptor, has made the most accurate investigation of the fragments, and agrees in this opinion. He notices that certain irregularities in the forms show that the sculptor was not a copyist but essentially an originator, working from his own ideal. The right cheek is rather larger than the left, and the corners of the mouth are not exactly alike, and the drapery is simple and finely designed so as to avoid all folds not essential to the position and not interfering with the harmony of the figure (*see* Louvre Cat., p. 171).

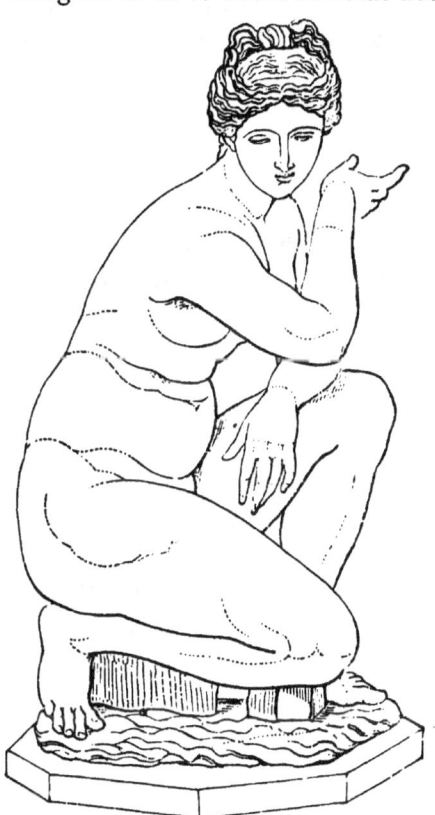

VENUS, Crouching. Pentelic m. Ht., 3ft. 7¾in. Vatican. Found at Salona at the end of 18th century, near Preneste. The plinth is inscribed ΒΟΥΠΑΛΟΣ ΕΠΟΙΕΙ, but this is regarded as modern ; the vase is, however, partly antique.

Restorations.—Hair, and upper part of head, and face retouched, right hand, left hand partly, fore-part of right foot and the two first toes of left. Visconti speaks of a bracelet, but this is not visible now. There was a famous statue of Venus at the Bath

FIG. 148.—THE CROUCHING VENUS. *Marble. Vatican.*

by Polycharmes, which Pliny speaks of as in the portico of Octavia (lib. xxxvi. c. 5), Venerem lavantem sese. Two similar statues once in the Giustiniani Palace are now in the collection of Prince Torlonia. A similar figure is in a bas-relief with two Cupids holding a cloth, in Ludovisi Villa.

VENUS AND CUPID. Heroic size; Parian m. Louvre. The goddess arming with the sword of Mars, with Cupid trying on the helmet. She has an armlet on left arm. A fine group, formerly in the Borghese Villa and Palazzo della Valle, and belonged once to Pope Julius III.

Restorations.—The whole surface has been rasped over; the right arm, left hand, left leg from knee to ankle, left arm of Cupid and right hand, his wings, and visor of helmet. (Clarac.)

VENUS, called the Crouching, or in the bath. Parian m. Ht., 2ft. 3¼in. Louvre. Has the right hand raised above the head. Differs also from the Vatican figure in being smaller.

Restorations.—Tip of nose, right hand, left arm and leg, part of thigh, and sole of foot.

VENUS KALLIPYGE. Life-size; m. Greek. Ht., 5ft. 2½in. Naples Museum. A nude statue holding drapery in front, and in the attitude of looking back over her shoulder as if admiring her own beautiful back, from which the statue takes its name (καλλίπυγος).

It was formerly in the Farnese collection with most of the sculptures at Naples, and was found in the ruins of the Golden House of Nero. It was once placed with all the Venuses in the Naples Museum in a separate room called after the name of this statue, and kept from the public view.

It has some few good points in the work of the body, but is not entitled to the reputation it has held of being copied from one of the Venuses of Praxiteles.

Restorations.—The head, the right leg and hand, part of the left arm, the hand and the breast are modern, and the work of the sculptor Albaccini.

(Venus Kallipyge.) The story goes that two pretty peasant girls disputed which had the best figure, and they appealed to a young noble of Syracuse passing near, who decided in favour of the elder one. Being desperately smitten with her charms, he confided his secret to his brother, who begged to see the two girls, and then preferred the younger one. ('Athenæus Deipnosoph,' lib. xii. ch. xc.)

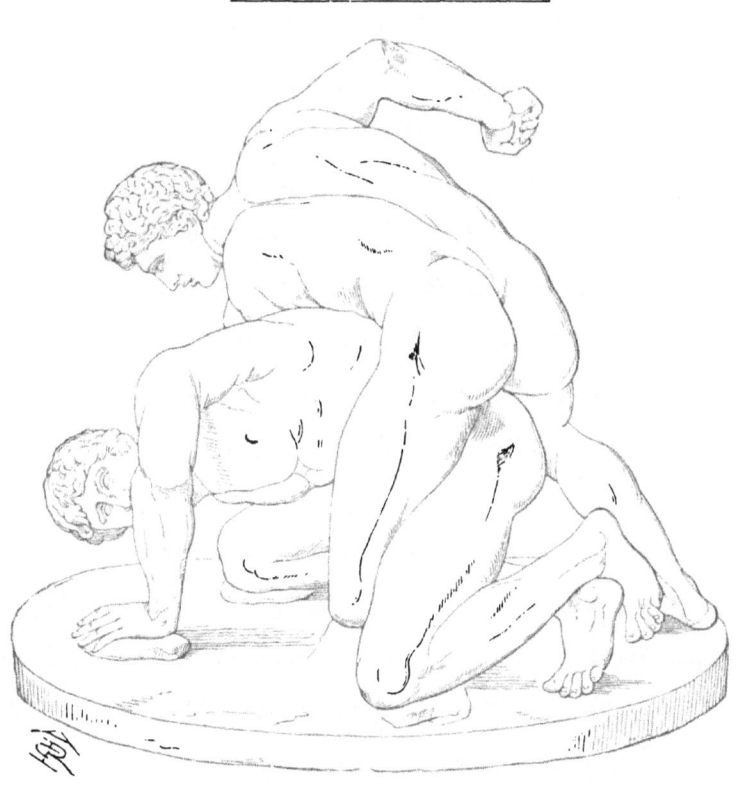

FIG. 149.—THE WRESTLERS.
In the Tribune of the Uffizi.

THE WRESTLERS. Group; m. Ht., 2ft. 10½in.; length, 3ft. 11in. Florence Gallery. A most remarkable group, although much of it is new. The immense difficulties of such a work are surmounted with wonderful skill, and in the knowledge of the figure shows a great mastery of the technical part of the art.

It represents a deadly struggle, not a mere throwing to the ground, which was another kind of game; in this the upper figure is about to deal a finishing blow upon his victim. It is a good example of choice of motive. It belongs to the later style of Greek art, and has been connected with the Niobe figures from having been found in the same place, and sold in one lot with them to the Medici family. Winckelmann thought they belonged to that group in accordance with another account of the Niobe catastrophe, which says that the sons were wrestling when it happened. In treatment it recalls the Laocoon group, and is classed in the school of Rhodes by some German critics.

Restorations.—The heads, the left arm and foot, right leg from knee of the upper figure, the right arm and leg above knee of the lower are modern. It is, however, maintained that they are antique; the head of the conquered wrestler being retouched only.

YOUNG SATYR, carrying a goat. M. Ht., 4ft. 6in. Madrid Museum. An excellent and spirited figure, the fir crown and *Syrinx*, or pipe on the tree trunk, left unfinished. Found in Rome near the church of S. Maria in Vollicella.

Restorations.—The arms from shoulders, the left leg from knee to middle of foot, done by Ercole Ferrata.

A good cast in the Royal Academy, London.

YOUTH SUPPLICATING THE GODS. Bronze. Ht., 4ft. 2½in. Berlin Museum. A young athlete invoking success, or giving thanks. A very fine and perfect work, found in the Tiber, and presented by Clement XI. to Prince Eugene of Savoy, from whom it passed to Prince Lichtenstein, who sold it to Frederick II. for 10,000 crowns. It resembles in style the bronze ' Spinario,' Fig. 123. A cast is in the Crystal Palace.

Restorations.—Part only of the right arm and hand.

ZEUS (the Jupiter of Versailles). Colossal; Carrara m. Ht., 11ft. 4½in. Louvre. This large decorative statue represents the god as the Giant-Slayer—' Gigantomachos.' The head is turned to the right, the hair floating behind as if by the wind. It was in the Medici Gardens, Rome, and was given to Cardinal Granvelle, who brought it to his Palace at Besançon in 1546. It was presented to Louis XIV. in 1668 and placed at Versailles. Mentioned in Montfaucon (Supplement) and Clarac, ' Musée,' pl. 312. There is another colossal Zeus in the Louvre, of Pentelic marble, about 7ft. 8in. high. Statues of Zeus are not common. A colossal seated statue much restored was in the part of the Canpana Collection sold to the Emperor of Russia. It was found on the shore of the lake of Alba. There is another colossal statue of Zeus,—No. 325, Vatican,—formerly in the Verospi Palace.

IMPORTANT BAS-RELIEFS.

ENDYMION. Alto-relievo ; life-size ; m. In the Capitoline Museum, Rome. Asleep upon a rock, his head, which is only blocked out, is inclined upon his breast ; the right side of the figure is shown, the arm fallen by the side, his spear resting on the left shoulder, his dog starting in the act of barking, as if he knew Selene was approaching. Selene (moon) came from heaven to kiss the beautiful youth. This fine relief was found upon the Aventine Hill during the Pontificate of Clement XI., according to Ficorini. It is thought that the head was left unfinished, as it was intended for some place where it would be in shadow and seen from below. Cast in the Crystal Palace, No. 33.

FEMALE FIGURE IN A CHARIOT. Bas-relief ; m. Athens Museum. An important example of the early Athenian sculpture of the time of Peisistratos (B.C. 560—490), which resembles the Xanthian bas-reliefs in the British Museum. It was found at Athens amongst the remains of the buildings destroyed by the Persians. The hair of this figure shows resemblance to the Xanthian figures, and the zigzag folds of the drapery are similar. A cast of this is No. 59, Crystal Palace.

PERSEUS AND ANDROMEDA. Alto-relievo; life-size; m. In the Capitoline Museum, Rome. Perseus with wings on head and heels, is nude, with the chlamys over the left shoulder and arm, falling down the left side of the leg. Andromeda is clothed in a long tunic and peplos, the head of the monster lying dead at her feet. The left hand of Perseus appears to hold the head of Medusa, which is not shown. Cast No. 35, Crystal Palace.

TWO COMBATANTS AND A HORSE. Bas-relief; m. Pentelic; above life-size. In the Villa Albani, Rome. This is one of the most beautiful bas-reliefs known, and is considered to have so much of the grand style that it may be classed next to the works of Pheidias. It was found near the arch of Gallienus, Rome, in 1764.

ANIMALS.

THE DOG 'Molossos.' M. Ht., 3ft. 8½in. Florence Mus. Two of these stand at the top of the stairs in the Uffizi. Fine examples of the life-like sculpture of animals by the ancient artists. There is another in the Vatican.

THE FLORENTINE BOAR. M.; life-size. The Boar of Calydon killed by Meleager. A copy in marble in the Louvre, and in bronze by Pierre Tacca in the Mercato Nuovo, Florence.

The most remarkable collection of animals sculptured in marble and hard stones of various kinds is in the Vatican.

The collection of casts from antique sculptures recently added to the South Kensington Museum, at the suggestion of Mr. Perry, affords many interesting and instructive examples, so that with those in the British Museum, and the Crystal Palace which is the most extensive collection of casts available for study to be found anywhere, the student is now enabled to acquire a complete practical knowledge of ancient sculpture.

A CHRONOLOGICAL LIST

OF

ANCIENT SCULPTORS,

AND THEIR WORKS.

---

*In this list the names of the sculptors and their works are spelt as in Greek.
In the text they are given as the Greek names were spelt by Latin writers.*

THE names of Egyptian sculptors of the earliest times (B.C. 5000) who designed those grand works still existing in so perfect a state, are not recorded. The same is to be said of the Assyrian sculptures, and of those called Phœnician.

The Shield of Achilles, described by HOMER, and the Shield of Herakles, the description of which is attributed to HESIOD, were worked in thin metal, embossed and chiselled ; but no names of the sculptors are recorded. The date of Homer and Hesiod is doubtful. The middle of the 9th century B.C. may serve for the time of Homer ; Hesiod was about a century later, about 735 B.C. The date accepted for the capture of Troy is B.C. 1184.

Certain names of Greek sculptors working in the primitive manner, to which the general term "Archaic" is applied, are mentioned by Herodotos, Pliny, and Pausanias as traditional, but their precise date is not known.

HERODOTOS was born at Halikarnassos 484 B.C., and wrote when an old man of 77. The date of his death is not known. PLINY was born at Verona A.D. 23, and perished in the eruption of Vesuvius in the year 79. PAUSANIAS (a native of Lydia?) wrote in the time of the emperor M. Aurelius, 161—180 A.D. Pausanias says—"Of my time the Emperor Adrian," &c. (*Taylor's Translation*, Book I., p. 14.) This Emperor was born A.D. 76, and died in July, A.D. 138.

ABBREVIATIONS : St. = Statue. W. = Wood. T. C. = Terra cotta. M. = Marble. B. = Bronze. G. = Gold. I. = Ivory. E. = Ebony.

B.C.

665 ? **Butades** or **Dibutades**—*Corinth*—Bas-relief in baked clay—Portrait of his daughter's lover—Said by Pliny to have been still at Corinth when the city was sacked by Mummius.

666— **Eucheir—Diopos—Eugrammos**—From *Corinth* to *Etruria*—Model-
500 ? lers in clay.

A.S.

B.C.

Damophilos—Gorgasos—From *Corinth?*—Statues in T. C. in the Temple of Ceres, Rome—Pliny, xxv. cap. 12—" Plastæ laudatissimi " &c.   Those on the right were by Damophilos, and the left by Gorgasos.

600 ? Rhoikos—*Samos*—Figures of Women in the Temple of Artemis at Ephesus, one called "Night" by the Ephesians—Mentioned by Pausanias, lib. x. p. 686.   Architect also of the Temple.

Theodoros, son of Rhoikos—*Samos*—Labyrinth of Lemnos, and Temple of Artemis—Theodoros, said to have learned the Egyptian canon of proportions in Egypt ; so that he at Ephesos made one vertical half of a statue (in wood ?) while Telekles of Samos made the other, the two fitting exactly when put together.

Telekles, brother of Theodoros—*Samos*—Statues in B. and W.

560 ? Theodoros, son of Telekles—*Samos*—St. in B. and W., and gem engraving.   B. St. of himself holding the ring, or scarab, his famous work—Flourished in the time of Kroesus and Polykrates, whose ring he made.

630 ? Glaukos—*Chios*—Iron-stand, or large vase with figures, at Delphi— Said to have invented soldering of metals.

540 ? Melas—*Chios*—St., M., none named.

Mikkiades—*Chios*—St., M., none named.

Bupalos—*Chios*—St., M., Tyche, at Smyrna.   St., G., The Graces draped.

580—Dipoinos—Skyllis—*Crete,* and to *Sikyon*—M., I., and E.   St., The
548 ?   Dioscuri at Argos.   St. of Artemis, Athena, Herakles, &c.— Called sons of Dædalos.

560 ? Dontas—*Sparta*—W., I., and G., Group, Herakles, Acheloos, Zeus, and other figures.   St. Hera, Athena.

560 ? Dorykleidos—*Sparta*—St., I. and G.   Athene.

Tektæos—Angelion—*Sparta*—W., I., and G.   Apollo at Delos. St., Athene.   St., Artemis.—Kallon of Ægina was pupil of these.

Klearchos—*Rhegium*—St., B. and W., Zeus at Sparta.—Master of Pythagoras the sculptor.

560—Smilis—*Ægina*—I. and G.   Group of the Seasons.

550 ? Cheirisophos—*Crete*—St., W. and G., Apollo, and St., M., of himself.

550 ? Enoidos—*Athens*—St., W., I., and M., of Artemis, for Temple at Ephesos.   Athene Polias.   St., W., with the Graces and the Seasons in M.

,, Gitiadas—*Sparta*—St., B., Athene, in Temple at Sparta.   Two tripods at Amyklæ—This St. was probably a pillar-like figure, ornamented with bands of reliefs described by Pausanias, as on a coin of Sparta.—See ' Hist. of Greek Sculpture,' by A. S. Murray. 1881.

,, Bathykles—*Magnesia*—W., B., and G.   Statue and Throne of Apollo at Amyklæ—Bathykles was the head of a band of sculptors whom he brought.

521 Eutelidas—*Argos*--St. of Athletes—Victors at Olympia.

B.C.

Chrysothemis—*Argos*—St. of Athletes—Victors at Olympia. Pausanias (lib. vi. p. 362, 25) gives the names as recorded in an inscription : Εὐτελίδας καὶ Χρυσυθέμις τάδε ἔργα τέλεστας 'Αργεῖυι, τέχναν εἰδότες ἐκ προτέρων.

521—**Ageladas**—*Argos*—1. Chariot group, at Olympia, B. 2. St., Ath-
455 ? letes, named. 3. Infant Zeus, at Ithone and Ægion. 4. Herakles, at Melite.—The master of Pheidias, Myron, and Polykleitos.

500 ? **Argeiadas—Atotos**—*Argos*—St. at Olympia—Argeiadas was son or pupil of Ageladas. His name is inscribed on a base found at Olympia, 1876 ; also another with names of Athanodoros and Asopodoros.

Aristomedon—*Argos*—Colossal statues at Delphi.

500—**Glaukos**—*Argos*—St. at Olympia—Groups of Amphitrite, Poseidon,
467 and Hestia—Mentioned by Herodotus.

Dionysios—*Argos*—St., Groups of Deities and Hesiod and Homer. St., Mare and groom, of Phormis, at Olympia—These horses and figures were of diminutive size.

Simon—*Ægina*—St., Horse and groom, at Olympia, in the Altis.

„ **Kanachos**—*Sikyon*—B., W., I., G., M.—St., B., Apollo at Branchidæ. St., W., Apollo at Thebes. St., G. and I., Aphrodite at Sikyon. St., A Muse. St., group, Boys riding—Bronze statuette, supposed to be copy of this, in B. Mus. His statues alluded to by Cicero as less soft than those of Kalamis.

Aristokles—*Sikyon*—St., A Muse at Sikyon—Marble Stele of a Warrior (fig. 70), bearing his name—He was brother of Kanachos, and though other works are not named, he was long acknowledged as founder of a school of sculpture, of which Sostratos and Ptolichos are named. (Murray, *loc. cit.*)

523—**Kallon**—*Ægina*—St., Persephone at Amyklæ. St., Athene at
480 ? Træzen.

477 ? **Onatas**—*Ægina*—St., Group (10) at Olympia—of Greeks casting lots to challenge Hektor. St., Group at Delphi. Chariot for Hiero of Syracuse at Olympia. St., B., Herakles at Thasos. St., B., Apollo at Pergamus. St., B., Hermes with a ram at Olympia. St., B., Demeter—'the black draped Demeter' at Phigaleia, a woman with head of horse. The marble statues of the Ægina Pediments in Munich Museum (fig. 74) may be by Onatas and Kallon. (*Brunn.*)

Kallitales—*Ægina*—Assisted Onatas.

485—**Glaukias**—*Ægina*—Chariot group, Gelo victor in the race at
477 Olympia. St., B. (3), of victors at Olympia—A base was found at Olympia inscribed ΓΛΑΥΚΙΑΣ ΑΙΓΙΝΑΤΑΣ ΕΠΟΙΕΣΕ.

Anaxagoras—*Ægina*—St., B., colos. Zeus at Olympia—Contemporary with Glaukias.

Aristonos—*Ægina*—St., Zeus at Olympia, in the Altis.

Serambos—*Ægina*—St., Boy, Victor at Olympia.

Theopropos—*Ægina*—St., B., Bull at Delphi.

B.C.

Philesios—*Eretria*—St., B., Bull at Olympia—The base of this bull has been found at Olympia, bearing his name.

510 **Antenor**—*Athens*—St., B. (2), Harmodios and Aristogeiton—Carried off by Xerxes, restored by Alexander. Many of this subject in the Ceramicum, Pausanias says, but that of Antenor the oldest. A fragment recently found on the Akropolis bearing the name ANTENOR.

480 **Kritios—Nesiotes** (*misread* **Nestokles**)—*Athens*—St., B. (2), Harmodios and Aristogeiton at Athens. Worked together in making a group to replace the old one. The group of the tyrannicides found on coins ; on a vase found in a tomb at Cyrene ; and a relief on a marble chair in Naples Museum ; and two separate statues in the same collection which would form a group. All these are of the style in the time of Alexander the Great. *See* p. 129.

Amphion—*Knossos in Crete*—Chariot group at Delphi.

Demokritos—*Sikyon*—St., Boy of Hippos, Victor at Olympia.

Amphikrates—*Athens*—St. of Leæna as a Lioness without a tongue, in allusion to her secrecy.

Hegesias *or* **Hegias**—*Athens*—St., Castor and Pollux at Rome, and Boys on race-horses—Mentioned by Pliny, Pausanias, and Lucan.

480 ? **Kalamis**—*Athens*—St., Race-horses for the chariot by Onatas at
460 ?   Olympia. St., Aphrodite (Sosandra) at Athens. St., Boys, at Olympia. St., Ammon. St., Apollo Alexikakos. St., Colossal Apollo at Apollonia. St., Zeus Ammon at Thebes. St., Hermes Kriophoros at Tanagra (A small marble statue of this is at Wilton House, and a terra cotta statuette in Brit. Mus.), called so from carrying a goat on the shoulders. St., M., Dionysos at Tanagra. The Quadriga on the Akropolis, Athens. Nikè Apteros at Olympia. St., Alkmene. St., Hermione. St., G., I., Asklepios. —Famous for his horses. The base of the Aphrodite has been found inscribed with his name.

Kallimachos—*Athens*—Surnamed 'Katatexitechnos.' Inventor of the Corinthian Capital.

Praxiteles (the Elder)—*Athens*—St., The charioteer for the quadriga of Kalamis.

Kleoitas—*Athens*—St., Warrior at Athens. Group of Zeus and Ganymede at Olympia.

480 **Pythagoras**—*Rhegium*—St., B., Philoktetes at Syracuse. St., B., Astylos, a runner of Crotona, at Olympia. St., B., Euthymos, a boxer, Olympia—The marble base discovered at Olympia inscribed with the names Pythagoras and Euthymos. St., B., Leontiskos, a wrestler, Olympia. Europa on a Bull at Tarentum (Marble of this is in Brit. Mus.). St., Mnaseas. St., Group, Etiokles and Polyneikos. St., Perseus. St., Apollo. Group (8 figs.) in the Temple of Fortune at Rome in Pliny's time.

470 **Myron**—*Athens*—St., W., Hekate at Ægina. St., Dionysos with Apollo and Muses, on Mt. Helicon. St., Erectheus, Athens. St., Colossal group, Zeus, Athene, and Herakles at Samos. St., group, Athene and Marsyas. St., Perseus and Medusa, Acropolis. St., R., A Cow lowing. St., Oxen (4). St., A Dog. St., Boy

B.C.

boxer Philippos. St., The runner Ladas. St., B., Diskobolos and other Athletes. St., Apollo (2). St., Herakles.—His style is by some recognized in the frieze of the Theseium, Athens. Also in the metopes of the Parthenon.

460 **Polykleitos**—*Argos* and *Sikyon*—St., B., Doryphoros, The Diadumenos. St., G. and I., of Hera at Argos, seated. St., B., Amazon, copy in the Vatican, and another. St., M., Amazon, Vienna Mus. St., M., Amazon, at Berlin Mus. B., Group of Astragalizontes. St., B., Aphrodite at Amyklæ. St., B., The Apoxyomenos, and another Athlete.—Pupil of Ageladas, with Pheidias and Myron. Was characterized by making his figures rest on one leg, as in the two st. of a Diadumenos in Brit. Mus. The author of the canon called after him. Coins of Argos represent his Hera. A Doryphoros is in Naples Mus. Contended with Pheidias, Kresilas, Kydon, and Phradmon with his statue of Amazon at Ephesos, and was awarded the prize. M. Head of Amazon in Brit. Mus.

464 ? **Pheidias** (b. 490 ? d.— ?)—*Athens*—St., B., colossal, of Athene Promachos. St., B., The Lemnian Athene. St., colos., I. and G., in Parthenon. St., I. and G., colos., Zeus at Olympia, Altis. The above four all destroyed—A small m. statue found at Athens, 1880; copied from the famous one in Parthenon. St., B., Amazon—leaning on a lance ; copy in the Vatican. The sculptures of the Parthenon. Those of the Pediments especially attributed to him (figs. 88, 89). St., M., Venus Urania. St., I. and G., Venus Urania, Elis. St., Apollo Parnopius, Athens. G., Athene and Apollo with the Heroes (Eponymi). The last four named by Pausanias.

460 ? **Strongylion** (Στρογγυλίων). St., Amazon, called 'Euknemon,' from the beautiful legs. St., A Boy. Plin. l. xxxiv. c. 8. St., Artemis. Group, Three Muses. Paus. l. 9.

440—**Agorakritos**—*Paros*—St., B., Aphrodite, called Nemesis Rhamnusia.
428 ? St., B., Athene Itonia. St., B., Zeus.—Pupil of Pheidias. Competed with Alkamenes for a statue of Aphrodite, and was beaten by him ; the 'Nemesis' was the name he gave to his statue.

444—**Alkamenes**—*Athens*—St., B., Aphrodite 'of the Garden.' St., B.,
400? Athene. St., B., Hephaistos. St., Centaur. St., Hera—Juno. St., Ares—Mars. I. and G., Dionysos. B., Hekate Tricorpor. St., Asklepios. St., Herakles, colossal. St., Eros. Sts. of the W. Pediment of the Temple of Zeus at Olympia. M., Battle of the Centaurs and Lapithæ (discovered 1879).—Pupil of Pheidias, who is said to have put the finishing touch on his Aphrodite. Contended with Pheidias for the statue of Athene.

435 **Paionios**—*Mende in Thrace*—Sts., M., in E. Pediment of Temple at Olympia—The contest between Pelops and Oinomaos—Discovered 1879. St., M., Victory with wings—A cast in Brit. Mus.

432—**Phradmon**—*Ephesus*—St., B., Amazon—Contended with Pheidias,
439 Polykleitos, and others : he was placed fifth.

Ktesilas (**Ktesilaus, Desilaos**)—*Lacedæmon*—St., Amazon wounded—The statue in Capitol, Rome, a copy (?). St., Perikles Olympius. St., A Doryphore.

B.C.

415 **Pyromachos**—*Athens*—Frieze of Temple of Athene Polias—Named as Phyromachos, φυρομαχος.—Grk. Anth., lib. iv. c. 12.

379 **Pythis (Pythios)**—*Athens*—M., Group on the Tomb of Mausolus—Discovered by Mr. Newton, 1857. In Brit. Mus. called Halikarnassus marbles.

Leochares—*Athens*—M., The sculptures of W. side of tomb of Mausolus - Also named by Pausanias as the sculptor of a Zeus, Apollo, and other statues.

Bryaxis—*Rhodes*—The sculptures of N. side of Mausolus tomb—A Pasiphaë, Asklepios, and Hygeia Liber Pater at Knidos.

Timotheos—*Athens*—The sculptures of S. side of Mausolus tomb—A Diana at Rome. A Ganymede; copy in Vatican.

364 **Skopas**—*Paros*—The sculptures of E. side of Mausolus tomb. 1. Venus, Pothos, and Phaeton. 2. Apollo Palatinus. 3. Poseidon, Thetis, and Achilles—In the shrine of Cn. Domitius Via Flamm. Rome. 4. Colossal Ares, seated. 5. Aphrodite Pandemon—Bronze. 6. Niobe group (?)—in Pliny's time at Rome. 7. Eros, Pothos, and Imeros at Megara—Same work as Venus, &c., No. 1 ? 8. Artemis. 9. Asklepios and Hygeia. 10. M., Herakles. 11. M., Hekate. 12. M., Drunken Bacchus. 13. One of the Columnæ celatæ of the Temple at Ephesus (?), begun B.C. 394. Architect of Temple of Athene Tegea.

364 **Praxiteles**—*Athens*—M., Aphrodite (Cnidian Venus)—carried to Constantinople. M., St. of Phryne, one gilt. M., Eros—carried off by Caligula; restored by Claudius; taken again by Nero to Rome, where it stood in the schools of Octavia; burnt in that building, reign of Titus. Faun—'Nobilem Satyrum,' περιβόητον. St., Sauroctonos. Group, Ceres and others, once at Rome. Flora, Triptolemos, Boni Eventus, Menades, Caryatides, Sileni, Apollo, Neptunus. Diana and Latona.—The Venus of the Capitol was thought by Flaxman to be copied from Praxiteles. The Niobe statues also attributed to him. Cast of Hermes and Dionysos, found at Olympia, 1879, is in Brit. Mus. Praxiteles was head of the later Attic school, with Skopas. A sculptor of the same name is mentioned in the time of Kimon, 480 ?

372 **Kephisodotos**, son of **Praxiteles**—*Athens*—Group at Pergamos ('*symplegma*')—perhaps the Florence 'Wrestlers.' St., Latona. St., Venus. St., Æsculapius and Diana—once at Rome, named by Pliny.

350 ? **Naukydes**—*Argos*—St., Discobolos, in Vatican. St., Hermes. St., Hekate. St., I. and G., Hebe.

330 **Polykleitos** (the younger)—*Argos*—A younger sculptor of the name, of the time of Lysippos.

340 **Lysippos**—*Sikyon*—(time of Alexander the Great—b. 356; d. 323;
320   æt. 32)—B., Statues of Alexander (celebrated), one holding a lance. Many of Hercules. B., Hercules of T. rentum—Glykon's well-known statue may be from this one, which was in the Capitol, Rome. Colossal Zeus at Tarentum. Equestrian Group of Alexander and the horsemen who fell at the battle of the Granicus, 334 B.C.—brought to Rome by Metellus, 146 B.C. St., B., Apoxyomenos—The statue in the Vatican considered to be copy of this.

B.C.

St., Hephaistion —He is said to have made 1600 works, mostly in bronze.

300 **Polykles**—*Athens*—Amyntas, wrestler. Hermaphrodite—whether recumbent is doubtful, but he is said to be the inventor of this kind of statue, one of which is in the Louvre, another in the Villa Albani, and another in Florence Museum.

290 **Chares**—*Lindus in Rhodes*—B., Colossus of Rhodes, erected 224 B.C. —Pupil of Lysippos.

Eutychides—*Sikyon*—Eurotam (River). St., Liber Pater. St., Timosthenes Eleus. St., Tyche (seated), with Orontes river as a youth at her feet, Seleucus and Antiochus crowning her.—Pupil of Lysippos.

Lysistratos, brother of **Lysippos**—*Sikyon*—Said to have invented the taking of casts of the face. Plin., cap. viii. sec. 44.

240— **Pyromachos**—*Athens* and *Pergamus*—St., B., Asklepios. Groups
295 of battles of Attalus and Eumenes, with other sculptures.—The Dying Gladiator is supposed to be a copy of a bronze statue in these groups at Pergamos; and also the group of Paetus and Arria in the Ludovisi Villa.

Isigonos—**Stratonikos**—**Antigonos**—*Athens* and *Pergamos*—Worked with Pyromachos—-Alto-reliefs, discovered at Pergamos, now in the Museum at Berlin. The school of Pergamos was founded on these.

160 **Timokles**—**Timarchides**—*Athenians*, worked at *Rome*—St., Asklepios. St., Athene Promachos at Elatea.—The shield of this statue was an imitation of that of the Parthenon statue.

Kleomenes—*Athens*—St., M., Aphrodite—'Venus dei Medici.' M. group, Thespiades—belonged to Asinius Pollio.

Kleomenes, son of the above—*Athens*—St. of Germanicus in the Louvre—The base inscribed as by Kleomenes, son of Kleomenes.

100? **Apollonios**, son of **Nestor**—*Doubtful* where from—St., M., Torso Belvedere—Inscription on the torso. Not the same Apollonios as he who did the Toro Farnese with Tauriscos. The name is found also on a statue of Æsculapius at Rome.

Agasias, son of **Dositheos**—*Ephesus*—St., The Fighting Gladiator in Louvre—the name upon the work. This statue formerly attributed to the time of Alexander, B.C. 330. Agasias is not mentioned by Pausanias or Pliny. Visconti suggests it was Hegesias.

90 **Pasiteles**—*Magna Græcia*—St., I., Jupiter in the temple, for Metellus.—Said to have written a book on art (Pliny).

Kolotes—*Paros*—None known—Pupil of Pasiteles. Another of the name said to have assisted Pheidias on the Zeus, Olympia.

80? **Arkesilaos**—*Greek*—St., Venus Genitrix, for the Forum of Cæsar. St., or B. rel., M., Lioness with Cupids, for Lucullus—Praised by Varro.

50 **Sauros**—**Batrachos**—*Not known, but Greek*—Sculptures in the Portico of Octavia. They carved a lizard and a frog, to signify their names, on this work. (Plin.)

B. C.

30 ? **Glykon**—*Athens*—St., M., Colossal Hercules, found in the Baths of Caracalla, Rome—His name not mentioned by Pliny or Pausanias, but his only work known bears his name. (Fig. 114.)

26   **Diogenes**—*Athens*—Worked on the Pantheon of Agrippa. Caryatides by him.

A. D.

50 ? **Apollonios** and **Tauriskos**—*Tralles*—Colossal Group, M., Dirké tied to the Bull, in Naples Mus. (Fig. 141.)

79   **Agesander—Apollodoros—Athenodoros**, son of **Agesander**—*Rhodians*—Group, M., Laocoon, in Vatican (fig. 136). The work of these three sculptors in the time of Titus.

60   **Zenodoros**—*A Gaul*—St., B., Coloss. of Nero—110 feet high, which stood before the Golden House. Afterwards dedicated as a Sol, in A.D. 75.

117—**Papias — Aristeas** — *Aphrodisias* — M., Two Centaurs in bigio,
138   marble.

Zeno—Attilianos—*Aphrodisias*—No works known, but the name found in inscriptions.

Pantuleios—*Ephesus*—   ,,   ,,   ,,   ,,

Zenophantes—*Thasos*—   ,,   . ,,   ,,   ,,'

Many more names might be added to this list, but those above given are the most important.

The great work of Franciscus Junius, '*De Pictura Veterum*' Fol. Roterodami 1694, affords an almost exhaustive collection of quotations from Greek and Latin writers referring to Sculptors and their works, with a very full catalogue, which will be found invaluable to students.

INDEX.

The names of Sculptors are in SMALL CAPITALS, and their works in *italic*.

SOME OF THE ATTRIBUTES SEEN IN ANCIENT SCULPTURE.

Ægis and spear of Minerva—Athene, as protecting and armed for combat. She sometimes in early works carried a lamp, in allusion to her wisdom.

Caduceus of Mercury—Hermes, a short round rod, with a pair of wings near the top, and two serpents twining opposite each other. Originally an olive branch served with the ribbons as the emblem of a messenger of peace. The ribbons ($\sigma\tau\acute{\epsilon}\mu\mu\alpha\sigma\iota\nu$) were changed into two entwined snakes, said by some to have been once separated while fighting by Hermes. It is seen also in a much simpler form as a staff with two short curved spiral ends at the top. A staff of this kind was carried by heralds and ambassadors in war. *The wings* of course told of speed, and are always seen on the cap or **petasus**, and attached to the heels as **talaria,** for the messenger of the gods to fly down to earth. As the god of commerce also they have a meaning.

Diadem—$\sigma\phi\epsilon\nu\delta\acute{o}\nu\eta$—to Juno—Hērē.

Eagle *and* **thunderbolt of Jupiter**—Zeus;—as the messenger and the weapon of the almighty god. The ruler of Olympus is represented seated with a figure of winged Victory standing in his right hand, and a sceptre in his left, with a 'patera' signifying culture; and with the Modius.

Modius—bearing the 'modius,' a measure for corn, on his head, as the Jupiter Serapis, all-bountiful. Pluto also has the modius as Serapis, the name of the corresponding deity in Egyptian mythology.

Hammer and **pincers** at his anvil, to Vulcan—Hephæstos.

Lyre, to Apollo, as the god of the day and of poetry. The **bow** and **quiver** also to him as the destroyer.

Mirror and **flowers** belong to Venus—Aphrodite—with the **tortoise** and **dolphin.**

Peacock to Juno, and the **Cuckoo** on her sceptre.

Pedum—the shepherd's crook-stick, is often given to satyrs and to Pan; sometimes to fauns and bacchanalians; to Thalia, as the goddess of pastoral life. The Centaur of the Capitol has one.

Pomegranate, fruit and flower to Proserpina—Persephone.

Poppy and wheat-ears to Ceres—Demeter.

Spear, two-pronged, to Pluto—Hades, who is sometimes represented with the **modius** on his head.

Thyrsus of Bacchus—Dionysos—a staff with a fir-cone on the top, tied with ribbons; given to Bacchante and other figures. The fir-cone is said to have been chosen on account of its giving the resinous flavour to wine which was so relished.

Torch belongs to Diana—Artemis, whose quiver and bow are later attributes. The spear and hound also belong to her. Ceres also carries a torch, signifying her search for Proserpina in Hades. *The torch reversed* is always funereal.

Trident of Neptune—Poseidon—as the sort of harpoon used by fishermen in the earliest times.

Turrets on the head of Cybele—Rhea.

GLOSSARY OF NAMES GIVEN TO STATUES, &c.

Apoxyomenos—The Athlete scraping himself with the strigil (from ἀποξύω, to scrape).

Diadumenos—Athlete wearing the victor's fillet (or diadem).

Dioscuri—Twin sons of the god Zeus (Castor and Pollux).

Discobolus—The Quoit (or Disc) thrower.

Doryphorus—The Spear-bearer.

Gigantimachia—Wars of the Giants with the Gods.

Panathenæa—Festivals in honour of Athene.

Parthenon—From παρθένος, a virgin. The Parthenon was dedicated to the virgin goddess Athene.

Sauroctonos—Apollo the lizard slayer (from Σαῦρος, a lizard, and κτονος, one who kills, from κτείνω, to kill).

CORRESPONDING NAMES OF MYTHIC PERSONAGES
IN ROMAN AND GREEK NOMENCLATURE.

ROMAN	GREEK	ROMAN	GREEK
Æsculapius	Asklêpios	Mars	Arēs
Aurora	'Eōs	Mercury	Hermēs
Bacchus	Dionysos	Minerva	Athēnē
Ceres	Dēmēter	Mors (Death)	Thănătos
Cupido *or* Amor	Erōs	Neptune	Poseidon
Cybele	Rhea	Pluto	Hades
Diana	Artĕmis	Pollux	Polydeukes
Parcæ (the Fates)	Moirai	Proserpĭna	Persephonē
Flora	Chloris	Saturn	Chronos
Furiæ (Furies)	Eumenides	Somnus	Hypnos
Gratiæ (Graces)	Charities	Sol	Hēlios
Hercules	Herakles	Venus	Aphrŏdītē
Juno	Hērē	Vesta	Hestia
Jupiter	Zeus	Victoria	Nikē
Latona	Leto	Vulcan	Hephaistos
Luna	Selēnē	Ulysses	Odysseus

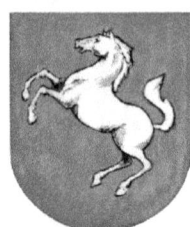

Featured Titles from Westphalia Press

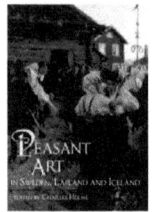

Peasant Art in Sweden, Lapland and Iceland
by Charles Holme

This particular work offers a carefully chosen selection of both the decorative and fine arts of Sweden, Iceland, and the northern most region of Finland. A comprehensive survey, it includes paintings, jewelry, textiles, metalwork, carving, furniture and pottery.

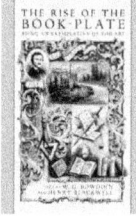

The Rise of the Book Plate: An Exemplative of the Art
by W. G. Bowdoin, Introduction by Henry Blackwel

Bookplates were made to denote ownership and hopefully steer the volume back to the rightful shelf if borrowed. They often contained highly stylized writing, drawings, coat of arms, badges or other images of interest to the owner.

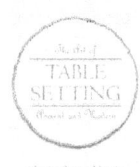

The Art of Table Setting, Ancient and Modern
by Claudia Quigley Murphy

The arrangement of a table in terms of cutlery, arrangement, serving style, and timing of courses has changed a great deal over time and now is enjoying renewed interest. The History of the Art of Tablesetting was written by a true expert in the field, Claudia Quigley Murphy.

Understanding Art: Hendrik Willem Van Loon's
How To Look At Pictures by Hendrik Willem Van
Loon, Introduction by Daniel Gutierrez-Sandoval

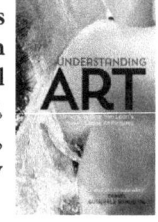

Hendrik Willem van Loon was a Dutch-American professor, journalist, prolific writer, and illustrator. His most famous work, "The Story of Mankind" earned him the prestigious John Newbery Medal.

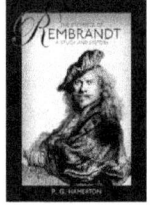

The Etchings of Rembrandt: A Study and History
by P. G. Hamerton

Philip Gilbert Hamerton (1834-1894) was an Englishman who was devoted to the arts in numerous forms. Due to the praise, Hamerton stuck with art criticism, and went on to write other works. He also wrote novels, biographies, and reflections on society.

Lankes, His Woodcut Bookplates by Wilbur Macey Stone

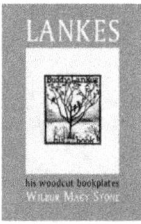

Julius John Lankes was born in Buffalo, New York in 1884, and became a prolific woodcut print artist, as well as an author and professor. As a child, he enjoyed working with the scraps of wood his father brought home from the lumber mill where he was employed. Lankes had a lifelong interest in art.

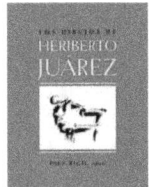

Los Dibujos de Heriberto Juarez / The Drawings of Heriberto Juarez, Edited by Paul Rich

That the drawings here are from life in México is not surprising because Juárez is constantly, and at times impishly, putting art into life and getting art from life. He doesn't think of art as something that is done just in a studio or for that matter kept in museums and looked at on Sundays.

The History of Photography: Carl W. Ackerman's George Eastman by Carl W. Ackerman, Introduction by Daniel Gutierrez-Sandoval

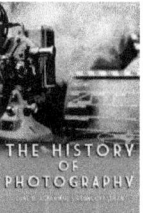

The life of George Eastman is very much a part of the history of contemporary photography. Founder of the Eastman Kodak Company, Eastman was an enthusiastic photographer himself who became instrumental in bringing photography to the mainstream.

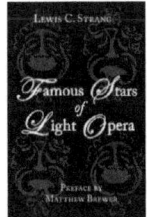

Famous Stars of Light Opera by Lewis C. Strang, Introduction by Matthew Brewer

Strang's attempts to quantify the humorous elements of each performer, as well as quotes from the performers themselves attempting to explain their own success, are an interesting exercise in attempting to explain the inexplicable.

The Historic Codfish by George H. Proctor, Samuel D. Hildreth, William Frank Parsons

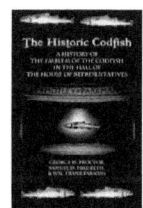

There may be 160 representatives in the Massachusetts legislature, but there is only one codfish. The nearly five-foot carving hanging from the ceiling is the third reminder of the importance of fishing to the state. The first was burnt in a 1747 fire and the second destroyed during the Revolution. The present fish was enshrined in 1784.